HARRIET MONROE AND THE POETRY RENAISSANCE

Harriet Monroe
and the
Poetry Renaissance

The First Ten Years of *Poetry*, 1912–22 §➤

ELLEN WILLIAMS

UNIVERSITY OF ILLINOIS PRESS
Urbana Chicago London

Publication of this work was supported in part
by a grant from the Andrew W. Mellon Foundation

Previously unpublished letters and one poem by Ezra Pound © 1976 by the Trustees of
the Ezra Pound Literary Property Trust. Published by permission of New Directions
Publishing Corporation and Faber and Faber, Ltd., publishers and Agents for the Trustees
of the Ezra Pound Literary Property Trust.

Previously unpublished letters by Wallace Stevens © 1976 by Holly Stevens. Published
by permission of Holly Stevens.

Previously unpublished letters by William Carlos Williams © 1976 by Florence H. Williams. Published by permission of New Directions Publishing Corporation, publishers
and Agents for Mrs. William Carlos Williams.

LIBRARY OF CONGRESS CATALOGING IN PUBLICATION DATA

Williams, Ellen, 1930–
    Harriet Monroe and the Poetry Renaissance.

    Bibliography: p.
    Includes index.
      1. Poetry (Chicago) 2. Monroe, Harriet, 1860–1936—
Biography—Editing career. 3. American poetry—20th
century—History and criticism. 4. Journalists—United
States—Biography. I. Title.
PS301.P623W5   811'.5'05 [B]   76-45403
ISBN 0-252-00478-7

to
R. J. W.

Contents ᔑᗥ

Acknowledgments ix

Introduction: The Background 3

Chapter One: A Confused Beginning, 1912–13 31

Chapter Two: The Great Years of *Poetry*, 1914–15 91

Chapter Three: "The Great Opportunity," 1916–17 175

Chapter Four: A Long Aftermath, 1917–22 221

Appendix: Figures on *Poetry*'s Income,
    Expenditures, and Circulation 295

Bibliography 297

Index 301

Acknowledgments ཀ

Sometimes human affairs change very rapidly, a storm of activity evolving out of apparent stagnation, as a tropical storm develops from a sunstruck sea. This book is the chart of such a change in literary affairs, a vortex whose lines of force converged from many places. One strong current came out of the architectural and social ferment that built Chicago; another from poets self-exiled to London; others from Boston and New Jersey, from Springfield, Illinois, from Ireland, from New York, from New Mexico, from Hartford, Connecticut. Near its center was Harriet Monroe, the quiet woman who edited *Poetry: A Magazine of Verse* at 543 Cass Street in Chicago. The correspondence that arrived at *Poetry* from many corners of the world is the record of a uniquely exciting period in American poetry. Something in Harriet Monroe brought out the personal flavor of her correspondents. Poets wrote to her with such direct self-revelation that their letters have immense biographical value and vitality. And the time when *Poetry* began, 1912, was germinal.

I am greatly indebted to Mr. Robert Rosenthal, Curator of Special Collections in the Joseph Regenstein Library, the University of Chicago, for permission to use the *Poetry* Papers, a collection in the Harriet Monroe Modern Poetry Library, and the Personal Papers of Harriet Monroe, and for his advice and assistance over many years; also to Mrs. Mary Janzen Wilson, Manuscript Research Specialist in the same library, for her generous help. James E. Miller, Jr., of the University of Chicago has been an unfailing source of counsel and encouragement.

Sherman Paul of the University of Iowa gave the manuscript a most helpful reading. At an early stage of the work, Robert E. Streeter and the late Morton Dauwen Zabel of the University of Chicago gave useful counsel. I owe to the late Napier Wilt of the University of Chicago my understanding that the affairs of *Poetry* must be related to the affairs of the other little magazines, that the history of the little magazines must be given as a whole if any part is to be clear. I have wanted to present the pattern of *Poetry* with maximum vitality, to stay close to the record, and to avoid the masterful overview that obscures more than it explains. Where the design has failed, or where it has created unnecessary clumsiness, the fault of course is mine.

Mr. Donald Gallup and Mr. Peter Dzwonkoski of the Beinecke Library, Yale University, have given very generous help. I am also indebted to Mr. K. C. Gay of the Lockwood Memorial Library, New York State University at Buffalo; to Diana Haskell of the Newberry Library; to Annette Fern of Burnham Library, the Art Institute of Chicago; to Mr. Donald A. Woods, the library of the University of Wisconsin at Milwaukee; to Jean R. McNiece of the New York Public Library; to Mr. David Farmer of the Humanities Research Center, the University of Texas at Austin; to Alderman Library, the University of Virginia; and to Houghton Library, Harvard College. Prof. Bernard Duffey, Mrs. Rose Hecht, Prof. Nicholas Joost, Miss Jane Lidderdale, Mr. William Mauldin, Prof. Arthur Mizener, Prof. Max Putzel, Prof. B. L. Reid, Prof. Robert H. Ross, Prof. Edna B. Stephens, and Miss Lydia Zelaya have kindly given advice or information.

The book would not be possible without the very kind generosity of many people who have given permission to print correspondence and manuscripts from the *Poetry* Papers. Most grateful acknowledgment is made to Mrs. Edwin S. Fetcher for permission to publish Harriet Monroe's correspondence and other unpublished writing from the *Poetry* Papers and an excerpt from a letter in the Ezra Pound Archive, Collection of American Literature, the Beinecke Rare Book Room and Manuscript Library, Yale University; to the Trustees of the Ezra Pound Literary Property Trust, to Mr. James Laughlin and New Directions

Publishing Corporation, and to Faber and Faber, Ltd., publishers and Agents for the Trustees of the Ezra Pound Literary Property Trust, for permission to publish excerpts from Ezra Pound's correspondence and from the manuscript of "From Chebar"; to Mr. James Laughlin and New Directions Publishing Corporation, publishers and Agents for Mrs. William Carlos Williams, for excerpts from the correspondence of William Carlos Williams; to Miss Holly Stevens for the correspondence of Wallace Stevens and for her kindness in describing Harriet Monroe's correspondence to Stevens; to Mrs. Edgar L. Rossin for the correspondence of Alice Corbin Henderson and for an excerpt from a letter in the Ezra Pound Archive, Collection of American Literature, the Beinecke Rare Book Room and Manuscript Library, Yale University; to G. D'Andelot Belin and Conrad W. Oberdorfer, Trustees under the Will of Amy Lowell, for Amy Lowell's correspondence; to Mr. Nicholas C. Lindsay for correspondence and manuscripts by Vachel Lindsay; to Mrs. Edgar Lee Masters for correspondence by Masters; to Mrs. Alfred Kreymborg for Kreymborg's correspondence; to the Estate of William Butler Yeats for Yeats's correspondence and manuscripts; to Mrs. Valerie Eliot for T. S. Eliot's letter; to Mr. Charles Schlessiger for the correspondence of Conrad Aiken; to Ann Elmo Agency, Inc., for Richard Aldington's correspondence; to Prof. Jack B. Moore for correspondence by Maxwell Bodenheim; to the Estate of Robert Frost and to Holt, Rinehart and Winston, Inc., for Frost's correspondence; to Mr. Clive E. Driver for correspondence by Marianne Moore; to Mr. James Kraft for Witter Bynner's correspondence; to Miss Helen Ranney for correspondence by Henry Blake Fuller; to Mr. John Hall Wheelock for his correspondence to Harriet Monroe; to Mrs. James Branch Cabell for Cabell's letter; to Janice Biala for the correspondence of Ford Madox Ford; to Mr. Allen Tate for his letter; to Mercantile Safe Deposit and Trust Company, Trustee under the Will of Henry Louis Mencken, for Mencken's correspondence; to Mrs. Hilda L. Petri for correspondence by John G. Neihardt; to Mr. Maurice C. Greenbaum for correspondence by Carl Sandburg; to Mrs. Annie Hays Rice O'Neil for Cale Young Rice's letter; to Laurence Pollinger, Ltd., and the

Estate of the late Mrs. Frieda Lawrence, the Viking Press, Inc., and William Heinemann, Ltd., for an excerpt from a letter by D. H. Lawrence. Excerpts from Sara Teasdale's letters are used by permission of Margaret Conklin, Literary Executor of Miss Teasdale's estate; correspondence by H. D. is published by permission of Norman Holmes Pearson, Literary Executor and owner of H.D. copyrights.

I am further indebted for permissions to reprint material from books or from the little magazines. I am particularly grateful to Mrs. Edwin S. Fetcher for permission to reprint Harriet Monroe's comment from *Poetry*, the *Dial*, and the *Chicago Daily News*, and to use material from *A Poet's Life* and from *Wallace Stevens: The Making of Harmonium* by Robert Buttel, published by Princeton University Press; and to Mr. James Laughlin and New Directions Publishing Corporation and to Faber and Faber, Ltd., publishers and Agents for the Trustees of the Ezra Pound Literary Property Trust, for permission to reprint excerpts from *Selected Letters, 1909–1941* by Ezra Pound, edited by D. D. Paige (copyright 1950 by Ezra Pound), from *Personae* and *Collected Shorter Poems* by Ezra Pound (copyright 1926 by Ezra Pound), from *Literary Essays* by Ezra Pound (copyright 1935 by Ezra Pound), from his letter of March 22, 1959, as quoted in Harry M. Meacham, *The Caged Panther* (copyright 1967 by Ezra Pound), and his letter to his father December 18, 1915, as quoted by Myles Slatin, "A History of Pound's Cantos I–XVI, 1915–1925," *American Literature* 35 (May, 1963) (copyright 1963 by Ezra Pound), and one phrase by Pound as quoted in Charles Norman, *Ezra Pound* (copyright Charles Norman, 1960, 1969); also to reprint excerpts from Ezra Pound's articles published in *Blast* (copyright 1914), the *Egoist* (copyright 1914, 1917), the *English Journal* (copyright 1930), the *Little Review* (copyright 1917, 1918), the *Criterion* (copyright 1932), and *Poetry* (copyright 1914, 1915). All rights reserved. Mr. James Laughlin and New Directions Publishing Corporation, publishers and Agents for Mrs. William Carlos Williams, have kindly given permission to reprint excerpts from *The Selected Letters of William Carlos Williams*, edited by John C. Thirlwall (copyright 1957 by William Carlos Williams), from *Collected Earlier Poems* by William Carlos

Williams (copyright 1938 by New Directions Publishing Corportion), and from Williams' articles in the *Egoist* (copyright 1916), *Others* (copyright 1919), and the *Little Review* (copyright 1919). All rights reserved. Grateful acknowledgment is made to Mrs. Edgar L. Rossin for Alice Corbin Henderson's comment in *Poetry*; to G. D'Andelot Belin and Conrad W. Oberdorfer, Trustees under the Will of Amy Lowell, for Amy Lowell's article in the *Poetry Journal* and for excerpts from *Tendencies in Modern American Poetry*; to Mrs. Edgar Lee Masters for exerpts from *Across Spoon River*, published by Farrar and Rinehart, Inc., and from Masters' criticism in the *Mirror*, edited by William Marion Reedy; to Mrs. Alfred Kreymborg for excerpts from *Troubadour* and from Kreymborg's criticism in *Poetry*; to Mrs. Valerie Eliot for excerpts from Eliot's criticism in the *Egoist* and the *Dial*; to Mr. Charles Schlessiger for excerpts from Conrad Aiken's criticism in the *Poetry Journal* and the *Dial*; to Ann Elmo Agency, Inc., for Richard Aldington's criticism in the *Egoist*, the *Little Review*, and *Poetry* and for excerpts from *Life for Life's Sake*; to Mr. James Kraft for Witter Bynner's comments in the *Little Review*; to Mr. Allen Tate for an excerpt from his article in *Poetry*; to the Mercantile Safe Deposit and Trust Company, Trustees under the Will of Henry Louis Mencken, for Mencken's comment from "A History of the *Smart Set* Magazine" by Carl Dolmetsch; to Mr. George Siegel for editorial comment by Margaret Anderson and Jane Heap and other material from the *Little Review*; to Dr. James S. Watson, Jr., for an excerpt from his criticism in the *Dial*; to Mr. John L. Clark for unsigned editorial comment in the *Dial*; to Mrs. Donald Davidson for Davidson's comments in the *Fugitive*; to Mr. John G. Alden for Raymond M. Alden's criticism in the *Dial*; to the Editor of *Poetry* for an excerpt from William Gardner Hale's criticism in *Poetry*; to Miss Margaret Haley Carpenter for an excerpt from *Sara Teasdale: A Biography* (New York: Schulte, 1960; copyright 1960 by Margaret Haley Carpenter) and for excerpts from William Stanley Braithwaite's criticism in the *Poetry Journal* and in his *Anthology of Magazine Verse* for 1915 and for 1916.

Grateful acknowledgment is made to Faber and Faber, Ltd., and to Harcourt Brace Jovanovich, Inc., for permission to print excerpts from *Collected Poems, 1909–1962* by T. S. Eliot, and to Faber and Faber, Ltd., for T. S. Eliot's introduction to *Ezra Pound: Selected Poems*; to Harcourt Brace Jovanovich, Inc., for an excerpt from *Complete Poems of Carl Sandburg*; to Alfred A. Knopf, Inc., and to Faber and Faber, Ltd., for excerpts from *Letters of Wallace Stevens*, edited by Holly Stevens (copyright 1966 by Holly Stevens), and from *The Collected Poems of Wallace Stevens* (copyright 1954 by Wallace Stevens) and *The Necessary Angel* by Wallace Stevens (copyright 1942 by Wallace Stevens); to the Estate of Robert Frost and to Holt, Rinehart and Winston, Inc., for excerpts from *Selected Letters of Robert Frost*, edited by Lawrance Thompson (copyright 1964 by Holt, Rinehart and Winston, Inc.); to Holt, Rinehart and Winston, Inc., for excerpts from *Robert Frost: The Trial by Existence* by Elizabeth Shepley Sergeant (copyright 1960 by Elizabeth Shepley Sergeant); to Houghton Mifflin Company for an excerpt from *The Complete Poetical Works of Amy Lowell*; to Horizon Press for an excerpt from *The Little Review Anthology*, edited by Margaret Anderson (copyright 1953); to the Macmillan Publishing Company, Inc., for an excerpt from Harriet Monroe's introduction to *The Congo* by Vachel Lindsay (copyright 1914 by the Macmillan Publishing Company, Inc., renewed 1942 by Elizabeth C. Lindsay) and for excerpts from *Collected Poems* by William Butler Yeats, *The Letters of William Butler Yeats*, edited by Allen Wade, and *Collected Poems* by Vachel Lindsay; to Michigan State University Press for excerpts from *The Chicago Renaissance in American Letters* by Bernard Duffey; and to the *New York Times* for the Yeats interview of February 22, 1914 (copyright 1914 by the New York Times Company).

Mrs. Josephine Elliott, formerly of the University of Chicago Library, and Sister Jean Harris and the staff of the Angus L. MacDonald Library, Antigonish, Nova Scotia, have helped with more details than I can remember to record. Finally, my loving thanks to Benedict, Sarah, David, and Catherine Williams, who have done their utmost to vary and relieve the stress of the work.

HARRIET MONROE AND THE POETRY RENAISSANCE

Introduction: The Background ᒰ

     In 1911 Harriet Monroe, a poet-playwright, essayist, and journalist based in Chicago, was at the age of fifty-one precariously established in a literary world which proclaimed that there was no American poetry worthy of the name. Although the revolution in modern poetry is often dated from the end of the first decade of the twentieth century, in 1911 that revolution was invisible. T. S. Eliot had the best part of his early poems written out in a notebook; Robert Frost had been a practicing poet for many years; Edgar Lee Masters had been publishing since the 1890s; Vachel Lindsay, loitering in Springfield, Illinois, had been discovered and forgotten by interested patrons several times. William Carlos Williams had published a small first book; so had Carl Sandburg. But none of these poets had surfaced as a recognized literary identity.

     The official literary landscape of 1911 was so empty of interesting poets that Harriet Monroe's decision to launch a small magazine devoted exclusively to current poetry seems to need explanation. *Poetry* at its inception was curiously without relations or connections, and more than one commentator has invented a meeting between Harriet Monroe and Ezra Pound in 1910 to supply the lack. Ezra Pound had surfaced, with some splash, the year before that with the publication of two books in London, but Harriet Monroe knew Pound only through those books. Although Pound vitally influenced the development of *Poetry*, he had no part in its origin.

     Harriet Monroe could not have had any definite knowledge

that many poets of considerable merit were unpublished or little known in the United States when she began to plan for the magazine in the summer of 1911. She was not acquainted with any of the poets who came to figure in the "new movement" or the "Chicago Renaissance." The poets whom she did know personally before *Poetry* appeared are not distinguished: Florence Wilkinson, Edith Wyatt, Agnes Lee, Cale Young Rice. Nor did she have contact with any group of young developing unknowns in Chicago. Probably no one could have anticipated the "Poetry Renaissance" which was to follow so quickly upon the first appearance of the magazine that in later years Harriet Monroe could claim, "The first number of *Poetry* appeared in October, 1912, and 'with it the new movement began.' "[1]

For twenty years editors had believed American poetry too thin and trivial to merit serious attention. With smug candor, literary men admitted the poverty of American poetry; the opinion attested to the purity of their critical perceptions. Here and there a commentator might give way to national passion, and find epic scope in James Whitcomb Riley or William Vaughn Moody, but the typical critic of the period 1900–1910 took pleasure in asserting a standard superior to time and place, concluding sadly that little American verse deserved so much as space in his paper. Thus Bliss Perry amiably rejected some poetry that Harriet Monroe submitted to the *Atlantic Monthly* in 1905, writing that he felt like an exhausted but determined tennis player obliged to slam poetry back to its contributors as quickly and as neatly as he could. The *Atlantic* had very little space for poetry; Harriet Monroe should judge the speed and the dexterity with which lesser poets were rejected by the celerity of her own rejection.[2]

Perry was defending his space against Robert Frost or Ezra Pound as much as against Harriet Monroe. Nevertheless, the American poetic tradition at the time was dull enough to justify his defensive posture. The leading North American poets of the

1. "An Open Letter," *Chicago Daily News*, June 20, 1915. When no other source has been given in text or notes for correspondence and manuscripts, the material is taken from the Papers of *Poetry: A Magazine of Verse*, a collection in the Harriet Monroe Modern Poetry Library, the Joseph Regenstein Library, the University of Chicago.

2. Letter of November 13, 1905, in Personal Papers of Harriet Monroe.

1880s and 1890s had been Thomas Bailey Aldrich, Edmund Clarence Stedman, James Whitcomb Riley, Bret Harte, Joaquim Miller, Eugene Field, Edwin Markham, Richard Hovey, Bliss Carman, Ridgely Torrence, and Edwin Arlington Robinson. The Harvard group of the nineties—William Vaughn Moody, Trumbull Stickney, George Cabot Lodge, and Percy Mackaye—did not fulfill its early promise. Stickney died in 1904, Lodge in 1909, Moody in 1910, and Mackaye turned to writing civic centennial pageants.

A good many American magazines in the first decade of the twentieth century were interested in printing serious fiction or essays—the *Century*, the *Atlantic*, the *North American Review*, *Harper's*, *Scribner's*, *Lippincott's*, the *Forum*, the *Bellman*, for example. But they used poetry only as humbler papers used advertisements for patent medicines, as a convenient filler for the unused half or quarter column at the end of an article. This practice bred what came to be a recognized type, the "magazine poet" whose melodious trivia was standardized to fill a little space without distracting a reader. The magazine system trained a horde of candidates for American laurels; the volume of verse produced frightened the editors. Ida M. Tarbell of the *American*, returning verse to Harriet Monroe in 1908, wrote that her stocks of accepted verse overflowed her files.[3] The *Dial* magazine, edited at Chicago by Francis Fisher Browne, greeted signs of increased poetic activity in 1912 with mild alarm: "As far as increasing its amount is concerned, we have grave doubts of the wisdom of any concerted propaganda." The *Dial* went on to describe the "emerged tenth" of the magazine writers, the least minor in a mob of minor poets. The list gives a good index to the poetic establishment at the moment when Harriet Monroe launched *Poetry*: Bliss Carman, Madison Cawein, Edwin Markham, Clinton Scollard, Ridgely Torrence, George Edward Woodberry, Olive Tilford Dargan, Julia C. R. Dorr, Josephine Preston Peabody, and Edith Thomas.[4] Other widely printed poets, perhaps beneath the *Dial's* notice, were Ella Wheeler Wilcox, Henry van Dyke, Lizette Woodworth Reese, Richard Bur-

3. Letter of November 18, 1908, in Personal Papers of Harriet Monroe.
4. "The Case of Poetry," December 16, 1912, pp. 478–79.

ton, and Theodosia Garrison. Harriet Monroe herself was not acknowledged; nor was Edwin Arlington Robinson.

Setting Robinson aside, one can sum up the poetic situation in 1911 by noting that the generation born after the Civil War had produced no poets. The reasons for such a breakdown of the poetic impulse are as mysterious as the reasons for the revival in the generation born around 1880. The relative poverty of English poetry in the 1880s and 1890s makes the break in American poetry more interesting, because it eliminates easy appeals to the strain of the Civil War or of industrialization. Yeats was one of the few poets of his generation in the British Isles who did not fade out early. His poetic voice, maintained through circumstances that silenced all his friends of the Rhymers' Club, seems fabulously tough. His friends were killed by a mysteriously fatal hostility between the mind of the age and the mind of the poet, in Yeats's account of it. By the turn of the century, the great mass of Yeats's contemporaries on both sides of the Atlantic seem to have felt, like his reviewer in *Reedy's Mirror* for January 9, 1913, that there was no impulse toward poetry in the modern world.

Harriet Monroe had felt that the indifference of the magazines was a cause, not merely a sign, of a decline of poetry in America. For the magazine editor of the period, the poets were a mass of small angry insects who would not quiet their shrill lyric whine. But Robert Frost was lost in that horde of contributors for almost twenty years. Susan Hayes Ward of the *Independent*, who published his first poem in 1894, was a sympathetic correspondent, but no one was able to give him meaningful help or encouragement. Between 1894 and 1913 Frost succeeded in publishing only fourteen poems. His rejected poems collected in *A Boy's Will* in the spring of 1913 were welcomed in London. Frost's experience bears out Harriet Monroe's contention that editors were perpetuating the weakness of American poetry. Manuscripts were being read by people who had no interest in or intelligence about poetry. American literary and cultural life had no structure. The literary world had no apparatus for finding poets, and did not know what to do with them when they somehow emerged into notice. Frost is the most conspicuous case of neglect, but there were others. Edwin Arlington Robinson, who

6

published books in 1896, 1897, 1902, and 1910, supported himself by working for the New York City Subway System. If Robinson is a special case—and his anonymous and lonely life seems chosen—Vachel Lindsay had been available for discovery since 1904, when Jeannette Gilder first published him in the *Critic*, and was in fact discovered several times before Harriet Monroe permanently discovered him in *Poetry* for January, 1913. Edgar Lee Masters had published books in 1898, 1905, and 1910 without attracting much attention from anyone except William Marion Reedy, who coached and criticized him after 1907.

Ezra Pound, who broke into the literary world in London in 1909, when Elkin Mathews brought out *Personae* and *Exultations*, knew the American literary scene. He put down his judgment of the American magazine editor of this period in many places. Here is a tirade in an undated letter to Harriet Monroe, sometime in the spring of 1915:

> Now the nasty thing about all other magazines, and the reason why I abominate the American magazines and why I think they should be exterminated in revenge for the damage they have done American poetry is that they specialize in two or three tones. . . .
>
> There is no literature for precisely this reason, that they are all stuck into uniforms. They chase a popularity, express one or two moods, usually cheap complacency, or, elsewhere, stereotyped pity. Since the death of Whitman there has been no literary figure, save possibly the suggested sketch (Hovey). The rest are blurred into the Century Magazine.

Pound's testimony confirms Harriet Monroe's assertion that the bad state of American poetry in 1911 derived from the editorial policies of the magazines.

There is one conspicuous exception to the rule that no one important in literary journalism before 1912 had any interest in poetry. William Stanley Braithwaite, after 1905, undertook for the *Boston Evening Transcript* a yearly survey of the verse published in the magazines. According to the *Dial*, "he continued year after year until his annual report became an influential contribution to the cause of better poetry in this country and even beyond its borders."[5] In 1913, and yearly after that, Braithwaite amplified his annual report into the preface of his *Anthology of*

5. "Casual Comment," February 1, 1915, p. 73.

Magazine Verse. When the Poetry Renaissance flared up, others besides the *Dial* credited Braithwaite for fanning the flame. But he can hardly be said to have been alert to the "new movement." His anthology got around to recognizing it by 1915; he mentioned the existence of Ezra Pound and of *Poetry* for the first time in 1916. Braithwaite acquired a position of considerable influence because he had the stamina to plow through a mass of magazine verse that daunted most readers, and because he began early, in 1905, when American poetry was an abandoned territory over which few cared to exercise authority.

Harriet Monroe, who intruded on Braithwaite's domain in 1911, had complex roots in the uneven culture of the nineteenth-century West. She was born in Chicago in 1860, the daughter of Henry S. Monroe, a lawyer prominent in the affairs of the very new and rapidly growing city, was educated in local schools, and was given a final polish at Georgetown Visitation Convent in Washington, D.C. From the publication of her first poem in Richard Watson Gilder's *Century* magazine in 1888, she was ambitious for a literary career. Her blank-verse tragedy *Valeria*, Shakespearean in diction, shadowy in character and plot, was praised by Gilder and by Henry Harland, later the editor of the *Yellow Book*. The play was privately published in 1892, and republished by A. C. McClurg in 1893. In 1892 her "Columbian Ode" was recited at the opening program of the World's Columbian Exposition in Chicago; she had been appointed the laureate of the White City, after protesting to the program committee that the art of poetry was insufficiently honored in the planned exposition. When the *New York World* reprinted her ode without permission from an advance copy of the program, she sued it for violation of copyright, and won a judgment for five thousand dollars in 1894. In bringing this case to court, she felt a sense of stewardship as representative of the poets, whose work had been routinely reprinted without permission, and she was helped by her father's experience with the legal problems of copyright.

Although Harriet Monroe belonged to Chicago's upper class, she was not wealthy. She supported herself through the middle years of her life, after 1889, by free-lance journalism, with some

teaching and lecturing. Between 1889 and 1912 she had frequent
articles or regular columns in the *Chicago Tribune*—for which she
was art critic at two different periods—the *Chicago Times Herald*,
the *New York Sun*, *Leslie's Weekly*, the *Atlantic*, the *Chicago American*, and the *Chicago Evening Post*. After she lost her job as *Tribune*
art critic in 1914, she had to draw a salary from *Poetry's* endowment.

Her situation as a poet in Chicago in the nineties was not very
secure. Edgar Lee Masters wrote her September 2, 1924: "But
you know what poetry was in 1898 [the year of Masters' first
book] and in the years that preceded it, and how difficult it
was for a writer in central Illinois in the late eighties and early
nineties to rise from the earth bound conditions. . . . Well,
what was Chicago then as an inspiration to the muse? There was
no market for anything and no interest in it after you did it.
Neither was I writing what Gilder and Stedman and Fawcett
and others were. . . ." In her autobiography she comments frequently on the cold public response to her poetry, and to all
poetry that "stepped out of the beaten tracks laid down by Victorian practice and prejudice." From her acquaintances in Chicago
who aspired to write poetry, there came in the period 1895–1910
"a steadily increasing silence."[6]

Harriet Monroe's Chicago was no cultural desert. It supported
an active group of architects and artists, including Louis Sullivan, Frank Lloyd Wright, and John Wellborn Root, who was her
brother-in-law. In the 1880s Root and Sullivan had been groping
toward the design of the skyscraper, not only in building but also
in lively public dialogues about their art. Harriet Monroe followed these with intelligent interest, and reproduced some of
them in her memoir of Root. Sullivan in his turn admired her art
criticism and thought of her as an ally in his campaign to create
an American, democratic, and twentieth-century art in the place
of the false classicism that sprouted everywhere after the Columbian Exposition. "The Little Room"—an informal social club
that met after the Friday matinees of the symphony orchestra for
many years—was Chicago's literary gathering place, and there
Harriet Monroe came to know novelists Henry Blake Fuller and

6. Harriet Monroe, *A Poet's Life*, pp. 180–81, 202.

Hamlin Garland, and journalists Francis Hackett and Floyd Dell of the *Friday Literary Review*.

This *Review* was a weekly supplement of the *Chicago Evening Post*; Hackett, who founded it in 1909, was later an editor of the *New Republic*. Under Hackett and Dell, it was considered "the most alert and most eager, and the most intelligent and the best-written discussion of literature in the United States."[7] Francis Hackett, an Irish Fabian Socialist, was an exotic in Chicago, but his review sustained a tradition begun in the town in the nineties by the *Chapbook*, a monthly published in 1894–98 by the publishing house of Stone and Kimball, "*avant garde* in format and content as was no other American magazine and, even more . . . alone in supplying the want of a lively, current literary periodical."[8] The *Chapbook* was publishing Verlaine and Mallarmé, Hamlin Garland, Thomas Bailey Aldrich, and Madison Cawein, among other poets, during Harriet Monroe's *Valeria* period and the years when she moved on to write verse dramas of modern life.

The *Chapbook* and the *Friday Literary Review* were brief lively episodes in the literary journalism of the city. The *Dial* was throughout this period the weightiest and most respected Chicago periodical. Founded in 1880 by Francis Fisher Browne, who picked up Emerson's old title, the *Dial* passed judgment on the books of the day with an Olympian loftiness that Robert Morss Lovett once attributed to provincial inferiority.[9] However, its high academic tone seems typical of the genteel tradition everywhere in the United States, and it was the only American journal that gave serious coverage to all current publications.

Despite this degree of cultural activity in her town, Harriet Monroe felt that poetry and the poets were shamefully neglected. The circular that she printed in April, 1912, to publicize her proposed magazine detailed endowments given by Chicagoans to the Art Institute and the orchestra, subsidies for drama, and the proposed Little Theater. "Poetry alone has no powerful friends. No endowment, prize, scholarship of any kind for origi-

7. Lucian Cary, "Literary Journalism in Chicago," *Little Review*, June–July, 1915, p. 1.

8. Bernard Duffey, *The Chicago Renaissance in American Letters*, p. 72.

9. "George Bernard Donlin," *Dial*, August, 1920, p. 149.

nal creative work in poetry is offered by any university or other institution, in this country or England."

Her feeling that the serious poet was ridiculed or ignored began with her youthful observation of Eugene Field, a neighbor and family friend, and was confirmed by her own literary career. Her poetry is ambitious in its subjects and its scope. From her early admiration for Shelley, she saw the poet as fire bringer, the maker of mankind, and her own poems are full of high purpose. Besides *Valeria*, she published *The Passing Show*, a collection of short verse plays, in 1903; *You and I* in 1914; *The Difference* in 1924; and *Chosen Poems* in 1935.

When Harriet Monroe gave up her first Shakespearean imitations, she became very serious about the need to give poetic expression to modern life, to bridge a gap between poetry and reality that many seemed to feel. This movement toward the real was encouraged by Henry Blake Fuller, who praised her *John Wellborn Root* in 1896 for a social realism worthy of *McClure's* magazine. In an undated letter he called it a "study of real life . . . tingling with actuality." Reality, the contact of the ideal with constricting fact, seemed the proper ground of developing art: "the systematic, unceasing succession of definite facts seems to have a cumulative effect that nothing can withstand." Root's Monadnock Building seems the best architectural expression of the pressure of circumstance against the form in the mind. In Harriet Monroe's own comments on Root, response to circumstance, to American conditions, implies also an openness to science, admiration for the power of commerce, and idealism about democracy. The democratic aspect of the cult of the real seems derived from Whitman, but was also a response to populist politics. In the gallery at the Democratic Convention of 1896 she had seen in amazement the passion of hope and faith aroused in the delegates by William Jennings Bryan's Cross of Gold oratory. She shared Louis Sullivan's attitudes, expressed in a 1905 letter: "now we are overwhelmed by the general foulness of feudalism and pessimism which permeates worn activity. I believe a reaction is near: but how near it is difficult to estimate. Until the trusts, and special privilege, are overthrown, democracy in any walk of life will have but little show, and a democratic art least of all."[10] For both of them democracy, the dream of the oppressed, meant the vital artistic intuition that worked in the present to create the future by overcoming the past.

Harriet Monroe's poetry arose out of such ideals, if it fell short of embodying them. Her work attracted a decent amount of notice from her contemporaries. William Archer admired her verse play *It Passes By*; two prose plays were good enough to interest Ethel Barrymore and Minnie Maddern Fiske as vehicles, although the negotiations petered out in both cases. H. C. Chatfield-Taylor, the most active patron of the literary arts in Chicago, underwrote a production of her play *The Man-Eagle*. Henry Blake Fuller praised *At the Goal*, the deathbed dialogue of a sick tycoon and the forgotten love of his youth, as an "inevitable" modern situation. Harriet Monroe's work was important compared with the other poetry published in America in her generation. Her statement that by 1910 she was so discouraged by many rejections that she had almost stopped trying to publish is not a confession of private failure.[11] In the five years before that date she had published several long, serious poems, "The Dance of the Seasons" in the *Fortnightly Review* in 1908 and "The Hotel" and "The Turbine" in the *Atlantic* in 1909 and 1910. But when she wrote publisher Mitchell Kennerley about bringing out a book of poems, he answered that although he loved to publish poetry, she knew as well as he that there was simply no sale for books of poems at that moment.[12] Since Kennerley became one of the busiest publishers of the poetic revival after 1912, his appeal to the commonly recognized fact that poetry cannot sell in the fall of 1911 marks a lower limit to the chronology of the Poetry Renaissance.

If the poetic scene was dull in 1911, Harriet Monroe's immediate motive in starting her magazine needs further explanation. She never gave any more definite account than the one in her circular of April, 1912: the poet was neglected and had no institutions to back him, so she decided to create one for him, mystically certain that a little encouragement would bear fruit.

10. Letter of April 10, 1905, in Personal Papers of Harriet Monroe.
11. *Poet's Life,* p. 189.
12. Letter of October 18, 1911, in Personal Papers of Harriet Monroe.

She assumed that America was due for an artistic awakening and that the business habits of magazine publishers stifled the very possibility of poetry. (Ezra Pound's account in *Patria Mea*, written in 1912 before he came in contact with *Poetry*, makes the same assumptions; it is significant that he pointed to the architecture of the skyscraper as evidence of American artistic vitality.) Perhaps the extra spark that drove Harriet Monroe into action came from the breakdown of her own literary career. Her combined failures to get a play on the stage and to get a book of poems published gave her, on return to Chicago from a trip to the Orient, a choice of retiring the literary figure Harriet Monroe or finding something new for her to do. She would not quit; she did not feel that her failure was personal. In *John Wellborn Root* she had celebrated the ideal of the artist whose personal form develops from the exploration of contemporary conditions, but her own artistic career had not been so happy. Like the prairie wheat farmer at the mercy of the banks and the railroads, she had been thwarted by corrupt institutions. A hostile environment had denied scope and ground to her efforts. Her play *The Thunderstorm* had developed such a theme, "the way environment and circumstances may nullify and silence a man born for creative art."[13] The intuition expressed in the Whitman motto that she posted on *Poetry*'s cover, "To have great poets there must be great audiences too," was deeply ingrained in Harriet Monroe.

In 1911, if she was personally undefeated, she was stymied. She could not continue to hurl poems into a void. No commercial publisher had issued her poetry since 1893 (*The Passing Show* was printed in 1903 with the help of a subsidy from a friend). The magazines were mostly not interested in her serious work. The degree to which she felt stultified by absence of response may be inferred from her image of an ideal relation between artist and audience. In an introduction to Lindsay's *The Congo and Other Poems*, she cited

> . . . Mr. Lindsay's plea for a closer relation between the poet and his audience, for a return to the healthier open-air conditions and immediate personal contacts, in the art of the Greeks and of primi-

13. *Poet's Life*, pp. 179–80.

13

tive nations. Such conditions and contacts may still be found, if the world only knew it, in the wonderful song-dances of the Hopis and others of our aboriginal tribes. They may be found also, in a measure, in the quick response between artist and audience in modern vaudeville. They are destined to a wider and higher influence; in fact, the development of that influence, the return to primitive sympathies between artist and audience, which may make possible the assertion once more of primitive creative power, is recognized as the immediate movement in modern art.[14]

If this seems too theatrical, imagined by a lonely poet contemplating rejection slips, it has some profound correspondences in twentieth-century poetic thought. The poet "fulfills himself only as he sees his imagination become the light in the minds of others" is Wallace Stevens' unprimitive version of the same idea, written thirty years later.[15]

Thus Harriet Monroe conceived the idea of *Poetry* when she saw clearly that poetry was not possible in the United States she knew. Her publicity circular of April, 1912, illustrates how the idea of *Poetry* developed out of the neglect of the poet. She cited the reasons for despair:

> First. Leading publishers of England and America have told me that they "almost never" publish a book of verse unless the expense of publication is paid by the author when the book is issued.
>
> Second. Editors of our most literary magazines state, in writing, that they cannot publish a poem of more than twenty or thirty lines, "no matter how meritorious," "more than once in a long time." Some of them say never, under any circumstances. And most editors are forced to accept verse from the standpoint of popularity rather than excellence.
>
> Third. Prices paid for the few poems accepted are less than one-tenth, sometimes scarcely one-hundredth, what a painter or sculptor would receive for an equally successful work requiring an equal amount of ability and time.
>
> Fourth. The poet who makes $200 a year through his art is

14. Introduction reprinted by permission of Macmillan Publishing Company, Inc., from *The Congo and Other Poems* by Vachel Lindsay, pp. viii–ix (copyright 1914 by Macmillan Publishing Company, Inc., renewed 1942 by Elizabeth C. Lindsay).

15. "The Noble Rider and the Sound of Words" reprinted from *The Necessary Angel* by permission of Alfred A. Knopf, Inc., and Faber and Faber, Ltd. (copyright 1942 by Wallace Stevens). The passage, pp. 27–30, is an illuminating comment on the values and the limits of the poet's relation to an audience.

fortunate. Thus he is forced to use up time and spirit in more remunerative occupations.

Fifth. If he or his friends raise money to publish a book of verse few buy it, the critics hardly notice it, and he rarely gets his money back.

Sixth. In short, the vast English-speaking world says to its poets: "Silence."

And found them grounds for action:

> For these reasons, as a modest attempt to change conditions absolutely destructive to the most necessary and universal of the arts, it is proposed to publish a small monthly magazine of verse, which shall give the poets a chance to be heard, as our exhibitions give artists a chance to be seen; which shall serve as an organ for Poetry, representing its interests, as numerous magazines, often heavily subsidized, represent those of the other arts.

Publication of a magazine, however modest, requires capital. The other impetus to the founding of *Poetry* came from H. C. Chatfield-Taylor, long-time patron of Chicago artists and an old friend of Harriet Monroe's. He suggested that she try to find a hundred businessmen in Chicago who would promise to give fifty dollars a year over five years. After that he assumed the magazine would be self-supporting. To this subsidy of five thousand dollars a year Chatfield-Taylor contributed the first fifty dollars.

Chatifield-Taylor, himself a man of letters, a novelist and biographer of Goldoni and Molière, had been a leader in projects to refine and improve Chicago for years. He was one of the most prominent agents in the "Upward Movement" that in 1890–1905 tried to reform the city's politics and helped to establish such institutions as the University of Chicago, the Chicago Symphony, the Art Institute, and the Newberry and Crerar libraries. So far as *Poetry* was modeled after institutions like the orchestra and the Art Institute—and Harriet Monroe often made the comparison—it was a last gesture of the Gilded Age, an anachronism in a Chicago whose impulse to patronize the arts was daunted by the theories of Thorstein Veblen.

Chatfield-Taylor's backing and encouragement were essential

to *Poetry*. Harriet Monroe dated the beginning of the magazine from June 23, 1911, the day he suggested the scheme of fifty-dollar contributions. Her father gave her another entree into the business offices of Chicago; although H. S. Monroe was dead and his law practice had dwindled away in the eighties, some wealthy and prominent men had been his friends. She used this connection as she worked her way through the office buildings of the Loop for almost a year, persuading bankers, lawyers, architects, and real estate men that the Chicago they were building owed something to the poets and to poetry.

When one considers that Harriet Monroe had nothing to give a donor in return for fifty dollars a year, no institution behind her that could impress a social climber or publicize his generosity, no art product more tangible than a small monthly pamphlet, it seems wonderful that she succeeded. The first published list of guarantors contains a hundred and eight names of people who gave mostly fifty dollars, a few twenty-five or a hundred. She must have impressed the businessmen, and they impressed her. She recorded in several places the new confidence in human possibilities that she gained when the grim citadel of Mammon responded to her appeal.

Many of the guarantors are well-known names. *Poetry*'s guarantors came from the same circles that had supported and patronized Chicago's earlier literary groups and its other cultural institutions. These would be people she reached through Chatfield-Taylor or through other "Little Room" connections: Charles L. Hutchinson, president of the Art Institute; Kate Buckingham, the great patron of the Art Institute; Charles Deering of the McCormick Harvester Company; the wife and son of Potter Palmer, the hotel and real estate man; Arthur and Owen Aldis of a real estate firm; Charles L. Freer, the Detroit collector; Chauncey and Cyrus H. McCormick and Edith Rockefeller McCormick, all of the harvester family; Mrs. Julius Rosenwald, wife of the president of Sears, Roebuck; Albert H. Loeb, vice-president of the same company; Edward L. and Martin A. Ryerson of Ryerson Steel; Charles H. Swift of the meat-packing company; and Samuel Insull, the utilities magnate.

Other guarantors seem less obviously eligible as patrons of a magazine of verse: Howard Elting of the Adams and Elting Paint

Company; George A. McKinlock, president of Central Electric Company, manufacturers of electric supplies; and Eames Mac-Veagh of Franklin MacVeagh and Company, wholesale grocers and manufacturers of coffee roasters. The occupations of most of the guarantors are less surprising: Anita McCormick Blaine was connected with the University of Chicago's School of Education; F. W. Gunsaulus was president of the Armour Institute of Technology and a well-known local clergyman; H. H. Kohlsaat, editor of the *Chicago Record-Herald*; Victor Lawson, editor and publisher of the *Chicago Daily News*; William A. Nitze, professor of Romance languages at the University of Chicago; W. D. McClintock, professor of English at the same university. Harriet Moody, widow of Wiliam Vaughn Moody, was glad to contribute to the cause, and so was Clarence Darrow. There were plenty of lawyers besides Darrow: Arthur J. Eddy, an art collector; Charles H. Hamill; Salmon O. Levinson, after 1914 the donor of the much disputed Levinson Prize; John S. Miller; John Barton Payne; Gilbert Porter; Wallace Heckman; and Andrew Sheriff. The following were bankers or brokers: Ernest A. Hamill, president of the Corn Exchange Bank; Augustus E. Peabody of Peabody, Houghteling and Company; George F. Porter; and Frank G. Logan. Howard Shaw and Arthur Heun were prominent local architects.

From these guarantors and others, Harriet Monroe had secured enough pledges by the spring of 1912 to move ahead with plans for the magazine. She and they had done something unique. No one else could develop or sustain a group system for support of the literary arts. The other meaningful literary patronages of the same era were relationships between wealthy individuals and individual artists; Harriet Shaw Weaver and James Joyce, and John Quinn and Ezra Pound, are examples that occur immediately. Ezra Pound probably spent as much time and effort as anyone in this era raising money for the literary artist, and his estimate of the difficulty of Harriet Monroe's feat is worth quoting. He wrote to her March 27, 1931, after almost twenty years' vicissitudes with the magazine:

> re/Poetry stopping. Having performed the great feat of manipulating the god damned boorzoi into spending a little money on the

best poetry at yr/disposal (given yr lights) it wd. be a crime to plug the hole.

You ought to leave as durable and continuing a monument as possible to the fact that you extracted from among the pork-packers a few less constipated and made them PAY money for the upkeep of poesy.

The five just men in Sodom were as nothing by comparison. I forget; I dare say they weren't to be found, and the angels morals had to be kept in the family.[16]

Poetry's system of annual pledges worked as well as it did because of the guarantors' confidence in Harriet Monroe's good faith and integrity, a confidence tremendously bolstered during the first five years by the new fashion for poetry. Despite grumbling over free verse, the guarantors' letters in her papers show a primary reliance on Harriet Monroe's personal integrity and sound judgment. Most of the guarantors were not deeply interested in literature, and left her almost as free in her editorship as if the five-thousand-dollar annual subsidy were her own money. Of course, they expected that she would so manage the magazine that the connection would be a credit to them, and the constant amorphous pressure of this expectation must have been a constraint on her. Also, the local financial backing made the magazine from the beginning a civic institution, rooted in its locality.

If the founding of *Poetry* can be taken as a sign of new activity in poetry in the twentieth century, the magazine's own sources were in the Dark Ages of American poetry. It began almost as pure reaction against the neglect of the poet, and the emotional base of its fund-raising drive was embattled idealism. The reforming zeal and the sentimental localism of nineteenth-century America were part of the first idea of the magazine. *Poetry* was the dawn star of the Poetry Renaissance because its own sources were in the black midnight. It was not conceived in response to other glimmerings. Surely never has a candle lit against the darkness been so suddenly rewarded with an explosion of light.

16. In Ezra Pound, *Selected Letters, 1909–1941*, ed. D. D. Paige, #247, pp. 252–53 (copyright 1950 by Ezra Pound). This and following excerpts reprinted by permission of New Directions Publishing Corporation and Faber and Faber, Ltd., publishers and Agents for the Trustees of the Ezra Pound Literary Property Trust.

Harriet Monroe turned to concrete plans for the magazine in the spring of 1912. The poets were to be informed of the magazine endowed for them and asked to contribute. Determined to overlook no one, she sat down in the Chicago Public Library and read through all the verse published in the important English and American magazines from 1907 to 1912 and all the recent books of verse, making a note of everyone who looked interesting. The list of poets solicited indicates that Harriet Monroe wanted to reach a wide audience. Local patriotism did not operate to select out middle-western poets: only Arthur Davison Ficke, resident of Davenport, Iowa; Floyd Dell, editor of the *Friday Literary Review* of the *Chicago Evening Post*; Vachel Lindsay; and John G. Neihardt, resident of Bancroft, Nebraska, could be so described. Better than a third of the writers were Englishmen or Irishmen—there is not even a strong national bias to the list. There is evident some anxiety to be up-to-date: several of the Englishmen—Lascelles Abercrombie, John Drinkwater, and Wilfred Wilson Gibson—were "Georgians," just come into notice during the past year; and Alfred Noyes and John Masefield were new reputations. Ezra Pound was still relatively new in 1912; Harriet Monroe had been introduced to his poetry by his London publisher, Elkin Mathews, whose shop she visited on her trip around the world in 1910. She had carried *Personae* and *Exultations* with her across Russia to China on the Trans-Siberian Railroad, and had read and reread them. Among the American poets whom she asked for verse, William Rose Benet, Witter Bynner, Fannie Stearns Davis, Floyd Dell, Arthur Davison Ficke, Hermann Hagedorn, Vachel Lindsay, Amy Lowell, Louis Untermeyer, Marguerite Wilkinson, and John Hall Wheelock were all comparative newcomers.

She did not want to get in touch with the prosperous "magazine poets" of the era; such names as Clinton Scollard, Olive Tilford Dargan, Edith Thomas, Julia C. R. Dorr, Richard Burton, Ella Wheeler Wilcox, Lizette Woodworth Reese, and Theodosia Garrison are absent from her list. *Poetry*'s only meaningful contact with the magazine establishment came the next year, in an exchange with Ella Wheeler Wilcox. Stung by a comment in the May, 1913, issue, Mrs. Wilcox wrote Septem-

ber 8, 1913, to hope that Harriet Monroe might grow at least
a sagebrush of heart to soften her desert of intellect.

Some more significant poets were overlooked in Harriet Monroe's painstaking survey. Frost had not published anything for
the three years before 1912. Orrick Johns, Joyce Kilmer, and
Conrad Aiken were very new. It is not likely that she came
across William Carlos Williams' privately printed *Poems* (Rutherford, N.J., 1909) or Carl Sandburg's little volume *In Reckless
Ecstasy*, published in 1904. Edgar Lee Masters was publishing an
occasional poem under the pseudonym Webster Ford, but she
did not notice him or run into any of his books. There is no
record that she asked Sara Teasdale for anything, though she
accepted poems from her by April, 1913, and their friendship
grew quickly after that spring. There is almost no one else, even
slightly remembered as an American poet who had published
before 1912, that she did not catch in her net. Among the established writers who received a circular advertising *Poetry* in the
summer of 1912 were Joseph Campbell, Bliss Carman, Willa
Cather, Frederic Manning, Edwin Markham, Alice Meynell,
Harold Monro, Ernest Rhys, Edwin Arlington Robinson, James
Stephens, Herbert Trench, and William Butler Yeats.

She wanted to start the magazine on a high plane. Having
qualms about her audience, she wrote Arthur Davison Ficke on
August 16, 1912, ". . . I must lead my subscribers gently to the
appreciation of poetry of that lofty kind," and she wrote to
another early contributor, "I can't tell yet just how the magazine
will develop—whether it will have room for . . . familiar poems
of various kinds."[17] The best full description of what she hoped
the magazine might be appears in the circular she mailed to the
poets in late summer of 1912:

> The success of this first American effort to encourage the produc-
> tion and appreciation of poetry, as the other arts are encouraged,
> by endowment, now depends on the poets. We offer them:
>   First, a chance to be heard in their own place, without the
> limitations imposed by the popular magazine. In other words,
> while the ordinary magazine must minister to a large public little

17. Letter of September 20, 1912, to Grace Hazard Conkling, a copy filed with the
Conkling correspondence.

interested in poetry, this magazine will appeal to, and it may be hoped will develop, a public primarily interested in poetry as an art, as the highest, most complete expression of human truth and beauty.

Second, within space limitations imposed at present by the small size of our monthly sheaf—from sixteen to twenty-four pages at present the size of this—we hope to print poems of greater length and of more intimate and serious character than the other magazines can afford to use. All kinds of verse will be considered—narrative, dramatic, lyric—quality alone being the test of acceptance. Certain numbers may be devoted entirely to a single poem, or a group of poems by one person; except for a few editorial pages of comment and review.

Third, . . . we shall pay contributors. The rate will . . . increase as the receipts increase, for this magazine is not intended as a money-maker, but as a public-spirited effort to gather together and enlarge the poet's public and increase his earnings. If we can raise the rate paid for verse until it equals that paid for paintings, etchings, statuary, representing as much ability, time, and reputation, we shall feel that we have done something to make it possible for poets to practice their art and be heard. In addition, we should like to secure as many prizes, and as large, as are offered to painters and sculptors at the annual exhibitions in our various cities.

In order that this effort may be recognized as just and necessary, and may develop for this art a responsive public, we ask the poets to send us their best verse. We promise to refuse nothing because it is too good, whatever be the nature of its excellence. We shall read with special interest poems of modern significance, but the most classic subject will not be declined if it reaches a high standard of quality.

On the back of the circular appeared for the first time the motto from Whitman, "To have great poets there must be great audiences too," which was to adorn the monthly issues of the magazine. Harriet Monroe hoped that *Poetry* could do something to create a "great audience" in modern America, poetry being "a reciprocal relation between the artist and his public,"[18] but her immediate motive in adopting the motto was to discourage harsh judgment of her contributors.

18. "The Motive of the Magazine," *Poetry*, October, 1912, p. 27.

The response to the circular was strong. William Rose Benet, Witter Bynner, Joseph Campbell, Bliss Carman, Arthur Davison Ficke, Wilfred Wilson Gibson, Alfred Percival Graves, Louis V. Ledoux, Vachel Lindsay, Amy Lowell, Percy MacKaye, Edwin Markham, Alice Meynell, Harold Monro, John G. Neihardt, Alfred Noyes, Ezra Pound, Cale Young Rice, John Hall Wheelock, Marguerite Wilkinson, and William Butler Yeats all sent in poems within six months of receiving it. By October, 1912, Harriet Monroe had enough material on hand that she could afford to be rigorous. *Poetry* was selective from the beginning.

Ezra Pound's response to the circular makes all other response feeble by comparison. His first letter to Harriet Monroe has been published in several places.[19] He wrote promising to make *Poetry* the exclusive American outlet for his own verse, offering to search out the work of other poets in London and to keep the magazine "in touch with whatever is most dynamic in artistic thought, either here or in Paris, as much of it as comes to me, and I *do* see nearly everyone that matters." He expressed concern that *Poetry* recognize the *art*—"an art with a technique, with media, an art that must be in constant flux, a constant change of manner, if it is to live"—and closed with hopes for an "American Risorgimento." These hopes chimed in with Harriet Monroe's, and she was delighted by the vigor with which he joined her project. It is rather surprising that Pound's letter replied to a routine request for help in a cover letter sent with the circular, August 7, 1912: "Your poetry has given me very special pleasure ever since Mr. Mathews introduced me to it in his London office, a fact which I am acknowledging in an article on American poets, in the *Poetry Review*. I strongly hope that you may be interested in this project for a magazine of verse and that you may be willing to send us a group of poems, for very early publication." Ezra Pound in London seems to have been on the alert for new publishing outlets, and for American literary allies. Harriet Monroe was glad to take him on, and in his next letter he agreed to accept the title of foreign correspondent.

Alice Corbin Henderson was Harriet Monroe's other confed-

19. In *Letters*, #5, pp. 9–10, dated "c. August 18, 1912" by Harriet Monroe.

erate in the early years of the magazine. They met through Lake Forest friends at the time when Miss Monroe was looking for an assistant. Mrs. Henderson, wife of painter William Penhallow Henderson, was a poet; her volume, *The Spinning Woman of the Sky*, was published in 1912. For almost four years, as associate editor, she gave first reading to the manuscripts that came into the office. Harriet Monroe always attached great importance to this first sifting of manuscripts, and never had another assistant whose quick sensitivity and clear judgment she could trust as she trusted Mrs. Henderson's. She was also valued for her wit and for the friends she brought into association with the magazine.

In addition to the editor, the associate editor, and the foreign correspondent, the personnel of *Poetry* included an advisory board, consisting for most of the first ten years of Hobart C. Chatfield-Taylor, Henry Blake Fuller, and Edith Wyatt. The function of this advisory board remains a bit shadowy. Its members were all old friends of Harriet Monroe's, members of the "Little Room" circle of Chicago artists and literati. Chatfield-Taylor had suggested the plan for financing the magazine and made himself the first guarantor. Fuller was a novelist of distinction in his generation, best remembered for *The Cliff Dwellers*. Edith Wyatt was also a novelist, and a poet and critic as well. It is not quite clear how much advice Harriet Monroe took from this committee; eventually it was reduced to a rubber stamp. She wrote in 1935, "The Advisory Committee has been for many years really an honorary affair, giving less advice than I would have welcomed, their chief contribution being the annual vote for prizes."[20] The influence of the advisory board during its first ten years is not distinguishable from the influence of its individual members. Fuller's words seemed always to weigh with Harriet Monroe, but Chatfield-Taylor and Miss Wyatt seem to have been pretty much under her thumb.

Chatfield-Taylor tried to resign without success. He wrote August 10, 1913, protesting his ignorance of the new movements in art and literature and suggesting she name to the committee someone more sympathetic to her ideals. She refused to accept

20. Letter of September 7, 1935, to Gordon J. Laing, a copy filed in Personal Papers of Harriet Monroe.

his resignation. Whatever persuasion she used worked for more than five years. His resignation dated September 3, 1920, was finally accepted, and Lew Sarett replaced him on the advisory board.

Harriet Monroe felt great respect for Edith Wyatt, and Miss Wyatt contributed a good deal to *Poetry*'s small editorial section in the first volume. But Alice Corbin Henderson, with "the sharp wit which would flash out like a sword,"[21] displaced her in volume two, after the spring of 1913, as the second-rank editorialist and reviewer, and the tone of the editorial matter is noticeably brisker. Miss Wyatt remained one of *Poetry*'s reviewers into the twenties, and often visited the office, but after the first six months she contributed within limits that Miss Monroe prescribed for her.

Henry B. Fuller seems the only member of the advisory board who seriously influenced editorial policy. He was personally reserved, and it is unlikely that he pushed his opinions. Ralph Fletcher Seymour, the first publisher of the magazine, thought he put most of his energy into proofreading. Fuller took the new movement in stride. He was even moved to experiment in a kind of free-verse short story that interested him as an alternative to the mechanical short stories published in magazines. Two of his free-verse narratives were published in *Poetry* in 1916 and 1917. Probably this advisory board, its members so much a part of Harriet Monroe's background, was listened to when its opinions happened to coincide with hers, which was probably quite often. And she could probably afford to disregard it when she disagreed with it. But it must have reinforced the conservative rather than the radical side of Harriet Monroe's sensibility.

By the autumn of 1912, as preparations for the magazine intensified, certain changes appeared in the literary landscape. Harriet Monroe undertook the magazine out of the feeling that the poet had no friends or comforters, but within the year that situation had altered. The list of young English poets whom she asked for verse in the late summer of 1912—Masefield, Noyes, Abercrombie, Drinkwater, Gibson—indicates new poetic activ-

21. *Poet's Life*, p. 317.

24

ity in England. Rupert Brooke, first published in 1911, and Walter de la Mare also belong to an English "poetic renaissance," often dated from the founding at the very end of 1912 of Harold Monro's Poetry Bookshop, or from the publication of the first *Georgian Poetry* in the fall of 1912. Edward Marsh spoke of renaissance in the brief preface to that anthology, announcing the beginning of a new Georgian period that might in time rank with the great poetic ages of the past.

By the fall of 1912 some literary circles in America were also discovering a poetic renaissance. W. S. Braithwaite's review of the year's poetry in the *Boston Evening Transcript* remarked on a "new era," and cited the number of books of poetry published in the fall of 1912, the founding of *Poetry* and of the *Poetry Journal* in Boston, and the publication of an anthology, *The Lyric Year*, as evidence of a revival.[22] Although the vigorous response which Harriet Monroe got from the poets suggests that she was launching her enterprise on a rising tide, this revival of American poetry in 1912 does not seeem quite genuine. Braithwaite anticipated any general awareness of a revival, and his account was not disinterested; the *Poetry Journal* was his own project. The *Dial*, which on December 16, 1912, noticed an increase in poetic activity, citing *Poetry*, *The Lyric Year*, and Harold Monro's Poetry Bookshop, was in this period very sensitive to English literary events and very slow to react to American ones. It was quite possibly aping English commentators when it talked about renaissance—by January 1, 1913, a *Dial* reviewer remarked on the new interest in poetry that characterized "the Georgian epoch."

But the history of Ferdinand Phinny Earle's *Lyric Year* anthology does give ground for believing there was an independent increase in verse writing in America in 1912, although Earle apparently got the idea for an anthology from "the English fervor of the Edwardian poets."[23] *The Lyric Year* was originally planned as an "Annual Exhibition or Salon of American Poetry," but it was never repeated after 1912. It printed a hundred poems,

22. Quoted in the *Dial*, January 1, 1913, p. 6.
23. W. S. Braithwaite, in Margaret Haley Carpenter, *Sara Teasdale: A Biography* (New York: Schulte, 1960), p. 154 (copyright 1960 by Margaret Haley Carpenter).

selected from among those submitted for a first prize of five hundred dollars and second and third prizes of two hundred fifty dollars. The prize contest was announced in 1911, and the book itself published some weeks after the first publication of Harriet Monroe's *Poetry*. The response was unexpected: the editor selected his hundred poems from ten thousand submitted by nearly two thousand poets. A controversy developed when Edna St. Vincent Millay's "Renascence" was passed over for the prize, and stirred up a good deal of excitement.

Elder statesmen like Bliss Carman, Madison Cawein, Richard LeGallienne, Edwin Markham, Ridgely Torrence, and George Edward Woodberry set aside, Earle's anthology did manage to select the minor poets who became the workhorses of the Poetry Renaissance. Of his younger contributors, probably only Edna St. Vincent Millay, Vachel Lindsay, and Sara Teasdale earned a higher rank. The reasons for refusing to take *The Lyric Year* quite simply as the first clear sign of a new vitality in American poetry are three. Magazine editors had been feeling overwhelmed by an avalanche of minor lyric verse for years, as letters to Harriet Monroe attest, throughout the period described by all as the Dark Ages of American poetry; a change would have to be in some sense qualitative. The quality of the verse published in the anthology is not high; "Renascence" seems the only memorable poem in it, and few serious poets entered the prize contest. And the book published few young poets who developed later into significant writers. But at the least *The Lyric Year* and the controversy over its prize made everyone aware that numbers of people in America were writing poetry. It was the beginning of the Poetry Renaissance for the American newspaper public.

Harriet Monroe felt that the other harbinger of the American poetry renaissance, W. S. Braithwaite's Boston-based *Poetry Journal*, was an impudent appropriation of her idea. In August of 1912 she was preparing for November publication when someone sent her a publicity circular for a magazine called *Poetry* to be published in Boston beginning in October, conceived in response to "the revived interest in poetry which has been revealed in the past few years."[24] She was put into a panic; it looked as if the

24. Harriet Monroe, letter of April 5, 1916, intended for *Reedy's Mirror*, filed in *Poetry*'s business papers.

goodwill and interest she had stimulated were to be deflected to this competitor. As it turned out, the *Poetry Journal* did not appear until two months after *Poetry*'s first publication, but Harriet Monroe always remembered the flurry in which the first number of her magazine was assembled. At first there did not seem enough good verse on hand to make an issue. She selected a little verse, "Poetry," sent in by Arthur Davison Ficke, to set the theme of the enterprise. She had two poems by Pound, "To Whistler, American" and "Middle-Aged," sent in with his first enthusiastic letter. Grace Hazard Conkling's long "Symphony in a Mexican Garden" went into the important closing spot in the issue, conventionally regarded as appropriate to the number two poet published.

Small poems by Emilia Stuart Lorimer and Helen Dudley were added, but the issue was like a dinner without a main course. Then Harriet Moody made available an unpublished poem of her husband's, "I Am the Woman"—a long, sonorous feminist meditation that went into first position in the number. William Vaughn Moody's status and Chicago ties, and the pathos of his untimely death, made it particularly felicitous that the magazine should begin with him. Harriet Monroe added editorial explanations of the magazine and of the place of the poet in an ideal scheme of things and an essay by Edith Wyatt, "On the Reading of Poetry," and rushed the manuscripts off to the printer. In October, 1912, *Poetry: A Magazine of Verse* moved into the light of day to test Harriet Monroe's ideals and aspirations—not so much, it turned out, against "reality" as against the conflicting ideals and aspirations of others.

PINE GROSBEAKS MOVE NORTH
For Robert Frost at Derry Farm

Red birds are quiet syllables
Deep in the orchard hollow,
Gentle gossips against hard weather.

No sign of sun or hope of green:
The great beaks tear the dormant buds,
Consuming summer hidden in the husk.

One stoops to autumn apples on the ground,
Remnant of a winter's rot.
His unexcited flight invokes the spring.

The snow, the dirty sky go down
Like pulpy apple smear beneath a claw.
The new bespeaks the end of everything.

ONE

A Confused Beginning 🙖
1912–13

The curious browser who looks over the first year or so of publication of *Poetry*, from October, 1912, to December, 1913, is apt to be disappointed. If he has the legend of *Poetry* in his mind, that the magazine served as a "forum" for Ezra Pound's movement from 1912 to 1914,[1] that Harriet Monroe's little magazine published the bulk of the poetry that made up the Poetry Renaissance,[2] he is apt to be bewildered. This beginning was more modest than the reflected glory cast upon it by the matured reputations of Ezra Pound, William Butler Yeats, Rabindranath Tagore, and William Carlos Williams. The Yeats work was poised between the early and the late; he was still working over Gaelic legend in the narrative "The Two Kings" published in *Poetry* for October, 1913. But "The Grey Rock," in *Poetry* for April, 1913, with the group of short lyrics in the issue for December, 1912, was the nucleus of *Responsibilities*, whose publication in 1914 is one conventional beginning for "the later Yeats." Pound's three publications in *Poetry* in this era likewise marked a transition in his work. Some of the most beautiful short poems in *Lustra* appeared in the "Contemporaria" published in *Poetry* for April, 1913, and in the group in the issue for November, 1913, but there is also a surprising amount of forced language in the poems. William Carlos Williams' first American

1. Ezra Pound, "Small Magazines," *English Journal* 19 (November, 1930), 692 (copyright 1930; all rights reserved). This and following excerpts reprinted by permission of New Directions Publishing Corporation and Faber and Faber, Ltd., publishers and Agents for the Trustees of the Ezra Pound Literary Property Trust.

2. Horace Gregory and Marya Zaturenska, *A History of American Poetry, 1900–1940*, pp. 141–42.

magazine publication, in *Poetry* for June, 1913, was made up of four small poems, of which only "Postlude" is memorable. One of Hilda Doolittle's best-realized poems, "Hermes of the Ways," appeared in *Poetry* for January, 1913, but the enduring reputation of Rabindranath Tagore is not based on the English translations of his Bengali poems that *Poetry* first published in December, 1912. John Gould Fletcher's "Irradiations" in *Poetry* for December, 1913, are among the best poems he ever wrote, but Fletcher's developed art did not come up to the promise of his beginning.

In addition, one finds several key figures in Ezra Pound's "movement" whose poetry is little remembered: Richard Aldington, who had three poems in *Poetry*'s second issue, November, 1912; F. S. Flint, who had "Four Poems in Unrhymed Cadence" in July, 1913; and Skipwith Cannell, whose "Poems in Prose and Verse" in August, 1913, were Pound's prize discovery of the year. There is further disappointment over the "tennis about ideas" that Pound remembered in *Poetry*'s first two years: there was not room for one good volley in the tiny prose section tacked onto the end of the small pamphlet. Over the fourteen months appeared Pound's accounts of Tagore and of Fletcher, Frost, Lawrence, Romains, and Jouve, among other short reviews; his accounts of the "Status Rerum" in London letters; of Imagisme and of "Don'ts by an Imagiste"; of Bohemian poetry and of "Paris"—a very short survey of the modern French poets. Ford Madox Hueffer's "Impressionism" was printed in two issues, there were editorials about Masefield, William Vaughn Moody, Mallarmé, Robert Bridges, and the Servian Epic, and a rising controversy over free verse that culminated in Harriet Monroe's article "Rhythms of English Verse." Short notices and reviews took up the rest of the space; there was no chance for give and take of the kind that Pound's metaphor implies.

But the disappointed reader is likely to be spoiled by years of reading the best work of the new movement in various anthologies. A magazine of verse cannot match the effects of an anthology, which can sift many years' production, but it has the advantage of showing poetry in development—"in . . . flux, [in] . . . change of manner," as Pound put it in his first letter to

Harriet Monroe. For a magazine that began just when *Poetry* began, the chance to body forth the development of the new movement as the poets grew and reacted to each other's work was unique. Anthologies and book publications had their place in promoting the new poetry, but at the beginning magazine publication was very important, much more than later when the poets were established and the movement a successful institution. Thus the unevenness of Pound's or Yeats's work in 1913 becomes a point of interest, and enthusiastic discoveries that quickly faded, like Skipwith Cannell, provoke curiosity rather than disappointment.

Most of the interesting work in *Poetry* in 1912 and 1913 came from Ezra Pound in London. It was printed against a background of verse selected in Chicago by Harriet Monroe and her associate editor, Alice Corbin Henderson. The great discovery of the year in Chicago was Nicholas Vachel Lindsay's "General William Booth Enters into Heaven"; it was noticed in *Current Opinion* by Edward J. Wheeler and created a sensation that permanently established Lindsay as a poet. The Chicago office also discovered Allen Upward, whose impressions from the Chinese strongly interested Pound and ended up in his *Des Imagistes* anthology in 1914. The rest of the Chicago contribution in 1912–13 was not very exciting: William Vaughn Moody, Grace Hazard Conkling, Joseph Campbell, Margaret Widdemer, Arthur Davison Ficke, Witter Bynner, Agnes Lee, Alfred Noyes, John G. Neihardt, Amy Lowell, John Hall Wheelock, Joyce Kilmer, Hamlin Garland, John Reed, and Ernest Rhys, with Harriet Monroe and Alice Corbin, seem the most significant names.

If Chicago at the beginning lacked the sense of a movement, of a group of poets whose mutual responses were creating a new poetry, Harriet Monroe remembered that *Poetry*'s first year was full of excitement. In looking back in 1922, she acknowledged first of all the "cordiality" of Pound's cooperation from abroad. But the little office on Cass Street was full of a sense of "adventure": "The novel enterprise hovered, in the mind of the public, on the delicate border-line between the sublime and ridiculous; and our own minds trembled between a thrill and a

33

laugh. . . . We were dashed between extremes, like a rubber ball in the play of a juggler; and the thing least expected was what happened next."[3] The office itself was lively. Poets felt free to drop in, look over manuscripts, and debate the new movement or free verse. Harriet Monroe mentioned among the early callers Tagore, Vachel Lindsay, Arthur Davison Ficke, Agnes Lee, Edith Wyatt, Helen and Dorothy Dudley, Sara Teasdale, and Maurice Browne of the Chicago Little Theater. Ezra Pound was an important part of the Cass Street debates; Harriet Monroe remembered that "each new letter from Ezra Pound sharpened the edge of them."[4]

The unflagging goodwill with which Miss Monroe described Pound's early correspondence is remarkable. His letters over the first fourteen months were voluminous, rich in exhortations and corrections, but erratic in timing and in tone. During October of 1912 he sent in a great deal of material. He wrote almost every third day, sending nine letters in all, alternating batches of manuscript with exhortations about editorial policy, anxious to establish an international tone that would be taken seriously by the elect. The verses of Richard Aldington, Hilda Doolittle, Rabindranath Tagore, William Butler Yeats, and Ezra Pound arrived in a glorious deluge. But among the foreign correspondence was Pound's first "London Letter," published as "Status Rerum" in *Poetry* for January, 1913, and this immediately created a difference with Miss Monroe.

Pound's article describes a London literary world in which there is very little new or exciting activity, outside the work of Yeats and Hueffer and a new group called the Imagistes, noted for their insistence on "precision" and the high value they put on the short poem. He chose to ignore the whole Georgian revival, which was the hot literary gossip of the moment; on the other hand, the Imagistes were at the moment known to no one but themselves and Ezra Pound. The little essay is arrogant in the grand manner, and perfectly unreasonable. As Conrad Aiken wrote Harriet Monroe from London,

3. "Moving," *Poetry*, May, 1922, pp. 89–90.
4. *Poet's Life*, p. 324.

. . . the Editor, or at least the Editor and Mr. Pound, are using Poetry too egotistically, in order to give expression and scope to their own personalities. . . . Must we share all of Mr. Pound's growing pains with him, pang by pang? And must we believe him when he says with lazy indifference . . . that there is no new poetry in England at present. . . ?

. . . Has America counterparts for Masefield, Abercrombie, Brooke, Davies, Gibson, de la Mare, Stephens, and Drinkwater, that she should be willing to ignore these men? Yet that is what Mr. Pound asks America to do![5]

When Harriet Monroe made some objection that the London letter was too egoistic, Pound replied with a long plea for understanding in a remarkable letter of October 22.[6]

Pound's whole notion of his role as poet, critic, and impresario of the movement is implicit in this long letter. He is the one honest man in a world that has lost all definition and all vitality, blurred by indifference, hypocrisy, and compromise: "Can't you see that until some one is *honest* we get nothing clear. The good work is obscured, hidden in the bad. I go about this London hunting for the real. . . . I'm sick to loathing of people who don't care for master work, who set out as artists with no intention of producing it, who make no effort toward the best." The only healthy communication in this world is created by uncompromising assertion of personal intuition—what a man really feels rather than what he knows the public expects. An honest assertion that is wrongheaded can still help discrimination: "It's only where a few men who know get together and *disagree* that any sort of criticism is born." And Pound judges work almost exclusively from the point of view of its immediate influence on other writers, or on his own writing. Here his sense of the movement is crucial:

When I say a thing is *good* I mean I can read it and enjoy it and do so without fear that it will harm my style . . . sap my energies or blunt my perception of *To Kalon*. I can find little contemporary

5. Letter dated "January, 1913" by Harriet Monroe.
6. Printed in *Letters*, #9, pp. 12–13, with cuts that tend to obscure the tone. Nine relatively conciliatory paragraphs are omitted and the conclusion is cut, so it is not clear that the letter covered a revision of the original article. Several passages in the text that follows were omitted from the printed version of the letter.

work—(some in france) which does not seem to me the worst possible stuff for a young poet to fill his or her mind with. Great God. if a man write six *good* lines he is immortal—isn't that worth trying for. Isn't it worth while having *one* critic left who won't say a thing is *good* until he is ready to stake his whole position on the decision.

Finally, Pound rather enjoys the role of revolutionary outcast: "Print me on asbestos, let them revile me, and perhaps some few will get mad enough to tell the truth in plain passionate language. . . . For one man I strike there are ten who can strike back at me. I stand exposed. It hits me in my dinner invitations, in my week-ends, in the reviews of my own work. Nevertheless it's a good fight. But you are welcome to believe me Thersites if you see it that way."

Pound's view of the poet as touchstone to honesty in a world rotted with cowardice and hypocrisy, his delight in the idea of poet as revolutionary, fitted Harriet Monroe's ideas. Her prose in this period laments the absence of organic, harmonious community life in America; she believed that really great poetry could only be written out of the life of a great civilization. And she hoped that the poet, that poetry, could create a great civilization, out of the give and take between the poet and his audience. Pound's "good fight," the launching of a new movement that would cleanse the word and also the world, found in her an ardent recruit. She printed the disputed "Status Rerum," with the minor revisions Pound sent October 22,[7] and ignored the furious letter of protest that Conrad Aiken sent for publication in January, 1913.

But two differences separate her idea of the new poetry from Pound's. For Harriet Monroe, the world would be restored by interaction between artists and nonartists, and great art itself is created by interaction between artists and nonartists: "To have great poets there must be great audiences too." For Pound, the nonartist hardly deserves to exist, and the new poetry is created

7. These include two minor alterations of phrasing—"any ass" to "any donkey," and "poet worth my serious study" to "poet worth serious study"—and deletion of a rather unrelated conclusion about Americans in Europe and émigrés. The original manuscript was dated September 24 by Pound.

out of interactions between the poets. Second, Harriet Monroe felt that a poet was born with his own peculiar imaginative grasp, and that no amount of harangue or comment could alter the scope of his work. Thus she saw a legitimate place for the consciously minor poet who turned out "delicate miniatures."[8] Pound, on the other hand, was "sick to loathing of people . . . who make no effort toward the best." The brief editorial "The Open Door," which Harriet Monroe published in *Poetry* for November, 1912, a public announcement that she intended to keep the magazine open to all poetic schools, to the small or consciously minor poet as well as to the ambitious or hopefully major poet, Pound read as a rejection of his point of view.

> The Open Door will be the policy of this magazine—may the great poet we are looking for never find it shut, or half-shut, against his ample genius! To this end the editors hope to keep free of entangling alliances with any single class or school. They desire to print the best English verse which is being written today, regardless of where, by whom, or under what theory of art it is written. Nor will the magazine promise to limit its editorial comments to one set of opinions. Without muzzles and braces this is manifestly impossible unless all the critical articles are written by one person.

A good bit of the enthusiasm went out of Pound's letters after November, 1912. An undated letter comments on "The Open Door": "Of course if *I* don't keep up this harping on art *art* ART, nobody will. I don't expect you or the contributors to agree with me, or if you agree can't expect you to go to the lengths that I do." He protested that Harriet Monroe's examples of the good minor poet—Loveless, Drayton, and Herrick—were really examples of his sort of poet, the man who would spend his heart's blood to write six *good* lines. And he distrusted the American appetite for the red-blooded and the cosmic. He stopped sending very many manuscripts, except for his own verse. Of course, he had probably sent everything immediately available in October, 1912, but from November, 1912, to March, 1913, he sent only one poem by William Carlos Wil-

8. "Aesthetic and Social Criticism," *Poetry*, October, 1918, p. 40.

liams, a prose poem by John Cournos, and something from Masefield that was not used. He also promised a poem by Frederic Manning, and recommended one by Frances Gregg.

When *Poetry* printed his people, his response was jaded. December, 1912, was pretty much the sample international issue he had asked for, led off by a group of Yeats lyrics and closed by the English translations of Rabindranath Tagore. Harriet Monroe had left the poems of H.D. until later because she feared to make the number "too exclusively English."[9] Pound did not refer to the issue except to say that Yeats saw it, and forthwith sent his battle poem elsewhere, and to deprecate Mrs. Henderson's statement that the *vers libre* movement in Paris derived from Whitman. His reaction to the January, 1913, issue, with H.D. and with Lindsay's "General Booth," was lukewarm. He called Lindsay's poem a "blague," "rather a good blague, and his own, ONLY he mustn't be let to use that manner of speech on other subjects," and felt that Harriet Monroe was apologizing for H.D. because she noted at the back of the issue that the poems "are not offered as exact translations, or as in any sense finalities, but as experiments in delicate and elusive cadences, which attain sometimes a haunting beauty." But he closed his letter with a plea for zeal and for faith: "I wish I could make you see that the standards I'm fighting for aren't merely a caprice of my own but that they are the standards of the few here who matter."[10]

Pound's "few here who matter" seem to have consisted for poetry of himself, Ford Madox Hueffer, the Imagistes—Richard Aldington and Hilda Doolittle, meeting with Pound in Kensington bun shops—Yeats, and some of Yeats's associates, remnants of the old Rhymers' Club, such men as Victor Plarr. He was more isolated in his London exile than he implied to Harriet Monroe. According to Wyndham Lewis, ". . . Pound arrived as an unassimilable and aggressive stranger: with his Imagism he

9. Harriet Monroe to Ezra Pound, November 9, 1912; Pound letter dated November 23, 1912.
10. Pound letter dated January 27, 1913, by Harriet Monroe. Her worry about translations from the Greek reflects the criticism that Paul Shorey of the University of Chicago had leveled at a fragment of Sappho translated by Richard Aldington. ". . . he wouldn't stand for it," she wrote Pound on November 9, 1912.

became aesthetically a troublesome rebel. It was not the fault of England nor was it his, but I hope I shall not seem sensational if I say that looking back I cannot see him stopping here very long without some such go-between as Ford Madox Hueffer."[11] The Imagistes, in the first public description of them at the back of *Poetry* for November, 1912, seemed to number more than two disciples and Pound—"a group of ardent young Hellenists who are pursuing interesting experiments in *vers libre*." But the other poets in the 1914 *Des Imagistes* anthology were either not Londoners (William Carlos Williams, Amy Lowell, James Joyce), not really young (Ford Madox Hueffer and F. S. Flint), or unknown to Pound in 1912. H.D. and Aldington remain, with no grounds for believing that in the fall of 1912 Pound had any other young disciples in London, unless one must consider Paul Selver, the translator of Bezruč, who was quickly alienated.

A common explanation of Pound's Imagisme is that it was a mere label, "invented to launch H.D. and Aldington before either had enough stuff for a volume."[12] But like many things in the movement, Imagisme has meant different things at different times. Pound's account in a letter of September 13, 1915, to Harriet Monroe shows a mixture of serious and unserious in it:

> By the way, merely for reference. Wherever the "Imagist" movement started it did not start with "Storer," who is the antipodes. Hulme was the only person I met in that 1909 group who had any sense and he quit verse for the translation of philosophy. . . . The name first appears in my introd. to T.E.H. at the end of *Ripostes*, and the whole affair was started not very seriously chiefly to get H.D.'s five poems a hearing without it's being necessary for her to publish a whole book. It began certainly in Church Walk with H.D., Richard, and myself. You will note that Flint writes in his first note ["Imagisme," *Poetry*, March, 1913,] as one coming to the group not as a founder.
>
> He does not say "we" but "they." Even when he came in he did not think of dragging in Storer, who was only dug up for the "obvious purpose" last May ["History of Imagism," *Egoist*, May, 1915]. I don't know whether the movement has been so cheapened

11. In Peter Russell, ed., *Ezra Pound*, p. 259.
12. Pound to Glenn Hughes, September 26, 1927, in *Letters*, #225, pp. 212-13.

as to make it advisable to renounce all connection, or whether one should be meticulous and try to retain some platform embodying the common sense of the original declarations.

I don't suppose it matters a t'upenny d. .n one way or another.

The degree of possible seriousness is measured by Pound's letter to René Taupin in 1928: "Ce que Rimbaud atteint par intuition (génie) dans certaines poèmes, érigé en esthétique conscient (??peutêtre)—je ne veux pas prendre une gloire injuste—mais pour tant que je sais. J'en ai fait une esthétique plus ou moins systématique. . . ."[13] A few years later, when Taupin had failed to make much of Imagism in his *L'Influence du symbolisme français sur la poésie américaine de 1910 à 1920*, Pound described the whole campaign as if Harriet Monroe made a manifesto of notes intended for a rejection slip without consulting him.[14] Although the "Don'ts by an Imagiste" were once intended as part of a rejection slip, Pound had waged a brief deliberate campaign for Imagisme in the fall of 1912.

Aldington says that Pound planned the anthology *Des Imagistes* from the beginning.[15] Perhaps Pound mounted the campaign to counter the projected *Georgian Poetry* announced September 20, 1912; the publicity he put into *Poetry* was meant to "reach England," as Harriet Monroe phrased it on another occasion. About the time Pound wrote the remarks on Hulme and the School of Images that appeared in *Ripostes*, he supplied the material for the note on the "group of ardent young Hellenists" that appeared in *Poetry* for November, 1912, unless Harriet Monroe developed the *Poetry* note from his "Status Rerum," dated September 24, 1912. In letters to Harriet Monroe written before November, 1912, Pound described Hilda Doolittle, himself, and Petr Bezruč, the Czech poet sent in translation by Paul Selver, as Imagistes. The "Status Rerum" in *Poetry* for January, 1913, describes the Imagistes rather negligently as one of the few stirrings of poetic activity worth notice in London; H.D.'s poems are signed "H.D., Imagiste," in the same issue, as Pound had instructed in October. The short articles in *Poetry* for March,

13. *Letters*, #229, p. 217.
14. "Small Magazines," p. 691.
15. Richard Aldington, *Life for Life's Sake*, p. 136.

1913, "Imagisme" by F. S. Flint and "A Few Don'ts by an Imagiste" by Ezra Pound, climax and conclude the campaign.[16] Pound seems to have tired of the Imagiste campaign long before March, 1913, for he did not promote it in his letters to Harriet Monroe after October, 1912, and did not again discuss Imagisme in them until Amy Lowell renewed the publicity in 1915. Pound sent no further Imagiste editorial material to *Poetry* after the "Don'ts." In referring to the "Don'ts" in March, he called them "instructions to neophites," without using the Imagiste label.[17]

The best evidence that Pound abandoned the Imagiste campaign in 1913 after the publication of his "Don'ts" is the fact that he introduced Skipwith Cannell to Harriet Monroe and to *Poetry*'s readers without making any use of the term. Cannell was in a situation analogous to Aldington's and H.D.'s—he was young and unknown, a discovery introduced to the world of letters under Pound's chaperonage. Although he was included with H.D. and Aldington in the anthology *Des Imagistes*, published in the spring of 1914, his verse appeared in the August, 1913, number of *Poetry* without any reference to Imagisme. When later in 1913 Pound revived Imagisme in his plans for the 1914 anthology,[18] he cut the connection with *Poetry*; he omitted all references to prior publications or publicity in *Poetry* from the book.

There is ground for believing that the Imagiste campaign in *Poetry* was a complete failure. After Amy Lowell made the term famous, Harriet Monroe had to remind her readers that she had discovered the school. A writer as close to the magazine and its Chicago milieu as Vachel Lindsay was surprised to learn that she

---

16. Flint was almost the nominal author of his article. In his "History of Imagism" in the May, 1915, *Egoist*, p. 70, Flint called it an interview over his signature, and in 1930, in "Small Magazines," Pound made himself the author of the three principles described in the article. Flint's first draft, with corrections by Pound, is printed in Christopher Middleton, "Documents on Imagism from the Papers of F. S. Flint," *Review*, April, 1965, pp. 36–38. The *Poetry* Papers give no evidence for the date of its composition.

17. Letter of March 10, 1913, in *Letters*, #16, pp. 17–18, as of March 30.

18. Pound wrote Harriet Monroe that plans for the anthology were under way November 7, 1913; by that time Aldington and H.D. were deserting the school. H.D. asked Harriet Monroe to cut "the affectation of 'Imagiste'" from her signature when her poems were printed in *Poetry* for February, 1914 (letter of October 24, 1913); Aldington's typescript of "Argyria," a poem published in *Poetry* for January, 1914, has the typed signature "R. A., Imagiste," scratched out and "Richard Aldington" written in Aldington's hand. The MS went to *Poetry* with Aldington's letter of July 5, 1913, or of October 6, 1913, or with an Aldington group Pound sent in September, 1913.

had been the first sponsor of the group. He wrote her November 30, 1915:

> Also I did *not know* that you introduced the Imagists until you told me when last I was in Chicago. What's more I did not realize that you were their especial partizan. I was thoroughly grateful for your championship of my work—but did not know who else you were championing in the same personal way. Certainly my human interest in the Imagists dates entirely from my last visit to Chicago—because they are particularly the sort of people hard for me to get at. . . . I thought you viewed them with something of the same polite effort to be fair that I do. . . .

Margaret Anderson, who was one of Chicago's youthful bohemians after 1911, did not discover the Imagistes until the middle of 1914, after the publication of *Des Imagistes*. The first four issues of the *Little Review* did not mention the school, except for a brief sneer by A. S. Kaun in June, 1914; then Imagisme exploded all over the July, 1914, issue. The effect is typical of Margaret Anderson's enthusiasms, and it is hard to escape the conclusion that Imagisme was a fresh discovery for her. Alfred Kreymborg, who recorded that the early issues of *Poetry* were exciting and encouraging to him in New York, did not take in Imagisme as such. In the spring of 1914, when he and Harriet Monroe had a misunderstanding about poems from *Poetry* reprinted without acknowledgment in *Des Imagistes*, of which he was nominal editor, he confessed March 16, 1914: "Pound's ms. had no reference anywhere to previous publication in other magazines—and I, for one, did not know of their publication in *Poetry*, all of whose numbers I am not familiar with."

The Imagiste aspect of Ezra Pound's foreign correspondence to *Poetry* seems built up of impulsive and contradictory decisions on his part. The story of Allen Upward's relation to the school completes the confusion. Harriet Monroe printed Upward's "Scented Leaves from a Chinese Jar" at the head of the September, 1913, issue of *Poetry*. Pound was impressed: "Upward is all to the good. I have just arranged to meet him. That Chinese stuff just is."[19] Pound himself had just begun to work with

19. Letter dated "August, 1913" by Harriet Monroe, in error for September.

Chinese materials: Ernest Fenollosa's wife gave him her husband's notes after reading his poems in *Poetry* for April, 1913. Upward's impressions from the Chinese seem an important influence on *Cathay*. This led to reprints of "Scented Leaves" in the *Des Imagistes* anthology. Upward wrote a poetical account of the business after he read "History of Imagism" in the *Egoist* in 1915:

> They [his poems] were sent back to me by the *Spectator* and *The English Review*.
> I secretly grudged them to the western devils.
> After many years I sent them to Chicago and they were printed by Harriet Monroe.
> (They also were printed in the *Egoist*.)
> Thereupon Ezra Pound the generous rose up and called me an Imagist.
> (I had no idea what he meant.)
> And he included me in an anthology of Imagists.
>
> This was a very great honor.
> But I was left out of the next anthology [Amy Lowell's project].
> This was a very great shame.
>
> And now I have read in a history of Imagism
> That the movement was started in 19 hundred and 8
> By Edward Storer and T. E. Hulme. . . .[20]

More important than Imagisme in *Poetry* for 1913, far more effective in arousing reactions from readers, were the poems of Ezra Pound published in April, 1913, as "Contemporaria." The group includes "Tenzone," "The Condolence," "The Garret," "The Garden," "Ortus," "Dance Figure," "Salutation," "Salutation the Second," "Pax Saturni," "Commission," "A Pact," and "In a Station of the Metro"—all, except for "Pax Saturni," which Pound did not reprint until 1968, substantially as they appear in the collected *Personae*. The group was selected out of a number of poems that Pound sent in several batches in 1912.

"Contemporaria" as printed in *Poetry* was the end product of a good deal of debate. Pound delighted in the poems that he felt

20. "The Discarded Imagist," *Egoist*, June 1, 1915.

were destructive of falsehood and revolutionary. Harriet Monroe was most interested in the poems that had some lyric sweetness,[21] and was upset by egoism and rash assertion in the satirical poems. The lines in "Pax Saturni" that lump "shopwalkers" and "employers of women" with "amateur harlots" and "disguised procurers" puzzled her. "How can one justly rail at employers of women? In this day and generation? It's the employers of children who need it!" The lines in "Commission" that call the three-generation family dwelling together "hideous" struck her as "rather bitter, and only occasionally true," and she wondered whether an artist could be great if he did not love. And she marked the lines in the same poem about "delicate lust" and "delicate desires . . . thwarted" as embarrassing, without further comment.

Harriet Monroe was willing to print the readings if they were important to Pound: "Although I balk at the above as rather strong for our struggling little magazine, please don't misunderstand me: if you say they must stand I shall pray the Gods for mercy and print them."[22] Pound, on his side, felt that some of the poems were rather too daring. He wrote December 3, 1912, "Of course I can stand 'Courtesy' ["The Bathtub" in *Personae*] and 'The Teashop,' but I think it might be very unwise to print 'em in *Poetry*." A little later when he sent the second batch of poems, he commented, "For GORD's sake don't print anything of mine that you think will kill the magazine but so far as I personally am concerned the public can go to the devil."[23] Miss Monroe printed "Pax Saturni" and "Commission" without alteration, but decided against printing six poems that Pound wanted in the series: "The Bathtub"; "The Teashop" (submitted in a longer version than the one printed in *Personae*); "Epilogue: To My Five Books"; "Salutation the Third"; "Our Respectful Homage to M. Laurent Tailhade," as eventually published in *Blast*; and an early version of the "Post Mortem Conspectu" published in *Blast* in 1914. Seven other rejected poems Pound did not particularly

21. Undated note by Pound about "The Garden" and "Dance Figure" being Harriet Monroe's preferences, while he preferred "The Teashop" and "The Bathtub."
22. Undated letter, copy filed in the Pound correspondence for spring, 1913.
23. Undated letter, about December, 1912, in *Letters*, #10, p. 13.

value; he did not include them in *Personae*. Finally, Miss Monroe rejected early versions of "Arides," "The Patterns," and the "Meditatio" of *Lustra*.

Nothing that Harriet Monroe left out seems much of a loss. Pound submitted more manuscripts than he had any wish to print, and was more frightened of his own daring in the satirical poems than he was to be later. A vigorous disagreement arose over a fragment from John Reed's "Sangar" that Pound posted over "Pax Saturni" as a prime example of fatuous chauvinism. Reed's poem, in *Poetry* for December, 1912, is heavily ironic, but Pound would not listen to remonstrances: "We simply must have the quotation to kick off from. . . . I've simply *got* to have the jem, Leid motif, Dio Santo! hasn't he, whoever he is, got the rest of his natural lifetime to shy pellets at my hide!!!"[24] Pound in the revolutionary role could not admit the existence of competitors.

The group as published in *Poetry* was very successful; Pound cited it later as a standard of effectiveness. The response of Chicago journalists was almost galvanic, and the free-verse controversy boiled in Chicago. As Pound later wrote in an "Epilogue" for *Lustra*:

> O chansons foregoing
> You were a seven days' wonder.
> When you came out in the magazines
> You created considerable stir in Chicago,
> And now you are stale and worn out. . . .[25]

Which does not seem fair to "The Garret," "The Garden," "Dance Figure," "In a Station of the Metro," and "Ortus," although the impudence of the satirical poems does not age very well. The group is of interest to the student of Pound's career, since it shows struggle toward a style that will take in a new range of subject and emotion. Even the more successful poems show strain. An oratorical overemphasis colors the expressions of personal emotion:

24. Undated note filed in the Pound correspondence for April, 1913.
25. Excerpt from "Epilogue" reprinted from *Personae* and *Collected Shorter Poems* by Ezra Pound (copyright 1926 by Ezra Pound) by permission of New Directions Publishing Corporation and Faber and Faber, Ltd., publishers and Agents for the Trustees of the Ezra Pound Literary Property Trust.

> Nor has life in it ought better
> Than this hour of clear coolness,
>   the hour of waking together.[26]

The frankly hortative poems are marred by tactless egoism. As in his earlier poems, Pound was most successful when most remote from contemporary tone and subject, despite all his struggles to write the "last obsequies of the victorian period."[27]

If Harriet Monroe, judging from the selection of this group of poems, had a good feeling for what was solidly achieved in Pound's poetry, she does not seem to have communicated her appreciation effectively. He seemed to feel that the new work which excited him frightened or bored her. When he sent in a new batch of manuscripts, he was less permissive about alterations: "I won't permit any selection or editing."[28] Then, a little later, in a letter of March 25, 1913, he weakened: "you will doubtless find it necessary to strike out a certain number of them before delivering them to the chaste american ear. . . . they'll cheer A.C.H. Doubtless you will yourself be horrified." Harriet Monroe responded to the new poems April 12, 1913:

> Your last bunch of poems, of course, we need not decide now which of them we had better use since we cannot use any for a few months. Some of these epigrams have a very complete little sting [the manuscripts titled "Xenia" in the Pound correspondence]. Others do not seem to me quite so firm. After all, Alexander Pope did that kind of thing pretty well. I like "Lustra" [another batch of manuscripts sent in March, 1913] but I rather wish that the next batch we print of yours might be an oblation to pure beauty, something in the vein quite different from "Contemporaria." However, of course, that is for you to decide.

Pound answered:

26. Excerpt from "The Garret" reprinted from *Personae* and *Collected Shorter Poems* by Ezra Pound (copyright 1926 by Ezra Pound) by permission of New Directions Publishing Corporation and Faber and Faber, Ltd., publishers and Agents for the Trustees of the Ezra Pound Literary Property Trust.

27. Letter of March, 1913, to Alice Corbin Henderson, undated in the correspondence, in *Letters*, #25, p. 23, as of October, 1913.

28. Ibid.

"Oblation to pure beauty"

Dear Miss Monroe:

What *could* be purer than the scarlet silk trousers [in "Further Instructions"]? Anyhow I'm afraid that's the purest you'll get for a little while.[29]

Harriet Monroe could not easily communicate her interest in Pound's work, and he seems almost to have taken her comments about beauty as a rebuff. At any rate, by June she had a rival American editor, who received many of the poems that Pound had already submitted to *Poetry*.

Pound had met Willard Huntington Wright of the *Smart Set* in June, 1913, and given him a number of manuscripts to select from. As he wrote Harriet Monroe, "his rate is higher than ours. ALso he has the good sense to divide all of the poets here into two classes: Yeats and I in one class, and everybody else in the other. Such illumination can not pass without reward."[30] His money apart, Wright's virtue as an editor was his evident enthusiasm for Pound's poetry, and Harriet Monroe suffered the consequences of a reserved and judicious tone. Although Pound implied in his letter that *Poetry* had been holding his manuscripts too long— "Of course if you wanted to use the first things sent, you ought to have done it when your first got 'em" — the complaint seems without foundation. Some of the "Xenia" he gave Wright in June had been at *Poetry* only since March, while "the first things sent" would be "Contemporaria" poems sent in October and December and not printed in April, 1913. But Pound, sending later work, including the "Xenia" and some "Lustra," advised Harriet Monroe on March 25, 1913, to hold all his poems in reserve: "They may stay your hand in case you should be tempted to accept anything worse. . . . There's no hurry about them as the book don't come out till autumn. . . ."

Harriet Monroe had reason to believe that all the Pound manuscripts were submitted for future publication in *Poetry*, with no very stringent time limitation. In his first letter to *Poetry*,

29. Letter dated "April or May, 1913" by Harriet Monroe.
30. Letter dated "August, 1913" by Harriet Monroe.

Pound had authorized an announcement that "for the present such of my work as appears in America (bar. my own books) will appear exclusively in your magazine,"[31] and while the gesture made to a stranger seems impulsively generous, Pound seems correspondingly feeble to revoke it the moment he got a decent chance at another American outlet. At any rate, several groups of Pound poems appeared in the *Smart Set* in the fall of 1913, and Harriet Monroe had to patch up the Pound group in *Poetry* for November, 1913, from the leftovers. The poems published in *Poetry* were "Ancora," "Surgit Fama," "The Choice," "April," "Gentildonna," "Lustra: The Rest, Les Millwin, and Further Instructions," and "Xenia: The Street in Soho, The Cool Fingers of Science, A Song of Degrees, Ite, and Dum Capitolium Scandet."

The "Contemporaria" group in the April, 1913, *Poetry* brought Pound and the movement to the attention of Chicago. Floyd Dell, speaking for the younger generation in the *Friday Review* of the *Evening Post*, was ecstatic: "Ezra Pound we salute you! You are the most enchanting poet alive. Your poems in the April *Poetry* are so mockingly, so delicately, so unblushingly beautiful. . . ."[32] Other newspapers parodied or attacked, and *Poetry*'s readers wrote in sputtering letters about "esoteric writhings," "insufferable snobs," "expatriate sensualists," and "plain blackguardism." Harriet Monroe enjoyed the fuss, and sent Pound clippings. "I don't know how you feel about jokes," she wrote April 12, 1913, sending parodies by Wallace Rice and B.L.T. from the *Tribune*'s Line O'Type column: "I don't mind them in the least." She had been feeling encouraged by local response to the magazine: "I am gratified by the kind of comment that the magazine is receiving over here, also our subscription list is growing gradually, and I begin to think we may have a Future. But I don't permit myself to think very much about that phase of it."[33] But in May, 1913, the *Dial*, which was the voice of the literary establishment in town, joined the newspaper attack on Pound's *vers libre*.

31. *Letters*, #5, p. 9.
32. Quoted in *Poet's Life*, p. 310.
33. Letter of March 31, 1913, a copy in the Pound correspondence.

Wallace Rice, the parodist of the *Tribune* column, wrote a letter printed in the *Dial* for May 1, 1913, that identifies poetry with technique, technique with tradition, and utterly damns both Pound and *Poetry* as violators of everything sacred in the past. Rice was a member of the local "Little Room" circle and of the Cliffdwellers' Club, a balladist and anthologist. He attacked Pound for intense egoism and weak-headedness, compounded by indecency, and was equally snide against the editor of *Poetry*. Harriet Monroe, he wrote, had confounded the hopes of her friends, seeking out the bizarre and the shocking, and printing a shabby little pamphlet unworthy in format and typography of the dignity of the cause. Moreover, she seldom printed a number without some of her own verse—which showed steady retrogression from her once high standard. (She had published two of her own poems in seven numbers: the very short "Nogi" in Nvoember, 1912, and the ambitious "Mother Earth" in April, 1913.)

Harriet Monroe wrote a reply to the *Dial* for May 16, 1913, that defended "Mr. Pound, who has devoted some years to an exhaustive study of metrical forms and variations in the poetry of eleven languages." She cited Moody's "I Am the Woman," John Reed's "Sangar," Lindsay's "General Booth," Charles Hanson Towne's "Beyond the Stars," Yeats's "The Grey Rock," Tagore's lyrics, and Pound's "Contemporaria" as poems published by her magazine expressing the social feeling, the growing strength of the women's movement, and the marvels of science, which Rice had written were crying out for poetic expression.

The next issue of the *Dial* finds Wallace Rice in the correspondence column gloating over an acknowledged victory, since Miss Monroe could cite only seven poems of special distinction. If he eliminated Mr. Lindsay's rubbish, the prose of Pound and Tagore, and the unpoetic lines of Yeats, it left a mere three poems that she could show after seven months of earnest effort. In the same number William Rose Benet of the *Century* joined the controversy. The free-verse issue raised by Rice did not interest Benet; he saw criticism as the expression of a personal taste necessarily dogmatic, but for what it was worth he found his own agreeing with Rice's. Of the poems that Miss Monroe had cited in her defense, only Lindsay's seemed to him a poem of distinction, and Pound's latest freak seemed calculated to drive away the admirers of the three decent poems he had written. Now he had placed himself in the ranks of the worthless.

Harriet Monroe replied in the *Dial* for June 16, 1913, avoiding further controversy with Rice but glad to take up Benet's praise of Lindsay. Her letter illustrates the defensive uses of her notion that the poet needs a "great audience." Publication of one poem of "very great distinction" is "an achievement which quite justifies the existence of the magazine and pays for all the labor and capital that have gone into it." How many of the publicized annual prize-winners of the art shows are similarly "distinguished," she goes on to ask. The excuse for her poets, if they need one, is the irascibility of men like Rice: "the poet—the artist of any kind—must have a public to speak to, else his art cannot grow, he can not go on. The people must grant a hearing to the best poets they have, else they will never have better. The great periods in any art come only when great energy of creation meets equal energy of sympathy,—that is inexorable law."

This controversy with Wallace Rice in the *Dial* over Pound's poetry has its comic side, since historically the *Dial* was on Pound's side, for an austere international standard in the arts. Francis Fisher Browne, the founder and editor, had fought this out in the nineties against Hamlin Garland's local color. Fragments of Rice's first letter sound more like Pound or Eliot than anything that Harriet Monroe was ever to write. And in many ways the literary issue was not the real one—*vers libre* was an ideally arguable instance of what was felt as the universal flouting of tradition and order.

Pound thought that "the question of 'vers libre' is such old game. It's like quarreling over impressionism or Manet,"[34] though he worried a bit that Harriet Monroe "might be bothered by the nasty things they say in foolish places."[35] But Harriet Monroe's correspondence with John G. Neihardt, of Bancroft, Nebraska, a poet who considered himself "accredited," shows a middle-western sensibility reacting with vigorous naiveté to the

34. Letter dated "April or May, 1913" by Harriet Monroe.
35. Letter dated June 21, 1913, by Harriet Monroe.

free-verse controversy. Neihardt, a writer of some reputation, reacted to "Contemporaria" in a letter of June 18, 1913:

Why do you take so much trouble to yourself by way of fighting sincere work? Noguchi and Tagore are wonderful poets, but what of the wretched drivel in the April number? In your heart you must know it is insincere and highly imitative of the worst in Whitman. Yelling isn't poetry. Billingsgate isn't beautiful. Rebellion gets no where. Only slow growth ever counts. There is no *new* beauty [reference to Harriet Monroe's editorial "The New Beauty," in April]. . . .

Why make your magazine a freak? You could print formless nonsense as an exhibit of transient tendency. But why defend the indefensible? My God! Have you forgotten that we are endowed with a great heritage? Will you and an impudent young man wipe out a tremendous past that has produced us?

Harriet Monroe in a letter of June 24, 1913, made a lively defense of Ezra Pound to Neihardt:

You say, "In your heart you know it is insincere and highly imitative of the worst in Whitman." Now, as a matter of fact, in my heart I don't know any such thing. I think that Ezra Pound is passionately sincere and that some of the poems are extremely beautiful and full of rare and exquisite rhythmic effects. . . . I think sincerity and careful workmanship are of very little use by themselves and I am tempted to say you must think so too. I fancy, from everything I hear, that Pound is one of the most sincere and careful workers we have—he writes poetry in no slap-dash fashion, but very slowly—or at least so I am informed by those who know.

You ask, "Why make your magazine a freak?" I don't see why a few poems or editorials that we print would place it in that category, even if they seem to you freakish, for surely we have been hospitable to all kinds and have not confined ourselves to any one school. You, at least, ought not to accuse us of limiting ourselves to the radical group.

The terms of Neihardt's letter suggest a cultural conflict raging between the sacred traditional and the revolutionary new. In its free-verse quarrel, *Poetry* came into contact with the vigorous young bohemia that existed in Chicago before World War I.

Young men and women were coming in from the smaller cities and towns of the Middle West, looking for a freer life and a world more full of possibilities. The hero of *Winesburg, Ohio* had many real-life precursors, and Chicago, around 1912, was one of the centers that drew them.[36]

The relation of *Poetry* to these young newcomers remained fairly remote, however; their lives did not center on the *Poetry* office. Floyd Dell and Margery Currey, Margaret Anderson, and Sherwood Anderson were among the leading spirits of the new generation in Chicago, and none of them ever had much to do with *Poetry*. Eunice Tietjens, who was a clerk for *Poetry* early in its history and later an associate editor, wrote for Margaret Anderson's *Little Review*, and Vachel Lindsay knew the Fifty-seventh Street bohemia founded by Dell. But the *Poetry* office was dominated by an older and more established group.

Indeed, Edgar Lee Masters had first reacted to *Poetry* as an "efflorescence" of the Little Room, the artistic and social group he hated, where he felt "dilettanti practiced a haughty exclusiveness, and where the lions were Henry B. Fuller, Hamlin Garland, and some of the literary set of the University of Chicago."[37] Floyd Dell, the leader and as it were founder of the new artistic bohemia, brushed aside Harriet Monroe's requests for poetry and prose, and had to defend himself against the charge of being "standoffish" not long before his departure for New York to join the staff of the *Masses*.[38]

Dell's departure reminds one that the turnover within the local bohemia was high. Perhaps 1912 was a significant moment in a progressive centralization of American society. Edgar Lee Masters, who had come up to Chicago in the generation before from a small Illinois town, had joined the local bar, married a local girl, and settled down to family life. But the young people with artistic aspirations who came to Chicago in 1912 from other, smaller middle-western towns departed in a few years for New York, or, after the war, for Europe. Thus Dell left for New York late in 1913; Margaret Anderson moved the *Little Review* to New

36. See Duffey, *Chicago Renaissance*, p. 142.
37. *Across Spoon River*, pp. 336–37.
38. Letter dated "Spring, 1913" by Harriet Monroe.

York late in 1916, after some two years' publication in Chicago; and Sherwood Anderson was spending more time in New York than in Chicago by 1918. This "upward" mobility of the leadership would tend to diminish the influence and weaken the identity of the local bohemia.

Several factors, then, kept *Poetry* from being the voice of the new generation in Chicago, whatever general stimulation it got from them or gave them. Ezra Pound, operating by letter all the way from London, remained the principal avant-garde stimulus in its editorial counsels.

Whether his material got a strong response, like "Contemporaria," or little response, like the Imagiste campaign, Ezra Pound was plainly the focus of interest in the first six months of *Poetry*. Even the Imagiste failure was a qualified one, for the reform of style preached in the "Don'ts by an Imagiste" strongly impressed the *Poetry* office. It was the doctrinaire aspect of Imagisme that drew no response in *Poetry*. Harriet Monroe took the stylistic tenets to heart but ignored the French label.

Nor was Pound's effect at the beginning of *Poetry* exclusively radical, although much of his material shocked *Poetry*'s small readership. A line in "To Whistler, American" in the first issue, which isolated Whistler and Abe Lincoln from "that mass of dolts," outraged national feeling and required editorial explanation by Harriet Monroe. She defended Pound with her habitual appeal to the need of a great audience. An American public whose indifference drove its best writers into exile could blame only itself if the poets labeled it "a mass of dolts," she wrote in *Poetry* for February, 1913.

Also, the detested exile sent in the poetry of William Butler Yeats, whose lyrics at the head of *Poetry*'s third issue could only create prestige for the magazine. And the award of the Nobel Prize to Rabindranath Tagore in the next year greatly enhanced *Poetry*'s status. The poems that Pound had sent in October, 1912, as part of his first deluge of material, published in December, 1912, gave *Poetry* credit for first publication of the Nobel laureate in the English language.

Compared to Pound's contribution, the material selected by the Chicago office is uninteresting. But the poets Harriet Monroe was printing—Margaret Widdemer, Arthur Davison Ficke, Witter Bynner, Joseph Campbell, Grace Hazard Conkling, Agnes Lee—represent a different level of aspiration from "magazine poetry," whatever the defects of their accomplishment. And Vachel Lindsay's "General William Booth Enters into Heaven" in the January, 1913, issue, was widely quoted and reprinted, striking the public as a splendidly original tribute to the founder of the Salvation Army. In its way it helped the struggling magazine as much as the publication of Yeats and Tagore: witness the comment of William Rose Benet in the *Dial* free-verse controversy. The Chicago office contributed enough substance to keep its part of the magazine afloat, whatever the disparity in permanent interest between its material and the London material. Thus Pound in an undated letter of March, 1913, took note of a lack of disgraceful weakness in the March *Poetry*: "while it contains nothing wildly interesting, it contains nothing or rather no group of poems which is wholly disgusting. I think the average 'feel' of the number is as good as you've done."[39]

In March, 1913, Ezra Pound's foreign correspondence, which had lagged after the spectacular beginning of October, 1912, showed new vitality. The big excitement of March was his discovery of Frost's *A Boy's Will*, but he also sent more poems by Tagore, and poems by Frederic Manning and F. S. Flint. The April issue, with his "Contemporaria" and Yeats's "The Grey Rock," cheered him and pleased his London set. He wrote April 10, 1913, from an Italian holiday: "Hueffer thinks that *at last* 'the little one is awakening,' or something of that sort. Can't remember the exact words, but he begins to have hopes. Yeats is interested, likes some of the things, trembles for my 'unrestrained language' (that was, I think, in a poem you're not using.) I shall change 'pot-bellied' and write 'obese.'" (In *Blast*, in "Salutation the Third," it ends up "slut-bellied.") The May number, which was given over entirely to John G. Neihardt's blank-verse tragedy, *The Death of Agrippina*, did nothing to reinforce the effect of the April one. Harriet Monroe had committed herself to

39. In *Letters*, #13, p. 14.

publishing the play sight unseen August 15, 1912, and wrote apologetically to Pound on March 31, 1913:

> Just a word to explain our May number, which I suppose will make you say "damn." I accepted Neihardt's play in the very beginning of the enterprise. I think it was before number one came out, when I was gratified to have a man of his strength offer me what he considered his best work. Even then I was terribly disappointed to find it a Roman tragedy of Elizabethan origin. Of late, I asked him to release me from my promise to print it in a single number, but he declined, so I am fulfilling the promise. It has some strong passages, I think in Nero's soliloquys, but much of it is bombast, and it isn't drama. However, we will get it off our hands and off our files and will never do such a thing again, please God.

Pound dismissed it good-naturedly at the time—"We'll cross off your Neihardt against my Vildrac and call it square"—although twenty years later he raked up her "secular crime of devoting a whole number to Neihardt in the year B.M. 1431."[40]

Pound's letters from abroad continued enthusiastic. In May he was excited about a long essay, "Impressionism," by Ford Madox Hueffer. In June he sent the verse of Skipwith Cannell—"By Jove this man Cannell is an artist to keep. Be sure to keep the first ten pages of August."[41] About the same time he gave a strong recommendation to Orrick Johns's "Songs of Deliverance," which Harriet Monroe had sent for his opinion. He wrote June 10, 1913, that the poems were "dam'd he-goatish Whitman, but that's better than peptomized Keats. It would be a great mistake not to print it. . . . *I* like it better than Lindsay, Oh a lot better . . ." and concluded that Johns was "about the best you've yet found on your side of the wet." In the same month Pound reluctantly decided that he had to do something to acknowledge the poetry of D. H. Lawrence: "Lawrence has brought out a vol., he is clever, I don't know whether to send in a review or not, we seem pretty well stuffed up with matter at the moment. . . . Detestable person but needs watching. I think he learned the proper treatment of modern subjects two years

40. Letters of April 10, 1913, and March 20, 1930.
41. Postcard of June 16, 1913.

before I did. That was in some poems in the Eng. Rev., can't tell whether he has progressed or retrograded as I haven't seen the book yet. He may have published merely on his prose rep."[42] A review of *Love Poems* came in a little later.

Thus *Poetry* in the spring of 1913 received a fresh transfusion of material from London. But it seems a sign of growth in *Poetry*, and in the Poetry Renaissance, that fresh contributions also came in from the American side of the Atlantic. The emergence of William Carlos Williams was an event in *Poetry* for June, 1913. The group—"Peace on Earth," "Sicilian Emigrant's Song," "Postlude," and "Proof of Immortality"—had been much negotiated before publication. According to Williams, the first batch of manuscript he sent in was rejected outright, but a second selected by his wife pleased the ladies at *Poetry* much better, and earned them the distinction—which he seemed in retrospect to begrudge them—of being his first magazine publishers in America.[43] In fact, it seems that Pound was instrumental in getting Williams a careful reading. He wrote, sometime over the winter, an undated letter sending "Postlude" and recommending attention to other things Williams was sending direct.

Harriet Monroe's letter of acceptance to Williams is another instance of cold welcome to a poet. The offer to publish, she seems to feel, is in itself a sufficiently positive response, and she goes on to discuss flaws in the work, so that the poet feels more rejected than accepted. She wrote March 3, 1913:

> I like best your Sicilian Emigrant's Song, but I am keeping also Peace on Earth and Immortality. Postlude seems to me to need revision. I find it does not appeal so much to me as Mr. Pound, but his word goes a long way and I should like to see the poem again when you have given it your last touch.
>
> Would it be banal to give a more explanatory title to Peace on Earth. Something that will give the reader a hint that you are talking about constellations. Perhaps it would be sufficient to capitalize their names. In Proof of Immortality you are using a fixed iambic measure in which the fourth and sixth lines do not seem to me to conform. They are both a syllable short. Will you

---

42. Letter dated "? June 1913" by Harriet Monroe, in *Letters*, #15, pp. 16–17, as of March, 1913.
43. William Carlos Williams, *I Wanted to Write a Poem*, p. 17.

please consider this point? I do not care much either for the title of this poem. Wouldn't "The Immortal" be better, or something else you may think of.

Williams clearly felt this a rebuff:

> . . . I had looked upon *Poetry* as a forum wherein competent poets might speak freely, uncensored by any standard of rules. "Poetry" seemed to me a protest against the attitude of every other periodical American publication. . . .
>
> Now life is above all things else at any moment subversive of life as it was the moment before—always new, irregular. Verse to be alive must have infused into it something of the same order, some tincture of disestablishment, something in the nature of an impalpable revolution, an ethereal reversal, let me say. I am speaking of modern verse. . . .
>
> I do not assail you because you fail to praise my exquisite productions but—in perfect good humor—I find fault with your expressed attitude toward my exquisite productions.
>
> Perhaps I am more than ever obscure. . . .[44]

It was the tone of Harriet Monroe's whole letter more than particular criticisms that had offended him—except for her query about irregular meter, which makes her seem the defender of static order. In his *Collected Earlier Poems* he made the title change to "Immortal" that she suggested, although the poem is still "Proof of Immortality" in its *Poetry* publication, and he also retained in the book the capitalized constellations that she suggested for "Peace on Earth." Williams must also have thought better of her selection of poems than he implied in *I Wanted to Write a Poem*, for all three of her choices are preserved in the fairly rigorous selection of *Collected Earlier Poems*, along with "Portent," which she rejected.[45]

Harriet Monroe had great sympathy for the point of view Williams expressed, that life is a perpetual revolution initiated by the poet. But she did not with him, or with any of her poets,

44. Letter of March 5, 1913, in *The Selected Letters of William Carlos Williams*, ed. John C. Thirlwall (copyright 1957 by William Carlos Williams). This and following excerpts reprinted by permission of New Directions Publishing Corporation, publishers and Agents for Mrs. William Carlos Williams.

45. Mentioned in a letter from Alice Corbin Henderson to Williams, with "Madonna Mia," which Williams did not print; the titles of other poems that may have been submitted are not preserved.

express her admiration vividly, and she was always clear about her hesitations and reservations. She expected the poet to understand the spirit in which she wrote, that her acceptance of a poem was the expression of admiration, and that her negative criticisms were mere suggestions made to a writer whose work on the whole interested or delighted her. But she did not often write a letter that communicated this spirit effectively. Her reply to Williams' complaint of March 5 is one successful expression of it:

> I wish I might make more criticisms, if they would call forth such pleasant expostulations. *Poetry*, I assure you, is as free as the air and you don't need to listen to my impertinent protestations. Yet I insist that you have improved "Postlude" [Williams sent a revision March 11, 1913], and I think you would improve it still further if you would leave off the last three lines, ending at the line, "Blue at the prow of my desire." You see I am quite an incorrigible.
>
> Perhaps it is inevitable that the Editorial mind should grow stilted, if you see evidences of it in *Poetry*, "Please punch my face in order to save my soul," as Ezra says, and I am very gratefully yours. . . .[46]

This letter disarmed him, and his reply of April 10, 1913, offered to make *Poetry* the outlet for everything he wrote:

> After all, you *are* a person of discernment. Thank you for your criticisms—one and all—though I can't see what it is that puts you so against poor Jason [in "Postlude"]. And by the way, may I adopt the habit of sending anything that I do from time to time piece by piece or would you rather have me collect the things and send the gist of them to you in yearly, two yearly, or four yearly installments? . . .
>
> P.S. It is always a delight to me to see Ezra saluted.

The harmony between Miss Monroe and Williams was fairly short-lived. She must have asked him to hold off his next batch of verses for six months or so—it was her custom to print the better poets twice a year, at roughly six-month intervals. A letter of October 10, 1913, shows Williams again angry at the emphasis on finish and consistency in her reaction to a rejected poem: "To

46. Letter of April 7, 1913, a copy in the Williams correspondence.

me, what is woefully lacking in our verse and in our criticism is not hammering out stuff but stuff to be hammered out. A free forum, there is the need, which asks only, 'Is it new, interesting?' I should think, even, that at times you would be concerned lest you get nothing but that which is hammered and worked out—except when the divine Ezra bludgeons you into it. . . ."[47] But the same day's mail brought a new batch of poems—"Get out your editorial piano, then, and try these. It was you suggested it—not me." Some of these Harriet Monroe accepted, according to a marginal note on the letter. Williams took her complaints about his obscurity with good humor in a letter of October 14, 1913:

> To tell the truth, I myself never quite feel that I know what I am talking about—if I did, and when I do, the thing written seems nothing to me. However, what I do write and allow to survive I always feel is mighty worth while and that nobody else has ever come as near as I have to the thing I have intimated if not expressed. To me it's a matter of first understanding that which may not yet be put to words. I might add more but to no purpose. In a sense I must express myself, you're right, but always completely incomplete if that means anything.
>
> But—by the gods of exchange—"the divine" shall be greeted and the words presented to him for the acid test.[48]

But after "the divine Ezra" wrote to say that he would find a place for the rejected poem—"The Wanderer: A Rococco Study," which ended up in the *Egoist* for March 16, 1914—Williams again expressed irritation. He remained, for some time longer, poised ambiguously between respect for Harriet Monroe's judgment and the view that she was only Pound's reluctant instrument. Miss Monroe on her side did not give his poetry any vigorous welcome: the group or part of a group accepted in October, 1913, was not printed until May, 1915. *Poetry* went almost two full years without printing any poetry by Williams, the longest wait imposed on a poet of stature by the magazine.

Besides Williams, another American poet of interest made a debut in *Poetry* in the summer of 1913. Amy Lowell had two

47. In Thirlwall, *Selected Letters*.
48. Ibid.

poems in July, "Apology" and "A Blockhead." These Harriet Monroe had winnowed out of a number of poems sent in. Miss Lowell, who was one of the few interested readers of Pound's Imagiste campaign in *Poetry*, had discovered that she, too, was an Imagiste while reading the poems of H.D. in January, 1913. Showing the energy and enterprise that were to make her a captain of poets, Amy Lowell wanted space in *Poetry* for her criticism as well as her poems. Harriet Monroe returned her review of Lawrence's *Love Poems* June 16, 1913, explaining, "I told you to write that review of Lawrence and now Ezra Pound has sent in one; without, of course, knowing anything about yours. I am afraid I shall have to use his, as it is really his preserves. Long ago I asked him to take care of England for us, and he has sent this review in response to that agreement."

A review of Fannie Stearns Davis by Miss Lowell was published in *Poetry* for September, 1913, but her offer to review John Gould Fletcher was refused, again because she was rushing in ahead of Pound, whose review of *Fire and Wine* and *The Dominant City* was published in December, 1913. Harriet Monroe authorized an article on Miss Lowell's immediate enthusiasm, French poet Paul Fort, but if it was written it was not printed. Amy Lowell's article "Vers Libre and Metrical Prose," on hand in June, 1913, was not used until March, 1914—a long wait for prose, which *Poetry* usually published within a few months of receipt. Harriet Monroe preferred to have her own say in "The Rhythms of English Verse," in November and December, 1913, before using the Lowell paper. In sum, Amy Lowell tended to be blocked out of *Poetry* because the very small editorial space was already reserved, and because Harriet Monroe was not disposed to accept her as leader or chief controversialist, although willing to take an occasional contribution.

The summer of 1913 also saw a second publication of Nicholas Vachel Lindsay in *Poetry*, following the conspicuous success of his "General Booth" in January. The "Moon Poems" had been in the *Poetry* office since October 29, 1912, when Lindsay sent them with "General Booth." Harriet Monroe had not been very eager to publish them. Apparently she objected that some of them were glib or trivial, for Lindsay wrote January 22, 1913, to defend himself: "I assure you I have thrown a great many rhymes into the waste basket of late, and these have been winnowed as far as I know how. If they have any weak spots it is my lack of art, not of application." Lindsay was eager to get them into print, and Harriet Monroe yielded to him. They did not add to his reputation when they appeared in July, 1913. One irate reader protested "those little *dingle dingles* about the moon." Pound concluded in a letter of July 12, 1913, that Lindsay was "semi-serious," "set to follow Bret Harte and Field and all that lot." Otherwise there was little reaction.

The discussion of precision of expression—"hammering out"—between William Carlos Williams and Harriet Monroe has an amusing sidelight. It is probably the echo, in her correspondence, of Pound's strictures in his letters to her that irritated Williams. The "divine Ezra" was not so inspiring at second hand. Pound again and again in letters to Harriet Monroe preached "hardness":

> I think you are probably taking the best of what comes in, but I do now and then have a twinge of curiosity about what is being cast out.
>
> Honestly, besides yourself and Mrs. Henderson, whom do you know who takes the Art of poetry seriously? As seriously, that is, as a painter takes painting. Who Cares? Who cares whether or not a thing is really *well* done? Who in America believes in perfection, and that nothing short of it is worth while?
>
> Who would rather quit once and for all than go on turning out shams?
>
> Who will stand for a level of criticism even when it throws out most of their own work?
>
> I know there are a lovely lot who want to express their own personalities, I have never doubted it for an instant. Only they mostly won't take the trouble to find out what is their own personality.
>
> What, what honestly would you say to the workmanship of U.S. verse if you found it in a picture exhibit??????
>
> I want to know, we've got to get acquainted somehow. I don't think I underestimate the difficulty of your position.[49]

49. Letter dated "March ? 1913" in *Letters*, #13, pp. 14–15.

Williams, in the same letter in which he rejected "hammering out" as a technique, rejected France as a standard: "France is France; we are not France. Would you not rather have anticipated a Lincoln than acclaimed a McMahon? Figure me, of course, the Lincoln." Apparently Harriet Monroe gave him a paraphrase of a Pound lecture, and he defended himself with an appeal to the rugged, autochthonous, American—a vein she usually mined herself.

If Miss Monroe's suggestions to Williams about revision seem high-handed, a good deal of editorial pedagogy was implicit in Pound's promotion of the new poetry. He wrote of the "Don'ts by an Imagiste": "I DO hope you'll print my instructions to neophites (sent to ACH) soon, that will enable our contributors to solve some of their troubles at home."[50] Pound and Harriet Monroe felt obliged to cleanse and prune the manuscripts that came under their editorial scrutiny. Pound went so far as to prune Yeats for publication without consulting the master, which resulted in an amusing series of letters from Pound to Harriet Monroe. One, dated November 2, 1912, asks her to correct his "emendations and changes" in the group of Yeats lyrics scheduled for publication in the December, 1912, issue. In "Fallen Majesty," Pound had eliminated "as it were" from the final line, ". . . that seemed, as it were, a burning cloud." In "To a Child Dancing upon the Shore," Pound had made two changes in Yeats's line "Nor he, the best warrior, dead," so that it read, "Nor him, the best labourer, dead." And in "The Mountain Tomb," "Nor mouth with kissing or the wine unwet" became "Nor mouth with kissing nor with wine unwet."[51] These

50. Letter of March 10, 1913, in *Letters*, #16, p. 18.
51. The reading "warrior" for "labourer" is implicit in the request in the letter of November 2 that it be restored; the other changes appear in Pound's hand on the typescript filed with the Yeats correspondence. Evaluation of Pound's alterations is confused by the fact that Yeats evidently looked over the typescript, which gives the reading "labourer," not "warrior." A note on one sheet in his hand asks Pound to check the punctuation of the poems. An alteration that Yeats apparently did not protest occurs in the typescript of "The Mountain Tomb": "eyes" is substituted for "sides" in what appears to be Pound's hand. *Poetry* printed "shut into its onyx eyes," and there is no record that the reading was protested. "To a Child Dancing upon the Shore" in *Poetry* reads: "Love lost as soon as won. / And he, the best warrior, dead / And all the sheaves to bind!" The text is based on the November 2 letter with three small changes taken from Pound's later note about the "final clinic." Again there is no record that Yeats protested the reading "warrior."

alterations angered Yeats at first; Pound's letter concludes with the image of an outraged monarch—"Oh *la la*, ce que le roi desire." After a little time Yeats became reconciled to one of them; an undated note on his stationary reads:

18 Woburn Bldgs.

Final clinic in the groves of philosophy.

read—

"Love lost as soon as won. (full stop)
And he, the best labourer, dead
And all the sheafs to bind!
What need that you should dread
The monstrous crying of wind?"[52]

Peace reigns on Parnassus,

E.P.

Later, in an undated letter of fall, 1913, Pound remarked of Yeats: "Also he is still revising the poems we've printed . . . [Pound's punctuation] they look more like the versions I sent first, at least it suits me to believe so." In each case, the final reading in Yeats's *Collected Poems* is substantially Pound's version.

Pound also undertook the emendation of Rabindranath Tagore's verse, the second group of poems sent for June, 1913, publication. Here is a sample of the minor changes Pound made:

Tagore: "watching had made my sight dim"
Pound: "watching has dimmed my sight"

Tagore: "worthies and workers, useful and clever,"
Pound: "worthies and workers, the useful and the clever,"

Tagore: "I'll shatter the memory's vessel,"
Pound: "I will shatter the vessel of memory,"

This rewriting worked less well. Harriet Monroe wrote April 5, 1913: "Tagore declines your emendations, and gives us carte blanche to do exactly as we please. To print however and whatever we want to. I must say I agree with him about your improvements with a few exceptions. You are alright for yourself

---

52. Excerpt from "To a Child Dancing in the Wind" reprinted by permission of Macmillan Publishing Company, Inc., from *Collected Poems* by William Butler Yeats (copyright 1916 by Macmillan Publishing Company, Inc.; renewed 1944 by Bertha Georgie Yeats).

but you had better let him run his own English." Pound replied April 22, 1913, that Tagore was in danger:

> . . . it will be very difficult for his defenders in London, if he takes to printing anything except his best work . . . his . . . philosophy hasn't much in it for a man who has "felt the pangs" or been pestered with western civilization. I don't mean quite that, but he isn't either Villon or Leopardi, and the modern demands just a dash of their insight. So long as he sticks to poetry, he can be defended on stylistic grounds. . . . Of course if he wants to set a lower level than that which I am trying to set in my translations from Kabir, I can't help it. It's his own affair.[53]

Pound was almost as willing to alter details in Williams. Sending "Postlude," he wrote: "Yes. Yes. I'll be responsible for submitting it. Its *real*. Also I'll write him to see if he'll emend the bad locution 'breasts of Amazon' etc.—probably a misprint. (Or an unknown substance, he has a scientific education.)" (The reading in *Poetry* is "Who wound me in the night / With breasts shining / Like Venus and like Mars.")[54] And Frost was revised by Pound about the same time: "He tried to [correct my verse], he asked me to join the little group of Imagistes who shortened one another's poetry: F. S. Flint, T. E. Hulme, H.D. and Richard Aldington. . . . But I had to work alone. Pound, to illustrate what it should be, took a poem of mine, said: 'You've done it in fifty words. I've shortened it to forty-eight.' I answered: 'And spoiled my metre, my idiom, and idea.'"[55]

Harriet Monroe was almost certainly playing the same game when she asked Williams to lop off the last three lines of "Postlude." The part of Pound's poetic credo she assimilated was the demand for a simplification and hardening of style, "to use no superfluous word." Thus she quoted Pound in her autobiography: "Objectivity and objectivity and again objectiv-

53. In *Letters*, #17, p. 19.

54. Excerpt from "Postlude" reprinted from *Collected Earlier Poems* by William Carlos Williams (copyright 1938 by New Directions Publishing Corporation) by permission of New Directions Publishing Corporation, publishers and Agents for Mrs. William Carlos Williams.

55. Elizabeth Shepley Sergeant, *Robert Frost: The Trial by Existence*, p. 106 (copyright 1960 by Elizabeth Shepley Sergeant). Reprinted by permission of Holt, Rinehart and Winston, Inc.

ity, and NO expression, No hind-side-beforeness, No Tennyso-
nianness of speech, nothing, *nothing*, NOTHING that you couldn't
in some circumstance, in the stress of some emotion, ACTUALLY
say. . . . When one really feels and thinks one stammers with
simple speech."[56] Her favorite words of praise for a style became
"stript" and "austere." It is clear that she saw her editorial task as
requiring the detailed criticism of manuscripts. When Pound
wrote her that he had an occasional "twinge of curiosity about
what is being cast out," she replied March 31, 1913:

> You needn't bother about the things we reject. You can be pretty
> sure that nothing that has any life in it gets by us. As for some of
> the stuff, you would dance a can-can if you could see it and your
> hair would stand on end.
>
> I am glad you like the March number fairly well. It is true that a
> lot of our versifiers think they must talk in Tennysonian or
> Elizabethan, but if you could see the letters we write them you
> will realize that we are trying to train them out of that. And
> frequently our suggestions for emendations result in distinct mod-
> ernizing of the tone and general improvement.

Sometimes one of the lowly horde became as disgusted as William Carlos Williams. Kentucky poet Cale Young Rice wrote
April 16, 1913: "Now my dear Miss Monroe, have you already
become so much the editor as to be amazed that a 'trained' poet
does not have every line perfect before submitting it anywhere? . . . Dear, dear! must editors and poets always secretly
wonder at each other's inferiority!"

Although Harriet Monroe's tendency to rewrite, revise, and
correct came to seem magisterial to a later generation of writers,
or simply philistine to a writer like Williams, intent to defend the
artist's right to freedom of expression, it originated innocently. It
belongs to the beginning of the movement. The test of any particular revision is the actual improvement wrought by prodding
the artist. Thus Yeats's revisions cast glory on Pound.

When Pound questioned Harriet Monroe in March, 1913,
about the manuscripts that were being cast out, he possibly had

---

56. In *Letters*, #60, p. 49. Harriet Monroe also printed the passage, from a letter dated
May, 1915, in *Poetry* for May, 1916.

one particular rejection in mind. *Poetry* turned down Robert Frost early in its career, before Pound found a copy of *A Boy's Will*. When Pound wrote to Alice Corbin Henderson full of excitement over "another Amur'k'n, VURRY Amur'k'n with, I think, the seeds of grace," promising to send "some of his stuff if it isn't all in the book,"[57] *Poetry* had already rejected some of Frost's work. Harriet Monroe wrote Pound on April 5, 1913: "Alice says *mea culpa* about Frost. For we find him among our returns and it was done while I was in New York. She has the grit to stand up however, and say if it was returned it deserved it, or at least these particular poems did. You can apologize for us and say we are very contrite and would like some more some day." Pound replied April 22, 1913: "I don't doubt that the things Frost sent you were very bad. But he has done good things and whoever rejected 'em will go to hell along with Harper's and the Atlantic. After my declaration of his glory he'll have to stay out of print for a year in order not to "disappoint" the avid reader—serieusement, I'll pick out whatever of his in-edited stuff is fit to print. . . ."[58] But Pound couldn't find any Frost poems immediately. He wrote in June, "Frost seems to have put his best stuff into his book, but we'll have something from him as soon as he has done it, 'advanced' or whatever you call it."[59] Frost did not give Pound much opportunity to rummage through his manuscripts. He had not been happy with the review of *A Boy's Will* in *Poetry* for May, 1913. He wrote Thomas Bird Mosher in July:

> You are not going to make the mistake that Pound makes of assuming that my simplicity is that of the untutored child. I am not undesigning.
>
> You will be amused to hear that Pound has taken to bullying me on the strength of what he did for me by his review in *Poetry*. The fact that he discovered me gives him the right to see that I live up to his good opinion of me. He says I must write something much more like *vers libre* or he will let me perish of neglect. He really

57. Letter dated "April, 1913" by Harriet Monroe, in *Letters*, #12, p. 14, as of March, 1913.

58. In *Letters*, #17, p. 19.

59. Letter dated "? June, 1913" by Harriet Monroe, in *Letters*, #15, pp. 16–17, as of March, 1913.

threatens. I suppose I am under obligations to him and I try to be grateful. But as for the review in *Poetry* . . . if any but a great man had written it, I should have called it vulgar. It is much less to my taste than the shorter reviews in *Poetry and Drama* and in *The English Review*. The more I think of it the less I like the connection he sees between me and the Irishman who could sit on a kitchen-midden and dream stars. It is so stupidly wide of the mark. And then his inaccuracies about my family affairs! Still I think he meant to be generous.[60]

Pound's enthusiasm for Frost was perfectly genuine. He wrote Harriet Monroe that Frost was "our second scoop," a discovery as important as Tagore,[61] but he could not control his tone, or get on any easy footing, with Frost. The misunderstanding is like his misreading of John Reed's poem, and like some of his responses to Harriet Monroe. When he found people who struck him as vividly "Amur'k'n," he was overcome by an itch to instruct and correct. He patronized Frost to a degree Frost found unbearable, but Pound also recognized Frost's qualities, and was eager to get his work into *Poetry*. He sent two short poems early in July, 1913, and when these were also rejected, he was sympathetic to the editorial judgment but interested in pleading for Frost. He promised to send another poem soon that "may be more pleasing than those sent in. I admit he's as dull as ditch water, as dull as Wordsworth, But he is trying almost the hardest job of all and he is set to be 'literchure' some day."[62] "The Code" finally earned Harriet Monroe's approval. She made no comment on receipt of the poem from Pound, but asked in a letter of September 15, 1913, if there was any hurry about publishing it and other manuscripts sent in the same mail—another instance of her habit of omitting positive comment on an accepted poem. Since the *Smart Set* had in the meantime turned down "The Death of the Hired Man," *Poetry* got the honor of being the first American magazine to print Frost after his English success, when "The Code" appeared in February, 1914.

60. Lawrance Thompson, ed., *Selected Letters of Robert Frost*, #55, p. 84. Reprinted by permission of Holt, Rinehart and Winston (copyright 1964 by Holt, Rinehart and Winston, Inc.).

61. Letter dated "December ? 1912" in error.

62. Letter dated "September, 1913" by Harriet Monroe.

Poetry's rejections and delays permanently irritated Frost, who said years later that Harriet Monroe never liked him, "for the reason, in her case, that she had refused all the poems I sent her until my reputation was established."[63] Like Williams, Frost believed that Pound forced his verse into *Poetry* over her obstinate objections. That, at least, is the view that runs through Elizabeth Shepley Sergeant's account:

> Frost had, in fact, recently sent Miss Monroe a batch of poems that she had rejected. (Later, she said that this had happened because she was away on a trip.) Now, seemingly, she was to have forced on her a review of *A Boy's Will*. Pound assured his new discovery that Harriet, though an old maid, was far less of a one than the editors of *Harper's*, *Scribner's* and the *Atlantic Monthly*.
> . . . .
> Miss Monroe had accepted "The Code—Heroics" for a February, 1914, issue of *Poetry*. Pound had kept pricking her, and it did seem time that something should appear in Frost's native land.[64]

But Pound was responsible for publicizing *Poetry*'s rejections of Frost in a way that exaggerated both the energy of his promotion and the vigor of Harriet Monroe's resistance. When Frost began to gain notice in the American press as an American poet who had won the attention of an English publisher and the praise of the English press, no one remembered Pound's similar success in 1909. Pound felt obliged to remind his fellow citizens that Frost had a precedent. He wrote a letter to the editor of the *Boston Evening Transcript* in which he went on to give himself the further credit of gaining Frost's first new American recognition over Miss Monroe's spirited resistance. Surely that is what his metaphor implies: "I hammered his stuff into *Poetry*."[65] This seems the origin of the tradition Miss Sergeant's account follows.

The tradition is exaggerated. There is no evidence that Harriet Monroe had any objection to Pound's review of Frost; she printed it without delay. Pound's recommendations of the poetry

63. Quoted in Sergeant, *Robert Frost*, p. 166. Frost never expressed this attitude to Harriet Monroe; he wrote her December 19, 1924: "My debt to you has piled up to some altitude above sea level since you first printed blank verse of mine in 1913 [*sic*]. We have grown to be old, if not quite first name friends. May we never be less."
64. Sergeant, *Robert Frost*, pp. 103, 115.
65. In *Letters*, #73, pp. 62–63.

were strong, but they were colored by his strained relation with Frost; he seems half to have sympathized with the second rejection. Harriet Monroe did not earn high marks for critical acumen, but there remains no record of the titles she rejected. They seem by Pound's account leftovers after all the best available poems had gone into *A Boy's Will*, and it is unfair to conclude that she stiffly resisted Frost's characteristic work. *Poetry* became enthusiastic about Frost after *North of Boston*. Both Mrs. Henderson and Miss Monroe seemed more responsive to the narratives of that book than to the lyrics of *A Boy's Will*. After 1914 the magazine was consistently friendly to Frost, although by 1915 his American reputation was booming and he no longer needed *Poetry*. After "The Black Cottage" failed to get into *Poetry* before its publication in *North of Boston*, Frost sent nothing at all for two years.

Besides rejections of Williams and Frost, one can add to Harriet Monroe's crimes against Pound a resistance to the poetry of Hilda Doolittle. "Hermes of the Ways," "Priapus," and "Epigram" were published within three months of their receipt at the *Poetry* office, but "the rest"—"Hermonax" and "Acon," published eventually in February, 1914—Miss Monroe was not eager to print. Pound nagged her from time to time about "the rest," but "nudging" describes it better than "hammering."

A contrast to this delay was Miss Monroe's eager response to the work of Richard Aldington. She thought his "Choricos," in *Poetry* for November, 1912, "one of the most beautiful death songs in the language."[66] She was pressing Pound for more of Aldington's work by April, 1913, and mentioned him after Yeats and Lindsay for a Guarantors' Prize for the most distinguished publication of the year. But Aldington has recorded, "My impression is that even so Ezra had to bully Miss Monroe to get her to accept the new poetry." "Ezra was a bit of a czar in a small but irritating way, and he had the bulge on us because it was only through him that we could get our poems into Harriet Monroe's *Poetry*, and no one else would look at them."[67] Occasionally one feels that Pound worked too hard at interpreting *Poetry* to its

66. *Poet's Life*, p. 292.
67. *Life for Life's Sake*, pp. 135–36.

contributors. Too many people had the impression that Miss Monroe deeply disliked the poetry that she somehow was forced into printing.

There is a similar misunderstanding about *Poetry*'s first publication of John Gould Fletcher, whose "Irradiations" appear in the number for December, 1913. Pound sent the Fletcher poems August 13, 1913, with the remark that he supposed it hopeless to expect that the full sequence would be printed. "Anyhow, do hack out ten or a dozen pages that will establish the tone and in some way present the personality, the force behind this new and amazing state of affairs . . . if you don't print a fairish big gob of him, you don't do him justice. . . ."[68] Fletcher himself wrote soon afterward, saying that Pound had refused to submit any of his work but *vers libre*, and asking if he could send some of his verse direct.[69] When he sent revisions of "Irradiations" October 17, 1913, he added a miscellaneous batch of his poems, in response to Harriet Monroe's request. She put a marginal note on this letter, "These the best," and she apparently flunked an examination that Fletcher thought fit to give her, because on January 23, 1914, after the publication of "Irradiations" in *Poetry*, he wrote her in a fury. Fletcher had been disgusted by a little poem that appeared in the same number with "Irradiations," "The Malay to His Master" by Cale Young Rice. When Harriet Monroe tried to excuse herself on the ground of old friendship with Rice—she had tried prodding him into revision without much success—Fletcher rebuked her savagely. An editor must be above personal friendship, he wrote. She ought to stop publishing if she were so easily persuaded. She ought to make Ezra Pound editor of her paper; he knew good work when he saw it. Fletcher went on to say that he had deliberately inserted some poor work into his miscellaneous batch of poems, to test her discrimination. Her reply made him despair that she would even bother to read him. She would be too occupied over the junk submitted by obscure and incompetent friends. The same Fletcher wrote Harriet Monroe two years later that *Poetry* was a proud achievement, that with it she had made an immense

68. In *Letters*, #22, p. 22.
69. Letters of August 29 and October 5, 1913.

contribution to the poetic revival.[70] He seems touchy and unreliable.

At any rate, these circumstances surrounding publication of Fletcher have become another instance of Pound's "hammering stuff into *Poetry*." In Horace Gregory's *Amy Lowell*, for example, Pound is said to have mounted a campaign in 1913 to discover Fletcher, and to have forced masses of his poetry on a very reluctant Harriet Monroe.[71] Pound patched up the quarrel between Miss Monroe and Fletcher, writing March 4, 1914: "I gather from Fletcher that he has written you a foolish letter. Please pay no attention to it. I've had another beautiful thing a 'Blue Symphony' from him which I will send on in time." Apparently Harriet Monroe was able to "pay no attention to it." Certainly the legend that she was hostile toward or sullen about the new poetry has monstrously outgrown the reality.

One can get further insight into what Miss Monroe "cast out" of the magazine in its first year of publication by studying the other rejections recorded in the magazine's correspondence files. The bias of them is in favor of the new poetry over the traditional and the Georgian; none of them seems sensationally interesting. William Rose Benet sent in a group in 1912 or 1913 that was "retd," according to a marginal note on his letter. John Hall Wheelock's long poem was rejected as trite and imitative of Rossetti. A poem from Percy MacKaye was returned with suggestions for revision, a group submitted by Edwin Markham was never printed, and three poems sent in by Francis Meynell were not used. Bliss Carman's group was "retd. very politely," according to a marginal note on a letter of December 17, 1913. Pound sent in poems by John Masefield and Charlotte Mew that were not used. Poems from John Drinkwater and Richard LeGallienne were not published. W. H. Davies was rejected twice. Conrad Aiken sent in a great deal of material, and after several rejections some poems were discussed for publication. Alfred Kreymborg was rejected twice in 1913 and 1914. Harriet Monroe put up a very stiff resistance to the translations of Bezruč by Paul Selver that Pound sent in October, 1912. He hammered

70. Letter of January 28, 1916.
71. Horace Gregory, *Amy Lowell*, pp. 90, 97.

them at *Poetry* in letters of March 25 and August 20, 1913, and August 17, 1914, without success.

But most writers who persisted—Benet, Wheelock, Carman, Drinkwater, Aiken, and Kreymborg—were eventually published in *Poetry*. Rejections were directed against poems, not against personalities. The established poets tended to take exclusion as final, and stopped sending manuscripts. Davies seems the most serious loss of this period. On January 20, 1914, he wrote a furious reply to his second rejection, protesting that Harriet Monroe was the very first to complain of a lack of spontaneity and intuition in his poetry, and promising to publicize her ignorance among young American poets of his acquaintance. Harriet Monroe replied, according to her marginal note, "Sorry I expressed an opinion," and that was the end of Davies as a *Poetry* contributor.

Miss Monroe was perfectly ready to reject the verse Pound sent when she felt it was inferior, but she labored to give him maximum freedom in London. A letter of April 12, 1913, shows her disagreeing with Pound's selection of poems by F. S. Flint but deferring to the possibility that he had committed himself: "I don't think Flint succeeds very well with his things. 'I Live Among Men' seems to me to fall down utterly toward the end. It becomes funny, that 'I am lonely' etc. 'In the Garden' seems to me to scarcely escape the ridiculous. . . . Shall I except these. I don't wish to veto anything you have said to him." In this case the resistance of the Chicago office was not unwelcome to Pound: "Chuck out the early example of Flint and use the ones you like. I think the later ones are better. It is very hard for me to do the rejecting in Flint's case, unless I can point a definite fault. He is very hard up and married and a father." [72] Like some other strains in the transatlantic cooperation, rejection at the Chicago office became an issue when it suited Pound to dramatize it. As a matter of editorial routine, Chicago was remarkably open to his recommendations.

Ezra Pound's attitudes toward Harriet Monroe are too shifting and confusing to allow any neat summary of the relationship

72. Letter dated "c. April 10, 1913" by Harriet Monroe.

established in their correspondence. The dominant tone of the letters is pedagogical—Pound delighted in instruction, and wrote long tirades that dramatize the defects of the work featured in *Poetry* and hold up the ideal of an art that will "hale a man naked into the presence of his God."[73] In letters of this sort, he often seems to be talking not to Harriet Monroe, but to his idea of America or of the young American artist:

> If I can help you make "Poetry" *the* center of the best activity, that will mean more to me than "rates." And I do want a high standard kept. There are a lot of men in the U.S. who've the real impulse and only need a little commonsense training, stuff hopelessly bad for lack of rudimentary knowledge which is so cheap really—& only needs a lot of transportation. . . . The charlatans!! They do more harm to the arts than any indifference. And it is to them that we owe so much the general mistrust of "the muse." When poetry is really good the people will take it fast enough. My war is not on the public taste, it is on editors and on pretenders.[74]

Pound's aspirations for art were not very distinct from his aspirations for America for some time in 1913, while his hopes for an "American Risorgimento" beat high. Like Harriet Monroe, he hoped to revolutionize American life by revolutionizing American poetry. In "From Chebar," a long harangue written in 1913, Pound urges America to perfection, and all but personifies the country as Harriet Monroe:

> I have not forgotten the birthright.
> I am not content that you should be always a province.
> The will is not enough,
> The pretence is not enough,
> The satisfaction-in-ignorance is insufficient.
>
> There is no use your quoting Whitman against me,
> His time is not our time, his day and hour were different.
>
> The order does not end in the arts,
> The order shall come and pass through them.

At some moments in the correspondence, Pound seems to delight in shocking Miss Monroe, expecting or requiring re-

73. Letter dated December 3, 1912, by Harriet Monroe.
74. Letter dated October 11, 1912, by Harriet Monroe.

sponses even more conventional than her real ones. After re-marking in a letter of March 25, 1913, that he supposed his new work would horrify her, he soared into joyous nonsense: "There are one or two old friends in the series, but Arma virumque cano. Non dico pueris. We celebrate the end of the erotico-swinburno-Oscaro movement. After 'Cato died' as the saying is. After our concert there was a visible slump in this sort of thing. The real swan song I dare not send you until it be shielded in a volume." Pound apparently had no sharp intuition of Harriet Monroe's identity. Throughout their long relationship, he seems unclear about her attitudes and reactions. As late as 1917, he questioned Alice Corbin Henderson whether Miss Monroe took him seriously. He felt he needed an intermediary to interpret him to her, and tended to see Mrs. Henderson in that light.[75]

As the year 1913 wore on, Pound seemed progressively disen-chanted with America and with the task of goading it to perfec-tion. He remarked of "From Chebar" in retrospect:

> It is increasingly hard to maintain an interest in "the american reader." GORRD!! By all means begin with the "Ancora." I have no intention of conceding an inch. The public is stupid, and any other opening, from me, would be the rankest hypocrisy. I know the "From Chebar" is dull as ditch water, and I am perfectly aware that, in it, I had stopped being an artist and was preaching. The only question is as to the value of the sermon. I want, in my rotten stinking weaker and sentimental moments I want, or delude myself into thinking I want America to "uplift." (Come on, Ezry, etc.) I know that this is a baser passion and that it is nothing to the immortal gods. What have they to do with political geography?[76]

He also became disenchanted about the possibility of operating through *Poetry*. Pound's reactions to the summer issues had been at least patient—"I think I've more or less quit grumbling and that I realize in some measure the difficulties," he wrote before going on to pick at the August issue.[77] But in September he

75. Alice Corbin Henderson to Ezra Pound, February 17, 1917, in Ezra Pound Ar-chive, Collection of American Literature, Beinecke Rare Book Room and Manuscript Library, Yale University. Mrs. Henderson wrote to reassure Pound that Harriet Monroe cared very much about his reactions, and that he had a perfectly good entree with her—there was no need to search out agents in Chicago.

76. Letter dated "August, 1913" by Harriet Monroe, in error for September.

77. Letter dated "September, 1913" by Harriet Monroe.

sounded seriously discontented with the magazine. Apart from Allen Upward, he felt that too much space in the September number was given over to mediocrity, and he suggested that Miss Monroe was spreading the good poetry too thin: "Of course a certain amount of space has to be charged to profit and loss, running leeway, etc. I know that. Still you would do better simply to jam in the best stuff as fast as you get it and trust to the gods to send more. Also with higher lights prompt appearance is valued. I still think you've got your files too much stuffed up. How about Johns?" (Orrick Johns's "Songs of Deliverance" had been sent Pound for an opinion in June.)[78]

At this point two poems by H.D., Pound's own poems sent in March, Yeats's "The Two Kings," and Fletcher's "Irradiations," which Pound had sent very recently, were the only Pound materials backed up in *Poetry*'s files. The poetry in the September, 1913, issue is not particularly strong. But *Poetry*'s handling of Pound's manuscripts does not seem to justify his remarks about stuffed-up files. Harriet Monroe got most of the things into print within three or four months of the date he mailed them from London. Pound seemed to be looking for excuses to send material to the *Smart Set*. In June, when he had first mentioned the possibility of using that magazine as a "New York Annex," he referred to stuffed-up files, again without much justification, and he used the same excuse for sending some D. H. Lawrence poems to the *Smart Set* before sending any Lawrence to *Poetry*: "I'd have sent some Lawrence, if I'd known you were going to get as much stuff out in the August no. but I thought you were so stuffed up that I sent it to the S.S. I'll provide you with some later, don't worry, all in good time."[79]

In response to this kind of talk in June, Harriet Monroe printed the poems of Skipwith Cannell, sent in the middle of the month with a request for quick publication, in August, 1913— about as early as was physically possible—and put the Hueffer article sent in May, a long swatch of prose for *Poetry*'s tiny editorial section, into August and September. But in September, Pound let her know that he had given a big batch of his own

78. Letter dated "August, 1913" by Harriet Monroe, in error for September.
79. Letter dated "September, 1913" by Harriet Monroe.

poems to the *Smart Set* in June, some of them already submitted to *Poetry*: ". . . I don't know in the least what he has used already and what he has set up and what he is going to use."[80] One gets the impression that he is backing away from the magazine. After sending the promised Lawrence poems in September and two short editorials, "Paris" and "The Tradition," he stopped sending in manuscripts. Except for an editorial blast at American nationalism in the arts, he sent no new material between September 23, 1913, and January 17, 1914.

At the end of September, Pound came to the conclusion that the arrangement with *Poetry* was unworkable and unendurable, and wrote September 24, 1913, to suggest that he be given a free hand to edit an expanded prose section from London. "We've got to carry on an educational campaign," he explained, ". . . with adequate space you might print stuff of lasting value. At present you can hardly do more than notes. . . . Definitely I want room enough to print essays by Yeats, Hueffer, and myself, and a French chronicle by Flint. I don't think there is any enlightened criticism in America, I don't see how there can be." He complained that he lacked authority to make final editorial decisions commensurate with the importance of his contribution to the magazine. Now he wanted a free hand to edit the prose as he saw fit, without interference or veto from Chicago:

> The magazine may be noticed a little over here but you can bet it is not the american contributions that have done it. Most of the list of contributors is beyond the pale of anything that can be taken seriously by the cognoscenti. . . .
>
> If I took on the job of gathering the four contributors named I should expect to edit the prose section, and have the selection of such other MSS as might come in. . . . I think you ought to recognize that a critical dept. simply cannot be steered from the provinces. When I say "I" should edit it, I practically say that Hueffer and I would edit it, and also that I should consult with Yeats, and that sort of consultation has to be done viva voce. Also nobody else will edit it for nothing. . . .
>
> Etc. I wish to God you'd take that advertising motto off the magazine and substitute Dante's "Quem stulti magis odissent."

80. Letter dated "August, 1913" by Harriet Monroe, in error for September.

After all he was a better poet than Whitman, and is more qualified to speak on such a matter.

This suggestion did not interest Harriet Monroe. She wrote back to Pound that the magazine was founded and edited to publish poetry, to provide what she felt was a much needed outlet, not to add to the volume of prose comment in the world. Furthermore, she felt that it was futile to try to "reach England," to influence literary opinion in London, with a magazine published and financed in Chicago.

In the meantime, Pound had become savagely angry over the award of a two-hundred-fifty-dollar Guarantors' Prize for the most distinguished publication of *Poetry*'s first year. The award went to Yeats at Pound's insistence; Harriet Monroe had felt it would be more "adventurous" to give it to Lindsay. Pound had further insisted that Yeats be informed of the prize before any public announcement, saying that Yeats would confer more honor in accepting the award than the committee would confer in giving it. Harriet Monroe enclosed the notification to Yeats in a letter to Pound and touched off an explosion:

> Either this rotten £50 is an honourable award for the best poem, or it is a local high school prize for the encouragement of mediocrity.
>
> Either it must be respectfully offered to Mr. Yeats, or the americans must admit that they are afraid of foreign competition. . . .
>
> You've got a second prize for the village choir. [A hundred-dollar second prize, limited to American contributors, was hastily raised for Lindsay. Harriet Monroe was working to get the money for it less than a fortnight before the official announcement, in a letter of October 21, 1913, to Albert H. Loeb.]
>
> . . . I cannot assist in this insult and you unfortunately try to make me party by leaving the letter open and asking me to read it. If you will think what the magazine would have been without the foreign contributions,!!!!!!! There is no american poem worth awarding, anyhow.
>
> You CAN not divide the arts by a political line. Mother of God!!! You accepted Yeats' stuff. You hung his pictures. You ought either to have specified the award as local, or you ought not to have accepted his stuff. . . .

I don't see how Yeats could possibly go on contributing after your letter.[81]

Apparently Harriet Monroe's note to Yeats betrayed her regret that the prize had not gone to Lindsay. It seems doubtful that she said anything extraordinarily impertinent. Her reply to Pound, dated October 13, 1913, shows amazing good nature under his abuse and a proper respect for Mr. Yeats:

We are obeying your orders—but I confess it would be with more pleasure if they had been uttered a bit more suavely. I do so for the same reason I asked you to read my letter to Mr. Yeats— because I appreciate your services to the magazine and do not wish to treat Mr. Yeats, whom you first brought to us, in any way which you disapprove. . . .

Now that the decision [about prizes] is made, there is no use in discussing the matter futher. In a more general way I would say, however, that it is easy for you, living in what one of our papers calls "the world's metropolis" to charge with imbecility us "in the provinces." If we are provincial, we shall always be so until we cease to take our art and art opinions ready-made from abroad, and begin to respect ourselves. This magazine is an effort to encourage the art, to work up a public for it in America. I realize perfectly, as you must when you think about it, that it will never, in any essential sense, reach England—that it would not if it were written in gold by Apollo and all the muses. A small handful of subscribers—mostly your friends no doubt—and an occasional [illegible word] are all we can expect from England. America takes English poetry as law and gospel, but England won't take ours; in a certain sense, the better ours might be, the more slowly and reluctantly England would take it, because of the inevitable instinct of jealousy which any mature man, or nation, feels for his aspiring and assertive offspring.

Therefore it hardly seems to me expedient that our prose section should be edited in London. The most disinterested effort there could not represent us over here, or be sympathetic with our efforts. I do think that we should increase the size of the magazine—I mean in thickness—as soon as we can possibly afford

81. Letter dated October 13, 1913, at the *Poetry* office. The prize for American citizens to which Pound referred was presumably the hundred-dollar second prize given to Lindsay in 1913. Otherwise, Pound meant the Levinson Prize, not awarded in 1913 but discussed in Harriet Monroe's letter of September 15, 1913.

it, which is not now, I regret to say. I am in doubt, though, about increasing the proportion of prose. There are so many magazines "about it and about"—my idea of this one has been that it should present the best we have, including the best of the young aspirants, as an exhibition does, and keep the prose within strict limits.

You speak of having often been irritated during the past year. I might say, so have I. Irritation is inevitable in any enterprise big enough to include more than one person. I think you must admit, however, that I have played fair with you, and I hope you may never accuse me of anything else.

Miss Monroe's remarks about reaching England provoked from Pound on November 7, 1913, a letter with a memorable image of the metropolis: it is New Jerusalem, a universal city discovered by those who have died to the sinful lusts of local pride and national sentiment.[82] Sometime the same day Pound received his copy of the November, 1913, number of *Poetry*. He wrote November 8, 1913: "Mother of God! You cut me down to seven pages at the hind end of a number on top of everything else. C'est trop *fort*." About the same time Pound wrote to Ford Madox Hueffer that he was transferring *Poetry*'s foreign correspondence over to him, and asked him to notify the Chicago office of the fact.[83]

The wonder is that the association of Ezra Pound and *Poetry* did not end there. He and Harriet Monroe seem to have arrived at a dead end in the road they had traveled together. Pound's position seems a truly difficult one. The strain of exercising influence all the way across the Atlantic Ocean was too much for him. He had his intuition of the movement, a series of brilliant hunches about who or what was valid in the new poetry. His own verse was in flux; he had been groping toward something new in his recent poems, and he wanted to place them where they would have most effect. He tried to organize all this so that it would make an impression, but he had to operate through *Poetry*, and see his movement draped with Harriet Monroe's apparently dowdy loyalties.

82. In *Letters*, #27, pp. 24–25.
83. Letter dated "November 1913" by Harriet Monroe, filed with the Pound correspondence.

Pound's movement, considered simply as literary politics, was always in danger of losing its forward way, and the fall of 1913 seems in general a disappointing time for it. He felt let down by Skipwith Cannell, whose work in the August *Poetry* did not "come up." "I saw more than there was in it," he wrote.[84] Imagisme seemed a false start. There were strained relations with Frost and with John Gould Fletcher, the brief erratic backer of Pound's literary department in the *New Freewoman*. Harriet Monroe's handling of the prize award threatened his relationship with Yeats, which was the solidest backing he had. She was sitting on two poems of H.D.'s that needed publication, and in October she rejected William Carlos Williams' "The Wanderer." The climactic insult was her printing of Pound's own verse behind Hamlin Garland, the old lion of Chicago letters, a leftover from the days of local color in Pound's view, who had the first place in *Poetry* for November, 1913. Whatever immediate hopes Pound had had for *Poetry* were dashed; some intricate maneuvering in literary London went for nothing. "The thing flopped so before that there has been no use talking it up," he wrote March 28, 1914.[85] On a practical level, *Poetry* was failing to "reach England," and Pound would have seemed well advised to direct his energy somewhere else.

But Harriet Monroe does not seem to deserve the abuse Pound gave her. When one inquires into each of his grounds for outrage, one finds reason for feeling that his reaction was exaggerated. In the particular case of the November, 1913, issue, for instance, she did not "cut him down to seven pages," but printed everything on hand that she did not believe committed to the *Smart Set*, except for two poems, "The Teashop" and "Epilogue: To My Five Books."[86] Pound's maneuvering with the *Smart Set* had confused the *Poetry* publication. As for the complaint about the hind end of a number, Pound had allowed Yeats to be put at the hind end of April, 1913, after his own "Contemporaria"; the position was not really so degrading. And there undoubtedly were good reasons in Chicago for giving recognition to Hamlin

84. Letter dated "September, 1913" by Harriet Monroe.
85. In *Letters*, #42, pp. 34–35.
86. Her marginal note on his letter: "Poems not used by us: Tea-shop, An Epilogue, Smart Set group."

Garland. H. C. Chatfield-Taylor tried to resign from the advisory board that August because the new movement in literature bewildered him. The one thing about *Poetry* that was unalterably middle-western American was its financial support.

One does wonder that Harriet Monroe had the stamina to endure Pound's irritated outbursts. She was free at any moment to break the association with Pound. Beyond the immediate circle that visited the *Poetry* office, she had no audience interested in contact with the movement. *Poetry* could gracefully have retreated to printing only Lindsay, Sara Teasdale, and John Hall Wheelock and worse. Harriet Monroe would have led a quieter life, and very few American commentators would have had the insight to reproach her. Plainly she must have maintained the connection because she was convinced of Pound's worth and of the worth of the new poetry, to the degree that she was willing to suffer personal insult for them.

Pound on his part kept up the connection because he had no other outlet available. The *Smart Set* proved unreliable, so he seems to have been forced to the cold decision that he would make use of what financial resources Harriet Monroe could marshal, in the absence of any decent material base of his own, and to channel his movement through her magazine, in the absence of a more appropriate publisher.

Pound's London set moved almost immediately to cancel out the effect of his resignation of November 8, 1913. Hueffer wrote Harriet Monroe a charming note on November 12:

> Could you not make it up with him or reinstate him—or whatever is the correct phrase to apply to the solution of the situation whatever that may be? I really think he applied himself to your service with such abounding vigour and such very good results that it is a great pity that you should part company. Besides, if I tried to help you that energetic poet would sit on my head and hammer me till I did exactly what he wanted and the result would be exactly the same except that I should be like the green baize office door that everyone kicks in going in or out. I should not seriously mind the inconvenience, if it would do any good, but I think it would really be much better for you to go on with Ezra and put up with

his artistic irritations; because he is really sending you jolly good stuff. That is the main thing to be considered, isn't it?

Richard Aldington wrote about the same time:

> I have been talking to Mr. Hueffer over this Pound affair. Of course it's no business of mine, but you know Ezra Pound does actually *know* more about poetry than any person in these islands, Yeats not excepted. Of course, he will insult you; he insults me; he insults Mr. Hueffer; he insults everybody; most of us overlook it because he is American, and probably doesn't know any better. On the other hand he is certainly the cleverest man writing poetry today, so you'd better do what he says. I don't know what the row is. I only know that Ezra came along to me at an unnaturally early hour breathing grim threats against someone; and that when I saw poor Mr. Hueffer at his at-home he was in a state of utter bewilderment and wondered what Ezra wanted him to do.[87]

By December 8, 1913, Pound reconsidered his resignation "pending a general improvement of the magazine,"[88] and in the January, 1914, issue of *Poetry* Miss Monroe acknowledged "her high appreciation not only of Mr. Pound's poetry, but also of his disinterested and valuable service as Foreign Correspondent."

In the same issue she announced that the bulk of the cash from the Guarantors' Prize, two hundred dollars, was going to Pound at Yeats's suggestion. Yeats had written November 7, 1913, that the money was wasted on him, and should go to some younger poet who needed it. He recommended Pound: "though I do not really like with my whole soul the metrical experiments he has made for you, I think those experiments show a most vigorous imaginative mind. . . . I know he is one of your staff, and it has occurred to me that some words of mine which you could quote . . . would enable you to get over that difficulty. . . ."[89]

One wonders why, if Pound was really exasperated beyond endurance, he did not resign quite simply, not pass the foreign correspondence, which was not in his gift, over to Hueffer. He wrote Amy Lowell during the month in a way which suggests that the resignation was not very serious: "I agree with

87. Letter dated November 28, 1913, at the *Poetry* office.
88. In *Letters*, #30, p. 27.
89. Excerpt from *The Letters of William Butler Yeats*, ed. Allen Wade, reprinted by permission of Macmillan Publishing Company, Inc. (copyright 1953, 1954, by Anne Butler Yeats).

you . . . that 'Harriet' is a bloody fool. . . . Also I've re-signed from Poetry in Hueffer's favor, but I believe he has re-signed in mine and I don't yet know whether I'm shed of the bloomin' paper or not." But Pound really was casting about for another magazine. He wrote Amy Lowell in January, 1914, ". . . I consented to return 'on condition of general improve-ment of the magazine' which won't happen—so I shall be com-pelled to resign permanently some time or other."[90] In fact, he was after Amy Lowell's backing that winter, but Miss Lowell was not a lady to hand over her purse. She described Pound's plan to Harriet Monroe in a letter of September 15, 1914:

> Do you remember, Ezra was very anxious for me to run an inter-national review, something on the lines of the "Mercure de France"? . . . it . . . transpired that he expected to become editor of said "review" with a salary. I was to guarantee all the money, and put in what I pleased, and he was to run the magazine his way. We talked over the cost of expenses, and we both thought that $5000 a year was the least that such a magazine could be run on. As I have not $5000 a year that I can afford to put into it, I based my refusal on that fact.

After his quarrel with Amy Lowell and the schism of the Imag-ists, Pound proposed to Remy de Gourmont that they collabo-rate on an international magazine, to be financed by individual contributions of two or three hundred dollars a year, a scheme resembling Harriet Monroe's guarantor plan. John Quinn's back-ing of Pound in the *Little Review* in 1917–19 was the fulfillment of these plans for a magazine of his own. That Pound delayed breaking the connection with *Poetry* reflects something more than the meager resources at his disposal in London. Chicago did in fact "improve" in 1914, and 1914 and 1915 were the great years of *Poetry: A Magazine of Verse*.

As Harriet Monroe's letter to Pound about expanding the prose makes clear, the business side of her enterprise did not flourish in 1913. The magazine was in financial difficulty before completing its first year of publication, and she wrote that she expected a deficit "before the end of the year." By the beginning

90. Letters of November 26, 1913, and January 8, 1914, in *Letters*, #29, p. 26, and #33, p. 29.

of 1914 she found that she had overspent available funds and thought she would need another two thousand dollars to finish the year.[91] Payments to contributors were maintained at a ten-dollar page rate, a little lower than the standard rate of the commercial magazines.[92] Through 1913 and 1914, Miss Monroe kept up the ten-dollar rate to contributors, while the circulation remained very low, much lower than she had anticipated in setting her rate. Paid subscriptions for 1912–13, volumes one and two, were 1,030, and for 1913–14, volumes three and four, 1,101. Within a year of launching her magazine with what seemed an enviably safe capital reserve, she was deeply involved in financial shortages and emergency appeals for funds, a condition that continued throughout the years in which she edited the magazine. Pound's comments that a few really excellent issues would send up the circulation and make all right, as the April, 1913, "Contemporaria" issue had sent up the circulation, were not realistic; the April, 1913, issue had not raised the circulation appreciably.[93]

But despite the dismal experience of *Poetry*, the "big" publishers and the "big" magazines, whose policies kept most significant twentieth-century poetry out of their columns, were beginning to pay more attention to poetry before 1913 was over. The *Dial* for October 1, 1913, tried to adopt a tone of mellow condescension toward the radical verse against which it had sponsored a hysterical attack in the spring, commenting that "a lively interest in things aesthetic, even if stimulated by the most ignoble examples, is better than no interest at all, for that way lies spiritual stagnation." Marinetti or Ezra Pound might be useful; even the tantrums of the Muse can remind one of the existence of Parnassus. As the *North American Review* had recently remarked, "Poetry has now become a mentionable subject in decent society." [94] During the year *Reedy's Mirror* became aware

91. Letter of February 24, 1914, to Howard Elting, a copy filed with the Guarantor Correspondence.

92. A survey described in *Reedy's Mirror*, July 18, 1913, p. 9, reports payment for poetry averaging fifty cents a line, with one dollar a line the top; very short poems averaged five dollars apiece, with ten dollars the top.

93. Harriet Monroe's draft of a letter of May 12, 1914, filed with the Pound correspondence.

94. "The Muse in a Pet," October 1, 1913, p. 246.

of "A Boom in Poetry": "Half a dozen periodicals devoted exclusively to poetry, an increasing popular demand for volumes of verse, more and more space given up to poems in the popular magazines, and an improvèment in the economic conditions of poets themselves—these are the recent phenomena that indicate a 'boom in poetry'. . . . A friend of the editor of the Mirror, connected with Brentano's, in New York City, writes that the sales of verse have increased two hundred per cent in two years."[95] Reedy's paper did little itself in 1913 to contribute to the boom. Most of the verse published was reprinted from other magazines.

If there was a rising market for poetry in 1913, the Boston *Poetry Journal*, edited by W. S. Braithwaite, did not find it, any more than Harriet Monroe's magazine did. Publication of the Boston periodical was irregular; after December, 1912, the next issue is dated February, 1913, and publication was suspended after July, 1913, until February, 1914. Numerous reprints of old favorites and the printing of single poems rather than groups make the typical issue look more like a scrapbook than a current periodical. The editor's favored poet was Amelia Josephine Burr. Her book *The Roadside Fire* is enthusiastically reviewed in the first issue, and her poetic play *Judgment* is printed in three installments in May–July. There is no editorial talk of a renaissance or a boom. At least Braithwaite's praise of *The Lyric Year* in February, "*England's Helicon* has been no more to English life and poetry than what the *Lyric Year* is certain to be to American life and poetry," reads more like rhetoric boiling out of the pot than like serious comment.

William Marion Reedy's note about a boom in poetry suggests that the revival was largely a commercial one, and that book publishers and booksellers were principally aware of it. One suspects some of this awareness was imported from London, for by 1913 a boom in sales of volumes of poetry was well established there.[96] An interview with William Butler Yeats in the *New York Times* confirms this:

95. July 18, 1913, p. 9.
96. E. H. Lacon Watson, "Literary Incomes in England," *Dial*, September 1, 1913, p. 138: Alfred Noyes and John Masefield were current best sellers.

It was Alfred Heinemann, the London publisher, who recently pointed out in an interview in the New York Times that a revival in the demand for poetry had recently arisen in England. Mr. Yeats concurs with Mr. Heinemann in that statement. His own books, he says, in the last year have doubled their sales.

"Though no one knows why," exclaimed Mr. Yeats. "And everyone who writes poetry is telling me the same story. . . . When I began to write, nobody of the poets was read but Tennyson; and he was read immensely. Then for a few years poetry was taken up again because people were looking for a new Tennyson. Then they stopped because they found that whatever they were going to get, it wasn't Tennyson. We were all of the trough of the wave. A curious thing is that the same thing happened in other countries. Art for art's sake, the disinterested service of the Muses passed away for a time, and everywhere now it is coming back. Paris, like London, is ceasing to be commercial in literature."[97]

"The movement" failed to get much benefit out of this new freedom for the Muse. Pound's plan to publish *Lustra* in the fall of 1913 fell through, and he had to make a clumsy transatlantic deal with Alfred Kreymborg and Albert and Charles Boni to get his anthology *Des Imagistes* published in February, 1914. Most of the new poets published by *Poetry* in 1912–13 did not find publishers for a volume until a season or two later, and thus did not make part of the book publishers' renaissance of 1913. Lindsay's *General Booth* came out late in 1913, Aldington's *Images* and Flint's *Cadences* in 1915, and H.D.'s *Sea Garden* in 1916. Fletcher and Amy Lowell published almost every year, but they had some capital to back their books. Pound's *Lustra* was not published until 1916. William Carlos Williams managed English publication in 1913, but did not publish a new book in America until 1917, when *Al Que Quiere!* came out. Harriet Monroe herself published *You and I* in 1914.

The Poetry Renaissance in 1913 was thus made up of Tagore; Frost, whose reputation had not yet reached America; Masefield; Noyes; the Georgians, including D. H. Lawrence; and lesser poets like the following, who had books of verse reviewed in

97. " 'American Literature Still in Victorian Era?'—Yeats," February 22, 1914, p. 10 (copyright 1914 by the New York Times Company). Reprinted by permission.

Poetry in 1913: John Hall Wheelock, Hermann Hagedorn, Percy MacKaye, Rhys Carpenter, Isabelle Howe Fiske, Florence Earle Coates, William Ellery Leonard, Amelia Josephine Burr, Marguerite Wilkinson, Clark Ashton Smith, George Wharton Stork, Margaret Root Garvin, Amy Lowell, Fannie Stearns Davis, Max Eastman, and George Edward Woodberry. The little magazines contributed almost nothing to this boom, except the controversy over free verse started in the correspondence columns of the *Dial*. The *Smart Set* had backed away from Pound and the new poetry by the end of the year; by February, 1914, Willard Huntington Wright was off the masthead. H. L. Mencken's notion, "The business of poetry . . . is to set up a sweet denial of the harsh facts that confront all of us—in brief, to lie sonorously and reassuringly,"[98] kept the magazine from printing interesting poetry during the next ten years.

Periodical contribution to the poetic boom seems limited to W. S. Braithwaite's first gathering of magazine poets, the *Anthology of Magazine Verse for 1913*, based on a systematic reading of *Harper's*, *Scribner's*, the *Century*, *Lippincott's*, the *Forum*, the *Smart Set*, and the *Bellman*, with odd poems added from the *Outlook*, the *Independent*, the *North American Review*, *Poetry*, the *Poetry Journal*, and the *Yale Review*. Braithwaite singled out for praise the poetry of Harry Kemp, Henry van Dyke, Edwin Markham, Robert Underwood Johnson, Rabindranath Tagore, Francis Thompson, Robert Bridges, Fannie Stearns Davis, William Rose Benet, Josephine Preston Peabody, Margaret Root Garvin, George Edward Woodberry, Mahlon Leonard Fisher, and Edwin Arlington Robinson. Although Tagore was cited, and Lindsay's *General Booth* was called the most important book of the year by an American poet, Braithwaite did not comment on *Poetry* or its work, except to credit the magazine for the one poem reprinted, Joyce Kilmer's "Trees."

The new American interest in poetry in 1913 seems stimulated by England, to the degree that it was not caused by the mysterious cyclical return to which Yeats referred. Nineteen thirteen was not a year in which much interesting poetry was published

98. Carl Dolmetsch, "A History of the *Smart Set* Magazine" (Ph.D. diss., University of Chicago, 1957), pp. 92–93.

in America outside the pages of *Poetry* and the *Smart Set*, and almost no one read *Poetry*. Although *Poetry*'s contents and tone steadily improved in the next year, the circulation did not rise. "Fit audience, though few" remained Harriet Monroe's throughout all her struggles for the sake of the great audience.

FOR EZRA POUND, IMAGISTE
—"a good minor poet and nothing more"

What he disdained to write is what was there.
Straining after the intensities,
The clear edges,
He built hallucinations
Lit up by radiant mind.

He seems like Kurtz to the retrospective scholar:
His death mask is an open mouth
Yawning to take in the beautiful,
Engorge it, digest it,
To utter forth again
          in great gulps of air.

He should be better remembered.
It is easier to enhance the commonplace,
Day in and year out,
Than to strive always with light and with air,
And the thin line, felt as motion,
Where they cross.

TWO

The Great Years of *Poetry* 🙌
1914–15

No plain evidence demonstrates that in one year *Poetry* was good, in another better, in the next declining into mediocrity. But a pattern exists in the issues of the magazine that cover the years of the Poetry Renaissance. Nineteen fourteen and 1915 are distinguished from 1913 as from 1916 by a sustained excellence in issue after issue. The magazine in 1913 published better verse than any other American periodical, but almost everything good came from Ezra Pound, and the contrast between his contribution and the local one was frequently ludicrous.

From January, 1914, to December, 1915, the files of *Poetry* would impress even the superficial reader. There is still a great deal of material to be passed over as weak or dated, but every issue has two or three poems or groups of poems that still engage the attention, and the contributions from Pound no longer stand out like flowers in a field of pigweed. Some poems stand out startlingly above the average level of the verse published, but these are "The Love Song of J. Alfred Prufrock" and "Sunday Morning," Fletcher's "Blue Symphony," Robinson's "Eros Turannos," or Pound's "Exile's Letter." And the lesser level they serve to define includes things any magazine would boast of: Hueffer's "On Heaven"; a fine group of transitional Yeats lyrics, including "To a Friend Whose Work Has Come to Nothing," "Song from the Player Queen," "The Magi," and "A Coat"; Sandburg's "Chicago Poems"; two interesting groups by D. H. Lawrence; Frost's "The Code"; Pound's play out of Fenollosa, *Nishikigi*, and his "Near Perigord"; two queer poems by Skipwith Cannell that seem to anticipate the early Eliot; Lindsay's "The

Chinese Nightingale"; Masters' "Silence"; and a group by William Carlos Williams. Even so long a list omits the first publication of Maxwell Bodenheim, the first American publication of Marianne Moore, a very good small group by H.D., three small Eliot poems, Rupert Brooke's war sonnets, two other groups of short lyrics and satires by Pound, and poetry by Amy Lowell, Sara Teasdale, James Stephens, Padraic Colum, and Richard Aldington.

Ezra Pound, in 1930 looking back over the literary wars, remembered that *Poetry*'s lively period lasted from 1912 to 1914. Pound's influence as foreign correspondent was less in 1914 and 1915, for two reasons. Some new poets cropped up who did not depend on him for access to the magazine: Wallace Stevens, Carl Sandburg, Marianne Moore, Edgar Lee Masters, and Maxwell Bodenheim. And most of the poets who had communicated with the magazine through Pound broke away and began to send in their things direct. William Butler Yeats, Skipwith Cannell, D. H. Lawrence, Richard Aldington, H.D., Padraic Colum, and John Gould Fletcher all sent work in late 1914 and 1915 themselves. In 1914 Pound contributed, in addition to his own work, poems by Yeats, Eliot, Hueffer, Masefield, Fletcher, Colum, Seamus O'Sullivan, John Rodker, Skipwith Cannell, Violet Hunt Hueffer, and Douglas Goldring. In 1915 he sent Eliot, William Carlos Williams—who was also in direct contact with the magazine—T. Sturge Moore, someone named Dewey, someone named Unde(?), and "Rosenberg, poor devil."

Pound commented in April, 1915, that the war caused a great shortage of good poetry. But the problem was more than World War I; the friendships and literary alliances on which Pound depended in 1913 weakened in 1914 and 1915. After the Imagist schism, he was no longer in a position to gather and sift the work of younger poets in London. Even his friendship with Ford Madox Hueffer was strained. He wrote September 15, 1914, that he was no longer close to Hueffer, and Amy Lowell wrote in the same month that Hueffer planned to publish in her Imagist anthology. That same fall Pound first met T. S. Eliot, and Eliot can be said to fill the gap left by F. S. Flint, Richard Aldington, and H.D. But Pound had a smaller volume of verse to contribute

in these two years than he had in 1912–13, and his influence as
foreign correspondent seems weaker.

At the beginning of 1914, Pound was backing away from
Poetry and casting about for another magazine that would give
him some income and an outlet for "the movement." The terms
in which he discussed a subsidy for the *Egoist* with Amy Lowell
make it probable that he would quickly have abandoned Harriet
Monroe if Miss Lowell had loosened her purse strings: "You can
'run' a paper in Boston and have a staff here. To wit me and
Hueffer and anybody you've a mind to pay for. 'Arriet, as you
know, has that recommendation. Only she will try to pick out
contributors for herself which is usually, from the point of view
of internationality or English circulation, fatal."[1] His correspondence with *Poetry* in this period continues to bristle with
outrage. The acknowledgment of the two hundred dollars that
he received at Yeats's suggestion, intended for publication in
Poetry, is arrogant for a public letter: ". . . I am very glad to
receive *Poetry*'s annual award at Mr. Yeats' suggestion as he is
about the only poet now writing in English for whom I have any
appreciable respect, or I might say more exactly for whom I have
any feeling of deference." He went on to ask that Harriet Monroe "give publicity to my own suggestion for the award," a division between Lindsay and Aldington that he had suggested after
he learned that Yeats intended returning the prize money.[2] And
he suggested a number of improvements necessary if the American side of the enterprise was to be worthy of his foreign correspondence: publication of Bliss Carman and Orrick Johns, and of
a French poem in each number.[3]

Harriet Monroe began to edit the letter, altering Pound's language so that he did not receive *Poetry*'s award, but Yeats's
money: "I am very glad to receive at Mr. Yeats' suggestion part
of the two hundred and fifty dollars sent to him as *Poetry*'s annual
prize as he is about the only poet now writing in English for
whom I have a feeling of deference." A little farther in the letter

1. Letter of March 18, 1914, in *Letters*, #40, p. 33.
2. Letter dated November 8, 1913, by Harriet Monroe.
3. Letter of January 20, 1914, with alterations in Harriet Monroe's hand.

she changed Pound's description of a "donation" for Mr. Lindsay into a "prize." But when she came to the request for publication of Orrick Johns, she stopped her editorial penciling, and abandoned the intention to publish the letter. Pound was disingenuous, since he knew Orrick Johns's "Songs of Deliverance" were scheduled for publication; they appeared in the February, 1914, issue. He expected Harriet Monroe to stage his act of "hammering stuff into *Poetry*" in her own editorial pages.

In a postscript to this letter of January 20, Pound wrote a protest against an alteration that Harriet Monroe had made in Richard Aldington's poem "Lesbia," in *Poetry* for January, 1914. Aldington had written, "Hermes, Thoth and Christ are rotten now, / Rotten and dank . . . " and Miss Monroe had asked him to substitute another name for "Christ." Aldington replied November 28, 1913, grumbling about "the idiocy of your readers" and "American prudishness": "a poet should *not* alter one fragment of his verse to please the mob, though he should labour always for the dilectation of the elect." But he was very young and high-spirited, and relented to suggest this list of substitutions: "Ra; Bel (an Assyrian Jehovah); Pound; Buddha (to annoy theosophists I will sacrifice my rhythm); Tanit; Mithra (who is Christ, at least of the second century); Adonis (who is also Christ)." Harriet Monroe printed the line with "Bel" substituted for "Christ." Three days after protesting for Aldington, Pound wrote again, asking the return of all his manuscripts on file, saying that he had sold some verse to Harold Monro's *Poetry and Drama*.

However, early in 1914 Pound began to send new manuscripts, for the first time since September, 1913: William Butler Yeats, Padraic Colum, and Seamus O'Sullivan, and his own translation of the Noh play *Nishikigi*, based on Ernest Fenollosa's notes, in January; Ford Madox Hueffer's long poem, "On Heaven," in March. In April he sent new manuscript copies of his own poems, with some new work of his own, John Gould Fletcher's "Blue Symphony," some new work by Skipwith Cannell, and John Rodker's "London Night." Necessity was constraining him to keep up the connection. He wrote March 23, 1914, "If that Nishikigi don't appear in April I shall starve in the gutter and then you *will* have to find a new thorn in the flesh." It occurred to him that he might have "opportunity of dissociating myself from certain policies of the magazine. A minority report is by no means an unheard of thing."[4] He seemed to be casting about for some set of terms that would allow him to coexist with Harriet Monroe, writing that he liked her editorial in January, 1914, "Sobriety and Earnestness," "but you cling to one pernicious heresy. That of the need of an audience. Once and for all dammmm the audience. They eat us. We do not eat them."[5] The upshot of these comments was the debate on "The Audience" between Ezra Pound and Harriet Monroe published in *Poetry* for October, 1914.

His tone toward *Poetry* continued extraordinarily haughty. The issue of May, 1914, containing his Noh play, *Nishikigi*, and a big group of Yeats's lyrics, he described to Harriet Monroe as representing a very high standard, as he well might. She seems to have worried that the tone of the issue would be too "sublimated," and he replied March 28, 1914: "'Sublimated number' be hanged! I dare say I'm vague and etc. but what I've been wanting all along is some such standard as that Yeats-Fenollosa number would be. Print it and don't fall below it. Don't accept until things hit at least that level, don't promise, leave the files open till the very going to press on the chance that a really good thing may come in. Then if nothing does come in use up some of your dead wood."[6] But this is how he noticed the May, 1914, *Poetry* in the *Egoist*:

This forlorn hope was started in Chicago about a year and a half ago. And in the dark occidental continent its editress raised the quixotic standard, "We intend to print the best poetry written in English." And the odd thing is that this provincial paper should, to some extent, have done it. I don't mean constantly or consistently, but every now and again some really good poem finds its way to the light in these small pages, and every now and again they print a presentable number. It is also safe to say that they print more important poems than all the rest of the American magazines put together.

4. Letter of February 12, 1914.
5. Letter dated "January–February 1914."
6. In *Letters*, #42, pp. 34–35.

One is not much concerned with American magazines, any more than one is concerned with the colonial press. . . . So it is all the more surprising to find an American paper that seems, every now and again, for the fraction of a number to be trying to introduce an international standard.

There have been numbers of *Poetry* that have bored us, let us however give praise now that we have the opportunity. . . . One must congratulate Miss Monroe on this number and one might even promise her that if she would modernize herself considerably more, and stay modernized, she might find some support from the more intelligent reader who won't be bored to support her paper as it has been, but who likes an occasional number.[7]

One wonders what brought Pound to feel that so patronizing a tone was appropriate. He seems to be addressing an audience of the heavenly elect and apologizing for *Poetry*'s appearance *sub specie aeternitatis*. Certainly the audience of the *Egoist* had no justification for feeling so superior to *Poetry*. Much of the poetry they read in the first six months of volume one, up to the date of Pound's notice, was reprinted from the Chicago magazine: F. S. Flint in the *Egoist* for January 1, 1914, was partly reprinted from *Poetry* for July, 1913; H.D. in the *Egoist* for February 2, 1914, was partly reprinted from *Poetry* for January, 1913; Fletcher's "Irradiations" in the *Egoist* for March 2, 1914, were another selection from the group that Harriet Monroe used in printing him in December, 1913; Allen Upward's "Chinese Lanterns" in the *Egoist* for May 15, 1914, were picked up from "Scented Leaves from a Chinese Jar," printed in *Poetry* for September, 1913. The other *Egoist* poets were such as *Poetry* was also printing—Frost, Lawrence, Aldington, Amy Lowell, William Carlos Williams ("The Wanderer," which Harriet Monroe had rejected), and John Rodker (the *Egoist* was six months ahead of *Poetry* in printing him)—or could easily match—Jack McClure, Isidore G. Ascher, Reginald Wright Kaufman, and Charlotte Mew. A regular department of notes on current French poetry

7. *Egoist*, June 1, 1914, p. 215 (copyright 1914; all rights reserved). Reprinted by permission of New Directions Publishing Corporation and Faber and Faber, Ltd., publishers and Agents for the Trustees of the Ezra Pound Literary Property Trust. Pound wrote under the pseudonym Bastien von Helmholtz.

by Muriel Ciolkowska is the only poetic feature of the *Egoist* that cannot be matched by *Poetry*. And the English paper apparently could not afford the poems of Pound himself, or of Yeats or Hueffer; at least it did not print them. With no "sublimated numbers" of its own, the *Egoist* comes off badly in the comparison with *Poetry*.

One other incident in the spring of 1914 seems a cold insult to Harriet Monroe and her magazine from the London side. Pound's anthology *Des Imagistes* came out in New York, published by Albert and Charles Boni, nominally edited by Alfred Kreymborg. It was part of a series of monthly publications under the collective title *The Glebe*, bound both in hard cover for sale as a book and in soft cover for sale as a periodical. Although thirty-one of the forty-seven poems in Pound's anthology had been first printed in *Poetry*, no acknowledgment was made to the magazine.

Harriet Monroe called in her lawyer, but when Kreymborg wrote her that he had acted in simple ignorance of previous publication in other magazines, she offered to drop the matter if a printed sticker of acknowledgment were added to all unsold copies of the book, and that was the end of the affair. The misunderstanding was occasioned by the ambiguous terms on which the *Glebe* was published. Pound thought of it as a book—he had written November 7, 1913, "the Glebe is to do our Imagiste anthology. There'll be various reprints from 'Poetry'"[8]—and he thought that *Poetry* had only the serial rights to the poems it had published. Even so, omission of all reference to publications in *Poetry* seems a great discourtesy, another sign of his disgust with *Poetry* over the winter, and another indication that he wished to cut the connection altogether.

Poetry's legal rights to the poems it had published were stronger than Pound recognized. The meaning of "copyright" was at the time a vexed question. Harriet Monroe's papers show magazine publishers asserting absolute rights, refusing her permission to reprint her own articles in a book, while book publishers assert in turn that serial copyright is an amiable fiction. But the courts favored the view that neither an author nor a book

8. In *Letters*, #27, p. 25.

publisher could move to print without honoring the copyright held by the magazine that first published the material. Harriet Monroe would have been sensitive to such questions; her lawsuit against the *New York World* for printing her "Columbian Ode" without permission, fought to a five-thousand-dollar judgment in her favor, would insure it. Pound wrote making much of the distinction between serial rights and book rights, but this seems a convention between publisher and author that had not been given legal definition. He conceded that he had been careless about the *Glebe* publication, but Harriet Monroe had never indicated, by sending contracts or forms, that she believed she was purchasing copyright on poems she printed. Pound had never consciously sold anything but serial rights, and he had not expected *Poetry* to take a rapacious businesslike view of its rights. He recognized no rights in such matters but the artist's. He went on to remark that *Poetry* could not expect other magazines, like the *Egoist*, to make acknowledgment when reprinting its poems until it had a much more prestigious reputation. The *Glebe* affair was his blunder—but how much was he supposed to pay in damages?[9]

If Pound made Harriet Monroe seem unattractively legalistic, he seemed on his side to deny her simple justice. He made her lapses from perfection an excuse to deny her ordinary rights. The heat of this disagreement, however, emanated entirely from Pound. Harriet Monroe had already settled her dispute with the Bonis and Kreymborg before Pound wrote his long, rambling letter about the *Glebe* and other matters. She wrote in reply on May 12, 1914:

> About the Glebe matter that incident is closed. Our letter to them could hardly have been milder, you must admit. I didn't want to bother you, but we could hardly stand for their highway robbery. I hadn't read their ad, or thought much about the Anthology—indeed I thought you were doing it in England. Just remember please, that we have the American rights on things we print, and that we ask proper credit when they are reprinted in books, or copied in other papers. I can't see why the *Egoist* would be injured—or any other paper—by giving us that credit. They ex-

9. Letter of March 28, 1914, in *Letters*, #42, pp. 34–36; the passage summarized is not printed.

pect their names to be plastered all over the place when American papers quote from them.

The first two issues of *Poetry* in 1914 are good ones, carrying most of the material Pound had sent in before the end of September, 1913: D. H. Lawrence and Richard Aldington are the features of January, and Robert Frost, H.D., and Orrick Johns the features of February. But March, 1914, marks a new strength in the magazine, for it is the first issue put together mostly by the Chicago office that can be called permanently interesting. Carl Sandburg's "Chicago Poems" lead off, followed by two good groups of quieter lyrics by Sara Teasdale and Frances Shaw, followed by Robinson's "Eros Turannos." Padraic Colum's "Irish Spinning Songs," sent by Pound in January, are not the freshest things in the number, and the impression of an enormous disparity between the London and Chicago offices is for the first time dispelled.

Pound recognized that the appearance of Sandburg represented some kind of American response to the material he had been sending overseas. He wrote April 18, 1914: "Good luck, glad to see Sandburg. I don't think he is very important, but that's the sort of stuff we ought to print." Later one interpretation of the movement would make Sandburg a disciple of Pound: "Some of his smaller verse is charming; but appears to be rather an echo of Mr. Pound, who has done it better," wrote T. S. Eliot in 1922.[10] Pound himself subscribed to the view that his work in London stimulated whatever new vitality manifested itself in America: "I think there is only one largish current error of this sort, namely that in America, the stay-at-home, local congeries did ANYTHING toward the *stil nuovo* or the awakening. Robinson is still old style. Lindsay did have a *rayon* of his own, the rest trundled along AFTER the hypodermic injection had been effected via London. Even Frost the prize autochthonous specimen had his debut in London, and was forced into the local New England bucolic recognition from Kensington, W.E."[11]

10. "London Letter," *Dial*, May, 1922, p. 512.
11. "Date Line," from *Make It New*, reprinted in *Literary Essays*, p. 80 (copyright 1935 by Ezra Pound; all rights reserved). Reprinted by permission of New Directions Publishing Corporation and Faber and Faber, Ltd., publishers and Agents for the Trustees of the Ezra Pound Literary Property Trust.

This view of his inspiration was apparently anathema to Sandburg. But it is easy to understand Pound's feeling as one reads the files of *Poetry* for 1913 and 1914. The effect is of a fire, which had been closely contained and in some danger of guttering out, suddenly shooting out and spreading in all directions. It is as if Chicago finally "caught on" after fifteen months of bellows work by Pound, and the appearance of Sandburg, whose manuscripts Mrs. Henderson had fished out of the pile of anonymous incoming contributions, is the first convincing spurt of new fire, whatever the cold biographical reality. The whole excitement of *Poetry*'s great period depends on the illusion that Pound and the new poets who turned up in America were part of the same movement, that the "stay-at-home local congeries," for that matter, had a common cause among themselves. The history of the composition of *Spoon River* is confused by controversy about the degree of Sandburg's influence on Masters. This kind of inference can be impertinent or misleading, as applied to the work of any individual poet, but it is crucial to creating the legend of a magazine.

Sandburg was confirmed as the first Chicago disciple of Pound by the *Dial*. "Chicago Poems" frightened that editorial office as even "Contemporaria" had not, and on March 16, 1914, it attacked in the same hysterical terms used against Pound the year before in Wallace Rice's correspondence, this time in a lead article: "The parlous times in which we live afford occasions innumerable for . . . calling out the old guard, for it has become the fashion with young people to reject everything that has been tested in the alembic of reflection, and to offer us in its stead all manner of raw and fantastic imaginings." The old was rejected as a matter of course, while the new was automatically reverenced; the more freakish it was, the more fervently it was acclaimed. For instance:

> Hog Butcher for the World,
> Tool Maker, Stacker of Wheat,
> Player with Railroads and the Nation's Freight Handler;
> Stormy, husky, brawling,
> City of the Big Shoulders.[12]

12. Excerpt from "Chicago" by Carl Sandburg reprinted from *Complete Poems of Carl Sandburg* by permission of Harcourt Brace Jovanovich, Inc.

"Here," continued the *Dial*, "a word of explanation is needed. The typographical arrangement of this jargon creates a suspicion that it is intended to be taken seriously as some form of poetry, and the suspicion is confirmed by the fact that it stands in the forefront of the latest issue of a futile little periodical described as a 'magazine of verse.'" No possible definition of poetry could admit this botch, for "all definition of art must say or imply that beauty is an essential aim of the worker, and there is no trace of beauty in the ragged lines we have quoted or in the whole piece of which it is the opening." Even doggerel has a rhythm, but "this composition admits no aesthetic claim of any description, and acknowledges subordination to no kind of law."

In its demands for absolute reverence for law, in the rigidity of alternatives such as "salutary tyranny" and "poetic anarchy," and in the blind fury of its diction—"futile little periodical"—the *Dial* seems almost the caricature of the bullying superior. There is joy in the battle and security in the justice of her cause in Harriet Monroe's reply in *Poetry* for May, 1914:

> Next to making friends, the most thrilling experience of life is to make enemies. Neither adventure being possible to the dead, the normal healthy person may accept hand-clasps and dagger scratches as tributes to his vitality. Both make his eye flash and blood tingle; both encourage him to go on his way rejoicing. . . .
>
> . . . perhaps our most outspoken enemy is our orthodox neighbor *The Dial*. For a year and a half it held aloof while we were introducing Mr. Tagore, Mr. Lindsay, and various other poets, but now, in presenting Mr. Sandburg, we go a step too far—his "Chicago" proves us a "futile little periodical."

It is possible that we have ventured rashly in "discovering" Mr. Sandburg and the others, but—whom and what has *The Dial* discovered? We have taken chances, made room for the young and the new, tried to break the chains which enslave Chicago to New York, America to Europe, and the present to the past. What chances has *The Dial* ever taken? What has it ever printed but echoes? For thirty years it has run placidly along in this turbulent city of Chicago, gently murmuring the accepted opinions of such leaders of thought as *The Athenaeum* and *The Spectator*. During all that third of a century it has borne about as much relation to the intellectual life of this vast, chaotically rich region as though it were printed in Glasgow or Caracas. Not only has it failed to grasp a great opportunity—it has been utterly blind and deaf to it, has never known the opportunity was there. Is its editor competent to define the word futile?[13]

Harriet Monroe's references to the "intellectual life of this vast, chaotically rich region" and to "a great opportunity" reflect the general excitement of the "Chicago Renaissance." In 1914 Chicago's literary awakening seems to have come to a climax. Edgar Lee Masters remembered a tide of free and delighted young people in town, reading Ibsen and Shaw, furiously debating the new poetry and the new theater. The reaction of the young bohemians to Sandburg gave *Poetry* new vitality.

But Miss Monroe had another ground for serenity in the face of the *Dial*'s attack. Her magazine had in the same month been given public endorsement by the man generally recognized as the best poet writing in English. She had written Yeats, who made a lecture tour of the United States in 1914, asking that he allow her to give him some kind of public reception while he was in Chicago. She felt that a festive social event might encourage those guarantors who were uncertain about the wisdom of their generosity.[14]

The scheme succeeded beyond her wildest expectations. Yeats not only gave *Poetry* the endorsement of his presence at a banquet, but climaxed the evening with some remarks that must have heartened the feeblest guarantors. Yeats praised *Poetry*'s first local discovery, Vachel Lindsay, in strong terms: ". . . I will address my remarks especially to a fellow craftsman. For since coming to Chicago I have read several times a poem by Mr. Lindsay, one which will be in the anthologies, 'General Booth Enters into Heaven.' This poem is stripped bare of ornament; it has an earnest simplicity, a strange beauty, and you know Bacon said, 'There is no excellent beauty without strangeness.'. . ." Yeats went on to describe his own early efforts to free his poetry from "the rhetorical poetry of the Irish politicians," comparing his situation to Lindsay's in the America of 1914: "I find that all we rebelled against in those early days—the sentimentality, the rhetoric, the 'moral uplift'—still exist here. Not because you are

13. "The Enemies We Have Made," *Poetry*, May, 1914, p. 63.
14. Her comment in the draft of the invitation to Yeats, penciled out.

too far from England, but because you are too far from Paris."[15]
Lindsay rose to the occasion, Harriet Monroe remembered:

> The keen spirit of the assembly was lifted to delight by the
> speaker's gracious compliment to Lindsay, who was still little
> known in spite of the acclaim given to "General Booth" over a year
> before. And when the new poet responded by reciting for the first
> time "The Congo," then still in manuscript, the "strange beauty"
> of the poem came to the audience with an accolade, as it were, of
> authoritative praise. Only a few of us had ever heard Lindsay
> recite his poems: the audience was quite carried away by his
> gusto, and if any dissenters from his method or manner were
> present they dared not express their feelings. The night, which for
> the Irish poet was merely one of many such occasions, was a
> triumph for the young poet of Illinois.

And a triumph for the editor who had sponsored him: "This also
was one of my great days, those days which come to most of us as
atonement for long periods of drab disappointment or dark despair. I drew a long breath of renewed power, and felt that my
little magazine was fulfilling some of our seemingly extravagant
hopes."[16]

Poetry, from March, 1914, onward, was established securely,
operating with a confidence that nothing had given it earlier.
Yeats's recognition of Lindsay was crucial to giving the magazine
security. Locally, one can see this in the response of the *Dial*.
The attack on Sandburg carried an incidental sneer at Yeats's
remarks on rhetoric at the banquet, and two weeks later, on
April 1, 1914, a fresh attack on Yeats, for comparing Lindsay
and Tennyson to the latter's disadvantage, was printed, indicating that the banquet speech still rankled. But by October, 1914,
the *Dial* praised Lindsay in a lead article and explained the circumstances of the Yeats banquet for the first time. Margaret
Anderson remembered the impact of the banquet speech so vividly that by 1930 she thought it had been addressed to the audience of the *Little Review*, and so implied in her memoirs. The
speech was printed in the second number of the *Little Review*,
April, 1914.

15. Quoted in *Poet's Life*, pp. 336–37.
16. Ibid., pp. 338–39.

Yeats's recognition also seems crucial to giving Harriet Monroe some serenity in her relationship to Pound. The situation created by the banquet was more than irritating to Pound. The high priest of his cenacle had recognized "strange beauty" in the poem that he had dismissed as a "blague." But Yeats could maintain sympathy with both Ezra Pound and Vachel Lindsay. He was able to insist on the "international standard" just as stiffly as Pound—he told Chicago at the banquet that it was "too far from Paris"—without abandoning an ideal of poetry rooted in the soul of a people. Yeats's point of view gave *Poetry* a breathing space that Pound's polarizations of "my side of the wet" and "your side" consistently denied it. The calm and cheerfulness of Harriet Monroe's letter of May 12, 1914, about the *Glebe*, seem to reflect a new confidence. She closed: "The only trouble with our living up to your standard is that you like nothing but importations—an ideal which, whether true or false, is impossible for an American magazine. However, I need scarcely repeat that we deeply appreciate what you have done for us. Moreover, we hope to keep climbing."

Poetry did not react to the new vitality in Chicago by setting itself up as the voice of a middle-western renaissance; nor were Lindsay and Sandburg given special favors. Sandburg did not publish significantly in *Poetry* after "Chicago Poems" until October, 1915; he has one small poem in the issue for June, 1914, and a poem entered in a War Poem Contest. In her editorial dealings with Lindsay, Miss Monroe had been and remained as judicious and finicky as she was with everyone else. Possibly because of this—in 1913 "The Blacksmith's Son," "The Traveler Heart," "The North Star," and "Incense and Splendor," as well as a batch of leftover moon poems, were considered and rejected—*Poetry* did not print "The Congo." Lindsay wrote February 16, 1914, to say that he had sent it to the *Metropolitan*. Besides the prizes given to "General Booth" in 1913 and to "The Chinese Nightingale" in 1915, the only evidence of Harriet Monroe's special preference for Lindsay is her sponsorship of his second book: she wrote the Macmillan Company recommending publication of *The Congo* and wrote an introduction to it.

Miss Monroe's preference for Lindsay was real enough, and

comes through strongly in her reviews of his books. She saw in him all the attributes proper to her ideal poet. In *Poetry* for February, 1914, her review of *General William Booth Enters into Heaven* is full of hope that Lindsay will reform American society, and full of the illusion that he wanted to. In January, 1918, defending *The Chinese Nightingale* against growing attacks on Lindsay's poetic merit, she found that the best of the poems were great, full of epic or mythical vastness: "they strip us all of sophistications, bring us back to primitive simplicities. They have what the advanced modern art movement is aiming at everywhere—a bold and broadly balanced composition of rhythmic figures, done in strong lines and masses of color. And they use always our own jargon, our own gesture. Without aping any style of the past, they have style."

Her infatuation is most simply evident in the fact that Lindsay, who was thirty-five in 1914, seemed to her exuberantly young and fresh—"the young poet of Illinois." Lindsay in his correspondence to her tends to play the role of a very young man; he writes a great deal about his crushes on a series of young ladies. The following postscript to a letter on November 4, 1913, gives the tone: "You have woven quite a web in giving me a spiritual introduction to Miss Teasdale. Our correspondence has become almost intimate—but a little humorous still—yes—still a bit humorous." He put himself in a romantic relation to Miss Monroe, also, writing October 26, 1913: "I think of you often. Be sure of that. Did you ever read May Sinclair's *The Divine Fire*? The heroine of that tale was something like what I fancy you are—only you have many rhymers, not one, to take care of." May Sinclair's heroine is incredibly learned—she recites Euripides and Sophocles with flawless accent and pointed wit—very beautiful, very delicate, very detached from practical affairs, and twenty-four years old. One does not know what to wonder at: that Lindsay took the character seriously, or that he would so grossly flatter Harriet Monroe. The heroine of *The Divine Fire* ends in the arms of the brilliant young Cockney poet who is its hero, and there Lindsay had a genuine intuition: Harriet Monroe's dedication to the poet had a great deal of romance in it, and Lindsay was not the only beneficiary of her ardent zeal.

But she did not let her enthusiasm for Lindsay overflow on the pages of *Poetry*. Lindsay would have been glad if it had. On May 1, 1914, he asked her to say in her introduction to *The Congo* that "*Poetry* magazine introduced me to the world [for years everyone ignored the list of Lindsay publications since 1904, carried away by the legend that Miss Monroe discovered him in 1913], and—though not necessarily in set terms—say your set in Chicago did much to get the Congo going. I want my work dramatized as it were, identified with the movements of your group." But such maneuvering with *Poetry* was quite alien to Harriet Monroe's notion that it was an exhibition where works of all schools were hung, though she was glad to express her own opinion that Lindsay represented "the immediate movement in modern art." Lindsay got the usual treatment accorded the better poets from *Poetry* in 1914: two publications over the year, "Aladdin and the Jinn" in April and a group of three "Poems to Be Chanted" in July. In 1915 *Poetry* published him only once: the ambitious "Chinese Nightingale" in February, winner of the Levinson Prize for the publishing year.

Lindsay also got the usual requests for revision and emendation when he sent manuscripts to the *Poetry* office. Miss Monroe asked him to put "The Blackhawk War of the Artists," from the July, 1914, group of "Poems to Be Chanted," through several revisions. Lindsay was fairly pliable about revising—if anything, he took too many suggestions from too many people. He wrote May 18, 1914, in response to her suggestions for "Poems to Be Chanted":

> Now I am much more tractable as to amendments to the Fireman's Ball than to the Trail—first because I have read it to you, and second I have not taken so many suggestions from *other* people before submitting to you, and my good humor is more on tap so to speak, and I am not worn out pretending to be meek, in this instance. But—first—please suggest cuttings—rather than tinkerings or amendments when you can. It is far easier for me to cut a cold poem than to mend it. And please send all criticisms in one fell swoop. *Mark* this copy all up.

This is the sort of thing Harriet Monroe objected to in Lindsay's manuscripts:

Here come the cat-horn, here comes the rat horn.
Listen to the dog-horn give fair warning.
Now comes the gad-horn, fad-horn, cad-horn.
Listen to the gold-horn, old-horn, cold-horn
Listen to the quack-horn, slack and clacking.

And:

Way down the road, trilling like a toad
Here comes the dice-horn, here comes the vice-horn
Then comes the nude-horn, rude-horn, lewd-horn
Followed by the prude-horn, bleak and squeaking.
(Some of them from Kansas, some of them from Kansas.)
Here comes the shank-horn, lank-horn, crank-horn,
Here comes the hod-horn, plod-horn, sod-horn
Listen to the cow horn—Listen to the plough-horn—
Never more-to-roam horn—loam horn—home horn
(Some of them from Kansas, some of them from Kansas.)[17]

This is the sort of improvement Lindsay would make: "The two passages to which you objected I have combined into one and made the whole passage five lines shorter. Also I eliminated several purely mechanical rhymes and beast phrases. Also I have cut off the last eight lines."[18] A manuscript of "The Santa Fe Trail" dated May 12 gives this reading:

Listen to the iron horns, ripping, racking—
Listen to the quack horns, slack and clacking!
Way down the road, trilling like a toad,
Here comes the dice-horn, here comes the vice-horn,
Here comes the snarl-horn, brawl-horn, lewd-horn,
Followed by the prude-horn, bleak and squeaking.
(Some of them from Kansas, some of them from Kansas!)
Here comes the hod-horn, plod-horn, sod-horn,
Never-more-to-roam horn, loam horn, home horn
(Some of them from Kansas, some of them from Kansas.)[19]

Lindsay seems disconcertingly willing to cut, as if he were aware that the poem he submitted was only half made. The second

17. Passages marked "?" in the MS of "The Santa Fe Trail" that Lindsay sent April 14, 1914.

18. Letter of May 13, 1914.

19. Excerpt from "The Santa Fe Trail" reprinted by permission of Macmillan Publishing Company, Inc., from *Collected Poems* by Vachel Lindsay (copyright 1914 by Macmillan Publishing Company, Inc., renewed 1942 by Elizabeth C. Lindsay).

version seems a real improvement over the first, but the original faults seem elementary.

In Lindsay's case, Harriet Monroe uniformly rejected the worst and printed the best of the poems submitted to *Poetry*. Here one sees the good side of the coolness of temper that often daunted her contributors. If she failed to communicate to Pound the degree of her admiration for his work, she was able, because of the same temperamental coolness, to keep her enthusiasm for Lindsay from overwhelming her. Thus Pound felt he could share the pages of the magazine with Lindsay without being contaminated: "he's all right but we are not in the same movement or anything like it. I approve of his appearing in *Poetry* so long as I am not supposed to want what he wants, but not in anything which I stand sponsor for [the proposed *Catholic Anthology*] as a healthy tendency. I don't say he copies Marinetti, but he is with him, and his work is futurist, it is also headed for the popular which is, in the end, hell."[20]

In fact, the magazine in its early years was more open to Pound than to Lindsay. This reflects a vacuum in Lindsay. He had no poetic platform to preach, no sense of a movement that needed guidance and direction, no very quick or clear understanding of his contemporaries. He missed the Imagiste movement in *Poetry* and had no interest in it, beyond "a polite effort to be fair" when he met it in Amy Lowell's version. He did not discover Sandburg until 1916, when the book *Chicago Poems* came out.[21] Lindsay contributed a note on "Primitive Singing" to the July, 1914, *Poetry*, but it reads like a mélange of Harriet Monroe's and Yeats's ideas, and he did not go on to preach a poetics of primitivism in later issues. He muddled through the Poetry Renaissance, absorbed in his own work and his own feelings. He had no particular use for a magazine of verse, except as an outlet for his own poetry, and he made no other use of *Poetry*.

According to one common account of Lindsay's career, the vaudeville style represented by "The Congo" and "The Santa Fe Trail" required a deformation of his original and best poetic voice. Lindsay eventually sickened of his "vaudevilles," but he

20. In *Letters*, #64, pp. 55–56.
21. Letter of June 11, 1916.

had no such feelings in 1914. Rather, he seemed boyishly delighted with his rough, tough style: "you . . . are to be the lusty pioneer and send forth the devil-work and the fire-crackers," he wrote Harriet Monroe on May 18, 1914. And he complained of some editors who rejected "The Fireman's Ball": "It appears they want me if I will roar gently, and have a care not to frighten the ladies."

Lindsay did sicken of the public identity he gained as the reader of these poems. Chicago, at the Yeats banquet, introduced him to the experience of taking an audience into his power. By the 1920s he felt that his reciting required a disgusting falsification of himself, but he was still susceptible to the delights of rhetorical power:

> That is not All, dear Harriet. I would give almost anything to escape forever the reciting and chanting Vachel. Except when immediately under the intense excitement which comes with facing an extraordinarily concentrated group of listeners, I dislike the very name of every poem I have recited very much, except the Chinese Nightingale, which, after all, I now recite very seldom. My whole heart is set on escaping my old self. . . . Everybody was very good to me, too good to me, in England, but I went there aping or recording, and as it were, shouting, the Vachel of ten years ago, for one gets into rhyme only a self that is long dead. I do not like that Vachel very well.[22]

The ironic possibility is that Harriet Monroe betrayed the poet she most admired into the hands of the audience she hoped he would ennoble. She created the situation, the banquet, which first seduced him, and encouraged him to think that the *frissons* he created in the lecture hall had something to do with "healthier open-air conditions and immediate personal contacts . . . the art of the Greeks and of primitive nations." Her view of Chicago was like Lindsay's vision of Springfield. Both kept hoping for organic, harmonious community life in cities that were as human communities undergoing progressive disintegration. But while Lindsay seems to have mortgaged his spirit to that disintegration with his life of public recitals, Harriet Monroe remained personally uncorrupted. She seems as much Lindsay's dupe as he seems

22. Letter of December 15, 1920.

hers, and the view that Lindsay's early poetry showed the spirit of Blake seems sentimental. He was capable of corrupting himself, if he was corrupted, without the help of Chicago or Harriet Monroe. Pound touched Lindsay's weakness when he called him "semi-serious." The attitude of the poetic speaker toward General Booth or toward the "fat black bucks" of "The Congo" is divided, half sympathetic and half supercilious. Pound seems right, that the combination of sympathy with superiority is essentially vulgar. Lindsay was capable of this sort of thing from the beginning, though his success as a vaudeville reciter led him to work the mine to exhaustion by 1920.

One feels some regret, in reading the correspondence between Ezra Pound and Harriet Monroe, that he never found a precise and dramatic formula for what he disliked in Lindsay. His objections never seem quite accurate, and he is left open to the suspicious inference that he resented Lindsay's popular appeal. Pound and Miss Monroe carried on a rather long debate about Lindsay in the first months of 1915; the issue was whether Lindsay merited inclusion in the projected *Catholic Anthology*. Pound insisted that Lindsay would prevent the book's having unity of tone and classified him with John Rodker as a futurist. But Rodker ended up in the anthology, whose very title proclaims its lack of unity of tone, and Lindsay remained out. Pound sent a parody, but the associations of idea in it are too arbitrary, the dominant mood too simply a frenzy, to be effective satire of Lindsay. When Harriet Monroe protested that Lindsay was expressing America, Pound answered May 10, 1915: "Now about Lindsey [*sic*], rubbish. Masters expresses America, and without letting all his steam off at the whistle, and besides he knows something, it isn't all froth and damn little beer. Effervescence is not vitality nor yet validity. All luck to Lindsey but there is no weight on his safety valve and he don't get up enough pressure."

Pound could not or would not take the trouble to arrive at the right formula for "Lindsey," just as he could not manage to learn the spelling of his name. Pound's letters describe a poet who has no shape, no style of his own, and Lindsay does emphatically have his own tone. Nor did Lindsay's style admit of endless easy duplications: in the twenties, when he became unhappy with the old reciting Vachel, his poetic vein ran out entirely. Pound was willing enough after 1930 to admit that Lindsay "did have a *rayon of his own*," but Harriet Monroe must have felt in 1915 that all his objections to Lindsay's "futurism" were unjust. The disagreement over Lindsay remained a wall between them.

Carl Sandburg and Vachel Lindsay were only the beginning of a parade of "discoveries" in *Poetry* in 1914. The next big find of the year really belonged to William Marion Reedy's Saint Louis paper, the *Mirror*, but *Poetry* played a small part in the introduction of the *Spoon River Anthology*. Its October, 1914, issue was given distinction and excitement by some reprints of Edgar Lee Masters' poem from Reedy's paper, where it had been running in installments since May 29, 1914. Alice Corbin Henderson, who wrote a brief appreciation of "Webster Ford" in the issue, had noticed the poems in an exchange copy of the *Mirror*. *Poetry* felt that it was Masters' discoverer and inspiration, that *Spoon River* followed from the Sandburg it had printed in March, 1914, and that its notice was the first critical recognition given Masters' poem. So Harriet Monroe wrote in *Poetry* for March, 1915:

> Edgar Lee Masters told . . . how *The Spoon River Anthology* was conceived nearly a year ago, when his mind, already shaken out of certain literary prejudices by the reading in *Poetry* of much free verse, especially that of Carl Sandburg, was spurred to more active radicalism through a friendship with that iconoclastic champion of free speech, free form, free art—freedom of the soul. At this acknowledgement that *Poetry* had furnished the spark which kindled a poet's soul to living flame, and burned out of it the dry refuse of formalism, this editor, in her corner, felt a thrill of pride, and a sudden warmth of unalterable conviction that, whatever may happen to the magazine now or later, its work can never be counted in vain.

Masters was willing to let this view of his inspiration stand in 1915; he saw the March issue of *Poetry* and commented March 11, 1915: "All in all it was excellent (the magazine). I always read yours and ACH's critical remarks—You are pretty 'subtile' both; and I concur in most of what you say." But in later years he soured, and was full of "insistencies, frequent and vehement, that Sandburg had no influence upon the conception or style of the poems and that he, Masters, had no use for Sandburg or his poetry."[23] Although Harriet Monroe's 1915 account seems valid, Masters was anxious to separate himself from *Poetry* by 1918. When Alice Corbin Henderson noted in a July, 1918, editorial that *Poetry* had given Masters his first appreciation, he wrote a formal denial and asked its publication: "my poetry received appreciation in England, and to an extent in America, before *Poetry* was founded," and he added that *Spoon River* was first noticed by Edward J. Wheeler in *Current Opinion* for September, 1914.[24]

As with Pound's inspiration of Sandburg, it is a case of the later record's belying inferences that were allowed to multiply in the general euphoria of 1914. Certainly Masters did not need *Poetry* to attract the world's attention to *Spoon River*. The *Mirror* commented as early as July 31, 1914, that the poem had been widely praised and that there was heavy demand for the issues containing the installments. But the excitement of Pound's response to the reprint in *Poetry* illustrates the aura of discovery that clings around it:

GET SOME OF WEBSTER FORD'S STUFF FOR 'POETRY'

Dear H.M.,

Please observe above instructions as soon as possible. Poetry is really becoming more or less what one would like to have it.[25]

Pound characteristically made the discovery his own. Harriet Monroe was negotiating for Masters' poetry by November; he promised her some "anthologies" after he had finished his commitment to Reedy. These were never forthcoming, but the "Silence" he also promised was printed in *Poetry* for February, 1915.

The November, 1914, issue, which followed the reprinting of Masters in October, should have been a disaster. Everyone but Alice Corbin Henderson, who had arranged it, deplored the War Poem Contest, the feature of the number. But the response of poets to the contest was strong, and among the contributions was

23. Duffey, *Chicago Renaissance*, p. 157.
24. Letter of July 20, 1918, printed in *Poetry* for September, 1918.
25. Letter of October 12, 1914, in *Letters*, #55, p. 43.

a group of short poems by Wallace Stevens, "Phases." Stevens had published before, while still an undergraduate at Harvard, and in September, 1914, in a New York little magazine, *Trend*. But he was unknown to Harriet Monroe, and she made an authentic discovery: "I was alone in the office when this group arrived almost too late for the War Number. I remember my eager reassembling of the page proofs to make room for two pages—all I could squeeze in—by this master of strange and beautiful rhythms." In the flurry of pulling apart the proofs, she was brought to more emphatic acknowledgment than she usually gave accepted poets. She wrote Stevens on October 21, 1914: "I was heartbroken that we could not use more of your poem, especially the first section. But our war number is terribly crowded—I could give you only two pages—and II through V seemed about the best of it. Also it stands well without the rest."

She showed the same enthusiasm in a postcard of January 27, 1915, although she rejected some poems whose titles are not recorded: "I don't know when any poems have 'intrigued' me so much as these. They are recondite, erudite, provocatively obscure, with a kind of modern-gargoyle grin in them—Aubrey Beardsleyish in the making. They are weirder than your war series, and I don't like them, and I'll be blamed if I'll print them; but their author will surely catch me next time if he will only uncurl and uncoil a little—condescend to chase his mystically mirthful and mournful muse out of the nether darkness."[26] The next time Stevens approached *Poetry*, it was with "Sunday Morning." Interpreting the beautiful, privileged woman in the poem as Stevens' Muse, the interior paramour, not as a representative liberated young person of 1914 (a reading suggested by the way her voice blends into the poetic speaker's voice), one can speculate that Harriet Monroe's remark about chasing the Muse out of the nether darkness planted the seed of "Sunday Morning" in Stevens' mind.

Stevens' quality does not come through "Phases," his little group of war poems, with striking clarity, but the publication is still a discovery to earn any little magazine a place in history,

26. *Poet's Life*, p. 342; Harriet Monroe's cards to Stevens reprinted from Robert Buttel, *Wallace Stevens: The Making of Harmonium* (Princeton, N.J.: Princeton University Press, 1967), pp. 231n, 187.

though it publish nothing else above the level of Amelia Josephine Burr and Olive Tilford Dargan. That it was occasioned by a War Poem Contest indicates that *Poetry* in 1914 was running so strongly before a rising tide that it could hardly make a mistake.

That is the legend of *Poetry* for 1914: discovery setting off discovery, wave after wave of new excitement. When one adds Pound's discovery of T. S. Eliot at the end of September, 1914, to the "discoveries" of Sandburg, Masters, and Stevens, the year seems truly astonishing. But essential to the legend is the belief that all the poets shared in one movement. Thus one finds Pound enlisting Masters in his school in a letter of October 12, 1914, written for publication but never printed. Pound's comments on Masters take off from these remarks by Alice Corbin Henderson in the October *Poetry*: ". . . Mr. Webster Ford unites something of the feeling and method of the Greek Anthology with a trace of the spirit of Villon; but the 'tradition' has only served to lead him to a little cemetery in a small town. . . ." Pound called this "a cross-cut at my note on The Tradition" (in *Poetry* for January, 1914):

> Mr. Ford's verses do not contradict that note. They are most welcome confirmation. His verses are excellent and they are excellent in measure as they approach "the method of the Greek Anthology and Villon" rather than the spirit of Milton and Tennyson, of the "Century Magazine" and of Henry Van Dyke. Let us have more of them in "Poetry" as soon as possible, and more of other people's verse like them . . . [Pound's punctuation] if it be obtainable.
>
> Mr. Webster Ford has set himself a most excellent standard, I would not willingly delay my open speech in his praise.

Masters in turn marked the conclusion of *Spoon River* in the *Mirror* for January 22, 1915, by writing a review of Harriet Monroe's volume of poems, *You and I*, in which he classed Sandburg and Pound together in a school of "modernity" sponsored by *Poetry*. Their poems are said to contain "genuine ideas of highly explosive character," while Harriet Monroe is praised for "a noble feeling for democracy, a high vision of the republic's mission, a passion for justice, an understanding of modern conditions, and a finished art." The effect of this timing in the *Mirror* was to sweep Sandburg, Pound, and Harriet Monroe up together in the triumphant wake of the *Spoon River Anthology*.

A little later, in March, 1915, Harriet Monroe in *Poetry* recorded Masters' tribute to Sandburg as an inspiration of *Spoon River* and her own exultation at *Poetry*'s role in kindling the poet to living flame. She went on in the same article, "The Fight for the Crowd," to express her passionate desire to carry the flame to the American people, and made her most fiery statement of the poet's redemptive mission:

> The crowd rebels against the universal theme of art—the littleness of man—or rather, the abysmal contrast between his littleness and his greatness. In old Chinese painting there is always some little weazened philosopher squinting at the cataract; and so in all great art stands the absurd, earth-bound, gnome-like figure of humanity facing the infinite with inadequate and unattainable dreams. Deep-buried in the heart of every man is some effigy of this figure, but most men are afraid of it, like to bury it deeper under conventional occupations, sentimentalities, moralities, instead of permitting artists and prophets to unearth it and expose it to the pitiless light. But every man's heart, however perverse with ignorance, however cluttered with knowledge, makes a secret confession of the truth. Poets and prophets, therefore,—the beauty of art, the sublimity of truth—appeal to him not quite in vain; and the appeal must go on so long as the race endures. To the last trench and the last despair certain spirits, in whom the common human spark of love becomes a flaming passion, must keep up the eternal impossible fight for souls, for "a kingdom of heaven on earth."

This is Harriet Monroe at her highest pitch, and the vision almost transcends her rhetoric, the imagery of battle, the drum-beating rhythm. Certain images are reminiscent of Yeats, who seems the person in her generation who could best reconcile the idea of the artist as Prometheus and the ideal of art as a common human possession. Her figure of the Chinese philosopher is very like the "ancient glittering eyes" of "Lapis Lazuli," except that his dream is prejudged "inadequate" and "unattainable." Yeats can say that every man is potentially a tragic hero:

All perform their tragic play,
There struts Hamlet, there is Lear,
That's Ophelia, that Cordelia;
Yet they, should the last scene be there
The great stage curtain about to drop,
If worthy their prominent part in the play,
Do not break up their lines to weep.
They know that Hamlet and Lear are gay;
Gaiety transfiguring all that dread.
All men have aimed at, found and lost;
Black out; Heaven blazing into the head:
Tragedy wrought to its uttermost.
Though Hamlet rambles and Lear rages,
And all the drop-scenes drop at once
Upon a hundred thousand stages,
It cannot grow by an inch or an ounce.[27]

Despite her missionary zeal, Harriet Monroe's idea that art clarifies the spirit's loneliness has some nobility. But Pound's reaction to this editorial, as to all her ideas, was reductive. He makes the image of the artist's desperate love a mere pandering to popular appetite: "can't you ever see the difference between what is 'good,' and good enough for the public, and what is 'good' for the artist, whose only respectable aim is perfection. . . . 'The difference between enthusiastic slop and great art' there's a text to preach on in your glorious unfettered desert for the next forty years. . . . You constantly think I undervalue elan and enthusiasm. I see a whole country rotted with it, and no one to insist that 'form' and innovation are compatible."[28]

Ezra Pound and Harriet Monroe are like two images from Yeats's crazy charts of the human personality, locked in irreconcilable misunderstanding. Pound seems all Mask, all Persona, the assertion of an idealized self against fate and circumstance and the common social ties that bind mankind. Harriet Monroe seems tied to that "Body of Fate," aware that the human person

27. Excerpt from "Lapis Lazuli" reprinted by permission of Macmillan Publishing Company, Inc., from *Collected Poems* by William Butler Yeats (copyright 1940 by Georgie Yeats, renewed 1968 by Bertha Georgie Yeats, Michael Butler Yeats, and Anne Yeats).

28. Letter of "March, 1915," in *Letters*, #64, pp. 55–56, a rather unspecific reaction to a number of Harriet Monroe's recent editorials, especially her "dry refuse of formalism" in "The Fight for the Crowd."

is shaped by circumstance and by society beyond his power to change, obliged to define himself as he exists in the eyes of his fellow men. Yeats seems relevant again because each seems to have hold of a truth, each seems unable to do justice to the other's truth, and Yeats's great poetic statements about art seem the place where the quarrel between them is reconciled.

For *Poetry* at its zenith, consciousness of difference was not yet sharp, and Masters, Sandburg, Pound, Yeats, Lindsay, Tagore, and Hueffer were part of the same crusade. Thus Lucian Cary described it in the *Little Review* in mid-1915: ". . . *Poetry* has printed poetry that nobody else dared print. *Poetry* has boldly discussed the poetic controversy when everybody else hid behind language. *Poetry* introduced us to Rabindranath Tagore, to Vachel Lindsay, in a way, to Edgar Lee Masters. *Poetry* printed Ford Hueffer's poem *On Heaven*. *Poetry* has heard of Remy de Gourmont and the *Mercure de France*—an incredible achievement for a Chicago literary journal. . . ."[29] But Pound was backing away from the public crusade by that time. His remarks on *Spoon River* in the *Mirror* for May 21, 1915, are notably more negative and more patronizing than his article on Masters in the *Egoist* for January 1, 1915, or his comments in the unpublished letter of October 12, 1914, to Harriet Monroe.

In 1914, for the first time in *Poetry*'s brief history, the problem of censorship, or of suppression of poems or parts of poems out of fear of the Post Office censor, began to loom. The Post Office was empowered to impound the entire issue of a magazine sent through the mails if its censor judged it obscene. In addition, Anthony Comstock and his New York Society for the Suppression of Vice liked to keep an eye on literature, and take an author to court if in their judgment his work was likely to corrupt the innocent young. It was an uncomfortable era for publishers. The passions released by the free-verse conflict suggest the public temper that permitted Comstock and the Post Office to decide what literature was fit to circulate in America. The threat of the Post Office was real enough. Among the victims of 1914 were George Sylvester Viereck, whose magazine, the *International*,

29. "Literary Journalism in Chicago," June–July, 1915, p. 2.

had an issue seized for a nude on the cover, and the *Metropolitan*, which had an issue temporarily impounded because it contained some photographs of nude statuary. Harriet Monroe recorded in her memoirs that *Poetry*'s War Poem issue of November, 1914, was threatened with Post Office impoundment because of ironically realistic detail in one poem by John Russell McCarthy. Her scheme for financing *Poetry*, which made her dependent on the vague goodwill of a group of guarantors who did not follow the new movement closely or have any firm convictions about modern literature, left her particularly defenseless against the threat of Post Office censorship. *Poetry* was established as a civic institution on a par with the Art Institute or the orchestra, and the suppression of an issue for obscenity would probably have demolished the financial base that Harriet Monroe had created for it.

She was not personally a Comstockian, although she had no interest in merely symbolic defiance of his society. In 1920 she joined in the protest organized by Mencken against the suppression of James Branch Cabell's *Jurgen*, and agreed to work with an association of writers that Mencken was creating to "tackle the Comstocks head on." But she felt that "we need a lot of money for a long legal battle." Otherwise she felt that the protest was pointless.[30] She was one of the very few Americans of any standing in the literary world who publicly expressed sympathy with the *Little Review* when its editors were taken to court over *Ulysses* by the New York Society for the Suppression of Vice. But as editor of *Poetry*, Harriet Monroe was not very courageous about printing poems that referred clearly to sexual love or human physiology.

Amy Lowell exemplifies amusingly the nervousness of the time over indelicate language. Miss Lowell's poem in polyphonic prose, "The Forsaken," was printed in *Poetry* for April, 1914, with a line omitted from the text, so that the lament of an unwed mother-to-be was changed from:

> My mother would call me a whore, and spit upon me;
> the priest would

30. Mencken letter of February 23, 1920; her note on a Mencken letter of March 15, 1920.

have me repent, and have the rest of my life spent in a convent.[31]

to:

> My mother would call me a whore, and spit upon me;
>   the priest would
> vent.

It seemed to Miss Lowell that "vent" could be read in its
"Elizabethan" sense of "evacuate the bowel," and she was willing
to go to any lengths to extirpate the error. She asked Harriet
Monroe on April 9, 1914, to suppress the edition and issue
another. If some copies were already in circulation, she asked
that the poem be reissued and sent out with an explanatory slip
to all subscribers. "I feel that my reputation as a poet, and as a
woman, is very seriously injured by such apparent coarseness,
and I do think that reissuing the edition is little to ask you. . . .
such a horrible coarseness . . . will have consequences which
may be very prejudicial to my future career." Miss Monroe telegraphed in reply: "April number mostly distributed. Will insert
correction in those left. No one here can see any vulgar meaning,
merely a manifest error." There was no public outcry. It is interesting that three years later the *Poetry Journal* had an issue seized
by the Post Office because a little poem by Scudder Middleton
used the word "whore"; neither Miss Lowell nor Miss Monroe
felt that the word was risky in 1914. The two incidents are possibly an index of the deepening hostility of the censors to the little
magazines. At any rate, the issue is more and more a vexed one as
the teens mount toward the twenties.

A group of short poems that Pound sent to *Poetry* in April,
1914, touched off a disagreement about propriety. Harriet Monroe did not think much of the group as a whole, and wrote May
12, 1914, to object to some in particular:

> First, your poems which arrived while I was away. We think—
> don't you—they are hardly up to your usual form—at least not up
> to the April group of a year ago. However, that's your lookout.
> But some of this group you must know we can't print, you should

---

31. Excerpt from "The Forsaken" reprinted from *The Complete Poetical Works of Amy Lowell* by permission of Houghton Mifflin Company.

know that without being told, viz:—The Temperaments, Erinna, Phyllidula, the Father and Lesbia Illa we would rather not. Oh little indoor England and its tiresome little adulteries! For the love of heaven, get outdoors! And I am dead against Valediction— what is the use of calling names? In this particular case your country *has* employed you. Why waste your time cussing? Does a poet in that slam-bang attitude convince anybody?

Then, in the rough draft, she scratched out the comments on indoor England and adultery, and left this reading: "we would rather not. What is the use of calling names? Does a poet in that slam-bang attitude convince anybody?" (She also scratched out the comment that the poems were inferior to the 1913 group.) The manuscripts of the poems she cites are substantially the same as the versions printed in the collected *Personae*, except for "The Father," which Pound did not print. She apparently found the poems shocking. They apparently *were* shocking for the time, because Elkin Mathews would not print "Phyllidula" and "Erinna" in a trade edition of *Lustra* in 1916, and did not print "The Temperaments" even in his private edition.[32] Harriet Monroe's objection to "The Father" is more mystifying except that the poem is dull, a four-line squib about a father who marries a barmaid to provide for his children by a dead aristocrat. Pound himself was puzzled by Miss Monroe's objection to "Lesbia Illa," which she in the end agreed to make part of the group in *Poetry* for August, 1914: "Cut out any of my poems that would be likely to get you suppressed but don't make it into a flabby little sunday school lot like the bunch in the November number. Now WHO could blush at Lesbia Illa??????*WHO*???"[33]

Pound in this exchange was less irritated by Miss Monroe's dislike of frank language than by what he felt was her desire to protect Christianity. The only clear incident of this kind earlier in the *Poetry* files is her alteration of "Christ" to "Bel" in Aldington's "Lesbia." Pound saw her objection to a line in John Rodker's "London Night" as similar; she wrote May 12, 1914: " 'to bring her to my couch' is rather strong language for God in

32. Charles Norman, *Ezra Pound*, pp. 186–87. See also the appendix in Forrest Reed, ed., *Pound/Joyce*.
33. Letter of May 23, 1914, in *Letters*, #45, p. 37.

these unbiblical days, even if he is singing about our battered planet. I request the poet to permit us the earlier reading, now crossed out, in which the symbol is more quietly put." The line in *Poetry* for December, 1914, reads "to bring her to me." Pound replied to her request: "Keep the Rodker as it is, one can't emasculate everything. I will spit in the eye of Gehoveh in my next lyric if it is necessary to establish free speech, tho' I doubt if Jehovah has an eye. . . ."[34] Two days later he sent "a few verses of simple piety," which must be "Printemps," which has not been printed, a poem that degrades Jehovah, a balding genie, to exalt the old gods of the furrow. Harriet Monroe penciled "Omit this" on the manuscript.

The group published in August, 1914, includes "To KALON, " "The Study in Aesthetics," "The Bellaires," "Salvationists I, II, and III," "Amitiés I, II, III, and IV," "Agathas," "Young Lady," "Lesbia Illa," "Passing," and "The Seeing Eye," as printed in *Personae*, along with "Abu Salammamm—A Song of Empire," which has been printed in editions of *Personae* since 1949. Poems submitted but not printed include "The Temperaments," "Erinna" ("The Patterns" of *Personae*), "Phyllidula," "Valediction" (MS not preserved), "The Father," "Printemps," and "Fodder," a little squib against Walter de la Mare and Ralph Hodgson that Pound withdrew. Miss Monroe made Pound alter some of his titles for publication, objecting to the "polyglot glossary" of "To KALON," "Amitiés," "Le Donne," "Agathas Intacta," "Lesbia Illa," "Passante," and "Abu Salammamm" in combination,[35] and one's sense of humor suggests she was right.

Evaluation of Harriet Monroe's objections to this group is confused by the fact that the poems are not particularly successful. She was right that the group was not equal to "Contemporaria." It is not even as good as the November, 1913, group—it is too much in one tone, and too full of bad temper. The satires are marred by a mock-prosaic vein that runs through most of them, ruining the flow of the lines and making the poetic speaker sound fatuous. In "The Temperaments," for instance, expressions like "quiet and reserved in demeanour," "on the contrary,"

34. Ibid.; passage omitted in *Letters*.
35. An odd sheet in her hand filed in the Pound correspondence for 1914.

"who both talks and writes of," and "accomplished this feat at some cost" seem to strain toward an effect of dandyish detachment, without achieving it:

> Nine adulteries, 12 liaisons, 64 fornications and something approaching a rape
> Rest nightly upon the soul of our delicate friend Florialis.
> And yet the man is so quiet and reserved in demeanour
> That he passes for both bloodless and sexless.
> Bastitides, on the contrary, who both talks and writes of nothing save copulation,
> Has become the father of twins,
> But he accomplished this feat at some cost;
> He had to be four times cuckold.[36]

And "The Temperaments" is more or less Pound's masterpiece in the genre. He noted on the manuscript that Yeats, who disliked his satires, felt that this one had the true Greek flair. It is not altogether clear how much Harriet Monroe was objecting to the flatness of these poems when she wrote that she did not want to print them. The Latinate poems of *Lustra* may have been a necessary discipline for Pound's style, but they did not offer many rewards to his readers.

There are two other occasions in this era when Harriet Monroe refused to print lines that seemed too outspoken. She would not allow John G. Neihardt the line "Run your swords through the belly that bore Nero" in *The Death of Agrippina*, though he pleaded the authority of Suetonius for it. And toward the end of 1914 she outraged William Carlos Williams by refusing to include "Conquest" in a projected group. He wrote November 13, 1914: "It is of course your prudence that has overcome your taste—because of which my groans are heard from New York to Chicago. Print your choice. Is there no one on your staff who could have saved me? (I am tempted here to explain in detail for the second time just the nature of the difference of the conflicting points of view of editor and poet but I will not.)" It is hard to see anything rashly frank in the poem Williams printed in his *Col-*

---

36. "The Temperaments" reprinted from *Personae* and *Collected Shorter Poems* (copyright 1926 by Ezra Pound) by permission of New Directions Publishing Corporation and Faber and Faber, Ltd., publishers and Agents for the Trustees of the Ezra Pound Literary Property Trust.

lected Earlier Poems, and the *Poetry* manuscript is not preserved; Williams at least thought the poem rejected because of frightened prudence. These relatively minor squabbles about rejection of poems and alterations of lines were the beginning of difficulties between Harriet Monroe and the more outspoken wing of the movement, which eventually divorced it from *Poetry*.

Nothing else in Ezra Pound's correspondence to Harriet Monroe equals, for sentimental and dramatic interest, the emergence of T. S. Eliot as Pound's friend in London, and Pound's discovery that he had at last a young ally whose poetry commanded his unqualified respect. The story begins quietly in a little letter of September 22, 1914:[37] "An American called Eliot called this P.M. I think he has some sense tho' he has not yet sent me any verse." The discovery of "The Love Song of J. Alfred Prufrock" followed in about two weeks:

> I was jolly well right about Eliot. He has sent in the best poem I have yet had or seen from an American.
>
> PRAY GOD IT BE NOT A SINGLE AND UNIQUE SUCCESS. He has taken it back to get it ready for the press and you shall have it in a few days.
>
> He is the only American I know of who has made what I can call adequate preparation for writing. He has actually trained himself AND modernized himself ON HIS OWN. The rest of the promising young have done one or the other but never both— most of the swine have done neither. It is such a comfort to meet a man and not have to tell him to wash his face, wipe his feet, and remember the date (1914) on the calendar.[38]

The first complication to the story followed in about a month: "Your letter—the long one to hand—is the most dreary and discouraging document that I have been called upon to read for a very long time. Your objection to Eliot is the climax."[39]

Part of Pound's irritation in this letter seems a reaction to the award of the Levinson Prize for 1913–14 to Carl Sandburg, for "Chicago Poems." Pound had nominated Ford Madox Hueffer's

37. Dated by Harriet Monroe at the *Poetry* office.
38. Letter of September 30, 1914, in *Letters*, #50, p. 40.
39. Letter of November 9, 1914, in *Letters*, #57, p. 44.

"On Heaven" for the major prize of the year: he thought it was the two-hundred-fifty-dollar Guarantors' Prize that had been given Yeats in 1913. He nominated Fletcher or Frost for the Levinson Prize, a two-hundred-dollar award that was new that year, and limited, by the wish of the donor, to a poet who was an American citizen.[40] Pound had also mentioned Lindsay, Orrick Johns, and Skipwith Cannell as possibilities for the "American citizen prize." He had not mentioned Carl Sandburg, and apparently considered him beneath notice.

The award to Sandburg does not now seem singularly misguided, but Pound thought Sandburg so unworthy to be ranked with Hueffer that he inferred that the two-hundred-fifty-dollar Guarantors' Prize, which had no nationality limitation, had been canceled to evade the necessity of recognizing Hueffer over a local rhymer. (Pound did not clearly express this attitude until 1916, when he wrote on May 3, "Certainly the dropping of the open to all prize that year had the definite appearance of sheltering American incompetence from foreign competition, though it was equally obvious that the original intention of the magazine was NOT to support foreign talent but local." He did not mention the prize to Sandburg in 1914, outside of the remarks on her long and dreary letter in his letter of November 9; Harriet Monroe would have been writing at the end of October to inform him of the prize vote.) The inference that Harriet Monroe was so anxious to exclude foreigners from her list of prize winners that she abolished the Guarantors' Prize seems altogether unlikely; she arranged the next year for a regular hundred-dollar second prize without nationality limitations. Probably money shortages made it impractical to give two prizes, one of two hundred fifty dollars and the other of two hundred dollars, in one year. In 1914 Harriet Monroe had to adjust to the loss of her income as art critic for the *Chicago Tribune*, and she had feared at one point that two thousand extra dollars would be needed to get *Poetry* through the year.

Pound digested his rage for a few hours, then wrote back the

40. Salmon O. Levinson specified the limitation in a formal description of the prize dated July 28, 1913. Harriet Monroe wrote Pound on September 15, 1913, that the limitation was Levinson's idea: "Mr. Levinson was determined that it should go to the best American poem."

same day about Eliot: "No, most emphatically I will not ask Eliot to write down to any audience whatsoever. I dare say my instinct was sound enough when I volunteered to quit the magazine quietly about a year ago. Neither will I send you Eliot's address in order that he may be insulted."[41] Harriet Monroe's "objection" to Eliot was a feeling that the end of the poem was weak. John Gould Fletcher wrote Amy Lowell in December, 1914, that Harriet Monroe had complained to him of an excess of social polish in the poem, too much atmosphere of Henry James.[42] She apparently disliked in particular the Hamlet passage and the note of futility in the conclusion. Pound wrote January 31, 1915:

> It is a portrait of failure, or of a character which fails, and it would be false art to make it end on a note of triumph. I dislike the paragraph about Hamlet, but it is an early and cherished bit and T.E. won't give it up, and as it is the only portion of the poem that most readers will like at first reading I don't see that it will do much harm.
>
> For the rest a portrait satire on futility can't end by turning that quintessence of futility Mr. P. into a reformed character breathing out fire and ozone.[43]

Pound's reaction to Prufrock the character is decidedly detached. He seems in his early reading to have taken Prufrock's failure as a not very interesting incident in a poetic universe full of richer meaning than the character could grasp. Thus, in the *Egoist* in June, 1917, he wrote of the sea passage in the last six lines: "The poetic mind leaps the gulf from the exterior world, the trivialities of Mr. Prufrock, diffident, ridiculous, in the drawing room. . . . Mr. Eliot's melody rushes out like the thought of Fragilion 'among the birch trees.' "[44]

It seems to later readers that Prufrock's is the mind that defines this poetic universe, and that the failure of love is all over it, on a scale larger than his individual plight, a failure that seems to

41. In *Letters*, #58, pp. 44–45.
42. An unpublished letter of December 22, 1914, cited in Stanley K. Coffman, Jr., *Imagism: A Chapter for the History of Modern Poetry*, p. 43.
43. In *Letters*, #61, p. 50.
44. "Drunken Helots and Mr. Eliot," *Egoist*, June, 1917, pp. 73–74 (copyright 1917; all rights reserved). Reprinted by permission of New Directions Publishing Corporation and Faber and Faber, Ltd., publishers and Agents for the Trustees of the Ezra Pound Literary Property Trust.

determine the shape, the smell, and the sounds of the city. The drawing room world in "Prufrock" is ugly and trivial enough, but one wonders how Pound could feel that the poetic mind leaped out of it. It reduces Prufrock's every attempt to get outside it, and makes him feel only his own fatuousness. He is reduced in scale to the very trivialities that humiliate him: "Should I, after tea and cakes and ices, / Have the strength to force the moment to its crisis?" At the end, when the sea comes in, one wants an affirmation, but Prufrock can only go under, not out of, his civilized plight, and the transitory music of the waves is neither a refuge for him nor an escape from him:

> I have seen them riding seaward on the waves
> Combing the white hair of the waves blown back
> Where the wind blows the water white and black
>
> We have lingered in the chambers of the sea
> By sea-girls wreathed in sea-weed red and brown
> Till human voices wake us, and we drown.[45]

When Prufrock immerses himself in the "destructive element," his "reality" destroys him.

Harriet Monroe's dislike of the conclusion of "Prufrock" throws some light on her general reaction to Eliot. It is at first surprising to discover that she was frightened of Eliot's poem. J. Alfred Prufrock has something in common with the emblem of humanity she described in the winter of 1915: "the absurd, earth-bound, gnomelike figure of humanity facing the infinite with inadequate and unattainable dreams." She should have been able to contemplate Prufrock's defeat calmly. In one sense, she loved to savor defeat; her reactions to the savage landscapes of the American West illustrate this. They gave her a desolate sense of mankind's puniness, but an exhilarating sense of the power of the mysterious nonhuman world by which man is reduced. She had no corresponding enthusiasm for images of civilized human fulfillment. She dismissed the landscapes of Italy: "Italy. . . . gives one a sense of things achieved rather than a stimulus toward a new revelation." In Arizona, on the

45. Excerpts from "The Love Song of J. Alfred Prufrock" reprinted from *Collected Poems, 1909–1962* by T. S. Eliot by permission of Harcourt Brace Jovanovich, Inc., and Faber and Faber, Ltd.

contrary, "we venture into those ultimate primitive ages—the beginning and the end of things—upon whose fundamental immensity and antiquity our boasted civilization blooms like the flower of a day." She valued the sense of becoming, of the annihilation of the human present in the name of the future, and so far as defeat made epoch-shaping, nonhuman power more present to her imagination, it became almost desirable.[46] She had the revolutionary temperament, despite her conventional situation. But the image of "Prufrock," of man denatured by his own civilization but unable to escape from it, is abhorrent to that temperament. The way Eliot's conclusion denies Prufrock any escape from himself, and suggests another level of reality in the sea only to deny it, would be shocking to Harriet Monroe. She tried to escape from the poem by making Prufrock's problem a personal problem of Eliot's—"modern sophistication dealing with the tag-ends of overworldly cosmopolitanism."[47]

But if Harriet Monroe would have had to make herself over to read "Prufrock" with relish, her reaction to the poem does not seem a sign of editorial incompetence. Pound's own reading seems an oversimplification after sixty years, but in 1914 or 1915 "Prufrock" was accessible on any terms to very few readers. Pound's account of reactions to the poem in London after its *Poetry* publication suggests that no one could make anything of it except Ford Madox Hueffer: "Hueffer having seen 'Prufrock' came in the other day to find out if Eliot had published a book, as he wanted to write about him. WHICH shows that you can't do a good thing without its being took note of. F.M.H. was just as quick as I to see that Eliot mattered."[48] The other interested English reader was Harold Monro, who had already rejected the poem for publication in his *Poetry and Drama* and had the chance of a second reading when the poem came out in *Poetry*. One gets the impression that every other London reader was stultified or stupified by the poem, because Pound almost rejoiced over these two interested responses.[49]

Poetry's American readership was equally confused. Very few

46. *Poet's Life*, pp. 166–67.
47. Ibid., p. 394.
48. Letter dated "July 1915" by Harriet Monroe.
49. Letter dated September 25, 1915, by Harriet Monroe, in *Letters*, #74, p. 63.

people commented at all. Louis Untermeyer was joyously amused that Miss Monroe should print a neurotic's muddle of infantile repressions and inhibitions. The only sympathetic comment that remains in the record came June 12, 1915, from Vachel Lindsay, the poet usually so abstracted about and unresponsive to his contemporaries: "Most of all I liked the Love Song of J. Alfred Prufrock—the best thing you have had for many a day." Harriet Monroe printed the poem when no other editor would, but commentators have so emphasized the nine-month delay between receipt of the manuscript and its appearance in *Poetry* that the fact of the publication is passed over.

The nine-month wait seems often interpreted as mere balky resistance to Eliot, but by mid-1914 *Poetry*'s files were in fact getting "stuffed up," and Harriet Monroe was not able to fit in Pound's London manuscripts as quickly as she had in 1913. She had written May 12, 1914: "About dates—we do our best to meet your wishes. But please give us as much leeway as possible, and let us know as long beforehand as you can. If a date is absolute, tell us why—that helps. Remember that people are clamoring also at this end." John Rodker's poem "London Night," in *Poetry* for December, 1914, was held up for nine months, and William Carlos Williams' work was held in the office for more than a year in 1914. In 1915, even Yeats had manuscripts held up for eight months. Harriet Monroe's resistance to Eliot was real, but given the theatrical element in Pound's established stance of "hammering stuff" into *Poetry*, one suspects that both its degree and its significance have been exaggerated. One can see both her resistance and Pound's recommendation set in the perspective of 1915, when "Prufrock" was not yet a sacred text, in an undated letter that Pound did not publish: "You mark my blossoming word, that young chap will go quite a long way. He and Masters are the best of the bilin'. If you think he lacks vigour merely because he happens to have portrayed Mr. Prufrock the unvigorous, vous vous trompez. His poem of Christopher Columbus is vigorous, and male, not to say coarse. I think however he may produce something both modest and virile before the end of the chapter."

Pound noted in the same letter that he had sent Eliot's "Portrait of a Lady" to Alfred Kreymborg's little magazine, *Others*, where the poem was published in September, 1915, "partly because you don't like him. . . ."[50] One is tempted to conclude that Harriet Monroe's unsympathetic response to Eliot provoked the consequence it merited: the loss of a most important new poet to a competitor, and the dissipation of the energy of Pound's movement among a number of little magazines. But the story is more complicated than that. *Poetry* had already survived a deflection of Pound's energies into the *Smart Set* six months after he first became foreign correspondent; the margin of tolerance that he extended to Harriet Monroe's magazine was thin from the beginning. Nor did Pound in 1915 make any new dramatic effort at a break. His letter went on about Eliot, "I want his next batch of stuff in *Poetry* to be made up exclusively of his newest work." In fact, Pound in 1915 came closer to *Poetry*, and the tone of his letters to Harriet Monroe became almost amiable; the storms of temper disappeared from them.

Pound's situation in London in 1915 was almost too ironic to be credible. His friendship with Eliot was developing, and publication of *The Portrait of the Artist as a Young Man* in the *Egoist* made a fresh contemporary statement of the meaning of his choice of exile as an artist. With Eliot, Joyce, and Yeats involved in his movement, his literary position was secure as never before. But on the material plane, Pound in 1915 was very much isolated. He sent in few manuscripts that *Poetry* could use because he had very few to send.

Pound's feud with the ex-Imagistes was at its height in the winter of 1914–15. As he wrote Harriet Monroe, "the whole lot of them are irritated, because having said they had certain poetic promise I later refused to accord to them a mature and judicious critical faculty. Having provided 'em with the weapons, i.e., the greater part of the publicity they have, I certainly should not complain if they use it, their editorial jobs etc., to attack me. I have only myself to thank for it."[51] The particular object of this

50. Partly, Pound sent "Portrait" to Kreymborg because "I was in a hurry for it to come out before the [Catholic] anth. as you know." Letter of September 25, 1915, in *Letters*, #74, p. 63.

51. Letter dated "May, 1915" by Harriet Monroe.

comment seems to be Richard Aldington, whose hostility blocked Pound's access to the *Egoist* from August, 1914, to March, 1916.[52]

Amy Lowell had kidnapped the Imagiste movement from Pound during the summer of 1914, on her visit to London. On July 20 she wrote Harriet Monroe a description of Pound's London set that seems pointed by malice. An "Imagiste" dinner she had given on July 17 was marred by Allen Upward's mockery of the hostess, mockery countenanced by the other guests:

> I have a lot to say to you about the situation here, but it is a little difficult to write it. [Marginal note above: "Of course this letter is private. I have met Allen Upward, he is quite unlike what one would suppose. I think he has a screw loose about his island."] I don't want to tell tales out of school, but it does seem as though you ought to know how things stand. I find our little group more or less disintegrated and broken up. Violent jealousy has broken out, whether because of the "Imagiste Anthology" and its reviews, I cannot say. Poor old Ezra has got himself into a most silly movement of which "Blast" is the organ—I will send you a copy tomorrow. He is annoyed with me because I will not finance a review for him to run. My feeling is that his slanging of the public, and his indecent poems, have flattened out his reputation, even Hueffer tells me that Ezra is very unhappy because he is so unsuccessful—the opinion of everyone is that he has nothing more to say. This would tally with your remarks to me about the last batch of his poems. Poor old Ezra, I am awfully sorry for him, but he is like a prickly pear to touch. My impression is that Hueffer is also in a gloomy way. I went to a lecture which he gave at which there were just nine people present, counting out his wife, the

52. Pound wrote, "This Egoist restart isn't good enough either, but if I can get a few stray £ I shall try to improve it," in a letter of March 5, 1916, in *Letters*, #83, p. 70, where the passage has been cut. Donald Gallup's bibliography attributes two Helmholtz articles in the *Egoist* for October 15, 1914, to Pound, as well as two pseudonymous contributions in the issue for December 1, and the *Egoist* for November 1 printed Pound's prospectus for the College of the Arts. But Pound's name disappeared after August, and he was excluded for almost all of 1915. Jane Lidderdale and Mary Nicholson, in their biography of Harriet Shaw Weaver, write that Pound stopped contributing to the *Egoist* because he lost interest in the paper (p. 100), but their account of the *Egoist* ruthlessly abridges the confusions of Imagist politics. Pound's new interest in the spring of 1916 seems complexly motivated by his growing regard for Harriet Shaw Weaver, by an offer of a subsidy from John Quinn, and by Aldington's prospective departure for the British army (Lidderdale and Nicholson, *Dear Miss Weaver*, pp. 116–21).

man who introduced him, and myself (who had to go because I dined with them). He is on the verge of nervous prostration, poor fellow—Flint, they all tell me, is writing very badly now, and that corroborates what you told me about the last batch of things he sent you. The Aldingtons seem to be the sanest and best working of the set, Except Fletcher, who is doing some good work. The craze for advertisement has swept Ezra off his feet. His Imagiste movement is petering out because of the lack of vigor in his poets, and the complete indifference of the public. Only one hundred copies of the "Imagiste" anthology have been sold in England! Much less than in America—It seems now as though it were simply a flair of young men with nothing in them. . . . With Ezra it is the poison of non-success brought about largely by his own foolish methods, which have done it—Another funny thing is that the reviews here are in such a bad way. That is the two which pretend to publish modern poetry, "The Egoist" and "Poetry and Drama." "The Egoist" is not sold at the newsstands of the largest news agency on account of its articles on sex, and "Poetry and Drama" is trying to get more funds, as it is practically bankrupt. I must say the outlook of the poor poets is not bright—and there is no such large and interested public for poetry here as there is in America— Within a decade, I feel sure that America will have all the poets writing in English.

Amy Lowell's instinct for success was clearly outraged by the small scale and bohemian atmosphere of Pound's movement, and she soon set to work to put it on a more businesslike basis. Richard Aldington, H.D., John Gould Fletcher, F. S. Flint, and D. H. Lawrence joined her in *Some Imagist Poets*, which came out in the spring of 1915 and was quickly a sensation.

Amy Lowell's account is biased, but the quarrelsome atmosphere she describes in London is confirmed from other sources. Richard Aldington was angry at Pound before the Imagistes disintegrated into Imagists, judging by the terms in which he recommended F. S. Flint to Harriet Monroe on July 8, 1914: "He has not the bravura and slap-dash methods of our friend Pound and is therefore a little apt to be overlooked." Aldington had been irritated by Pound's involvement with Wyndham Lewis in Vorticism. His review of *Blast* number one in the *Egoist* for July 15, 1914, is unsympathetic:

> As to Mr. Pound. . . . as the uncleanness of his language in-
> creases to an almost laughable point the moral sentiment of his
> writing becomes more and more marked. . . . his contributions
> to "Blast" are quite unworthy of their author. It is not that one
> wants Mr. Pound to repeat his Provencal feats, to echo the
> nineties—he has done that too much already—it is simply the fact
> that Mr. Pound cannot write satire. Mr. Pound is one of the
> gentlest, most modest, bashful, kind creatures who ever walked
> this earth; so I cannot help thinking that all this enormous arro-
> gance and petulance and fierceness are a pose. And it is a weari-
> some pose.

Pound's poetry in *Blast* was not a new departure, but a continua-
tion of the satirical strain that failed to make much impression on
Poetry that spring. Pound felt that having published in *Blast*, he
could abandon his efforts at contemporary satire. He wrote Harriet Monroe on August 17, 1914: "Be comforted, I have probably
finished my series of satires. BLAST has relieved me. BLAST is
comfort and cooling water. Even Bill Williams felt the gracious
relief. With Blast to keep going one will have only one's most
gracious mood for the Muses."

The larger bearings of *Blast* are difficult to determine. Wyndham Lewis sounds simply opposed to literary propagandizing,
futurism in particular, rejecting the sentimental future and the
"sacripant past" for the reality of the present. Lewis' Vortex
might be interpreted as an annihilation of time perspectives by
assertive personal will, but Pound defined the Vortex by making
the past the dynamic focus of its energy: "All experience rushes
into this vortex. All the energized past, all the past that is living
and worthy to live. ALL MOMENTUM, which is the past bearing
upon us, RACE RACE MEMORY, instinct, charging the PLACID NON-
ENERGIZED FUTURE." [53] Pound invented the term "Vortex" for
Lewis' movement just before the distribution of the first *Blast*,
sometime in June, 1914.[54] By August, 1914, he had borrowed it
for his version of Imagisme. Pound wrote Harriet Monroe on
August 17 that an article on Imagisme written sometime earlier

---

53. "Vortex," *Blast*, June 20, 1914, p. 153 (copyright 1914; all rights reserved). Reprinted by permission of New Directions Publishing Corporation and Faber and Faber,
Ltd., publishers and Agents for the Trustees of the Ezra Pound Literary Property Trust.
54. Hugh Kenner, *The Pound Era*, pp. 237–38.

had been retitled "Vorticism" for publication in the *Fortnightly Review*. This terminological switch was motivated by difficulties with the Amy Lowell group, surely; but Pound's Vortex seems a legitimate development of his Image: the instant of time set revolving about itself, drawing in the past. Among other considerations, Pound was casting about for a theory, an approach to writing, that would sustain a long poem.

Blast is not closely related to the history of *Poetry*; most of Pound's Vorticist associates were not poets. In 1915 Pound put a great deal of energy into promoting Lewis' and Gaudier's work, as well as Joyce's. But if Vorticism produced little that Pound could send over to *Poetry*, the respectable English press, as well as the *Egoist*, ostracized him because of it, and he became more dependent on Miss Monroe. The boycott was lifted by the spring of 1916, when Pound wrote Harriet Monroe that the *Times* had praised his book on Gaudier-Brzeska and that the editor of the *Quarterly* had forgiven him for appearing in *Blast*. In March, Pound wrote about an *Egoist* "restart": John Quinn offered him a subsidy of a hundred twenty pounds for the literary department of the *Egoist*, an offer eventually refused by the editors of that paper. In May arrangements were completed with Elkin Mathews for the publication of *Lustra*; several earlier projects for the book had fallen through.[55]

In sum, Pound lived through a rather dry period from the publication of the first *Blast* in July, 1914, to the spring of 1916, during which *Poetry* was one of his few sources of income, and Harriet Monroe one of his few sympathetic correspondents. In a letter of June, 1915, he wrote, "it is a lamentable fact that you and A.C.H. (with her noble efforts on *Drama* etc.) [a Chicago quarterly that published several of Pound's Fenollosa translations] are all that stands between me and a life of shame." In 1913, 1914, and 1915 *Poetry* paid him altogether about fifty pounds a year, which was about half the sum he calculated was necessary for a poet's decent subsistence. *Poetry* in 1915 seems instrumental to his survival. In that year his correspondence with

55. Letters of March 25, 1913, April 6, 1914, and May 4, 1916, discuss publication plans for *Lustra*. See Noel Stock, *The Life of Ezra Pound*, p. 187, and Kenner, *Pound Era*, p. 244, for Pound's financial difficulties.

Harriet Monroe became warmer and more relaxed. Long, rambling letters give his views about Amy and her Imagists, his estimates of his contemporaries, and his speculations about the movement.[56]

The *Catholic Anthology*, which is one of the principal subjects of this correspondence, was another of Pound's losses of 1915. It seems plain in his discussion of *Des Imagistes* and of Amy Lowell's projected anthology that one motive of *Catholic Anthology* was to counter *Some Imagist Poets*:

> The problem is HOW, how in hell to exist without overproduction. In the Imagiste book I made it possible for a few poets who were not over-producing, to reach an audience.
>
> That delicate operation was managed by the most rigorous suppression of what I considered faults.
>
> Obviously such a method and movement are incompatible with effusion, with flooding magazines with all sorts of wish-wash and imitation and the near-good: with yards and pages of "application."
>
> If I had acceded to A.L.'s proposal to turn "Imagisme" into a democratic bear-garden, I should have undone what little good I had managed to do by setting up a critical standard.
>
> My problem is to keep alive a certain group of advancing poets.[57]

A letter dated the next day gives the plan for *Catholic Anthology*: "the only way to get *Poetry* in on this side. I should not call it an Imagist anthology, but should select from the newer schools,—stuff on modern subjects, mostly *vers libre*." Despite Pound's declared intention to "keep the book in one tone," the contributors are rather an odd mixture: Yeats, Eliot, Douglas Goldring, Alice Corbin, T.E. H[ulme], Orrick Johns, Alfred Kreymborg, Edgar Lee Masters, Harriet Monroe, M[axwell] B[odenheim], Harold Monro, Carl Sandburg, Allen Upward, W. C.

56. Two letters dated January 31, 1915, give the tone; excerpts from them are printed in *Letters* as nos. 59, 60, and 61, pp. 48–50. The text seems based on *A Poet's Life*, where Harriet Monroe used a composite of the January 31 letters and one dated January 5, 1915, with added material that she had printed in *Poetry* for May, 1916, some of it taken from a letter dated "May, 1915."

57. "Second Letter" of January 31, 1915. in *Letters*, #59, p. 48. The two paragraphs between "standard" and "My problem" in *Letters* have been inserted from a letter dated January 5, 1915.

Williams, Pound, and John Rodker. Except for Kreymborg, Monro, and T.E.H., the group has a certain historical raison d'être: it is an assemblage of the people who made the first three years of *Poetry* memorable, minus Amy Lowell and her Imagists —H.D., Aldington, Fletcher, Flint, and Lawrence—and Vachel Lindsay, Wallace Stevens, Rabindranath Tagore, and Ford Madox Hueffer.

Pound has said that the motive of the book was "getting sixteen pages of Eliot into print at once,"[58] but when he first began to plan it, Eliot was a relatively unknown quantity—"Eliot is intelligent, very, but I don't know him well enough to make predictions," he wrote January 31, 1915. Probably by the time the book went to press, the negative motive, countering Amy, had faded from his mind, and the positive one of promoting Eliot was foremost. But however glorious the Eliot looks in retrospect, the book failed to find a public. The common cause of Chicago and London that seemed so exciting in 1914 did not have enough reality to make a good anthology by late 1915. Pound lost the battle of the books, resoundingly, to Amy Lowell's *Some Imagist Poets*.

Throughout the whole of the Imagist furor, Harriet Monroe was conspicuously faithful to Ezra Pound. Even before *Some Imagist Poets* was published, she protested in *Poetry* for March, 1915, the omission of Pound from the anthology: "Mr. Pound, whose early authority and present vitality in the school Miss Lowell . . . would be the last to deny. Indeed, probably no one regrets more than she that he will not be represented in it." Pound wrote to squelch any too partisan defense; he evidently had no wish to engage in a public squabble over the ownership of Imagism.[59] Miss Lowell commented March 15, 1915, "I had rather you had left the matter [Ezra's omission] unmentioned, as this will give Ezra the feeling that I am whining for him, which I am far from doing."

For six months Amy Lowell had been struggling to win Harriet Monroe from Pound. She had followed her disparaging letter

58. Norman, *Ezra Pound*, pp. 181–82.
59. Letter dated "March ? 1915," in *Letters*, #64, p. 55.

of July 20, 1914, about the breakup of the Imagistes, with a long, full-dress account of the schism in a letter of September 15, 1914, which is the primary source for the historian of Amygism. A letter of November 2, 1914, gave Harriet Monroe the inside story of Pound's rage over exaggerated claims made in an ad for Amy Lowell's book *Sword Blades and Poppy Seed*. Miss Monroe's soothing reply provoked an ambiguous flattery from Amy Lowell on November 9: "you are quite right about my being too sensitive and I greatly admire the way you go on regardless of what they write to you." On January 15, 1915, Miss Lowell wrote anew to warn Miss Monroe that Ezra had sent to the Macmillan Company a long, libelous attack written for the *Egoist*, suppressed there by Richard Aldington's threat to resign: "That he [Ezra] should have done such a thing to you, who have shown him nothing but kindness is outrageous. . . . I felt you ought to know this, as 'Poetry' has championed him so much—I do not want in any sense to 'get back' at Ezra, but I care very much for 'Poetry' and you are my friend, so I thought I ought to tell you." When Harriet Monroe failed to show an appropriate degree of alarm about the article, which apparently never reached Macmillan, Amy Lowell tried one final round of insinuation:

> Of course I never expected you to do anything about the article, and it would be the greatest mistake in the world for you to quarrel with Ezra and lose either his contributions, his contributors, or his interest. I merely wanted to warn you to keep your eyes open. You remember he "did" you a year ago about the prize, and got the money himself by what I cannot help thinking was a trick; and I only wanted to show you what kind of person he is and that, while keeping on good terms with him professionally, you should be always on the lookout to be sure that he is not up to something prejudicial to your interests. But, as I said before, I ought not to have done it at all. You naturally put it down to my jealousy, which I assure you it is not. . . .[60]

Miss Monroe's strong public stand in the spring of 1915 for Pound's prestige as an Imagist was a rejection of the temptations to self-pity that Amy Lowell had been offering her.

60. Letter of January 23, 1915.

If Amy Lowell wished to push her campaign against Ezra further, she suppressed the impulse. She wanted a good deal of notice from *Poetry* that spring, and she asked for it with surprising bluntness and with maddening particularity. On February 23, 1915, she telegraphed a request that John Gould Fletcher's article on her polyphonic prose appear in *Poetry* for March, 1915, putting particular stress on the timing: "Have done everything possible to show my loyalty and appreciation of Poetry and except for reviews of my books no pleasant encouraging word about me has ever been printed in its pages while many other people are constantly booked. Must say am distinctly hurt about this. You are always writing and helping Ezra."

Miss Lowell was also busy maneuvering about the publication date of her poems submitted to *Poetry*. Since *Some Imagist Poets* was to publish several of the group at the end of March, 1915, Harriet Monroe ought logically have been instructed to print them in the March *Poetry* or earlier. (She would use nothing that had appeared elsewhere in print.) On January 13, 1915, Amy Lowell gave such instructions about the work of other Imagists that *Poetry* had in the accepted file—H.D., Aldington, and F. S. Flint. But she felt that her own group could be held off until April: "the book will certainly not be more than just out and I hardly think it will affect you in any way." Ezra Pound was printed at the head of *Poetry* for March, 1915, with a solid group of poems, including "Exile's Letter," and Harriet Monroe seems to have inferred that Amy Lowell wanted to avoid appearing beneath him. Miss Lowell next wrote that Ezra's presence in the March issue had nothing to do with her preference for the April issue; rather, she preferred that her poetry not appear in the same number with John Gould Fletcher's praise of her polyphonic prose. But when Harriet Monroe finally arranged that both Miss Lowell's poetry and the Fletcher article appear in *Poetry* for April, 1915, there was no objection from Brookline.[61] Harriet Monroe's inference seems fair, that Amy Lowell was maneuvering for place in *Poetry*, and most unwilling to appear beneath Pound in an issue of the magazine.

61. Amy Lowell letter of March 3, 1915, makes it clear that she consents to the April publications.

Once her anthology was published, Miss Lowell was energetic in promoting it. She asked that *Poetry* notice the Imagist number of the *Egoist*. " 'The Egoist' has such a small circulation that it will never be seen unless you mention it," she argued disarmingly on March 26, 1915. But the only notice that *Poetry* gave the *Egoist* issue was a reprint of Allen Upward's poetic attack on it, "The Discarded Imagist," in September, 1915. Miss Lowell next wrote April 18, 1915, to suggest how *Poetry* should review *Some Imagist Poets*: "please don't lay stress on the schism with Ezra. I don't want to make the row important—Rows are a mistake, and their perpetuation shall be none of my doing." In the same letter she asked a favor with an outrageous piece of wheedling:

> Do you know, my dear, I have had occasion to go over all the numbers of "Poetry" since its beginning . . . and I was immensely struck by the fact that there is not a single poet of distinction among the younger generation whom you have not printed. Go on, my Child, never mind any of us when we criticize, taken in its entirety your review is a magnificent achievement. And the impartiality with which you represent all schools is fine. Now I have a suggestion to make. You will remember that you still have six little poems of mine, and that you are going to lead off with me sometime. . . . Will you take "Lead Soldiers" to precede them? It is the best thing I have done, I am sure. You remember you liked it, but I wanted to try the "New Republic" people with it.

This letter shows the Amy Lowell who inspired flaming disgust in Alice Corbin Henderson: "There is only one way to handle Amy, and that is with a pair of tongs"; "the worst thing Ezra Pound ever did was to spill her on the world. Amy *uber alles*! and her place in the sun."[62] Harriet Monroe was more tolerant of Miss Lowell, and when she felt the power of her push responded with admiration for her nerve. No irritation comes through the sketch she wrote for *A Poet's Life*:

> Imperious and meticulous, sometimes exasperatingly critical of one's literary offenses—things said or omitted in the magazine— she was yet wholeheartedly loyal in friendship. . . . Amy Lowell, true daughter of the Puritans, was no flatterer, but "straight as

62. Letters of January 23, 1918, and "April, 1916."

a die" in all her words and dealings. Sometimes she hit from the shoulder. . . . But temperamental outbursts were part of her excitable make-up, and I did not take her too seriously. She was "great fun," as even Ezra admitted—one could laugh at her and with her, and whatever she did or said, one had to acknowledge her power and unfailing charm. I still think she had "everything but genius"—but whether a great poet or not, she was a great woman.[63]

Genuinely unperturbed by Amy Lowell's proddings, Harriet Monroe went on in June, 1915, to print a review of *Some Imagist Poets* that was just the reverse of the one Miss Lowell had requested. The first half of her review is a discourse on the difference between Amy Lowell's Imagism and Pound's Imagisme, with a recapitulation of Pound's "Don'ts by an Imagiste" and a claim that the "finest entries" in the book had first appeared in *Poetry*. Amy Lowell herself is given faint praise, characterized as a "painter poet," her polyphonic prose work tending to self-consciousness and prosiness. H.D. by contrast is praised as presenting "perhaps the very essence of Imagism," some of her poems almost ranking with Pound's "most magical." Amy Lowell complained June 23, 1915: "You referred constantly to the people who are not in the anthology. Would it have been disloyal to Ezra, and would it not have been graceful to me, had you confined your remarks to the things which were in the book. . . ?" "Don't you want to cease referring to the break between Ezra and the rest of us? If I am willing to be silent, you, as Ezra's friend, should be thankful." Richard Aldington joined the protest, writing July 8, 1915, that although *Poetry* had given the Imagists their first publication "in the U.S.," the *Egoist* was their " 'official' organ." He went on to snipe at Pound: "You also don't quite recognize the insignificance of Ezra Pound's recent work, in comparison with the new work of Amy, Fletcher, and H.D. . . . he has done practically nothing in the last two years, whereas all the other Imagists have produced their best work during that time."

Harriet Monroe fended off Amy Lowell's reproaches with little sign of embarrassment:

63. *Poet's Life*, pp. 400–401.

. . . I can't agree that I was at all unkind to your group in my review. Of course, as your preface did not speak of us, we had to make some claim. As for the mention of Ezra, I don't think that showed any disloyalty to you. I did not in the least blame you or anybody else for the omission, and certainly there was no covert accusation in the article, but merely the expression of my feeling that Ezra is an important member of the Imagist group and that his refusal to appear in this anthology is unfortunate. As to the "History of the schism" that has nothing to do with the merely artistic question of his position in the school.[64]

Nevertheless, she made a point of granting the next favor Amy Lowell asked. Miss Lowell had been stung by a review written in the *Poetry Journal* for July, 1915, by Conrad Aiken, the most lively of the critics of Imagism who began to fill the journals in 1915. Aiken suggested that if the Imagists acted on their principles, they would confine themselves to a mere *reportage* of sensations. He called them "delicate tea-tasters," neurasthenics lacking in genuine emotional response: "they have the myopia of the microscope, and lacking intensity of any feeling save the purely aesthetic, they are constitutionally incapable . . . of singing. Hence their comparatively rhythmless forms." Amy Lowell asked Harriet Monroe to write an answer, since she did not want to dignify Aiken's attack with a personal response. Miss Monroe responded with an editorial in September, 1915, that made a general defense of Imagism, against several separate Aiken attacks, as a reforming and clarifying influence in poetry, "the beginning of a search for the Chinese magic."

But Amy Lowell was unappeasable, and six months later, under the mistaken impression that Harriet Monroe had cut some substantial praise out of Agnes Lee Freer's review of *Six French Poets* in *Poetry* for January, 1916, she was more injured than ever. She wrote January 29, 1916:

If you pushed nobody and showed no favouritism, no one could complain, but you do show favouritism. You have pushed Ezra Pound against all possible odds down the throats of your readers; you print not only his poems in large quantities, but his opinions, which is less defensible. You boom him in editorial paragraphs,

64. Letter of July 1, 1915, a copy in the Lowell correspondence.

and you give him enormous space to boom himself, although Ezra's work no longer ranks in importance with that of many other poets, and he has never produced a work of criticism to compare with my book on the French poets. You do not seem to be able to feel the public pulse, and realize which poets are making successes and which are not.

You have also pushed Vachel Lindsay. Your editorial paragraphs in his favour have been many and fulsome. I have never received a single editorial paragraph from you, outside the reviews of my books. Now I have no objection whatever to your pushing either Pound or Lindsay, I like and admire much of Lindsay's work. I admire much of Pound's poetry (never his prose), but I do not recognize myself as inferior to them in any way, nor do my publishers recognize me so. Nor do other magazines accept my poems less than they do these two men's. Why is it that you alone conspire to keep me in the back seat, when neither my own talents nor the public appreciation of them keep me there. Surely you must realize by this time that I am among those contributors of yours who are making good.

Her particular complaints are not well founded. Very little more editorial notice is given Pound, and much less is given Lindsay, from December, 1912, to January, 1916, than is given Miss Lowell.

Of course, Ezra Pound had been given "enormous space to boom himself," and Miss Lowell probably resented the relative coolness of the editors to her own prose contributions. In 1913 she had been willing to function as a discoverer of poets, to take over the role that Pound was playing. Harriet Monroe had turned down reviews of Lawrence and Fletcher, explaining that Pound had first rights on English publications. Amy Lowell's correspondence also shows her proposing to review Lindsay's *General Booth*, but Harriet Monroe was ahead of her there; Masefield's *Pompey the Great*, but Miss Monroe felt it unwise to review a reprint; Frost's *North of Boston*, but Pound again had priority; and Charles Hanson Towne's *Beyond the Stars*, but she concluded that Harriet Monroe was afraid to publish that review. Miss Monroe reviewed the Towne book herself. On March 19, 1914, Amy Lowell wrote that she considered herself one of *Poetry*'s family: "I am not nearly as busy as you are, and the compensation for having no family, and no one dependent upon one, which has its drawbacks in certain ways, is that one has more time for other things. Therefore, please realize that I consider myself a kind of unofficial member of your staff, and glory to myself in the situation, and that anything I can write for you, and any labor which I can take off your hands, I consider to be a privilege." But by October, 1915, Miss Lowell rejected a suggestion that she review a book on Maeterlinck. The periodicals open to her with the success of her Imagist publicity made her less anxious to use *Poetry* after 1915. Although *Poetry* published a fair amount of her prose in 1913 and 1914, the sum total of Harriet Monroe's acceptances and rejections justifies some of Miss Lowell's outrage in January, 1916. It was not so much a policy of exclusion as a policy of containment. If Harriet Monroe had had all-powerful influence over American poetic criticism, Miss Lowell would never have achieved the status she arrived at.

Miss Lowell's anger over Lindsay, who had been given less notice than she received herself and who had only two prose contributions printed before January, 1916, had a different cause. Notice given Lindsay is unreservedly enthusiastic, while notices of Amy Lowell are moderate in their praise. The review of *Six French Poets* that occasioned her outraged letter is simply rather flat. As Miss Lowell wrote February 3, 1916, after seeing the original manuscript, ". . . I find that you only left out things which could in no way add to the value of the review, and which, had I been editing the manuscript, I should have left out myself."

This exchange set the pattern of the relationship between Harriet Monroe and Amy Lowell for the next several years. Miss Monroe was more and more openly a hostile critic of Miss Lowell's work, and Miss Lowell protested with unabashed persistence that justice and deference to the general opinion required that she be noticed more enthusiastically. Amy Lowell was willing to quibble over very small details in her campaign to get decent notice out of *Poetry*. She found a "studied insult" in Harriet Monroe's omission of her name from a list of poets visited during an eastern trip reported in *Poetry* for May, 1916.[65] She was pacified when Miss Monroe promised to mention her lec-

65. Letter of May 8, 1916.

tures, but a paragraph sent in advance of publication for her approval only entangled them in new difficulties. Miss Lowell protested May 21, 1916: "As your paragraph read, it made me consider the starting of 'Poetry' to be directly responsible for the New Movement. Of course I did not mean that, for the poets were already writing or 'Poetry' would have had nothing to make its hit with—Therefore to suggest that Ezra and Co. were experimenting as early as 1910, is beside the point; for we were all experimenting. You make me say tacitly that 'Poetry' introduced *all* the important poets of the New Movement, whereas, as you will see from my telegram, it didn't. . . ." The paragraph was doctored up to please Miss Lowell for publication in the editorial "Various Voices" in *Poetry* for June, 1916, but Harriet Monroe was in her own way as tenacious as Amy Lowell, and wrote of Miss Lowell's lecture twenty years later, "Miss Lowell's subject was 'the new movement,' which had begun, she was gracious enough to say, with *Poetry*'s first number, in October, 1912."[66]

Miss Lowell continued to complain that she was "grossly neglected" in the editorial pages of *Poetry*:

> In your paper "Colonialism Again," you mention the names of all the American poets who seem to you of especial value. . . . You do not mention one or two Americans, but a number. Here I find the names of Masters, Frost, Lindsay, Pound, Sandburg, Fletcher, and H.D., but not the faintest reference to myself.
>
> I know quite well that you neither like nor appreciate my poetry *con amore*, but whatever may be your personal opinion on the subject, surely in any consideration of present day American poetry mine should not in fairness be left out. You know as well as I how I am considered by the world at large—whether liked or disliked, I am certainly not ignored—and I think I may say that you are the only editor who would have so insulted me.[67]

In a letter of May 26, 1917, she insisted that justice required that Miss Monroe express admiration for her poetry, whether she liked the work or not:

> I was not contending for recognition by other people, but by you. It was *your* words which I thought I had a right to receive, and *your* pronouncements which I regretted your withholding from

66. *Poet's Life*, p. 406.
67. Letter of May 4, 1917.

me. . . . In one sense of course I do not "need" it, but what is a little newspaper talk and discussion. That is not what I am out for, I want the serious recognition of thinking people, and I want you to accord me the place which I have won for myself, as well as to have others accord it to me. . . . Perhaps in the next editorial you write dealing with American literature as a whole you will find a niche for me.

Harriet Monroe held out against such persuasions for a little while, but in *Poetry* for October, 1917, in a review of the magazine's first five years, she knuckled under and called Miss Lowell's poems in the April, 1914, issue the "special excitement" of the fourth volume. The remark is a manifest exaggeration. Miss Lowell's group was made up of "The Cyclists," "The Foreigner," "A Lady," "Music," "The Bungler," "Anticipation," "A Gift," and "The Forsaken." For excitement it cannot compare with the Pound-Fenollosa-Yeats number of May, 1914, with Hueffer's "On Heaven" in June, 1914, with John Gould Fletcher's "Blue Symphony" in September, 1914—which got a marked response from *Poetry*'s readers—or even with the first publication of Maxwell Bodenheim in August, 1914. It did Miss Monroe no good to perjure herself, moreover, for Amy Lowell misread the comment, and thought she was called the "special excitement of the War Number," November, 1914, which was number two of volume five. She wrote back October 10, 1917: ". . . O Harriet, I seem to remember you gave the prize in that war number to Miss Louise Driscoll, and I also seem to remember that, although I had withdrawn from the prize [She withdrew from consideration for the war poem prize in a letter of September 10, 1914.] and that that was the reason I did not receive it, it would have been handsome of you to have mentioned it. This is ancient history, of course, but—another effort to forgive. Positively you strain me, my dear."

In fact, Harriet Monroe seems to have made room for Wallace Stevens in the war number by squeezing out Miss Lowell, who had submitted two long poems, "The Allies" and "The Bombardment." "The Allies" got as far as the proofs, but was not used in the end. Miss Monroe went so far toward excluding Amy Lowell from the list of significant contemporary poets that one

wonders why she refrained from open attack. She went too far as
it was to spare Miss Lowell's feelings. Like the treatment given
Lindsay in *Poetry*, it seems an instance of editorial detachment,
of an impersonal stewardship that kept *Poetry* open to all schools.
With artists who had achieved a certain degree of competence,
inclusion or exclusion based on Harriet Monroe's personal preferences was an impertinence. It was up to the audience to dispose
of Amy Lowell, if she needed disposition. In the meantime
Poetry continued to publish her poems and to notice her books
with civility.

The verse in *Poetry* for 1915 was generally good but relatively
unsensational, as Pound remarked October 2, 1915, in his survey
for the prize nominations: "Eliot's poem is the only eligible thing
in the year that has any distinction. The average of the year has
been perhaps better than the two years before but there has been
no particularly notable work, except Prufrock (and, *si licet*, the
Exile's Letter)."[68] Pound complained April 10, 1915, that very
little good work was being done in London: "The war is making
itself felt, I think, in a great dearth of good work." The war was
not yet a factor on the American side, but in 1914 and 1915 the
monopoly that *Poetry* had had over the movement since Pound
lost out on the *Smart Set* was broken. By 1915 Harriet Monroe
had American competitors for the good poetry.

The first of these was Margaret Anderson, who founded the
Little Review in Chicago in March, 1914. Direct comparison of
the *Little Review* with *Poetry* is difficult, for Margaret Anderson's
magazine published relatively little verse and a great deal of
personal comment, as well as reviews and fiction. It is altogether
a difficult magazine to assay. Margaret Anderson the personality
dominates it, and this is the note on which she began her venture:

> Life is a glorious performance. . . . and he who changes his role,
> with a fine freedom and courage, discovers that he's not acting but
> living his part! . . . And close to Life—so close, from our point
> of view that it keeps treading on Life's heels—is this eager, pant-

68. In *Letters*, #75, p. 64.

ing Art who shows us the wonder of the way as we rush along. . . .

The Little Review means to reflect this attitude toward life and art. Its ambitious aim is to produce criticism of books, music, art, drama, and life that shall be fresh and constructive, and intelligent from the artist's point of view.

Ezra Pound was not at first impressed. He wrote Harriet Monroe on August 5, 1914: "I'm glad *The Small Review* has started. All the best sellers, all the popular cries, almost up to date. A jolly place for people who aren't quite up to our level. You should find it a great comfort and relief to have a place where the meritorious A2 writers can go and console each other." Much of the poetry the *Little Review* published in 1914 and 1915 is of the caliber that Pound described—*Poetry*'s rejects. Maxwell Bodenheim, first published in *Poetry* for August, 1914, had tried to give himself entirely to the *Little Review*. He wrote Harriet Monroe on June 19, 1914: "If you had written poetry for six years without seeing a line of your work in print, would you not be a trifle impatient? Miss Anderson promised to print three of my poems in the July number of her magazine, and I yielded to the temptation of immediately seeing my work in print." One of the poems given Margaret Anderson was part of the group scheduled for *Poetry* publication, but editorial courtesies prevailed, and the *Little Review* held off printing the Bodenheim poems until the month after he appeared in *Poetry*. *Poetry* lost the honor of the introduction of Scharmel Iris, self-characterized as the first Italian in America to write poetry in English; his "Lyrics" in the December, 1914, issue of *Poetry* followed "Lyrics of an Italian" in the *Little Review* for November, 1914.

Like Bodenheim and Iris, many other of the *Little Review*'s poets were local, but the rule that the magazine depended on the Chicago Renaissance for material in its first years does not hold for poetry. The names of F. S. Flint, Amy Lowell, John Gould Fletcher, and Richard Aldington among the contributors for 1914–15 indicate that the *Little Review* was an outlet for Imagism in that era. Indeed, Margaret Anderson had something of the relation to Amy Lowell's Imagism that Harriet Monroe had had to Pound's Imagisme; the *Little Review* in 1915 sometimes reads like the American annex of the *Egoist*. Margaret Anderson had first discovered the school in Pound's *Des Imagistes*, but most of the editorial notice given Pound in 1914-15 is condescending. Amy Lowell, on the other hand, was passionately courted by the *Little Review*. She wrote Harriet Monroe on September 15, 1914, about the magazine: "I am afraid it strikes me as rather amateurish and effervescent, but the Editor is so fearfully enthusiastic about me that I have given her some things of me. However, I am afraid her magazine does not stand much chance of making any real place for itself."

Over the next year the *Little Review* got a great deal of material from and about the Imagists, including what may be Amy Lowell's best-remembered poem, "Patterns," in August, 1915. Richard Aldington's review of H.D.'s work in the *Little Review* for March, 1915, indicates the thoroughness with which the first Imagiste campaign was buried by the second. "I believe her work is quite unknown in America," Aldington wrote, quoting from "Hermes of the Ways," which *Poetry* had published in 1913. In August, 1915, Margaret Anderson's enthusiasm for Imagism reached its climax: "it has been the aim of most poets to put nature into poetry, but the Imagists *have done it:* their medium is not only a more direct one: the point is that they have dispensed with a medium. Their words don't merely convey color to you; they *are* the color."

The *Little Review* in its first two years put relatively little emphasis on Chicago poetry, although Masters came on strong in the fall of 1915 as the Imagists faded, and Lindsay had some small poems in the issue for June, 1914. One does not, in reading *The Little Review* for 1914-15, get the feeling that Chicago was the center of poetic ferment. The Chicagoans who appear in its pages were little fish: Bodenheim, Ben Hecht, Eunice Tietjens, Helen Hoyt, Scharmel Iris, Mitchell Dawson. One could summarize Margaret Anderson's first eighteen months' publication of poetry by noting that she missed the most exciting local work and imported a secondhand poetic revolution.

Such a summary would miss the special charm of the early *Little Review*. The magazine carried on a controversy against the Imagists concurrently with its promotion of them. In October,

1914, Witter Bynner described Imagism as an effort to imitate the Japanese hokku: "If only they would acknowledge the attempt for what it is and not bring it forward with a French name and curious pedantries." In August, 1915, when she declared that the Imagists had annihilated language as a medium to present color pure, Margaret Anderson also printed a review by Mitchell Dawson that dismisses the people who derive Imagism from the hokku: "They may eventually discover that they are building on the shaky premise that 'Imagism' exists other than as a clever word." And Witter Bynner was permitted to remark of the Imagists, "These people wring tiny beauties dry. . . . Poetry gave signs of becoming poetry again and of touching life—when these fellows showed up, to make us all ridiculous." The *Little Review* seems like a live conversation, full of contradictions, unexpected allusions, and false starts. The first public response to the printing of "Prufrock" appears in the *Little Review* for September, 1915, when Arthur Davison Ficke begins his poem "Cafe Sketches" with "I want to see dawn spilled across the blackness / Like scrambled egg on the skillet." Margaret Anderson's magazine had a vitality that kept it interesting on the brink of chaos, but the editor was in constant danger of seeming silly.

Miss Anderson had one other strong point as an editor, one that stands out sharply when comparing her to Harriet Monroe. She knew how to make a poet feel her admiration. Amy Lowell gave Margaret Anderson "Patterns" at the time she was wheedling Harriet Monroe to take "Lead Soldiers," possibly because she felt Miss Anderson "so fearfully enthusiastic about me." Margaret Anderson got Maxwell Bodenheim to give her a poem he had already submitted to *Poetry*. She made Lindsay feel that "to get the earnest attention of a faction that boils itself down to twenty poetry-readers is worth far more than to be scattered through ten conventional magazines—and get no particular attention or earnestness aroused anywhere."[69] When Harriet Monroe asked John Gould Fletcher for "The Old South," which she ultimately published in July, 1915, he answered March 2, 1915, that he had been about to send it to the *Little Review*,

69. Letter of May 1, 1914.

because he knew that Margaret Anderson was always interested in fresh and lively experiments. Margaret Anderson could pour out ardent appreciations of a poet, without committing her magazine to him, without taking sides with him against his rivals and competitors. The judicious and disinterested Harriet Monroe seems very cold by comparison. She herself admired Margaret Anderson's adventurous editorial tone, and defended it to Amy Lowell, who responded, ". . . I agree with you that it is better than dull professionalism, but I wish she had your power of making her magazine a first class one."[70]

But if Harriet Monroe managed to keep *Poetry* comfortably ahead of the early *Little Review*, Alfred Kreymborg's little magazine, *Others*, which began publication in July, 1915, put the corresponding summer issues of *Poetry* quite in the shade. Here comparison is easily made, for *Others* published nothing but poetry, usually putting out an issue without editorial comment of any kind. The first number had no major poem, but groups by Mina Loy and Orrick Johns had a crazy wry tone, enormously quotable and much parodied in the newspapers, which made the magazine a success overnight. The August issue had groups by Amy Lowell, William Carlos Williams, Skipwith Cannell, and two poems by Wallace Stevens, including "Peter Quince at the Clavier." The September issue was headed by Eliot's "Portrait of a Lady."

No magazine could sustain such a beginning, and the rest of *Others* for 1915 was rather an anticlimax. Publication of a poem by Carl Sandburg in the December, 1915, issue blurred any special reaction against *Poetry* that may have been part of the first idea of the magazine. Helen Hoyt, who was identified with *Poetry*, having worked as a clerk in the office in 1913, was also quick to contribute to *Others*. Thus any suggestion of a polarity between eastern and western schools of American verse was quickly dissipated, although *Poetry* seems the object of reaction against which *Others* first defined itself. Kreymborg said that the magazine originated with Walter Conrad Arensberg's feeling that *Poetry* admitted too many compromises, but Kreymborg himself is hard to pin down on the meaning of his title. In 1919

70. Letter of September 26, 1914.

when he started up the magazine after a lapse, he blandly posted what he called "the initial motto" of the magazine at the top of the January issue: "The old expressions are with us always and there are always others." The motto had never appeared on an earlier issue of the magazine. It had been posted on the first *Others Anthology*, published in the spring of 1916.

Harriet Monroe wanted *Others* defined as the people who were too youthful or too radical to get into *Poetry*. She wrote Kreymborg on July 2, 1915, when he asked for information for a feature story he was writing for a New York paper: "*Poetry* you know tries to publish the best we can get of ALL the different schools. We have printed a good deal of rather radical experiments and shall no doubt continue to do so, but I assume that 'Others' stands exclusively for the radicals and for a rather more youthful effervescence than I am quite ready to endorse publicly. . . . Please make it very clear that we were the first in the field and the beginning of the present Renaissance." The letter suggests a dangerous degree of self-satisfaction; Miss Monroe was rather smug over her successful institution. However, Alfred Kreymborg, who seems always good-natured, was tolerant of Harriet Monroe although he had been exposed to her prickly side, notably during the misunderstanding over the poems reprinted from *Poetry* in *Des Imagistes*. He rather triumphed in his memoir over the "number of her contributors who appeared in the newer periodical—with poems, on more than one occasion, she had rejected and regretted rejecting," but he felt that "one had to revert to beginnings and acknowledge the courage and ability she had brought to the practical solution of a dream that had seemed utterly incongruous."[71] He replied calmly July 6, 1915, to her demand that he acknowledge her priority, ". . . *Poetry* will, by all that is in accordance with the facts, have precedent over all other publications with the possible exception of *The Egoist*." It is interesting to find afloat as early as 1915 the impression that the *Egoist*, which began publication as the *New Freewoman* in June, 1913, and made considerable use of reprints from *Poetry*, was the first magazine to promote the new poetry.

Despite Kreymborg's remarks about *Poetry*'s rejections pub-

71. *Troubadour*, pp. 287–88.

lished in *Others*, most of the poets published in his magazine were not *Poetry*'s rejects. Several facts give some substance to the idea that Kreymborg fostered talents that *Poetry* had no room for. Kreymborg himself had been several times rejected by *Poetry*, and did not appear in its pages until 1916. Harriet Monroe had given "Prufrock" so cold a welcome that Ezra Pound had sent the "Portrait of a Lady" to Kreymborg. Pound also sent Kreymborg some of his own satires that Harriet Monroe had not wanted to print, not all of which Kreymborg printed.[72] And *Poetry* had been sluggish about printing William Carlos Williams and Marianne Moore, although both appeared in *Poetry* before *Others* was founded. *Others* might have been the showcase for these distinguished poets if they had contributed to it regularly and indicated that they felt at home in its pages, but only Williams had this relation to Kreymborg's magazine. It belonged as much to William Zorach, Horace Holley, Robert Carlton Brown, and Robert Alden Sanborn as to the more illustrious names. Thus Pound wrote to Harriet Monroe on December 15, 1915: "We must be harder for new writers to get into, than is 'Others' . . . . Kreymborg gets too many stars for them all to be genuine." Nevertheless, Kreymborg's magazine got off to an enviable start, with the best work of T. S. Eliot and Wallace Stevens.

If the competition from the *Little Review* and *Others* drained off significant poems and flattened *Poetry*'s effect, the publication record of 1915 is still remarkable. On the American or Chicago side, the literary interest centered on Edgar Lee Masters. Although Lindsay won the Levinson Prize that year with his "Chinese Nightingale," he was no longer a new phenomenon. The literary world watched to see whether the *Spoon River Anthology* would be followed by more verse as interesting, or whether it was a pocket struck by a poet whose other productions were valueless.[73]

72. Pound mentioned a long, disagreeable poem sent to Kreymborg—possibly "L'Homme Moyen Sensuel"—in a letter of "C. June, 1915"; nothing answering the description was printed in *Others*.

73. Eunice Tietjens' letter to Harriet Monroe, December 28, 1915. See also the *New York Times Review of Books* on *Spoon River*, "A Year's Harvest in American Poetry," November 18, 1915, p. 464; and the review of Masters' *Songs and Satires* by Caesar Zwaska in the *Little Review*, August, 1916.

Spoon River itself had compelled attention. Raymond M. Alden, the *Dial* reviewer who was a sharp critic of "the new movement," could not dismiss it. He called it "the *reductio ad absurdum* of certain of the new methods—such as the abandonment of conventional form and the fearless scrutiny of disagreeable realities. There is nothing here, to be sure, of the vaporings of some of our imagists, but a stern virility to which one might warm were it not so deliberately unlovely."[74] But Alden was able to triumph over *Songs and Satires*, which Masters published a year later. Ezra Pound, who wrote a friendly notice of *Spoon River* for the *Egoist* in January, soon began to have qualms about Masters. His note published in *Reedy's Mirror* for May 21, 1915, was patronizing and self-centered, reminiscent of the Helmholtz notice of *Poetry* in the *Egoist*. (The article was first intended for the *New Age*, but A. R. Orage refused to publish criticism of free verse. Pound's London tone persists in the Saint Louis publication.) Reedy was irritated: "Mr. Pound's praise of Mr. Masters as a partial realization of his hope for American letters is, for Mr. Pound, most generous. But—read his article."

Poetry in 1915 took no part in this game of waiting to see if Masters could go beyond *Spoon River*. Alice Corbin Henderson wrote an enthusiastic review of it in June, 1915, placing Masters with Frost and Robinson as a developer of an indigenous American poetic tradition. In an exchange of compliments, Masters wrote April 1, 1915, that an American renaissance was imminent and could probably be traced to "543 Cass Street." In *Poetry* for August, 1915, Mrs. Henderson attacked the *Dial* for its condescending and negative treatment of Masters. In print *Poetry* became the sponsor and partisan of Masters, while in private Harriet Monroe shuffled through his manuscripts, looking for a really good poem to print. He had sent "Silence" in November, 1914, and it appeared in *Poetry* for February, 1915; people seem to have taken it for granted as an afterimage of the graveyard in *Spoon River*. Masters had sent in about the same time "The Moon Rises," and over the winter "The Loop" and "Room 634"; none of these poems was printed in *Poetry*. In September, Harriet Monroe had declared a strong interest in "Arabel," among other

74. "Recent Poetry," June 24, 1915, p. 28.

manuscripts on hand. The poem, published in *Poetry* for November, 1915, satisfied some watchers that Masters would last. Pound's first enthusiasm for Masters was temporarily restored by "Arabel," and he liked the poem well enough a year later to nominate it for the Levinson Prize, "with the proviso that he [Masters] spend the money on a trip to Europe as soon as peace is declared. His work is going to pot and if he don't get into an atmosphere where quality is more valued than quantity he will very nearly undo all the good he has done."[75] Harriet Monroe's selection from Masters' manuscripts seems well judged, but Masters perhaps did not relish having so many poems held and finally returned, for after 1915 he never again gave her so much opportunity for selection.

Ezra Pound in 1915 had little interesting work to send, besides his own poems and T. S. Eliot's. In London he was reduced to building up an alliance with Sturge Moore, for lack of more congenial collaborators. His review of Moore's *Hark to These Three* in *Poetry* for June, 1915, makes him the type of the secluded craftsman working for a small audience of his peers. He sent in Moore's long poem "Isaac and Rebekah" on November 16, 1915, anticipating agonized protests from Chicago: "I suppose you will loathe it. However, he has written more good poetry than any other living native of these islands except Yeats, and you are very lucky to get it."

Pound's own poems published in *Poetry* over the year bear out his promise to abandon satire and reserve his gracious moods for the Muse. The group published in the issue for March, 1915, includes "Provincia Deserta," "Image from D'Orleans," "The Spring," "The Coming of War: Actaeon," "The Gipsy," "Dogmatic Statement Concerning the Game of Chess," and "Exile's Letter." Pound felt great excitement over "Exile's Letter," as if he had broken through to something in the poem, after a series of relative failures. Later he sent another "nice 'poetic' poem. . . . It attacks no one's finer feelings."[76] This was "Near Perigord," published in *Poetry* for December, 1915.

Another source of excitement in 1915 was *Poetry*'s publication

75. Letter of August 30, 1916.
76. Letter of June 5 [1915].

of Rupert Brooke's war sonnets in April, just ahead of the news of the poet's death in the Aegean. Brooke had looked in on the *Poetry* office on his way through Chicago the year before, and spread the glow of his glamorous presence around it. He sent the war sonnets to Harriet Monroe in January, 1915, and the news of his death cast a pathetic reflected glory on the *Poetry* publication in April.

Poetry's issue for May, 1915, looks exciting in retrospect, with William Carlos Williams' second publication in *Poetry*, and the first American publication of Marianne Moore. But Pound felt at the time that the feel of the whole number was bad: "MY GAWDD! THIS *IS* A ROTTEN NUMBER OF POETRY."[77] The issue was ill-starred, for it marked the end of really friendly relations with both Williams and Miss Moore. Williams, who had been irritated by a rejection of "Conquest" in November, 1914, was beginning to find *Poetry* rather stale by April 13, 1915: "Best wishes to 'Poetry' though I haven't relished it as much recently as in the past—for no reason that I can see either." One suspects the influence of Kreymborg's developing plans for *Others*. By January 6, 1916, outraged by some remark or action of Harriet Monroe's now lost from the record, Williams wrote: "Charmed I'm sure. Whatever intellectual significance 'Poetry' ever had has long since departed. Maybe I can sell you something. Yours in good faith." This outburst did not end Williams' relation with the magazine, but it marks a moment in his correspondence with Harriet Monroe. He never again wrote as if he trusted her editorial judgment. "Our taste in matters of verse seems to differ hence these occasional outbursts first of extravagant love for you then equally extravagant outbursts of indignation," he wrote October 28, 1916, trying to analyze and excuse his mercurial attitudes.

The break with Marianne Moore was more complete. *Poetry* had discovered her; at least one of her poems printed in May, 1915, had been sent with a letter of July 10, 1914. The *Egoist* beat *Poetry* to first publication, however. Two Marianne Moore poems appeared in the *Egoist* for April 1, 1915, a month ahead of the *Poetry* group, "That Harp You Play So Well," "To an In-

77. Letter dated May 17, 1915, by Harriet Monroe, in *Letters*, #70, p. 60.

tramural Rat," "Conseil to a Bachelor," "Appellate Jurisdiction," and "The Wizard in Words." From the beginning Marianne Moore felt that *Poetry*'s welcome was cold, for she added a postscript to a letter of April 8, 1915: "I thank you for your suggestions as to title and am grateful for criticism, even adverse." When she was encouraged by the May publication to send more poems, they were "Retd," according to a note on her letter of May 22, 1915, and Marianne Moore responded, with a politeness that seems pained, "Printed slips are enigmatic things and I thank you for your criticism on my poems. I shall try to profit by it."[78] She did not send another poem to Harriet Monroe until February 22, 1932.[79]

The June, 1915, number, which is memorable for the publication of "The Love Song of J. Alfred Prufrock," was also fairly good as a whole, as Pound commented in a letter of June 15. But the following issues of *Poetry* for 1915 were ominously empty, tending to confirm William Carlos Williams' intuition that the magazine was going flat. Richard Aldington wrote July 8, from his vantage point on the *Egoist*: "Why don't you print more prose and less but more rigorously selected poetry? I don't believe that poetry by itself will go very far, but people are always interested in discussions about poetry. Monro has pretty well come to the conclusion that poetry by itself is no go—there isn't enough good stuff written to make a magazine. What do you think?" Small as *Poetry* was, it could only fill most of its pages with *good* poetry if it had a monopoly on the movement. This seems the crucial injury in the competition offered by the *Little Review* and *Others*. These new little magazines did not take very many poems away from Harriet Monroe, but for every "Portrait of a Lady" or "Peter Quince" that she did not print, she had several pages to be filled by someone like Georgia Wood Pangborne. Every month she courted the risk that such bland but hopeful aspirants would set the tone of the whole issue and define the magazine itself.

78. Letter of June 6, 1915.

79. Marianne Moore did write several reviews for *Poetry* in 1918—of Jean de Bosschère's *The Closed Door* and of Eliot's *Prufrock* in April, of Yeats's *The Wild Swans at Coole* in October. Harriet Monroe seems to have asked her for these critical notes; there is no covering correspondence, but there is a letter without a context written May 10, 1918: "Poetry's approach to art is different from my own; I feel it therefore to be very good of you to imply that I am not ipso facto an alien."

Aldington's suggestion, that she solve the problem by printing prose in place of the journeyman poetry, contradicted her basic program for the magazine, crowding the poets out of their own place in favor of commentators on poetry. She had rejected a similar suggestion from Pound in the autumn of 1913.

But the problem remained unsolved. Even the quickening of tempo usual in the fall issues does not seem to have helped the magazine in 1915. Probably either the September or October issue is superior as a whole to any issue of 1913, except the April, 1913, issue with Pound and Yeats, but the excitement of new discovery, which radiated in *Poetry* in 1913 and 1914, is no longer there. Eliot's poem "Cousin Nancy," printed in October, created some factitious excitement when it embroiled *Poetry* anew with the *Dial*. The *New York Times Review of Books* first attracted attention to "Cousin Nancy." An editorial in the issue for October 17, 1915, noted with approval the *Dial*'s latest criticism of *Poetry*—what *would* Walt Whitman think of the magazine he had fathered?—and printed Eliot's poem as a random sample of hashed free verse. The *Dial* editors in their turn leaped on the line from Meredith at the end of the poem, and displayed it triumphantly in their columns as an outright "plagiarism."[80] John L. Hervey, who had been carrying on a long-winded attack on Harriet Monroe in the correspondence columns, generated by her refusal to place William Cullen Bryant "among the mighty dead," brightened at this new evidence of her editorial stupidity. He set Miss Monroe a dilemma: she was proved incompetent, for either she was ignorant of Meredith's line or she was an accomplice to a plagiarist.[81] In the same issue, the *Dial* waved away attempts to explain Eliot by asserting "an elementary law of literary ethics that quotations must be enclosed in quotation marks," and by refusing to acknowledge a quotation not listed in *Bartlett's* as well known and easily recognized. The *Dial* overreached itself in the whole affair and stood revealed as a nasty, stupid, and pompous intellectual bully.

However, genuine excitement was restored to *Poetry* in

80. "Casual Comment," November 25, 1915, pp. 476–77.
81. "Some Further Remarks about Bryant," December 9, 1915, pp. 555–57.

November, 1915. Wallace Stevens' "Sunday Morning" appeared at the end of an issue headed by Edgar Lee Masters' "The Conversation" and "Arabel." Wallace Stevens had published elsewhere, notably in *Others*, since Harriet Monroe pulled apart her war number to fit in his little group of "Phases." But *Poetry*'s printing of "Sunday Morning" confirms the magazine as his discoverer and sponsor. Unfortunately, Harriet Monroe was not equal to the honor. She asked Stevens to cut the poem. He wrote June 6, 1915: "Provided your selection of the numbers of *Sunday Morning* is printed in the following order: I, VIII, IV, V [marginal note by Harriet Monroe: "Also VII as V"], I see no objection to cutting down. The order is necessary to the idea."[82]

Miss Monroe apparently did not recognize the poem as a whole, but reacted as if she were dealing with eight separate poems on a common theme. Stevens wrote June 23, 1915:

No. 7 of *Sunday Morning* is, as you suggest, of a different tone, but it does not seem to me to be too detached to conclude with.

The words "On disregarded plate" in No. 5 are, apparently, obscure. Plate is used in the sense of so-called family plate. Disregarded refers to the disuse into which things fall that have been possessed for a long time. I mean, therefore, that death releases and renews. What the old have come to disregard, the young inherit and make use of. Used in these senses, the words have a value in the lines which I find it difficult to retain in any change. Does this explanation help? Or can you make any suggestion? I ask this because your criticism is clearly well-founded.

The lines might read,

> She causes boys to bring sweet-smiling pears
> And plums in ponderous piles.

[This version of the lines was printed in *Poetry*. Stevens had originally written the two lines that he printed in 1923.]

But such a change is somewhat pointless. I should prefer to keep the lines unchanged, although, if you like the variation proposed, for the sake of clearness, I should be satisfied.

The order is satisfactory. Thanks for your very friendly interest.[83]

82. No. 193 in *Letters of Wallace Stevens*, ed. Holly Stevens (copyright 1966 by Holly Stevens). This and following excerpts reprinted by permission of Alfred A. Knopf, Inc., and Faber and Faber, Ltd.

83. In *Letters*, #194.

Stevens made a final comment on the cut version September 23, 1915: "The lines seemed perfectly all right to me in the proof and I am satisfied to have them go through in their present form."

Harriet Monroe perhaps had last-minute qualms about the cuts, but Stevens shows a detachment about cutting and criticism of his manuscript that seems almost superhuman. The politeness he sustained through the exchange over "Sunday Morning" is not, like Marianne Moore's about the same time, pained or strained. When a year later Harriet Monroe wrote that his *Three Travelers Watch a Sunrise* had won a prize for verse drama, and suggested certain minor changes to counter complaints that the play was not actable, he replied May 19, 1916: ". . . I am most interested in the thing and shall be glad to work over the play. . . . You are an encouraging person, if there ever was one and I am grateful to you not only for that, but because, in addition, you give me an opportunity to do what you want, if I can. I shall try."

One can consider 1915 the beginning of the end of *Poetry*'s period of influence. One need only list delays in publishing T. S. Eliot and William Carlos Williams, rejection of Marianne Moore, and cutting of Wallace Stevens to make a case that Harriet Monroe had offended the best of the new poets. When one adds to these irritations the award of *Poetry*'s Levinson Prize for 1914–15 to Vachel Lindsay's "The Chinese Nightingale" over "The Love Song of J. Alfred Prufrock," the case is strengthened. The slight to Eliot was much worse than the slight to Hueffer that had angered Pound in 1914, for Eliot was an American citizen eligible for the award, and Lindsay was doubtfully eligible, having already received a hundred-dollar "American citizen award" hastily raised for him in 1913. Eliot was also passed over in 1915 for a hundred-dollar second prize, which went to Constance Lindsay Skinner for her West Coast Indian songs, and for a special prize for a lyric poem, which went to H.D. "Prufrock" got third honorable mention.

But an offense is relative, in some degree, to the injury felt by the victim. Wallace Stevens chose not to be injured by the cutting of "Sunday Morning." William Carlos Williams' anger against Harriet Monroe became almost chronic after 1915, but never became crucial; against the grain of his outrage he continued to send in poems. Marianne Moore quietly removed herself from the roster of *Poetry*'s contributors. T. S. Eliot remained silent, in communication with the magazine only through Pound. And Pound was surprisingly deficient in outrage at the end of 1915. One turns to the correspondence, expecting the geyser of wrath that the subject of prizes had released in him in 1913 and 1914, and finds him writing December 1, 1915, "Yes the prizes were peculiarly filthy and disgusting, the £10 to H.D. being a sop to the intelligent, however I knew it would happen, I know just what your damn committee *wants*."[84] Since Pound had gone on record October 2, 1915, against prizes to Lindsay and Skinner in casting his own vote for "Prufrock," and had made the point that Lindsay already had a prize and could be presumed ineligible, his acquiescence is the more surprising.

Two weeks later, on December 15, 1915, Pound wrote a very long, diffuse, and interesting letter in which he took note of increased competition from rival magazines—*Others*, the *Little Review*, and *Poetry Journal*—and planned a new editorial program for *Poetry*:

> We have obviously led the reform in style. Now we must *go in for weight and mass attack*. We must keep a monopoly of the BEST six or ten poets.
>
> We have Yeats, I can keep Eliot out of the Poetry Journal which is fishing for him. I fear Hueffer won't write anything more until the end of the war. I can stop spilling unimportant scraps into other magazines. But we must have the pick of Masters, Frost, Yeats, Eliot, and probably H.D.—even if it means printing fewer authors and giving them more room. THAT is the only way I see to keep the audience we've got.

The letter suggests a number of interesting things about the Pound of 1915, but what is most unexpected is the assumption of common cause between "his side" and "her side" in *Poetry*: suddenly, "we." The correspondence to Harriet Monroe is more amiable in 1915 than it was earlier, and this letter marks the climax of that amiability.

84. In *Letters*, #78, p. 66.

One of the causes of the improved relation between Ezra Pound and Harriet Monroe may be the controversy that they carried on in the editorial pages of the magazine after October, 1914. The disagreement about the relation of the poet to his audience, which developed early between them, takes on the proportions of a formal debate in *Poetry* for October, 1914. Earlier, in January, 1914, Harriet Monroe had written a defense of the independent creative spirit, against the forces that urge "Sobriety and Earnestness" on the artist, which illustrates vividly the inconsistency of her view of the artist:

> . . . sobriety and earnestness are precisely the two attributes of mediocrity which need no institute to encourage them; without such aid they win most of the prizes and sit at most of the banquets. The original creative spirit is earnest, no doubt, but his is the earnestness of fire, which scorches and destroys and gives light; not that of the fog, which decently veils the sun. If the torchbearer is not encouraged, if he batters his head against the blind wall of public apathy, it becomes physically and psychologically impossible for him to keep his soul and his light alive. For only when the creative impulse meets an equally strong impulse of sympathy is the highest achievement possible in any department of human effort.

She is as willing as Pound or Williams to describe the poet as a being set apart from his fellows, leading an existence they can hardly comprehend, but she will not allow him the prerogatives of an aristocrat or a superior being. A primary commitment to an ideal of human brotherhood prevents her developing her image of the poet as a sun "which scorches and destroys and gives light." Instead, she goes on to make the sun's light dependent on the sympathetic response of the vegetables it fosters.

Pound, in "The Audience" in *Poetry* for October, 1914, gives a full statement of his view that the artist is the source of vitality and value in human life, that other sorts of men and other sorts of activity are only the raw materials to be disposed in his transforming vortex:

> The artist is not dependent upon the multitude of his listeners. Humanity is the rich effluvium, it is the waste and manure and the soil, and from it grows the tree of the arts. As the plant germ

seizes upon the noble particles of the earth, upon the light-seeking and the intrepid, so does the artist seize upon those souls who do not fear transfusion and transmutation, which dare to become the body of the god. . . .

It is true that the great artist has in the end, always, his audience, for the Lord of the universe sends into this world in each generation a few intelligent spirits, and these ultimately manage the rest. But this rest—this rabble, this multitude—does *not* create the great artist. They are aimless and drifting without him. They dare not inspect their own souls.

It is true that the great artist has always a great audience, even in his lifetime; but it is not that *vulgo* but the spirits of irony and of destiny and of humor, sitting with him.[85]

Harriet Monroe's reply in the same issue shows her willing to agree with Pound that the "great audience" of her Whitman motto may be a very small one. But she also believed that art, at its best, takes in the whole of the reality of the life of an age, and that the conditions of twentieth-century life are such that it can be "taken in" only by a writer sensitive to the feelings of the mass. The "coterie" will necessarily limit its darling poets. Her reforming zeal entered into the debate; to Pound's talk about people who dare not inspect their souls, she replied that it is the poet's ultimate function to show them how. Her vision of the "great audience" at its perfection was a mass or mob transformed into an aristocracy that numbers in the billions:

. . . Of course, as Mr. Pound says, there is a sense in which a "great audience" can be a very small one. That was hardly Whitman's meaning, nor is it the hint we intend to convey by our motto. Modern inventions forcing international travel, inter-racial thought, upon the world, have done away with Dante's little audience, with his contempt for the crowd, a contempt which, however, disregarded the fact that his epic, like all the greatest art, was based upon the whole life of his time, the common thought and feeling of all the people. No small group today can suffice for the poet's immediate audience, as such groups did in the stay-at-home aristocratic ages; and the greatest danger which besets modern art

85. "The Audience," *Poetry*, October, 1914, p. 32 (copyright 1914 by Harriet Monroe; all rights reserved). Reprinted by permission of New Directions Publishing Corporation and Faber and Faber, Ltd., publishers and Agents for the Trustees of the Ezra Pound Literary Property Trust.

is that of slighting the "great audience" whose response alone can give it authority and volume, and of magnifying the importance of a coterie. . . .

Art is not an isolated phenomenon of genius, but the expression of a reciprocal relation between the artist and his public. Like perfect love, it can be supreme only when the relation is complete. There is a magic in it beyond the reach of reason, a magic which Whitman felt when he wrote the sentence printed on our cover. Science is explaining more and more the reactions and relations of matter, of life. It becomes increasingly clear that nothing can stand alone, genius least of all.

Despite her modern insights, Harriet Monroe seems insensitive to the problems of evaluating art by majority vote. On the other hand, it is Pound's metaphor that breaks down in this exchange, implying as it does that the germinating seed selects or elects those elements in the soil that it needs for growth. It is the seed's dynamism that puts it in need of nourishment; its vitality makes it dependent upon the inert elements in the soil around it. The metaphor illustrates Miss Monroe's view better than his own.

Pound felt the controversy was "quite well worth going on with,"[86] but Harriet Monroe decided that the debate in October, 1914, was as much formal discussion as the subject would bear. However, the interplay of contending opinions runs through much of the editorial matter printed in *Poetry* in 1915. Pound's long, three-part essay, "The Renaissance," gives a fairly elaborate presentation of his view that art is produced by an elite, of the literary tradition by which the elite is formed, and of the role of the capital as a vortex that draws the best to itself. Harriet Monroe's "The Fight for the Crowd" in *Poetry* for March, 1915, is her most intense expression of her conviction that the artist works to redeem and ennoble his fellow man through his creation. Pound made his final statement in the audience controversy in his review of Sturge Moore in *Poetry* for June, 1915. "I am always at war with the motto on the cover of this magazine," he wrote. Moore, he said, had almost no audience, but had won the admiration of Lawrence Binyon, Maurice Hewlett, Yeats, and

86. Letter of October 12, 1914.

Wyndham Lewis. The consciousness of an audience could only hurt an artist. Pound cited the "charm" of so many first books, never recaptured in later publications: "if the gods have no pity the very middle of his thought is interrupted with the thought that too many must hear it."[87]

This controversy does not seem to have aroused much response from readers. John Gould Fletcher was highly irritated by Pound's review of Moore, writing to complain that Moore's work was not even mentioned: instead, Ezra went on with his usual tedious complaints about reviewers and editors, about an imaginary cabal of New York writers. Pound's notions of America were wildly distorted, and he exaggerated his own importance in a tiresome replay of Oscar Wilde's old act. Much more of this sort of reviewing, Fletcher felt, would wreck *Poetry*; if he read much more of it, he would faint with nausea.[88] But Fletcher and Amy Lowell were furiously campaigning against Pound in this era. Otherwise there was little interest or opposition, and after the summer of 1915 Harriet Monroe seems to have lost interest in much of Pound's prose. She began to turn down his propaganda pieces. An editorial sent in December, 1915, protesting the tariff on books imported into the United States, was not printed; an article of January, 1916, that asked for a "living wage" for verse writers—payment for poetry at a twenty-five-dollar page rate—was not used; "Nothing in this for us," she noted on a passionate protest against the censorship of works of art in the United States sent in May, 1916. It appears that she decided against involving *Poetry* in the kind of practical or material literary campaign—against tariff, against censorship, against institutional policy—that more and more interested Pound.

One cannot say that these editorial exchanges in 1914 and 1915 brought Harriet Monroe and Ezra Pound closer to agreement. If anything, each was driven to a progressive exaggeration of his point of view, so that they ended up further apart than they

87. "Hark to Sturge Moore," *Poetry*, June, 1915, pp. 143–44 (copyright 1915 by Harriet Monroe; all rights reserved). Reprinted by permission of New Directions Publishing Corporation and Faber and Faber, Ltd., publishers and Agents for the Trustees of the Ezra Pound Literary Property Trust.

88. Letter of June 3, 1915.

began. On the audience question, an agreement seems hopeless
from the start, because each had taken up a position in advance of
the debate that committed him beyond persuasion. Pound was
already the artist in exile, and Harriet Monroe had created her
magazine out of Chicago's willingness to make poetry a civic
institution. But they knew each other by December, 1915, as
they had not known each other in 1913, and as a result their
editorial cooperation involved fewer surprises and nasty nervous
shocks. To this extent the editorial debate may have contributed
to the amiability of Pound's correspondence.

But neither a financial dependence on *Poetry* nor a clearer
understanding of Harriet Monroe's premises accounts altogether
for Pound's tone in the survey of the new poetry that he made in
his letter of December 15, 1915. After proposing that *Poetry* work
to get the front rank of poets—"Masters, Frost, Yeats of course,
Hueffer . . . myself if permitted and Eliot"—he goes on to discuss the poets of the second rank in a rambling way, then inter-
rupts himself:

> Now DO LISTEN A MOMENT even tho I have been vilely diffuse. We
> have broken down the old hedge. We, more than everyone else
> have established the right of vers libre to get printed. 60 young
> people are all trying to express themselves with a fair directness of
> statement, instead of tying up their meaning in pink ribbons.
>   Now
> All that counts is
>   a. *Knowledge of life*,
>   b. Great *technical skill*.
> A. Knowledge of life, *that is to say*, direct knowledge, (Masters as
>   opposed to Aldington, as opposed to all theoricians and rhetori-
>   cians.)
>   Ideas got from seeing *life in arrangement*, the designs in life as it
> exists.
>   NOT the trying to see life according to an idea (vide, poor
> Hagedorn, to whom I am indebted for starting me off on several
> trains of activity at the moment). [Hermann Hagedorn's poem
> "The Cabaret Dancer," published in *Poetry* for December, 1915.]
> As you shall see in a day or so.
>   Almost anyone can now describe a sunset, a cloud, a sea gull

with fairish delicacy. On the other hand Frost has seen a form of life—despite his surface dullness.

ETC.

Yeats, knows life, despite his chiaroscuro and his lack of a certain sort of observation. He learns by emotion, and is one of the few people who have ever had any, who know what violent emotion really is like; who see from the centre of it—instead of trying to look in from the rim.

60 young people can describe their *sensations* almost as well as some others can describe external nature, or pick up a delicate shade. That's *not* the same thing. Timbre, sap, fibre, is what we've got to hunt for. Skill only comes through endless practice, endless castigation, endless fastidiousness, which must *not* be simply a refinement, a *raffinement*, a dilutation into half tones.

In hunting for pure colour we had to refine and refine, perhaps, but that set of experiments is made. We must no longer sacrifice weight. No longer simply whittle away.

Then Pound's letter falls back into a catalog of writers and their possibilities. There is one "Addendum" about Masters that is related to the remarks about life in arrangement: "GRASP, Masters has it—and then he slips, he drags in 'views.' Some profound sense of life, as opposed to a slither, usually an optimistic slither over the top."

The letter clearly marks the end of something and the beginning of something for Pound. He said goodbye to the intaglio method, to effects created by the absence of the stone. He put an end to a long clarification that had exorcised Rossetti and Swinburne from his style. As a critic, as impresario of the movement, he had tended, in the period when his emphasis was on refinement, to require too much single-mindedness or unity of emotion in a poem, almost too much simplicity of mind. He had been irritated by Harriet Monroe's praise of Emily Dickinson as an "unconscious and uncatalogued Imagist" in *Poetry* for December, 1914: "Imagism consists in presentation of the Image, it certainly does not consist in talking about abstractions like 'Finite infinity.' That sort of thing is precisely what we are avoiding with greatest intensity."[89] His criteria—clarity, objectivity, precision,

89. Letter dated January 5, 1915, by Harriet Monroe.

presentation, proof color—did not allow him to make useful distinctions between Shakespeare and Poe, or between Emily Dickinson and Rupert Brooke. Possibly it was the strong cerebral element in Wallace Stevens' early poems that kept Pound dubious about him. Nowhere in his voluminous correspondence to Harriet Monroe does he make a remark about Stevens or about his work. In the year "Sunday Morning" was published, Pound on August 30, 1916, made his usual canvass of candidates for the Levinson Prize without noticing Stevens' poem amid the "overwhelming amount of rubbish" he found in the magazine. The Stevens and Dickinson cases are unique, for usually when Pound chose to reject or ignore a poet of some merit, he did it with awareness of his qualities; Frost and D. H. Lawrence are the obvious examples.

In coming out for "GRASP" and for "life in arrangement," full of temporary new enthusiasm for Masters stimulated by "Arabel" in *Poetry*, "The Cocked Hat" in *Reedy's Mirror*, and "So We Grew Together" in the *Little Review*, Pound was shifting away from his Imagistic emphasis on style, from the reforms preached in the "Don'ts." The difference is merely one of emphasis, for Pound's Image—"that which presents an intellectual and emotional complex in an instant of time"[90]—had been itself a form of life in arrangement. But now he seems interested in something less tidy than the instant, in a more fluid sort of order influenced by time and change, in the struggles and linguistic confusions of the mind stubbing up against alien and irreducible fact. For Ezra Pound, the difference in emphasis is considerable.

The consequences for his own poetry seem very exciting. He began 1915 stuck where he was when his satires failed to develop into something interesting. The translations out of Ernest Fenollosa, like "Exile's Letter," that he published in 1915 are among his most beautiful poems, but they did not give him a clear direction for his own work; nor did the new "poetic" poems out of his old subject matter of Provence, like "Near Perigord," seem to provide the possibility of new developments. But by De-

90. "A Few Don'ts by an Imagiste," *Poetry*, March, 1913, reprinted in *Literary Essays* (copyright 1935 by Ezra Pound; all rights reserved). Reprinted by permission of New Directions Publishing Corporation and Faber and Faber, Ltd., publishers and Agents for the Trustees of the Ezra Pound Literary Property Trust.

cember, 1915, Pound was in the first stages of the work that was to dominate the rest of his life. He wrote his father on December 18 that he had completed four cantos of a "big long endless poem."[91] The exuberance of his letter to Harriet Monroe on December 15, the new sense of larger perspectives in it, was part of an exhilarating renewal in his work.

Some students of Pound's poetry have emphasized the influence of Joyce in the genesis of the *Cantos*. Indeed, it hardly seems likely that Ezra Pound read the conclusion of *A Portrait of the Artist* in September, 1915, without a significant response to the idea of forging in the smithy of his soul the uncreated conscience of his race. But his letter to Harriet Monroe on December 15 suggests strongly that some specifically poetic influences were at work, notably the Edgar Lee Masters of the *Spoon River Anthology*. The letter to *Poetry* also reflects the immediate excitement of writing the poem Pound mentions in it, "To a Friend Writing on Cabaret Dancers." One would even speculate that the several trains of activity on which Hermann Hagedorn's "The Cabaret Dancer" started Pound included something in the first draft of the *Cantos* itself, but the insignificant little poem can hardly support itself, much less bear up under any responsibility for initiating Pound's epic. However, Pound's "To a Friend Writing on Cabaret Dancers" does, without reference to the *Cantos*, lead in a new direction for his poetry, one that ends in *Mauberley*.

The consequences for *Poetry* of Pound's new outlook in December, 1915, seem also very exciting. For the first time since he became Harriet Monroe's foreign correspondent, he writes with candid hope for their common cause, and puts the "Amur'k'n" poets as high as the exiles. His project to channel Yeats, Eliot, himself, Hueffer, and H.D., with Masters and Frost, into *Poetry*, to the exclusion of lesser poets—allowing an occasional poem by Lawrence, Aldington, Colum, Rodker, William Carlos Williams, Maxwell Bodenheim, Sandburg, Alice Corbin, Harold Monro, and Sturge Moore (the other poets mentioned in

91. Myles Slatin, "A History of Pound's Cantos I–XVI, 1915–1925," *American Literature* 35 (May, 1963), 185 (copyright 1963 by Ezra Pound). Reprinted by permission of New Directions Publishing Corporation and Faber and Faber, Ltd., publishers and Agents for the Trustees of the Ezra Pound Literary Property Trust.

the letter of December 15, 1915)—meant a chance to recapture the ideal unity of the movement that had given *Poetry* its force in 1914.

The revival of poetry in England, which seems the source of the Poetry Renaissance that American publishers and journals began to notice in 1913, was blighted by World War I. Rupert Brooke's death in the spring of 1915 is the symbol of this, and Pound's comments from London, as well as Richard Aldington's remark in July, 1915, that he and Harold Monro agreed that there was not enough good verse to fill a magazine, bear it out. But the American poetry renaissance reached a zenith in 1915. Before 1914 was over, the "new poetry" had become respectable if not fashionable in the Middle West.[92] John L. Hervey's attack on Harriet Monroe in the *Dial* in 1915 mocks the modishness of the new poetry.[93] Miss Monroe wrote Alfred Kreymborg in the summer of 1915 about "the present Renaissance" as if it were universally recognized. Pound's series of articles in *Poetry* in the spring of 1915, "The Renaissance," has some of the same implication.

William Marion Reedy acknowledged a renaissance in writing Harriet Monroe on June 1, 1915, and remarked that he felt *Poetry* was responsible for it. Indeed, as early as February 6, 1914, before the *Spoon River Anthology* began, *Reedy's Mirror* had sounded a little weary of the Poetry Renaissance, which had been talked up for about a year at that point. Reedy visited the annual banquet of the Poetry Society of America in New York, and the sleekness and propriety of the assembled poets made him feel grubby. "I take it," he wrote, "that the poetry business must be just about the most prosperous in New York." He felt irritated by the sheer volume of verse poured out: "Never before were there so many pleasant, well-phrased, melodious poems written as there are today, and at no other time has there been such a dearth of really distinguishable poetry."[94]

By spring, 1915, the Poetry Renaissance needed some new

92. "Mr. Vachel Lindsay," *Dial*, October 1, 1914, p. 282.
93. "Bryant and 'The New Poetry,'" August 15, 1915, pp. 92–93.
94. Comment on a poem by R. L. Gales, March 26, 1915, p. 15.

phenomena, and three were ready to hand: the *Spoon River Anthology* in book form, the American publication of Frost's *North of Boston*, and Amy Lowell's *Some Imagist Poets*. The response to these books suggests a journalistic world delighted to find poetry of sufficient individuality to give definite shape to the long-rumored renaissance. The newspapers became alert for news in poetry: Amy Lowell, reading her poem "The Bath" to a monthly meeting of the Poetry Society of America in New York, created an uproar,[95] and *Others* came out in July, 1915, to find the newspapers ready for it. The *New York Times Review of Books*, summarizing the year's publication, noted that the older poetry had been rebuked, and that rhymeless and meterless verse had won approval.[96] It gave special attention to a "time-spirit" school derived from Whitman, including Edwin Markham, James Oppenheim, and Louis Untermeyer. But it had praise for Amy Lowell among the Imagists, for *North of Boston*, and for *Spoon River*. Everything indicates that "New York" found out about the new poetry in 1915, that Masters, Amy Lowell, and Robert Frost arrived in time to give substance to the rather vacuous publishers' renaissance that had developed in 1913.

At the end of the year the forces making up the renaissance took on a new configuration, with an alliance between Amy Lowell and W. S. Braithwaite, a move foreshadowed by Amy Lowell's comments in a letter of March 26, 1914, to Harriet Monroe: "You have no idea how the trail of William Stanley Braithwaite lies all over the growth of poetry here in the East. It never occurred to me that the man had any standing, with his Magazine anthology, until the other day in New York, when Edwin Arlington Robinson and Louis Ledoux informed me that they thought his opinion carried a great deal of weight. . . ." Braithwaite's 1915 survey of magazine verse for the *Boston Evening Transcript*, a preliminary to his annual anthology, announced that "Patterns" was the most distinctive poem published in the year; it also gave special notice to "The Adventurer" by Odell Shepard, "Needle Travel" by Margaret French Patton,

95. Horace Gregory, *Amy Lowell*, p. 116.
96. "A Year's Harvest in American Poetry" and "Poetry," November 18, 1915, pp. 464, 474.

"The Road Not Taken," and "Peter Quince at the Clavier," in that order. The Imagists and Masters were praised, and Braithwaite defined poetry as having for its essence "the mental and emotional image." The existence of *Poetry* was not acknowledged, nor did Braithwaite mention Harriet Monroe's magazine in the preface to his *Anthology of Magazine Verse for* 1915, where Frost and Masters are called "the two great successes of the year," and Amy Lowell's Imagists get special notice. Braithwaite had finally been brought to recognize the existence of the new poetry, as *Poetry* commented with satisfaction in December, 1915. The further fruits of his alliance with Amy Lowell appear in the monthly numbers of his new magazine, the *Poetry Review*, in 1916.

Thus in the mature Poetry Renaissance *Poetry* the magazine had almost no part. Braithwaite's silence is typical: the publishing history of *Poetry* tends to be passed over in the excitement over the Imagists, Frost, and Masters. Amy Lowell, after her conquest of the metropolis, wrote Harriet Monroe on June 11, 1915: "The attitude of New York [toward *Poetry*] is utterly incomprehensible to me. I am bound to confess, I think perhaps Ezra's articles, pitching into everything American, from the beginning of the magazine, up to date, have had something to do with it." The magazine's financial position did not improve, although circulation went up slightly. In the spring of 1915, when poetry was burgeoning elsewhere, Harriet Monroe cut her rate of payment to contributors, from an average of ten dollars a page to eight dollars a page. Even with that economy, she needed a special emergency donation of five hundred dollars to finish her publishing year.

But if *Poetry* was deemed too tenuous and avant-garde to deserve recognition from a critic like Braithwaite, the young avant-garde began in 1915 to express the attitude that *Poetry* was too conservative and too provincial for it. There were overtones of such an attitude in the founding of *Others*, but the first to articulate it was Conrad Aiken, who had been offended by Harriet Monroe ever since she published Pound's "Status Rerum" in 1913, and demonstrated indifference to the Georgians. In November, 1915, writing in the *Poetry Journal*, which had passed from the editorship of Braithwaite to the keener management of Edmund R. Brown, Aiken lumped Harriet Monroe's magazine with Braithwaite's anthology as an institutional rhinocerous: "November is a deadly month for poets: simultaneously, then, appear two annual phenomena against which I am sure the fastidious must rage: Mr. Braithwaite's selection of the year's best poem, Miss Monroe's prize-giving and list of honorable mentions." Despite the injustice of bracketing *Poetry* and the Braithwaite anthology, the attack was a telling one, for it isolated the weakness in Harriet Monroe's effort to present impartially the best of all the schools. The annual award of the Levinson Prize aroused a disproportionate amount of attention and emotion, and of all the magazine's editorial gestures, it was most suspect of regional bias, with awards to Yeats and Lindsay, then to Sandburg, then to Lindsay again. The controversy stirred up by Aiken's attack continued into 1916. The developments of that year did a great deal to settle the question of *Poetry*'s public identity.

At the Museum

Wallace Stevens, 1916

The loneliest person
Moves among locked cases,
Down aisles where glass reflects to glass.
He sees, beneath the polished ghost
Of his own image, the rose, deep rose
And sea green jade of ancient porcelain.

He knows this rose, this green.
He cups them in his mind,
Leaving the museum,
Carrying earliest fire, a current of earliest sea,
Through the mouse-grey tentative city,
Past minds which catch no color from his own.

THREE

"The Great Opportunity" 🔊
1916–17

The events of 1916 canceled *Poetry*'s chance to win wide recognition as the chief publisher of the new poetry, and the magazine began to decline toward relative mediocrity. The numbers for much of the year are uneven like the later issues of 1915: for each that seems dead, another seems full of interest, but there is no sense of burgeoning development as there was in 1914. And by 1917 the magazine falls well below its past standard.

A number of people wrote Harriet Monroe during 1916 to plead for "concentration," for a rigorous editorial selection of the best eight or ten writers from among the hordes produced by the Poetry Renaissance. Ezra Pound characteristically followed up his letter of December 15, 1915, which had nominated an elite for promotion, with a practical program for sustaining his poets. He suggested on January 23, 1916, that *Poetry* raise its rate to five pounds (twenty-five dollars) a page to allow the better writers to earn a living wage while publishing no more than twenty pages of poetry a year:

> A multitude of magazines is good in one way, but if it encourages diffuseness it is bad. And anything which tends to concentrate the force is much better. If there is too great a flood of loose verse, we shall kill the enthusiasm, the present enthusiasm, bore everyone, and lose all we have gained. Besides if people could only get decently paid for a small amount of good work (by decently I mean "living wage") they would be less pushing, less anxious to "place" all their trash. We all want the concentrated good in one place not scattered in ten little magazines.

As often when he was in a practical mood, Pound in his proposal to raise rates was at cross-purposes with *Poetry*, for Harriet Monroe had reluctantly cut her rate to eight dollars per page the year before. Pound was not aware of this; apparently she had retained the old rate in paying for his poems in the December, 1915, issue. In March he wrote angrily because T. Sturge Moore had been offended by a lower payment than Pound had promised him. The misunderstanding eroded the confidence in *Poetry* that Pound had expressed over the winter. His March letter holds Harriet Monroe liable to penitential compensation for any and all sharp practices that American publishers had inflicted on his English acquaintances, and hints that payment to Ford Madox Hueffer for "On Heaven" had been reduced out of deliberate malice, a sly provincial nastiness that had clouded his intimacy with Hueffer. *Poetry* usually paid less per page for a very long poem or a very long group of poems; this was probably the basis of Hueffer's disappointment. Up until the spring of 1916 Pound seems unaware of *Poetry*'s precarious finances. Images of wealthy plutocrats, unconstipated pork-packers, welled up in his mind when he thought of *Poetry*'s endowment fund, but a glance at the magazine's yearly expenditures reveals that year in, year out, as all expenses rose, the funds available for distribution to poets remained remarkably constant, between twenty-five hundred and three thousand dollars per year. *Poetry* was not Maecenas, as Pound would have it: "either Poetry is Maecenas, upholding a principle that poetry ought to be decently paid, or else it is a sheet begging for favors—which last it of course is not. But. . . . As W.B.Y. writes to his sisters: 'Are you a convent, or are you not?'" [1]

One part of Harriet Monroe's problem, as *Poetry* failed to prosper despite all the renaissance publicity, was to conceal from her contributors as well as from the world at large how shaky was the financial base on which she operated, how nearly *Poetry* was a charity, how nearly its contributors were foundlings in the imagination of the editor. In the fiscal year 1915–16 she pushed payments to contributors above three thousand dollars, but the

1. Letter of March 5, 1916, in *Letters*, #83, pp. 70–71. The note, p. 78, that this letter was printed in *Poetry* is in error.

strain on her resources was great. That spring she visited New York and met for the first time some of the people associated with *Others*—Alfred Kreymborg, William Carlos Williams, Skipwith Cannell, and Horace Holley. Williams' reaction to a personal meeting is most interesting. He recognized in Harriet Monroe a strong personality inhibited, he felt, by a false sense of mission, by a sentimental overemphasis on the poet's need for succor. He wrote April 11, 1916:

> Come again and stay longer. I have a fine bed waiting for you in my tumble down spare room.
>
> As soon as I get the time I'm going to write you a real love letter—tell you your faults etc.
>
> Two things I want to say to you now however: 1 Verse doesn't *pay* and no boosting by "Poetry" will ever make it pay—quit trying or you'll strangle yourself. 2 Print the better folk oftener and quicker.
>
> Why so much Christliness? Why try to help the poor artist—what help can you give the poor artist (the poor, poor artist) other than Harriet Monroe's personal understanding of him? Is "Poetry" a poetic stock yard? For God's sake let's have more Harriet and less "Poetry." I despise "Poetry." There never was a more stupid commercial magazine than "Poetry"—come to life, let's have what Harriet likes (if she likes anything) and not what she thinks is helpful for us. Good night if you don't listen to me. . . .
>
> [P.S.] If "Poetry" were printed free in a garret on toilet paper—it couldn't help but have a meaning.
>
> Now it has none.
>
> The sad thing is that with Harriet back of it, it only needs to be let loose to get a meaning.

The imagery of the privy is not humor aimed against Miss Monroe, but Williams' recurring metaphor for creative expression: "what I have done clings to me horribly until someone relieves me by ridicule, praise or any possible action. 'Poetry' cuts the rope between the ox and his dung. Pardon the coarse allusion."[2] Despite the striking contrast between his view that poetry cannot *pay*, and Pound's campaign for a living wage, it is evident that Williams belongs with Pound in the group that pleaded for con-

2. Letter of May 22, 1914, in Thirlwall, *Letters*.

centration. He abated his mysterious rage of January, 1916, to write March 1, 1916:

> Mrs. Williams is a sincere believer in your openmindedness even in spite of my occasional ravings against you, however I still believe that if I were in your place I would be still more marvelous than you in the looseness of my policy.
>
> My frank opinion is that "Poetry" pays too much for its verse and that it is too anxious to be inclusive.
>
> Less money and a more defined policy would keep away many a foolish rhymster. Of course you want them all "to come unto" you but if the policy of a periodical of poetry is of any less steely fiber than that of the best verse the result will be disastrous.
>
> Ah how pleasant it is to give advice!

Pound's proposal that a selected group of "les jeunes" be kept up by *Poetry*, published in the magazine for April, 1916, got support from an unexpected quarter. John Gould Fletcher wrote October 25, 1916, to endorse the suggestion for selection. He felt that *Poetry* had been largely responsible for the poetic revival in America. But the general vague fashion for poetry was useless. He was delighted to find himself for once agreeing with Ezra Pound—the Poetry Renaissance might be only a cheap, hot blaze of paper. The *Poetry Review, Contemporary Verse, Others*, and the *Poetry Journal* were now all busily trying to create Harriet Monroe's great audience, but the audience was ready, waiting, eager for verse with some substance. Good poets, not new poets, were needed, and a criticism that could discriminate the poetry that would mean something to the future. Fletcher offered to send all his best work, to be printed without payment, if *Poetry* would make out a list of contributors, each guaranteed two appearances a year, and if Harriet Monroe would notify the world that she intended to print no more new people. Without some clear standard, he felt that the poetic revival would quickly come to nothing.

Conrad Aiken, writing in the *Poetry Journal* for February, 1916, continued his attack on *Poetry*'s prize awards by relating the question of prizes to the question of concentration: "Poetry is already, thanks to Mr. Braithwaite and Miss Monroe, too much rather than too little recognized in this country. There is a dead level of praise and recognition abroad which confounds issues, which obliterates all distinctions, which makes it difficult, almost impossible, for the genuinely good to make its way in the chaos." Harriet Monroe had defenders against attack from Aiken. Amy Lowell wrote a strong tribute for the *Poetry Journal* of January, 1916: "Miss Monroe manages the prize-giving with infinite care and integrity. It is impossible to imagine Miss Monroe doing anything otherwise than honestly; it is her unique single-mindedness which brought her magazine to the high place it now occupies." Ezra Pound counseled her to ignore the attack: "it is from a rival paper with no prizes to give, from a man never likely to take a prize."[3] *Poetry* published a note from Pound in March, 1916, defending any award, pension, or grant to the artist, citing the funds made available to French and English writers. For a while this was the last of the debate about *Poetry*'s prizes. Aiken remained hostile to Harriet Monroe on more general grounds, and the habit of lumping her with W. S. Braithwaite, which originated in his first article about prize giving, continued in his criticism.

Despite these signs that strong editorial leadership was required in 1916, despite pleas for clearer definition coming from London and New Jersey, from Imagist and Vorticist, from friend and enemy, Harriet Monroe did little in 1916 to alter the magazine's established policies. The selection of verse shows the usual effort to cover the whole poetic spectrum. The year's publication is clearly weaker than the publication record of 1915. Too much space is given to local dignitaries who lacked significant poetic stature—Henry B. Fuller, Mary Aldis, Cloyd Head, and Edith Wyatt. When Harriet Monroe tried to include "all the schools," the more literary among the guarantors, the advisory board, and the personnel of the Chicago Little Theater perhaps demanded their share of space. But the speculation is probably unfair: Henry B. Fuller's poem in February, 1916, interested Pound; Mary Aldis, though she was the wife of a guarantor, was generally recognized as a poet and published in other little magazines; *Grotesques*, the play by Cloyd Head that won the Levinson Prize for 1916–17, is one of those manipula-

3. Letter of December 15, 1915.

tions of basic dramatic convention that always seem startling. Only the publication of Edith Wyatt in December, 1916, seems a clear piece of ward-heeling literary politics.

The publication record of 1916 looks weak on the middle-western side because the poets who had been the chief source of excitement were not writing much or were not writing well. Edgar Lee Masters' contributions to *Poetry* in 1916, "In Memory of Byron Lathrop" and "All Life in a Life," might have been written by Edith Wyatt, for all the difference they make in the magazine. The latter poem, a sententious life of Christ that makes a 1914-style liberal of him, won the Levinson Prize for 1915–16. There was a consensus that Masters deserved recognition that year; both Pound and Alice Corbin Henderson voted the prize to him, though Pound nominated "Arabel," not the poem about Christ. Carl Sandburg published nothing at all in *Poetry* in 1916. Vachel Lindsay's three "Booker Washington" poems in *Poetry* for June, 1916, are the best that the Chicago Renaissance contributed in the year.

Poetry's bravest single gesture in 1916 was the prize awarded Wallace Stevens' *Three Travelers Watch a Sunrise* in a contest for poetic drama jointly sponsored by *Poetry* and Aline Barnsdall's Players' Producing Company. Harriet Monroe explained in June that, with one dissenter from the award, the judges had abandoned standards of actability and human warmth to honor "extraordinary poetic beauty. . . . the original creative impulse . . . the outreaching experiment." Stevens' play was certainly not written to a formula for winning prizes, and strongly aided the cause of concentration when it was printed in *Poetry* for July.

The issue for November, 1916, is one that also seems to make for concentration: it features Frost's "Snow." The appearance was Robert Frost's second in the magazine; he had not published in *Poetry* since "The Code" in February, 1914. By 1916 Frost had many outlets for his verse, and asked Harriet Monroe for "not much less than two hundred dollars" in sending "Snow" on March 8, 1916. She noted on his letter that she "offered $100," which he apparently accepted. William Carlos Williams also had a group in the November issue, his first appearance in *Poetry* since the "ROTTEN" number of May, 1915. The poems, "Love Song," "Naked," "Marriage," "Apology," "Summer Song," and "The Old Worshipper," had been sent at the beginning of 1916, possibly with the snarling note that concluded, "Maybe I can sell you something." Williams had warmed to *Poetry* over the year, to the point where he had contributed ten dollars to the magazine, writing October 6, 1916, "You make one feel it worth while to be alive." But discussion of line arrangements and capitalizations of first letters of lines in the proofs for November embroiled him in a new quarrel with Harriet Monroe: "Let it go. No one will notice anything wrong and as long as nothing is noted to disturb the gently flowing accord of the magazine from Vol. 1 number 1 until the year of Grace which is to see its end I suppose the major part of its mission is accomplished."[4] Harriet Monroe wrote back something soothing, and Williams' reply makes the comment about outbursts of extravagant love followed by outbursts of extravagant indignation that seems to characterize the whole correspondence, alterations as rapid as the pace of a slapstick comedy.

However, two or three good issues are not enough "concentration" to redeem the rest of a year. Unfortunately, Ezra Pound's London group was weakly represented in *Poetry* in 1916. Yeats sent no verse during the year. Possibly he resented Harriet Monroe's proposal to put him into an anthology, a proposal he firmly rejected: "It means being paraded before the public with a lot of people to whom one hasn't been introduced."[5] Possibly he resented a delay in publishing the poems in the February, 1916, issue, which were held in the *Poetry* office for eight months, almost as long a gestation period as Harriet Monroe had imposed the year before on "Prufrock." Possibly he had no poetry needing American publication that year.

Pound in 1916 continued to complain that very little verse was being written in wartime England. "Production in England at present very low," he wrote April 21, 1916, in sending some poems by Iris Barry.[6] He did, however, send five of James

4. Letter of October 26, 1916, in Thirlwall, *Letters*.
5. Letter of "January 1916."
6. In *Letters*, #90, p. 79.

Joyce's lyrics January 29, 1916, arguing that they were good in their way, though it was not his way, and that the group would convey its own atmosphere, having a certain distinction, "though it would perhaps be difficult to say why. At any rate Joyce's name on list of contents will be an excellent thing in saeculum saeculorum." Harriet Monroe found the poems "uninteresting,"[7] and did not print them until May, 1917, when "Simples," "Tutto è Sciolto," "Flood," "A Flower Given to My Daughter," and "Night Piece" appeared in *Poetry*.

Pound also sent June 22, 1916, a long poem by Jean de Bosschère, "Homère Mere Habite Sa Maison des Planches," which has attracted later notice as an influence on T. S. Eliot's "Mélange Adultère de Tout." Again Harriet Monroe delayed publication; she wrote Pound on July 3, 1917, "I rather like his poem, and still intend to use it—but it's a good deal of space for a French poem when we have so much waiting." *Poetry* publication eventually was forestalled by book publication of the poem in the fall of 1917. The four poems by T. S. Eliot that appeared in *Poetry* for September, 1916—"Conversation Galante," "La Figlia Che Piange," "Mr. Apollinax," and "Morning at the Window"—came from Pound on May 29, 1916, along with "Death of St. Narcissus," which Eliot withdrew. The same issue had a group by Pound—"The Fish and the Shadow," "The Three Poets," "Pagani's," "The Lake Isle," "Impressions of François-Marie Arouet," "Homage to Quintus Septimius Florentis Christianus," and "Dans un Omnibus de Londres"— the whole of his *Poetry* contribution in 1916, except for a poem that Harriet Monroe felt she could not print, "To a Friend Writing on Cabaret Dancers."

"To a Friend Writing on Cabaret Dancers" is the poem on which Pound was working when he wrote his long, excited letter of December 15, 1915, about the difference between seeing "life in arrangement, the designs in life as it exists," and "trying to see life according to an idea (vide, poor Hagedorn, to whom I am indebted for starting me off on several trains of activity at the

---

7. Pound, May 3, 1916: "Yes, Joyce's verses are uninteresting, but he is worth keeping up, tremendously worth it."

moment). . . ." Hermann Hagedorn, whose "The Cabaret Dancer" appeared in *Poetry* for December, 1915, is the friend of Pound's title. The letter marks an important change in Pound, with his excitement over "Grasp, Masters has it—and then he slips, he drags in 'views,'" with the announcement that the experiment in refinement, clarification, and simplification of style "is made. We must no longer sacrifice weight. No longer simply whittle away." He seems interested in more complex patterns, more involved in time, in human accident, and in historical change than the Image caught up in an instant of time that he had promoted in 1912. He had begun to work on his *Cantos*; he sent in the first long draft of "Three Cantos" over the next winter.

The "Cabaret Dancers" poem itself perhaps cannot justify the excitement communicated in Pound's letter; one might not find much in it, if the letter did not put one to searching. It is hard to understand Pound's enthusiasm, given the jerky rhythms and transitions and the bluntly personal tone of the poem. But despite its loose and rather garrulous pace, the poem carries Pound's homage to Gautier:

"Carmen est maigre, un trait de bistre cerne son oeil
de Gitana"
and "rend la flamme,"
You know the deathless verses.

It is the beginning of a nameless movement he described, comprising himself and T. S. Eliot, leading to Eliot's 1920 *Poems* and to his own "Mauberley": "at a particular date in a particular room, two authors neither engaged in picking the other's pocket, decided that the dilutation of vers libre, Amygism, Lee Masterism, general floppiness, had gone too far. . . . Remedy prescribed: 'Émaux et Cameés' (or the Bay State Hymn Book). Rhyme and regular strophes. Results: Poems in Mr. Eliot's *second* volume (not contained in his first . . .) also 'H. S. Mauberley.' Divergence later."[8] The technical emphasis in Pound's description of this change, and the implication that it began in reaction

8. "Harold Monro," *Criterion*, July, 1932, p. 590 (copyright 1932; all rights reserved). Reprinted by permission of New Directions Publishing Corporation and Faber and Faber, Ltd., publishers and Agents for the Trustees of the Ezra Pound Literary Property Trust.

away from "Lee Masterism," are additions after the fact. Masters was an important influence leading Pound toward more fluent and dramatic patterns, more involvement in history, when he wrote "To a Friend Writing on Cabaret Dancers."

Eliot in his turn reacted to Pound's poem. It contributed something to "Sweeney among the Nightingales":

> Euhenia, in short skirts, slaps her wide stomach,
> Pulls up a roll of fat for the pianist,
> "Pauvre femme maigre!" she says.
>   He sucks his chop bone,
> That some one else has paid for, grins up an amiable grin,
> Explains the decorations.
>   Good Hedgethorn, they all have futures,
> All these people.
>   Old Popkoff
> Will dine next week with Mrs. Basil,
> Will meet a duchess and an ex-diplomat's widow
> From Weehawken. . . .[9]

The lines seem the remote ancestors of

> The person in the Spanish cape
> Tries to sit on Sweeney's knees
>
> Slips and pulls the table cloth
> Overturns a coffee-cup,
> Reorganized upon the floor
> She yawns and draws a stocking up;
>
> The silent man in mocha brown
> Sprawls at the window sill and gapes ...
> . . . .
> Branches of wisteria
> Circumscribe a golden grin. . . .[10]

And the use of Old Popkoff and Mrs. Basil is reminiscent of Eliot's polyglot names in "Gerontion": "De Bailhache, Fresca,

9. Excerpts from "To a Friend Writing on Cabaret Dancers" reprinted from *Personae* and *Collected Shorter Poems* by Ezra Pound (copyright 1926 by Ezra Pound) by permission of New Directions Publishing Corporation and Faber and Faber, Ltd., publishers and Agents for the Trustees of the Ezra Pound Literary Property Trust.

10. Excerpts from "Sweeney among the Nightingales" reprinted from *Collected Poems, 1909–1962* by T. S. Eliot by permission of Harcourt Brace Jovanovich, Inc., and Faber and Faber, Ltd.

Mrs. Cammell. . . ."[11] "To a Friend Writing on Cabaret Dancers" gives a view of the new poetry at a very interesting crisis, suggesting influence between Masters and Pound and between Pound and Eliot, and leads straight toward important later developments in Pound's and in Eliot's work, after Masters had fallen by the wayside.

This sort of vision of poetry in development seems just what a magazine of verse exists to communicate, and Harriet Monroe's rejection of the poem seems a great loss to *Poetry*. One's imagination becomes overheated in contemplating the rejection. It seems to include the rejections of all the poems to follow in the wake of "Cabaret Dancers," the developed work of Pound and of Eliot. For this seems a consequence of *Poetry*'s failure to print Pound's newest work in 1916. Whatever motives lay behind his cordial and uncondescending letter of December 15, 1915, were squelched; any new confidence in *Poetry* that had survived the misunderstanding about payment to Sturge Moore in March was extinguished. In the spring of 1916, new opportunities were opening up for Pound. He wrote to Harriet Monroe on May 3, 1916, a long letter that he said was "to have been . . . about a definite and conscious programme for 'Poetry.' Certain definite positions ought to be taken, and certain policy decided on, IF you are going to keep Poetry above the various other new magazines." Instead, the letter wobbled between protests about the rejection of "Cabaret Dancers" and rehashings of the confusion about rates, and Pound remarked parenthetically: "America has at least one great man in it and that man is John Quinn. Now about Tarriff [sic: the tariff levied on books imported into the United States], are you going to fight it in Poetry or am I to move on to the 'Little Review'?" After the spring of 1916, with the rejection of the work that so excited Pound, there was never again a possibility of genuine harmony between London and Chicago in *Poetry*.

Although in retrospect one can draw these consequences from the rejection, Harriet Monroe could hardly have been aware of the importance of the decision at the time. The poem itself is

11. Excerpt from "Gerontion" reprinted from *Collected Poems, 1909–1962* by T. S. Eliot by permission of Harcourt Brace Jovanovich, Inc., and Faber and Faber, Ltd.

garrulous and half realized, and her judgment of it seems more accurate than that of Pound, who wrote, "The Cabaret thing is the best I have done since The Exile's Letter, and the best original thing since 'The Goodly Fere.'" Her chief motive for rejecting it was fear of the censor; the phrases "advertising bitch" ("advertising spade" in the version published in *Personae*) and "prudent whore" put her off. She also wrote something about the poem as a whole lacking "beauty," because Pound replied, "As for beauty, I've enough in the 'Fish and Shadow' to satisfy the few people who can understand it,"[12] and he was sarcastic a month later about "the desire of the editor for the candy box." Pound agreed to leave it that "expediency and the assininity of your guarantors" required the rejection.[13]

Harriet Monroe's management of *Poetry* in 1916 suggests that she could not respond effectively to the calls for strong editorial selection that she received over the year. She seems distracted during 1916, and the most important cause of her distraction was the loss of Alice Corbin Henderson, who had been her associate editor from the beginning of *Poetry*. Mrs. Henderson was very important to the magazine. She had by custom given the first reading to all the manuscripts that came in the mails, she was a clever and incisive critic, and her presence in the office was witty and stimulating. In the spring of 1916 she was exiled to New Mexico with tuberculosis. Eunice Tietjens returned to Chicago and took over the work in the *Poetry* office from July, 1916, to June, 1917, but Mrs. Henderson remained associate editor on the masthead. Harriet Monroe perhaps left her name there because she continued to function by correspondence from Santa Fe. Her letters are full of detailed and challenging reactions to the work published in *Poetry*, rather similar in spirit to the letters Pound had sent.

Harriet Monroe welcomed Mrs. Henderson's sharp but informed comments from outside. Remembering the welcome she gave to Pound's correspondence, even when its tone was very angry, one speculates that she wanted the stimulation this criti-

12. Letter of May 3, 1916.
13. Letter of June 5, 1916, in *Letters*, #94, p. 81.

cism gave her. Harriet Monroe seems to have functioned on two levels. Sara Teasdale described her, rather melodramatically, to Louis Untermeyer as a divided person—cold and even harsh on the surface, loving and alive beneath—but "on to herself," not just the prisoner of the division in herself.[14] Her surface personality, the conventional, upright, and judicious gentlewoman who inspired so much confidence in the guarantors, was not as perceptive as her deeper personality, but that level in her needed some kind of shock before it could function effectively. "Please punch my face in order to save my soul," she wrote to William Carlos Williams in 1913. People who were fond of her liked to describe her as a fighter. "Harriet is one of the hardest fighters on American soil,"[15] wrote Vachel Lindsay. Alfred Kreymborg's little sketch in his memoir makes much of her "scrappiness." Since she was not a combative person, these comments must mean that she seemed most alive when answering a sharp challenge. One can see that she might need and value the sort of comment that Mrs. Henderson wrote from Santa Fe: "And oh, Harriet, whatever you do—*don't* speak of '*boosting the art*.' It is dreadful. You can *boost* a magazine—but art is above and apart from all *boosting*."[16] Eunice Tietjens might take over the work of manuscript sorting and minor reviewing, but the important loss of Alice Corbin Henderson from the *Poetry* office was the loss of someone who could say "Oh, Harriet!" at the right moment. And fortunately, she was able to sustain that function, to some degree, in her correspondence.

Mrs. Henderson had not been long in Santa Fe before she joined the chorus urging Harriet Monroe to select among the poets more rigorously, to concentrate the best in one magazine. She wrote June 7, 1916:

> I very much fear at times that "Cinderella" is going back to her ashes, and that she may feel more comfortable there than in her automobile—that this supposed popularity of the art is a good deal of dust. . . . By that I mean especially that one sees so much stuff passing itself off as poetry that is nothing of the sort. The

14. Louis Untermeyer, *From Another World*, p. 174.
15. Letter of February 16, 1925, to Harry A. Maguire.
16. Letter dated "June 1915" in error, commenting on *Poetry* for September, 1916.

need for a perfectly fearless high standard was never greater than
it is at this moment. What we need to do is to forget schools,
forget Imagism, forget vers libre (now that that's back history) and
talk poetry. . . .

Keep Poetry *up*, *up*! The need is all the greater because the other
magazines are so poor—you don't want to be classed with them. I
shiver when I think of the left-overs in the file! Are there many?

Except for Stevens' play in July, the summer issues of *Poetry* did
not reassure her. She wrote August 8, 1916, that the August
issue was "pretty sad, honestly. Once into Isaac and Rebeccah it
is not so bad and it is the best thing in the number and certainly
should have had first place—Amy—well Amy is not so bad—but
the rest is *triste*." She prescribed concentration:

There is *absolutely* no use in encouraging the poet who has *one*
passable poem in a lot of bad ones, and who hasn't the *germ* of
development, who will never—(so far as we can see)—*get* anywhere. Encourage him to keep on trying all you want to. But let
him try outside the magazine. Now *concentrate* on Masters,
Lindsay, Sandburg, Ficke, Fletcher, Frost, Pound, the English
ones—W.B.Y., Hueffer, Manning—etc.—when you can get
them. Also of course *Wallace Stevens*—and get something from
Arensberg—also Wm. Carlos Williams. There is nothing absolute
about this list. . . . But try not to let any number go out without
some outstanding contribution. *This is all important*.

Another distraction for Harriet Monroe in 1916 was the labor
of preparing an anthology, a project to which she had committed
herself before Mrs. Henderson became ill. Like Pound's *Catholic
Anthology*, Harriet Monroe's anthology, *The New Poetry*, was intended to oppose and to correct Amy Lowell's *Some Imagist Poets*.
She suggested the project to the Macmillan Company, claiming a
need for a "much stronger more representative anthology," the
month that Amy Lowell's book came from the press. Despite
Pound's assertion that Harriet Monroe had no right to sponsor an
anthology, "considering the awful rabble that has been admitted
to *Poetry*," [17] and his grumbling over strained relations with English writers who had resented the request to contribute poems
with no arrangement for royalties, *The New Poetry* was very suc-

17. In *Letters*, #83, p. 70.

cessful. But a good deal of time and energy that she needed for her magazine in 1916 went into her book. The strain of the work shows in her comment to Ezra Pound on July 3, 1917: "Glad you liked the collection, on the whole. It has many faults, no doubt, but Alice dropped out of the work early, and I had too much to do. . . . the bibliography . . . I assure you, was the meanest job I ever undertook. No more Anthologies for me."

Harriet Monroe, in sum, was overworked and shorthanded in 1916, and inattentive to appeals for a new sort of concentration in the magazine. Money worries also troubled her, of course. Pound's new program had been based on the assumption that *Poetry* could somehow pay twenty-five dollars a page for the best work of the elite, and he followed the letter that made that proposition with an ill-natured and suspicious tirade about rate reductions to Sturge Moore. Her reply is not preserved, but one can infer that it was rather testy, for Pound wrote back May 3, 1916, about money:

> Now now, I know well enough that it's not your fault that you don't give £60 a page, and also that you've worked yourself nigh to death keeping the magazine going, and I don't (*DO NOT*) forget it. But you live in a desert of people always talking about "things paying" etc. etc. and it is just as well to remember your original thesis that poetry ought to be paid as well as the other arts. No not paid, but that poets should be fed. Anyhow, that is a perfectly good position, and the plutocracy need to be reminded of it now and again.

Harriet Monroe believed *Poetry*'s limitation lay in her failure to attract enough subscribers for financial security, and she may very well have been right. But she does not seem sufficiently sensitive to the problems of censorship in 1916, or to have much insight into what her rejections meant for poets. Pound in his long letter of May 3 raged on about "Cabaret Dancers": "If one only had a public that was acquainted with eighteenth century literature, *or* the classics, *or* the elizabethans, or anything else save Wordsworth, Tenny, and the nincompoopy Victorian parsons————Gawd!! Of course you are welcome to print it with asterisks, saying that 'modesty forbids you etc.' . . . If verse can't have the freedom of a classic, or a russian novelist, or an elizabethan author, or of De Goncourt, or De Gourmont, it is ridiculous to consider the public who read it." About this same time he sent the article "Is Poetry Serious?," a flaming protest against censorship of works of art. Harriet Monroe noted on the manuscript, "Nothing in this for us." She simply did not see the problem, of American public policy suppressing literature, as *Poetry*'s problem. Yet in practice she became the agent of the Post Office censor, as fear constrained her editorial decisions and kept certain poems or parts of poems out of her magazine. It seems an issue that had no middle ground: one had to be for the freedom and dignity of the artist, or against it. In failing to recognize this, Harriet Monroe became the enemy of her poets. Printing the work of Pound or of Williams with asterisks, even, would have been useful. It would have publicized the conflict between the poets and the American public consciousness, and been the beginning of some new solution, while in no way threatening *Poetry* with Post Office confiscation. But the serene face that *Poetry* presented to the public further injured the poets, by denying the existence of their problem.

In the fall of 1916, inattention, distraction, or panic betrayed Harriet Monroe into her most damaging editorial suppression, one without parallel in her career, for at no other time did she cut a poem without securing some permission from the writer. In the September, 1916, number of *Poetry*, Pound's poem "Phyllidula and the Spoils of Gouvernet" appeared with the word "bloody" omitted from the line "And dine in a bloody cheap restaurant,"[18] without Pound's prior knowledge or permission. Much worse, in the same issue she cut "He laughed like an irresponsible foetus"[19] from T. S. Eliot's "Mr. Apollinax" without consulting the poet. The cut obliterated the central metaphor of Eliot's poem, and it is hard to see what advantage it secured to *Poetry*. The line does not seem censorable, any more than Pound's "bloody" does (Pound changed the word to "soggy" for publica-

18. Excerpt from "Phyllidula and the Spoils of Gouvernet" reprinted from *Personae* and *Collected Shorter Poems* (copyright 1926 by Ezra Pound) by permission of New Directions Publishing Corporation and Faber and Faber, Ltd., publishers and Agents for the Trustees of the Ezra Pound Literary Property Trust.

19. Excerpt from "Mr. Apollinax" reprinted from *Collected Poems, 1909–1962* by T. S. Eliot by permission of Harcourt Brace Jovanovich, Inc., and Faber and Faber, Ltd.

tion in the collected *Personae*). The decision to cut seems foolish, distracted, or panic-stricken. Perhaps she gave way to an ill-founded impulse in a last-minute check of the proofs, for the Eliot manuscript on file with his correspondence shows no editorial deletion of the line, which means that it went to the printer as Eliot originally wrote it. (The Pound manuscript of "Phyllidula" on file shows the deletion of "bloody.")

Ill-founded impulse or not, its consequences were irreparable. T. S. Eliot never again submitted prose or verse to *Poetry*. He had agreed that summer to contribute an occasional short article or review, but the only fruit of this arrangement was a review of H.D.'s *Iphigenia* sent September 7, 1916. Pound later tried to arrange for a series on the French in *Poetry*, and wanted articles on Rimbaud and Tristam Corbière from Eliot, but these were not completed for *Poetry* publication. Eliot answered in 1918 to Harriet Monroe's request for verse that he had nothing available. She apparently never again requested a contribution,[20] and Eliot never again sent anything.

The quarrel was Pound's more than Eliot's, since he had mailed in Eliot's poem. He wrote a formal protest September 16, 1916, which is not preserved, and followed it up in private: "Sept to hand. I have this A.M. written you what I think of the alterations in text. The editorial office ought at least to have the courage of its own prudery. If you are going to knuckle under to the super-degenerate now reigning in the place of the dead decayed dung-minded Comstock of putrid memory, at least you ought to leave dots (in my case and in Eliot's), indicating that the author has written something which the editors blush to reproduce and NOT that the poet respects superstition and the local Dorcas society." Pound, loudly and abusively as he suffered under Harriet Monroe's editorial policies, was more willing to make allowances for her than was Eliot, who wrote nothing at all about the mutilation of his poem. The graduate student who arrived in London in 1914 with "Prufrock" already behind him was far ahead of Har-

20. Harriet Monroe apparently would have been glad to print Eliot; she was sufficiently impressed by the 1920 *Poems* to mention it for a P.S.A.-Columbia Prize when she acted as judge in 1921. (Copy of a letter of August 14, 1921, to Richard LeGallienne, filed in the LeGallienne correspondence.)

riet Monroe. The demonstration that Eliot frightened and bewildered Harriet Monroe is her handling of "Mr. Apollinax"
rather than her handling of "Prufrock."

If Chicago had little to contribute to *Poetry* in 1916, and if
Pound's London contribution was half choked off in its pages,
the poets whom Mrs. Henderson called "the *Others* people" were
not much of a resource over the year. *Others* had outlived the
glories of its beginning, of the summer of 1915. By June, 1916, it
had lost both its publisher, John Marshall, and its editor, Alfred
Kreymborg; a system of guest editorships was to be tried in
future numbers. William Carlos Williams gave the magazine an
exuberant obituary in the *Egoist* for September, 1916, although it
was still being published at that date: "And then, the MSS of
our native artists beginning to fail to appear; Marshall having
failed to gauge matters rightly . . . financial ruin staring *Others*
through, no more meetings with strange cousins of Isadora Dun-
can, etc., strange French 'Artists,' no stir in the newspapers, no
verse but the worst being accepted by the magazines, the anthology [the first *Others* anthology] having failed to sell well because
of one silly poem—not by Cannell—our minds began to go to
sleep."[21] Harriet Monroe described an overripe Poetry Renaissance in her account in May, 1916, of a visit to New York and of
an *Others* party. She commented that poetry had become almost
dangerously fashionable, "because poets need an audience, not
fitful and superficial, but loyal and sincere." As evidence of the
fashionable interest in poetry, she cited the large volume of
bookstore sales of poetry, the proliferation of little magazines,
and the growth of quarrelsome poetic cliques. Alice Corbin
Henderson wrote a squib on the *Others* anthology, on the "I-am-
it" school of poetry, which used excerpts from the poems to
deride heavy use of the first-person singular by *Others* poets.
When this was published in *Poetry* for May, 1916, it roused a
storm.

The intensity of the reaction suggests that panic and disinte-

21. "The Great Opportunity," *Egoist*, September, 1916, p. 137 (copyright 1916; all
rights reserved). Reprinted by permission of New Directions Publishing Corporation,
publishers and Agents for Mrs. William Carlos Williams.

gration dominated New York. Maxwell Bodenheim, who had migrated from Chicago that year, was sententiously furious in a letter of May 16, 1916:

> The cheaply satirical article in your May issue, in which a group of poets is ridiculed, in which the work of these poets is deliberately misquoted, and their names twisted and mutilated—this cheaply sarcastic article will probably deprive you of the good will and friendship of the poets unjustly libelled, and of myself. The "Others Anthology Group" would have silently accepted a critical, fair attack upon its work, but your magazine's doubtfully humorous slander, cannot be allowed to pass unnoticed. The article is deliberately false. It attempted to prove its thesis (or jest) by citing isolated fragments from individual poems—a very poor method. And also, I have no recollection of ever having read anything in your magazine, in which Edgar Lee Masters became Ed Masters, or Nicholas Vachel Lindsay was altered to Nic' Lindsay, or Arthur Davison Ficke to Art Ficke. Your magazine is evidently careful with whom it takes liberties.

Apparently even the easygoing Alfred Kreymborg was brought to rage. William Carlos Williams wrote Harriet Monroe on May 3, 1916:

> Alfred tells me he has asked you to send his stuff back to him because of that foolish review by A.C.H.
>
> For the sake of humor give him the ha, ha! Take a chance on it please for it means a lot to me. Tell him he is a simp and that I say so. Send this letter to him if you want to.
>
> Please do this for me if you love me for I refuse to see Alfred cut his throat and not go with him. If you allow him to take back his things, back come mine too and that would break me all up.
>
> The review is to my mind trivial. Valueless as the Others anthology may or may not be it is a fine thrust out into the dark. It has at least been a free running sewer and for A.C.H. to ignore its positive qualities for the mere accident of its contents is too bad.
>
> Poetry, if it had half the convictions that straightforward little magazine possesses, would be a great gainer.

Kreymborg had not written the request for return of his manuscripts that Williams described. He answered May 15, 1916, to Harriet Monroe's letter of inquiry: "At first, I took ACH's stunt as a joke—later—after seeing some of the boys—there were reactions of sorrow, spleen, fun again, and one or another of confused emotions. Since then, I've learned indirectly from M.B. and Helen Hoyt that the thing was intended in fun. So we'll let it go at that as far as I'm concerned. Unfortunately, we all thought the business was intended in place of a review."

Mrs. Henderson reaffirmed her dim view of *Others* a month later: ". . . I've just re-read the Others Anthol. and ninety-nine per cent is sheer bosh. . . . both Fletcher *and Ezra* liked the I-am-its. As I said before, I am personally sensitive to altercation etc. but a magazine has got to have a fighting edge to it. Braithwaite's first page [the new *Poetry Review*, edited by W. S. Braithwaite] makes you think that he is conducting a revival meeting, and that poetry is the chief mourner at the Mercy Seat! to be prayed over! and shouted at!"[22] In June, 1916, Harriet Monroe published a long review of the *Others Anthology* by Max Michelson, respectful but not interesting, little more than a catalog of the contents. Kreymborg got in the best hit of the exchange with a squib that *Poetry* published in June, on the "You-are-it" school of Carl Sandburg: Harriet Monroe had praised *Chicago Poems* the month before for trying to express the national life in the large, "in the deepest sense a poet's business." She editorially regretted the current rash of conflicts and controversies, and pleaded for more humor and detachment. One must remember that Amy Lowell also wrote that spring, finding a "studied insult" in the omission of Brookline from the account of Harriet Monroe's eastern trip in May, and began her long series of requests for special editorial notice.

The "I-am-it" controversy seems developed out of general nervous fatigue as the movement lost its sense of direction. *Others* appeared irregularly after the summer of 1916 under various editors, William Carlos Williams among them. There were two more versions of the *Others Anthology*, in 1917 and 1920, edited by Alfred Kreymborg, and the magazine was resurrected under his editorship at the end of 1918. *Others* continued to be important in publishing the new poetry, but it was no longer a New York focus for the new writers—for William Carlos Williams,

22. Letter dated "June 1916."

Wallace Stevens, and Marianne Moore, in particular. *Others* followed Kreymborg to Chicago in 1917; he even edited a "Chicago number" in June, 1917. The loss to the East Coast, which had no organizing center for the serious poets, seems considerable.

A sharp focus on Harriet Monroe's rejection of "Cabaret Dancers" and cutting of "Mr. Apollinax" is misleading, for 1916 was a year in which distraction and nervous breakdown were general. Pound wrote October 21: "'Poetry' has gone to sleep. Masters has gone to pot. Kreymborg and New York have *quit*. Sandburg says his book is coming but it hasn't arrived. He may be the lone exception." Under the circumstances, Pound felt that stimulating the American young was rather like arousing a morgue.

Harriet Monroe got more backwash from the swamping of *Others* at the end of the year, when Maxwell Bodenheim returned to the attack, ostensibly furious because she had mentioned his play *Brown* in an editorial without citing William Saphier as coauthor. Bodenheim wrote December 4, 1916, to withdraw everything he had in the accepted file of *Poetry*, including the manuscript of the play: "You can, of course, keep the poems as security until I pay the money borrowed from you, but after that, I should like their return." Somehow *Poetry*'s survival where *Others* had failed made Harriet Monroe an accomplice to the murder of Kreymborg's magazine, for Bodenheim went on to pure denunciation:

> You are an intangible coward. You will not advance a poet whose work you respect beyond the mere printing of him, until that poet has become "safe"—until his work is widely mentioned. Sometimes you will aid a poet who has won favor with one of the influential members of your magazine-staff. That is your only deviation.
>
> The championing of any poet who is a bit ahead of his time and therefore unpopular, is impossible to you, even though you may greatly admire his work. The scarecrow of material failure always stalks at your side and often counsels you to veil your actual opinions. One Alfred Kreymborg, who bravely shouts his youthful challenge to the philistine and pompous literary-arbiters of this country and then dies as many others have died, is worth ten

timid editors like you—editors who blow their careful challenge through a muffled trumpet.

You were among the first to print the "new poetry" in this country, but it would eventually have gathered impetus, even if you had not noticed it. You were, I think, shrewd enough to foresee the wave of attention it has secured, but I doubt whether, at the beginning, you brought it forth because of a deep feeling regarding its beauty and importance. You have done little for the less popular "new poets" beyond printing their excellent poetry now and then. Your favors have been reserved for those "new poets" whose work has won at least budding popularity. . . .

Harriet Monroe sent Bodenheim's poems to him December 6, 1916, and restrained herself to the comment, "Perhaps sometime you will feel like telling me you regret your rather absurd letter." That did not end the affair, for William Carlos Williams intervened solemnly December 18, 1916: "I appeal to you for Bodenheim. I do not know that he will accept my mediation but should I be able to get him to reconsider his withdrawal of the verse and play you had accepted would you print them for him. It seems to me that a man as young as Bodenheim, as willfully unattractive as he is and as unfortunate—physically, not spiritually—being the artist he is should be forgiven much—one might even be exceptionally generous with him at no great loss. I await your answer with great interest." He wrote again a month later, on January 15, 1917: "The matter of an apology is between Harriet Monroe and Maxwell Bodenheim—this has no relation to 'Poetry.' 'Poetry' should print work by M.B. regardless of animosities between editor and poet. If work of sufficient merit is received in your office from the pen of Bodenheim would you for a personal reason block its acceptance or not? I am anxious to have word from you on this point." Williams does not seem consistent in reproaching Harriet Monroe for expressing personal bias as editor of *Poetry*: only the spring before he had urged her to let herself loose in the magazine, reproaching her for making an impersonal institution of *Poetry*. The full ground of the quarrel between Harriet Monroe and Bodenheim, which also involved his exclusion from a lecture series sponsored by *Poetry* in the fall of 1916, does not appear. She wrote an account to

Williams that got this reply: "I am sorry to hear of Bodenheim's rotten taste in treating you as he did. I am trying to get in touch with him."[23] That was the end of Williams' involvement in the quarrel.

Bodenheim made it up the next year, but remained embroiled with Harriet Monroe, in a series of letters that are comic but painful, marking the course of a progressive disintegration in Bodenheim. "Harriet Monroe," he wrote September 16, 1919, "you often seem to me as unreal as a character taken from a melodramatic page by Dickens: I write this very sadly." She replied, "As for your further observations, and the general tone of your letters and conduct during the past three years, I despair of our ever understanding each other, so discussion would be useless."[24] Bodenheim next wrote to announce his permanent departure for England to join the ranks of the exiles, but he returned in three months, writing August 6, 1920, that England "does not offer much material hospitality to aliens, British subjects dominating all lines from brick-laying to magazine-poetry. . . . I feel now that I have shown little ability to separate the personal from the impersonal in my decision never to appear in your magazine." Bodenheim made an impression in London, for Harriet Monroe wrote back to *Poetry* from a European visit in 1923: "I am questioned more or less about Maxwell Bodenheim by these English poets. According to Aiken, M.B.'s brief visit to London made him, and American poets in general, so unpopular as to put back the cause for twenty years."[25]

Bodenheim's disintegration, which was to prolong itself for years, was only an episode in the general disintegration of 1916. Alice Corbin Henderson thought none of it serious, and wrote December 11 to console Harriet Monroe:

> . . . I hasten to tell you . . . not to bother about Bodenheim. As for E.P.—he can easily be set right and so can Dr. Williams if need be. I am sorry that you had the experience and sorry for your sake that you didn't keep the poems and print them and get back at least $35 worth of your own money! But I can not help being

23. Letter of January 26, 1917.
24. Copy of a letter filed with the Bodenheim correspondence.
25. Letter of May 27, 1923, to Margery Swett.

relieved that you did not print "Brown." That sort of stuff is *impossible*. I read it, you know, before I left. . . . As for his perverted similes that he calls "quaint images," we can do without them too. He doesn't *grow* a bit—and the first things we accepted, I think, remain the best. The others are patches of D. H. Lawrence and Fletcher stuck together with a little Bodenheim adhesive tape.

The common denominator of the quarrels and discomforts of 1916 seems an overdeveloped Poetry Renaissance. In the *Dial* for November 22, 1917, Conrad Aiken explained why the conspicuous fashion for poetry produced a sense of suffocation in the serious poets:

> The confectioners . . . are the prettifiers, the brighteners of life, the lilting ones. They fill our standard magazines; they are annually herded by Mr. Braithwaite into his anthology; and now, taking advantage of the poetic decuman wave and the delusions of publishers, they are swamping the land with their sweet wares. The conservative press flings garlands at them, the "Literary Digest" quotes them, the Poetry Society of America (alas!) fetes them. Hourly they grow more numerous, more powerful. The courageous and creative ones, and those who look to poetry for truthfulness and for a consciousness of life always subtler and more individually worked will soon have to fight for their lives. And how, indeed, shall they be able to fight? There are no giants to be slain—rather, a host of pigmies, and all alike. A poem by one might bear the signature of any. They sing in chorus rather than singly.

Renewed competition among the little magazines in 1916 and 1917 added to the glut of poetry. Two new poetry magazines appeared: *Contemporary Verse* and the *Poetry Review*, a new pulpit for William Stanley Braithwaite. A new journal with the ambition to enhance American national self-consciousness, the *Seven Arts*, which appeared at the end of 1916, published a fair amount of poetry. *Reedy's Mirror* published no poetry of significance, but *Others*, the *Egoist*, and the *Little Review*, as well as *Poetry*, printed some important verse. The publication record of these other magazines does not suggest that concentration would have been easy for *Poetry*. Nineteen sixteen was not a year in which Harriet

Monroe lost many beautiful poems to her rivals; there is no parallel to the *Others* publication of the "Portrait of a Lady" and "Peter Quince at the Clavier" in 1915. If concentration would have helped *Poetry* to stand out from the rest, it is hard to see where the poetry was to come from. The period 1916–18 was a time of transition and adjustment for most of the new poets. Undoubtedly World War I had much to do with the general distraction.

Nevertheless, *Poetry*'s situation altered so radically from 1916 to 1917 that it is difficult to restrain the judgment that Harriet Monroe had squandered an unparalleled editorial opportunity. If she had printed Pound's manuscripts as quickly and willingly as she printed them in 1913, she would not have had to face the loss of Pound, Eliot, and Yeats as contributors. Of course, she was trapped between fears of the censor on one hand, and money shortages on the other. It seems a case of falling between two stools. She did not please her guarantors well enough to have any chance of increasing her rate to contributors, as Pound had urged; on the other hand, she remained too dependent on their goodwill to operate without considering the Post Office censor. In another arrangement of stools, she had cooperated with Pound to a degree that seemed irresponsible to the respectable literary world; on the other hand, she had not cooperated with Pound to a degree that impressed Pound. One cannot help feeling concern for her desperate efforts to keep all the warring factions in balanced relation. Even without her paralyzed response to Eliot, they seem foredoomed to failure. If she managed to reconcile Kreymborg with Sandburg, and soothe Lowell and Fletcher about Pound's propaganda while restraining theirs, if the guarantors and the censor were both appeased, and the huge successes of Masters and Frost acknowledged but kept in proportion, if Pound was at least quiet about Lindsay, Harriet Monroe could not indefinitely continue to keep all the important elements of the pattern in balance. In 1916 she seems to have lost track of Yeats, for example. *Poetry* remained out of communication with him after the publication of his group in February, 1916, and in March, 1917, Ezra Pound had a group of Yeats poems promised for publication in the *Little Review*.[26] The pressure of the conflicting demands on her distracted Harriet Monroe's attention away from Yeats, and he interpreted distraction as lack of interest.

Heroic as were her efforts to present a broadly balanced spectrum of all the poetic schools, they seemed futile in 1916. James Branch Cabell wrote a few months later to express a judgment of *Poetry* that is substantially the one Ezra Pound has perpetuated:

> . . . after considering intently the magazine as published during the last two years, I have come to the unwilling conclusion that *Poetry* is really a pernicious publication. You had, I think, a wonderful chance: and—again, of course, this is mere personal opinion—you missed it, with mildly dangerous results. . . . Pray understand me—I don't question that you honestly admire your selections. And I too admire quite honestly your ardor and industry, and your motives, even while I regret their manifestations.[27]

Lacking the money that would provide the elite with a living wage, and a volume of good poetry sufficient to fill the pages of her magazine, Harriet Monroe decided at the end of 1916 that some new editorial emphasis was necessary. She chose to promote the young and the unknown. With the pressure of all the schools on her, the future was perhaps the only direction that lay open. Temperamentally, the option for the future seems natural to her, and it was the choice that had worked in 1914, when the "discoveries" of Sandburg, Masters, and Stevens had restored the balance in her awkward relationship to Pound. She replied November 22, 1916, to John Gould Fletcher's suggestions that she publish no more newcomers but concentrate on the best work of the established poets:

> In regard to what you say about the management of the magazine, I think a little reflection will convince you that it would be impossible to run it on that basis. The magazine was started and the guarantors were secured primarily to give the young poets a chance to be heard. If we should change it to be the organ of a special group it would lose its use, and the guarantors would, I am sure, one and all, discontinue. As for my part in it, I should

26. Pound to John Quinn, March 26, 1917, cited in B. L. Reid, *John Quinn*, p. 285.
27. Letter of April 20, 1917, without context in a very small correspondence file.

become merely a kind of register, and all the pleasure of gambling on the young and unknown would be gone. If that had been the policy of the magazine from the beginning think how many of your friends would never have been in it at all. You tell me to stop asking people for poems. The truth is that I have never asked anybody: before the magazine started I issued circulars generally asking for the cooperation of poets, but since then I have not asked more than three persons to contribute, and those requests were a kind of courtesy extended when I asked for the loan of poems for an anthology. It is an awkward thing to ask for contributions, because an editor might not like them when they came.

Fletcher was not one of Harriet Monroe's confidants, and one need not take this letter quite literally. Probably she asked Robert Frost and William Carlos Williams for verse while arranging her anthology, for both suddenly reappear among her contributors in 1916, without explaining themselves and in no very sweet temper with her. It seems unlikely that the guarantors would have revolted one and all if she had minimized the publication of young, unknown poets. But her account of her own motives seems genuine; the pleasure of the quest for young, unpublished genius sustained her through the ugliness of the literary wars in which *Poetry* became involved. Beyond the figure of any concretely realized irate genius glimmered the consoling image of the still more powerful poet whom no one had yet read. But 1916 was a bad year in which to renew the quest for the unknown. All the discoveries had been fished out of the sea.

The depth of *Poetry*'s troubles is measured by the recognition given it in W. S. Braithwaite's *Anthology of Magazine Verse for 1916*. Braithwaite, who had maintained a hostile or bewildered silence during *Poetry*'s great years, failing to acknowledge the existence of the magazine in his annual survey, showed a ghoul's instinct for calamity. In analyzing the Poetry Renaissance in his preface for 1916, he suggested that "the point of departure from conservatism may be dated from the establishment of *Poetry: A Magazine of Verse*, the instrument of Ezra Pound's radicalism." But he recognized only to dismiss: ". . . Mr. Sandburg, a much-heralded innovator, has not lived up to prophecy; the radical influence of *Poetry* itself has waned, the collected poems of

Pound . . . find it difficult to obtain an American publisher, and the magazine *Others*, largely supported by his disciples, has, I understand, ceased publication." Braithwaite named Alfred Kreymborg, Amy Lowell, Masters, Frost, and James Oppenheim, editor of the *Seven Arts*, the significant survivors of the experimental stages of the Poetry Renaissance.

Harriet Monroe felt that this attack required a reply, and wrote in *Poetry* for January, 1917: "this is the first time the Boston dictator in these annual reviews has even mentioned *Poetry* or its influence. We should be duly grateful that he has finally discovered us, though—alas—with polite deprecation, as 'the organ of Ezra Pound's radicalism,' and with the long-delayed admission, not yet intended as a compliment, that 'the point of departure from conservatism'—he should have included his own conservatism—'may be dated from the establishment of *Poetry*. . . .'" Her position must have seemed weak to her, that she was driven to wring endorsement from such a mean attack. Braithwaite's annual collection was always noticed seriously by the *Dial*, and his distortions were apparently influential in confusing people. Alice Corbin Henderson thought Braithwaite's attack the work of Amy Lowell, who was to some extent associated with him: "Tell Carl not to make too much of Amy's spectric kisses. Braithwaite is her tool. Amy can't dictate to *Poetry*. Amy will raise herself by any means, whether it is a rotten prop like B. or a sound prop like Pound or Fletcher; and once up she will kick the prop aside. I can't help but suspect Amy of being secretly pleased by having it stated that the radical influence of *Poetry* has waned. She could never bear to have Boston's supremacy supplanted by Chicago."[28]

Ezra Pound's reaction to the Braithwaite attack was not immediately clear; he drifted altogether out of touch with *Poetry* over the winter of 1916–17. He sent two editorial notes in letters of October 21 and November 3, 1916. On December 22, 1916, he wrote full of enthusiasm for a paper read by Edgar Jepson at the Poets' Club: "The outburst of a man whose critical sense has kept him from publishing any verse for nearly twenty years. It was not gentle and wandering theoretic, nor was it so suggestive as

28. Letter of December 1, 1916.

Hueffer on Impressionism, but it was in its own way as important." Jepson was a member of the Rhymers' Club of the nineties who had developed into a writer of popular fiction; he was coauthor of some of the Arsène Lupin thrillers. His paper is presumably "Words and the Poet," published in *Poetry* for May, 1917. Pound sent other short letters to *Poetry* discussing a review of the Sitwells' *Wheels* and proposing a series of articles on French poets by himself, Eliot, and Jean de Bosschère. He sent Alice Corbin Henderson the manuscript of his long first draft of "Three Cantos" sometime over the winter. She mailed it from Santa Fe, commenting in a letter of February 6, 1917: "E.P. has sent me a long poem for *Poetry*. He sent it so I could read it and then send it to you. Of course, it will be caviar to the general, no doubt, but I like it." Between January 5 and April 18, 1917, Pound did not communicate with the *Poetry* office at all.

Harriet Monroe herself was out of the office for six weeks in the late winter of 1917, stricken with influenza. She sent Pound's "Three Cantos" to Robert Frost for an opinion, presumably because she was ill and unable to cope with the manuscript; nothing in Frost's correspondence invites a share in the editorial responsibilities of the magazine. His relationship to Harriet Monroe was detached from beginning to end, although he came closer to *Poetry* in 1916 and 1917, with a series of letters about the publication of "Snow," and letters of September 4, 1916, and January 9, 1917, sending poetry by English friends, notably Edward Thomas. He became expansive when "Snow" won a hundred-dollar second prize in November, 1917: "it is my first real prize in a long life. Hitherto my utmost had been a few dollars for running at a Caledonia Club Picnic, a part interest in a pair of ear-rings, and a part interest in a gold-headed cane for impersonations at a masquerade, a gold medal for sheer goodness in a high school, and a Detur for scholarship at Harvard."[29] But after that he did not send another poem until July 21, 1920.

Picking up the threads of *Poetry* after her illness, Harriet Monroe inquired of Alice Corbin Henderson about the long-silent foreign correspondent, but Mrs. Henderson had not heard from

29. Telegram of November 2, 1917, in *Selected Letters*, #171, p. 222.

him recently. His vehement critiques of the monthly issues of *Poetry* had not been produced that winter. Mrs. Henderson wrote: "Don't worry about Ezra's condoling with me over *Poetry*—he hasn't done it, and I have imagined that his thunders must have gone direct to you. . . . A propos of Bodenheim who evidently made a remark about your favoring other poets or something foolish, E.P. told B. he was a fool, etc. etc. He's asked me to forward some suggestions about the prose, and I will, if I can lay my hands on them."[30] A few days later, on April 18, 1917, Ezra Pound wrote, enclosing the receipt form for payment for his few short editorial notices in *Poetry* over six months, and suggesting that *Poetry* might prefer to do without him in the future. Whatever a foreign correspondent was worth to *Poetry*, he wrote, he considered that his services over six months rated more than $7.68. He added that *Poetry* payment for the full year 1916 had shrunk to seventeen pounds. He thought that Harriet Monroe might want to break the connection but was constrained because of his long association with the magazine. He wasn't sure, because the great number of his poems that she printed in *The New Poetry* suggested that she still admired his work, but he knew that many people wanted him off the magazine, and he preferred a clean break to reluctant doles.

This note crossed a letter from Harriet Monroe in the mails, for Pound wrote again April 24, 1917, glad to hear from her, sorry about her illness, pleased by her decision to print "Three Cantos" in three numbers of the magazine, sorry she herself didn't much like the poem, and asking her to write more often if she expected him to keep in touch with the magazine. The acceptance of "Three Cantos," as well as the twenty pages of his verse that Harriet Monroe selected for *The New Poetry*—the biggest block of verse by one poet in the book—reminded Pound that she had been one of his relatively enthusiastic readers over the years, and deflected his intention to resign from *Poetry*. He did not give any notice of his fully developed plan to act as

30. Letter of April 16, 1917. Pound's suggestions about the prose seem to be the letter dated "March, 1917," in *Letters*, #121, p. 108. The letter in the *Poetry* Papers is two half sheets cut from a longer letter, with this comment in Pound's hand: "you can send these pages to H.M. as they stand." The only date is a note in Harriet Monroe's hand, "Ansd. June 28, '17."

foreign editor for Margaret Anderson's *Little Review*, but explained himself in the opening pages of the *Little Review* for May, 1917:

> My connection with the *Little Review* does not imply a severance of my relations with *Poetry*, for which I still remain Foreign Correspondent and in which my poems will continue to appear until its guarantors revolt.[31]
>
> I would say, however, in justification both of *Poetry* and myself, that *Poetry* has never been "the instrument" of my "radicalism." I respect Miss Monroe for all that she has done for the support of American poetry, but in the conduct of her magazine my voice and vote have always been the vote and voice of a minority.
>
> I recognize that she, being "on the ground," may be much better fitted to understand the exigencies of magazine publication in America, but *Poetry* has done numerous things to which I could never have given my personal sanction, and which could not have occurred in any magazine which had constituted itself my "instrument." *Poetry* has shown an unflagging courtesy to a lot of old fools and fogies whom I should have told to go to hell tout pleinement and bonnement. . . .
>
> Had *Poetry* been my instrument I should never have permitted the deletion of certain fine English words from poems where they rang well and soundly. Neither would I have felt it necessary tacitly to comply with the superstition that the Christian religion is indispensable, or that it had always existed, or that its existence is ubiquitous, or irrevocable, or eternal. . . . If any human activity is sacred it is the formulation of thought in clear speech for the use of humanity; any falsification or evasion is evil. The codes of propriety are all local, parochial, transient: a consideration of them, other than as subject matter, has no place in the arts.
>
> I can say these things quite distinctly and without in the least detracting from my praise of the spirited manner in which Miss Monroe has conducted her paper. She is faced with the practical

31. The peculiar timing which has Pound asserting that he will continue as *Poetry*'s foreign correspondent, in a magazine published within twelve days of his note of April 18 that offered to break the connection with *Poetry*, is explained by the fact that the *Little Review* usually published late. Pound wrote John Quinn on April 18 (Reid, *John Quinn*, p. 290) that he had written an attack on *Poetry* for the *Little Review*, which sounds like a reaction against Harriet Monroe's defense of the minor poet in *Poetry* for March—"Hard Times Indeed." But the editorial that appeared in the *Little Review*, with its comment about future publication of his verse, probably was revised after Pound got word about the publication of "Three Cantos."

problem of circulating a magazine in a certain peculiar milieu, which thing being so, I have nothing but praise for the way she has done it. But the magazine does not express my convictions. Attacks on it, grounded in such belief, and undertaken in the magnanimous hope of depriving me of part of my sustenance, can not be expected to have more than a temporary success and that among ill-informed people. . . .

I can not believe that the mere height of the Rocky Mountains will produce lofty poetry. . . . I can not believe that the mere geographical expanse of America will produce of itself excellent writing. . . . Neither can I look forward with longing to a time when each village shall rejoice in a bad local poetaster making bad verse in the humdrum habitual way that the local architect puts up bad buildings. The arts are not the mediocre habit of mankind. There is no common denominator between the little that is good and the waste that is dull, mediocre. . . .

. . . the patron is absolutely at the mercy of the artist, and the artist at the cost of some discomfort—personal, transient discomfort—is almost wholly free of the patron, whether this latter be an individual, or the hydra-headed detestable vulgus.

There is no misanthropy in a thorough contempt for the mob. There is no respect for mankind save in respect for detached individuals.[32]

This manifesto is Pound's sharpest assertion of the qualitative superiority of the artist, and about as good a description as one could want of his incompatibility with *Poetry*'s ideal of the great audience, and with Harriet Monroe's attachment to the cause of the minor poet.

Pound's editorial looks rather odd in the *Little Review*, however, for that magazine had not been functioning in vigorous support of the poetic elite. The *Little Review* wobbled badly over the period, late in 1916 and early in 1917, when it moved from Chicago to California to New York. Jane Heap, Margaret Anderson's new associate in the magazine, had a more steady literary sense than Margaret Anderson possessed, and was the mistress of the peculiar intimidating wit that is the hallmark of the

32. "Editorial," *Little Review*, May, 1917 (copyright 1917 by Margaret C. Anderson). Reprinted by permission of New Directions Publishing Corporation and Faber and Faber, Ltd., publishers and Agents for the Trustees of the Ezra Pound Literary Property Trust. All rights reserved.

later *Little Review*. Her influence seems the explanation of a new editorial policy emphasizing art over anarchism. But before Pound came in as foreign correspondent, the change was not propitious. The paper and the proofreading of the numbers declined, issues appeared irregularly, and the editorial address shifted around confusingly. The level of literary criticism was not exalted. Jane Heap in March, 1917, defended Amy Lowell against Harriet Monroe's slighting review of *Men, Women, and Ghosts*, asserting that Miss Lowell "has not come the way of Masters or of Dreiser. She is really the first poet in America to express in her writing something of that leisure from which they tell us art flowers best. . . . *Men, Women and Ghosts* is a beautiful book, full of stately measures." Results of a *vers libre* contest were announced in the April, 1917, issue, with copious quotations from the three judges, William Carlos Williams, Eunice Tietjens, and Helen Hoyt, and protest against their judgments, this by Margaret Anderson: "Now I hope these judges will not get provoked with me or feel that I am being personal or any of the other things that one is usually accused of when one is most impersonally talking his 'cause.' I am simply overflowing with criticism of their valuations and I must speak it out. These two poems are pretty awful, I think. Where are the winged words that make poetry something more than thoughts or ideas of emotions?" There is no need to slight the *Little Review*, but Pound's May editorial requires some perspective. In leaving *Poetry* he was not abandoning middle-class mediocrity for a journal that had achieved aristocratic critical poise. He was only exchanging the great audience as an ideal for "winged words."

This move of Pound's stimulated some painful reactions and lengthy mutual explanations at the *Poetry* office. Alice Corbin Henderson was at first outraged. She wrote Harriet Monroe on June 9, 1917:

> As you know, I have always been a staunch advocate of E.P. and I would hate now to do anything to cut off his income or anything of that sort. But obviously we have different ideals of conduct. I can not understand why he should so calmly assume that he was at liberty to be foreign correspondent of the Little Review *and* Poetry, unless he had made arrangements with you in advance? It

isn't as if the L.R. were paying him handsomely. I know he has felt that Poetry has held up his reviews lately and has not paid much for them—otherwise I don't know anything of your relations. I suppose the real trouble is that Ezra *has no sense of values.* To connect oneself with the L.R. as it has been for the last two or three months is perhaps suicidal enough to be a sufficient punishment in itself! Isn't he a great idiot?

But on further reflection she softened. She wrote June 15:

About Ezra, I think I would simply write him a letter and say that you were surprised that he should assume, without saying anything to you, that he could continue as F.C. for Poetry and for the L.R. as well, and that his policy of washing linen in public is not exactly in good taste, nor gentlemanly, etc. Whatever else you care to say of course I can't dictate. At first I was simply furious, but I am honestly too sorry for E.P. to continue mad. He ruins his own case continually and perpetually. I told him he was an idiot to tie up with the L.R. before I saw this last no. Haven't written since. Of course Eunice [Tietjens] doesn't like E.P., but I am very sensible of the many benefits conferred by E.P. not only upon *Poetry* editorially, but upon poetry at large—upon Eunice incidentally whose later work has been decidedly Poundish, and Amy Lowell's Lacquers ["Lacquer Prints" in *Poetry* for March, 1917] were very much so, but I mean more than this—he has helped criticism and has made for less sentimentality and softness etc. Of course he has his own quite noticeable faults. Do just as you think best.

Harriet Monroe scribbled a note on the back of the receipt form sent out with the check (twenty-one pounds) for "Three Cantos" June 11, 1917: "I have much to say, but no time to say it now, so I won't delay this draft. This is the best I can possibly do for the poem—just now anyway. Poetry is strapped—and terrible bills coming in for paper etc. H.M." She was at that time preoccupied with her campaign to raise a new endowment for *Poetry*; the original five-year pledges were to run out in the fall of 1917. When Pound next wrote, July 2, 1917, he was back on his old footing as foreign correspondent, with a rambling letter full of comment on the current issues of *Poetry*, on the current state of the movement, and on plans for future issues. His divided allegiance seems to have been no problem to him. He wrote that Harriet Monroe should return unwanted editorial manuscripts promptly; he could speak his mind in the *Little Review*, and having few friends in America besides herself, he needn't pull his punches. The *Little Review* would on occasion pay a higher rate for poems than *Poetry*; perhaps the guarantors would thereby be prodded into more generous subsidies. Pound said he had no love either for New York or for Chicago, but wanted food for the very few poets worth sustaining, and would cooperate for that end with thieves, if necessary—and all nationalities and political persuasions be damned. With the help of God, he wrote, he would use the *Little Review* to scourge the elders who had worked so long to stifle American literature.

Harriet Monroe had formulated her attitude toward Pound's double correspondenceship by the end of June, and wrote Pound a letter that crossed his in the mails. The essential problem, as she saw it, was that Pound might now be using his influence in London against rather than for *Poetry*. She cited the Yeats poems in the June *Little Review*—a beautiful group including "The Wild Swans at Coole," "Presences," "Men Improve with the Years," "A Deep Sworn Vow," "The Collar Bone of a Hare," "Broken Dreams," and "In Memory of William Pollexfen"—and in the August *Little Review*, "Upon a Dying Lady," for which Yeats had rejected *Poetry*'s offer.[33] Her letter is dated in draft July 3, 1917:

My dear E.P.:

I have been somewhat surprised at your taking up with the *Little Review* without saying a word to me about it; still more at your airing in public matters which I should have thought anyone would have held confidential—and in a misrepresenting sort of way moreover, for there has been no spirit of compromise in *Poetry*. I never pretended to hand over the Editorship and make it your "organ." Also I have marvelled somewhat over the bad taste, and, I must confess, the dullness of your slam at Tagore, whom you once admired. And though Eliot is clever, I am not over-

33. Harriet Monroe had offered Yeats's agent eleven dollars per page, when her standard rate was eight dollars, but the poems were withdrawn because the price was too low. (Harriet Monroe to C. Paget, June 8, 1917, a copy in the Yeats correspondence.)

whelmed by your first numbers. But all this may be according to your ideas of good faith—I could with some effort perhaps try to understand them. The item which strains most severely the belief I have always had in your fundamental loyalty is the Little Review's printing of poems by Yeats in July [*sic*] and August— poems, which, apparently, if you are still acting for us, should have been sent to us. This, taken in conjunction with the fact that Mr. Yeats has recently refused, for another poem, the highest rate per page we ever offered him, would seem to indicate that your influence with him of late has not been in our favor. So I should like to know what is your idea of our present relation—are you still expecting to send us the best verse you can get hold of, and to confine your *Little Review* activities to prose?

I am more sensitive than you seem to be over any connection with such a magazine as the Little Review has been over the past year or so, when I thought even its Editor—in fact, everyone except its creditors—was losing faith in it. Perhaps you can pull it up—doubtless you would not try unless someone (perhaps Mr. John Quinn?) were giving it more solid financing than it has ever had.

She went on to explain various delays in printing Pound's editorials and reviews, and defended several rejections that had angered him in 1916:

Your prose, when you take the trouble, is good hard stuff, done with style. But some that you send us, like one or two editorials now in the office, may be called "slop" with possibly more justice than anything which troubles you in our prose section—loose, shapeless, full of repetitions, etc. And when it is slop thrown in other peoples' faces that antagonizes without other result, I have to draw the line. For example, that squib against some honor—I forget what—to Longfellow: it seems rather late in the day for us to bother with Longfellow, but if not, the beard-pulling should be done with more air, more manner. And your violence against all things American doesn't strike home as it would if you used a more Gallic stroke; also of course, the effect is left-handed, because you are expatriate. You are your own worst enemy, alas! Something in you fails to recognize that a little rudimentary tact is not compromise; that anyone who carries a bludgeon for friend and foe finds himself before long, butting the empty air. My very

respect for your work makes me wish you would not plant yourself so violently in front of it.

Pound's reaction to Harriet Monroe's letter of July 3 marks the
effective end of his foreign correspondence for *Poetry*, although
the break was not made explicit for two more years. His reply,
dated July 23, 1917, was long, repetitious, and disconnected.
Pound began with the point that *Poetry* was committed by its
original program to support poets as bountifully as sculptors and
painters were supported. He therefore felt "a freeze-out" when
his own income from *Poetry* fell to thirty shillings for six months,
and he felt that the offer of thirty-five dollars for Yeats's "Dying
Lady," when

> any sculptor or painter of any standing . . . would get £1000 for
> work of equivalent calibre, was a gratuitous insult. I think the
> guarantors have come to look on our art as too much a matter of
> private charity, and to think their doles may be reduced in-
> definitely. I shall certainly bull the market on Yeats' and Eliot's
> stuff. If the guarantors want the swank of making Chicago THE
> center, they can fork up. If with infinitely less cash at my disposal
> I can concentrate the best verse in the L.R., so much the worse for
> Chicago. It will of course be difficult to buy good stuff for less
> than ten dollars a page.

Pound softened this by putting the blame on the guarantors, but
the essential argument is clear: Harriet Monroe and *Poetry* were
worth exactly what they could pay. A number of comments in
the letter blurred the edge of this assertion without changing it.
Pound explained that Yeats had given his poems to the *Little
Review* for June because he did not trust *Poetry* to get them out in
time to synchronize with English publication. Pound had no
apologies for anything else. *Poetry* had always gagged him.
Braithwaite had paid him a left-handed compliment by attacking
Poetry at a time when he had contributed very little to it. He
responded to Harriet Monroe's remark about belief in his fundamental loyalty, that his idea of loyalty did not require that he
huddle in her fortification forever. The *Little Review* would push
things ahead. He meant to publish mostly prose there, anyway,
on subjects that would not be appropriate for *Poetry*.

Earlier in the letter Pound had said that his own verse would continue to go to *Poetry*, barring the "L'Homme Moyen Sensuel" in the September *Little Review*, which he knew Harriet Monroe would never have accepted. These various definitions of his foreign correspondence for the *Little Review* are confusing. At one point, he wrote that he would concentrate the best verse, Yeats and Eliot in particular, in the *Little Review*; at another, he asserted that he would send his own poetry to Harriet Monroe; at another, he wrote that the *Little Review* would be mainly for prose. But the confusion vanishes when one looks at the three remarks from a financial point of view. Yeats and Eliot would go to the *Little Review* unless *Poetry* outbid him for their verses; if *Poetry* put up its rate to corner the market on poetry, the *Little Review* would be mainly an outlet for prose; whatever happened, Pound would sell his own verse to Harriet Monroe, because he wanted the extra income a *Poetry* payment would give him. John Quinn's subsidy for the *Little Review* provided a very modest allowance for Pound's services as foreign editor, and if Pound were to pay himself a decent rate for his own poetry, he would have to reduce the sum available to pay for the contributions of other artists.[34]

Pound went on in his letter to acknowledge that mere bad communications had something to do with his impression that he was a burden to Harriet Monroe and that the advisory board longed to be free of him. Possibly he had not taken sufficient account of her illness that winter, and of the problems of getting news from Chicago. He offered to look up the young English poets, in search of new contributors, if *Poetry* intended to renew its endowment. But he did not see any useful function for *Poetry* outside the one he had outlined in a letter of January 23, 1916: the payment of a high page rate would give poets a living wage without overproducing, which would attract all the poets worth printing and drive the "old skin-the-gut" magazines out of the poetry business. "Poetry should put up her rates of payment and finally finish off Harpers, Scribner, Century, Atlantic. They have gone on long enough. . . . I know this is repetition. Still it

34. See Reid, *John Quinn*, p. 284, and Pound to Margaret Anderson, in *Letters*, #120, p. 107.

is a fact. Chicago, America in general has got nothing but money. If they want to be an art centre they must at least contribute *that*, they must at least give what they've got. IT IS NOT SO GOOD as creative ability, not by a damn sight. It is not so good as critical ability, not by a damn sight. But if they don't even show a readiness—Basta."

When one remembers Pound's irritable and inconsistent behavior through most of *Poetry*'s first two years, his eagerness in 1913 to branch out into the *Smart Set*, whose rate was higher, and his vehemence about the award of money prizes in 1913 and 1914, it seems as if his attitude toward the Chicago magazine and its editor was consistent throughout. *Poetry* was a cash box improbably made available in Chicago, where neither poetic creation nor the enlightened understanding of poetry was to be expected. This cash box he felt was his by right of creative superiority, and he used it until it ran out of funds. When it did he left it, glad to be rid of a connection that he found embarrassing from every point of view but the financial one.

The nastiness of Pound's attitude toward *Poetry* is veiled by three complicating factors. Chicago did have some creative and critical identity of its own, and when this became obvious, toward the middle of 1914, Pound had to bank down the arrogance of his tone. In addition, he seemed briefly carried away by a genuine sympathy for the Masters of *Spoon River*, one that led him to feel a common cause with Chicago. By coincidence, most of his other allies and resources deserted him in 1915, and made the *Poetry* connection crucially important for him. But when he emerged from that bad period, newly subsidized by John Quinn, to find the American poetry renaissance disintegrating and Masters "gone to pot," he returned easily and naturally to his first attitude. Nor would he feel any nastiness in his treatment of Harriet Monroe. She furnished the manure that had nourished the tree of his art; having exhausted whatever nourishment she could provide, he left her in the dust. If she had some spark of nobility in her, of "light-seeking," she would feel repaid by the beauty of his art. If she chose to nurse injuries based on illusions that she deserved some "loyalty" from Pound, it was only the comic presumption of a clod aspiring to be a fruit tree. Pound

213

had put his notions of the relation of the artist to his fellow men in that metaphor during the audience debate of October, 1914. He really meant it, and he acted in accordance with it.

He closed his long, disjointed letter of July 23, 1917, with hopes for the *Little Review*, and with the offer to allow Chicago to continue its subsidy of his poetry movement if the money could be raised. With Joyce, Lewis, Yeats, Eliot, Waley, and Lady Gregory in its pages, the *Little Review* did not seem likely to discredit him. But he would not mind restricting the *Little Review* to prose if Harriet Monroe wanted, if the guarantors would do their bit, and if the work were printed quickly. But he couldn't wait for Mrs. Moody.

This letter marks the effective end of Pound's foreign correspondence for *Poetry*, for there was no new money available in Chicago, and the connection was inevitably broken. Harriet Monroe was busy in the summer of 1917 with the campaign to get her 1912 guarantors to renew their pledges for another five years, a campaign that had limited success. The new financing left *Poetry* with a smaller endowment: the income from guarantors in 1918 was $4,605, down from $5,990 in 1917. Her original appeal for funds had been based on "Gilded Age" patterns of patronage. The newly rich of America after the Civil War had been eager to construct symphonies and libraries and art museums, to build up the institutions of a cultural life in their raw new cities and to put themselves in a princely role. But these motives were fading in 1912, and had pretty well exhausted themselves by 1917. In the middle of World War I, with the confusing social changes of the twentieth century already manifest, the appeal to combined motives of local pride, personal display, and yearning for beauty and tradition no longer worked very well. As Harriet Monroe explained to Edward Ryerson, October 10, 1921, "I find it difficult to get new Guarantors—people seem to expect the old friends of an enterprise to carry it on." Since Pound contended that *Poetry* needed a twenty-five-dollar page rate to insure a living wage to the few decent poets, and that *Poetry* served no other useful function, it follows mathematically that the few decent poets under Pound's generalship would abandon *Poetry* as the meagerness of its financial base became apparent.

The break with Pound and his poets, which did not become absolute until 1919, was painful for Harriet Monroe. A detached observer might conclude that given her squeamishness and Pound's arrogance, the exigencies of literary politics, and a shortage of cash, *Poetry* had to lose many of the new poets. The ideal unity of the movement that the magazine embodied in 1914 was a glittering illusion, impossible to sustain for long. But some creative ideal of a periodical that could present month by month the unfolding reality of the new poetry lay behind Harriet Monroe's efforts to hold all the schools together in her magazine. When she had to acknowledge that the balance was broken and the schools scattered, she felt a profound sense of failure.

In 1922, looking back over the magazine's first ten years of publishing, she expressed a good deal of regret. "You have wasted a great opportunity," she quoted one correspondent, apparently James Branch Cabell, who wrote in April, 1917, that *Poetry* had missed "a wonderful chance." ("The Great Opportunity" is William Carlos Williams' title for his 1916 *Egoist* essay on the breakdown of *Others*; he probably picked up the phrase from Harriet Monroe's fiery reply to the *Dial* in May, 1914.) Her various misdeeds and mistakes haunted her: "the editor realizes only too deeply the magazine's many errors and derelictions; whatever it has done for the cause, unquestionably it might have done much more under the all-wise guidance of complete and perfect competence."[35] But she concluded that her magazine's basic weakness had been financial; she thought she might have found more subscribers somehow. *Poetry*'s failure to reach Harriet Monroe's ideal of the great audience lost it Pound's ideal, the concentration of the elite.

However, Harriet Monroe never gave enough weight to the censorship problem in *Poetry*'s history. If Pound had managed the audience debate cleverly, he might have awakened her imagination on the other irritating issue, because the censorship question and the audience question were related. Pound's letters do not make the connection, but it is plain in the letters of William Carlos Williams. Williams made the case that the function of a magazine of verse is to put a poem into the public or

35. "Mea Culpa," *Poetry*, September, 1922, p. 323.

objective world, to rescue the poet from the merely private relation he has to his poems: "What I have done clings to me horribly
until someone relieves me by ridicule, praise, or any possible
action. 'Poetry' cuts the rope between the ox and his dung."
Williams' idea of an audience was neither great nor small; it was
only the indefinite outside, the not-self, but even so dimly defined he found it crucial to his development as a poet. He stood
on Harriet Monroe's side of the question, not on that of Pound,
whose "dance, danced for the dance's sake, not a display"[36]
seems independent of any need for an audience or an "outside."

An exchange between Harriet Monroe and Williams during
the time when Pound joined the *Little Review* illustrates how
censorship for Williams destroyed the relation between the artist
and the "outside," simply by denying him free access to it. Williams had written to Miss Monroe on March 28, 1917, acknowledging a copy of *The New Poetry*, and almost seemed to be saying
good-bye: "Thank you for the new anthology: it is a very fine one
and should be popular if I am a good guesser. The world moves
fast doesn't it: I wish I felt as close to 'Poetry' as I used to. Good
luck." She must have replied asking him for verse, for he wrote
April 25, 1917, sending two poems. A note in her hand appears
on the letter: "*Smell* acd May 22 *History* acd if certain lines on
page 1 and 2 are omitted." Two passages are marked for omission
on the manuscript of "History" filed with the Williams correspondence:

> to mingle faience dug from the tomb,
> turquoise colored necklaces and
> belched wind from the stomach;
> delicately veined basins of agate, cracked
> and discolored and the stink of dried urine!

and

> Love rubbed on a bald head will make
> hair—and after? Love is
> a lice comber!

> Gnats on dung![37]

36. "Arnold Dolmetsch," in *Literary Essays*, p. 435 (copyright 1935 by Ezra Pound).
Reprinted by permission of New Directions Publishing Corporation and Faber and
Faber, Ltd., publishers and Agents for the Trustees of the Ezra Pound Literary Property
Trust.

37. Excerpts from "History" reprinted from *Collected Earlier Poems* by William Carlos

On May 25 Williams wrote again: "First of all I express my deep personal sympathy for you in your illness—happily passed. . . . Next I pay tribute to your extraordinary gentleness with me which I have always treasured for its great value. I recognize both the difficulties of a practical kind you are facing as well as certain habitual reactions of your own sensibilities which you cannot overcome and I think I have not been slow to express how unfortunate these are in my opinion but I cannot stop for these in writing what I find should be written." He went on to suggest that Miss Monroe leave out each objectionable word, "replacing the letters of those words with full stop points. The lines are to remain the same and all words not objectionable are to remain in position."

A week later Williams got word from his publisher that *Al Que Quiere!* was scheduled to come out before *Poetry* could be expected to print his two poems. He wrote Harriet Monroe on May 31, 1917, "If . . . you have a chance to publish the poems first—do what you please in the matter of omissions only please indicate the omission in some way." Harriet Monroe published the two poems, with her cuts in "History," in *Poetry* for July, 1917. Williams was resigned to this censorship, but not pleased by it. He wrote back June 18, 1917, forgiving the editor of *Poetry* in person of his wife, an attitude that became rather a habit with him:

> My wife says you have been "very decent" with me "far more decent than I would have been." I cannot get her to understand that our relationship is not that of a commercial house in need of a commodity and an individual with a first class article to dispose of. "I seem to imagine," I tell her, "that I am far more important than *Poetry*." But she still persists in wishing me to reform and be nice. . . .
>
> I certainly must thank you for printing my stuff in such an early issue as of course I realize it may be one thing to print work previously accepted on short notice but to have work sent to you with a request that it be printed at once is quite another. I hardly expected you to meet my wishes. Thank you.

Harriet Monroe must have strained her resources in making a large payment to Williams for these two poems. In this she was surely responding to the campaign for a living wage that Pound had been making.

But Williams had disagreed with Pound about the feasibility of a poet's supporting himself as a man of letters from the very beginning of their careers, and wrote July 11 that generous payments for verse would only create a false market, attracting imitative and opportunistic poets. Harriet Monroe's answer to this letter apparently betrayed the strain of her half-successful campaign to renew her endowment, for Williams on July 17 scolded her for jeopardizing the magazine by paying too much, and gave her an account of the function of a magazine of verse that differed from the one Pound sent a week later: "What you are doing by paying what you do for poems is this: you are jeopardizing the existence of your magazine in the mistaken notion that what poets want is money when in reality—though money is sorely needed also—they need space, an opportunity to gain print often and at will. This lack of space, this lack of opportunity to appear is the hell. And you will add to it by going bankrupt!"[38]

More effectively than Pound's assertions of the superiority of the artist, Williams made the essential case against the censorship of literature, and it is strange that Harriet Monroe continued so insensitive to the artist's side of the question, when she was so acutely aware of the poet's need for an audience. Perhaps she failed to take Williams seriously because he tended to define a magazine of verse as the mere extension of the poet—a "free running sewer," as he wrote of *Others*, in which the poet can gain print "at will." Their disagreements over conformity to conventions of capitalization and punctuation in his verse were symptomatic of the more important disagreement, whether a magazine could set any standards or conventions for its contributors, whether a magazine as a magazine had any right to an identity. Harriet Monroe's very personal commitment to *Poetry* made her answer to that question different from Williams'.

38. In Thirlwall, *Letters*.

DISTILLATION OF LEAF AND MUD

For William Carlos Williams

Along the creek bed
Damp humors proliferate;
Leaf litter impedes the stiff ginseng
And lichen streaks the tree trunks.
Here everything has been doing nothing quietly
        for a long time.

It distills a presence—
Wry, volatile, unpredictable,
Not altogether trustworthy,
A physician inclined to bully the layman.
He came to brace himself against
        empty spaces,
Like this one, and to speak the thereness of there.

FOUR

A Long Aftermath &

1917–22

Harriet Monroe's retrospective sense of waste, of loss of a great opportunity, gave Ezra Pound's break with *Poetry* a portentous emphasis that it lacked in 1917. Pound continued as foreign correspondent, sending an occasional contribution until April, 1919. *Poetry* continued to publish the familiar balanced array of the schools; if Eliot were lost to it, it still had a little of Pound and an occasional poem from Yeats. Pound as late as January 28, 1918, could describe *Poetry* as "*The* official organ for that art in America." It was not until 1920, with the competition of Scofield Thayer's new *Dial*, that most of the major new poets disappeared from its pages.

During the war years and the first postwar year in America, literary affairs were full of frustration and anticlimax. One of the keenest disappointments of this disappointing period was Pound's career as foreign editor of the *Little Review*. The glory of Pound's *Little Review* was the printing of *Ulysses*, but looking past Joyce to the poets, one does not find much interesting work published. T. S. Eliot was clearly the prize horse in Pound's stable, but he was worth relatively little in 1917; the *Little Review* printed "Le Directeur," "Mélange Adultère de Tout," "Lune de Miel," and "The Hippopotamus" in July, but nothing else of Eliot's until the fall of 1918. Harriet Monroe was right to isolate Yeats as the important loss to *Poetry* in Pound's move; his poems in the June, 1917, *Little Review* are very beautiful. But this loss was not absolute. When she wrote June 8, 1917, to Yeats's agent, "We should greatly dislike to give up printing poems by Mr. Yeats," she evidently corrected some misunderstanding. Yeats wrote back June 25 that he felt one pound per poem too small a price for "Upon a Dying Lady," but would "let you have something else if I can. I have nothing at the moment." On July 21 he sent "Ego Dominus Tuus," saying, "You can have it at any price you think fit."

Yeats and Eliot apart, the *Little Review* in the first year of Pound's direction printed the poetry of Maxwell Bodenheim, Louis Gilmore, Emanuel Morgan, John Rodker, Iris Barry, Robert Alden Sanborn, Arthur Waley, William Carlos Williams—"Improvisations" from *Kora in Hell*—Jane Heap, J. R. White, Hart Crane—one small indefinite poem, "In Shadow"— Jessie Dismorr, Ben Hecht, and Ezra Pound—most of "Langue d'Oc" and "Moeurs Contemporaines" of the collected *Personae*.[1] In June, 1918, Jane Heap, in a qualified rebellion, organized an American number: "It was made with no compromise to Margaret Anderson and Ezra Pound. It is not a revolt against our 'foreign all-star cast.'" The poetry of Wallace Stevens, William Carlos Williams, Amy Lowell, Carl Sandburg, Mark Turbyfill, S. Foster Damon, Alfred Kreymborg, and Max Michelson in the number was patronized by Margaret Anderson as "interesting . . . second interest" work. Ezra Pound looked back over the first year in the next issue, and congratulated himself with justice on Yeats's poems. But the only other poetry he could cite was "the small bulk of Mr. Eliot's poetry that has been written during the current year." Comments in the "Reader Critic" correspondence column in the same issue, on the American number, illustrate the silly rivalry between "English" and "American" poets that Pound's direction of the *Little Review* fostered:

> What a disparity! Endlessness of Hecht's desolate adjectives, the sillyness of Kreymborg, Amy Lowell the female poet, the endeavors of Williams to create a stir, the Rollo Peters stage scenery of Wallace Stevens. . . . But give us more of Lewis, Lewis, Wyndham Lewis, and Eliot! And what happened to Jessie Dismorr?

> T. S. Eliot makes a writer like Stevens look like a schoolgirl straining for originality.

1. These Pound poems were sent to *Poetry* with a letter of January 1, 1918; there is no evidence in the *Poetry* Papers about the reasons for returning the MSS.

Wallace Stevens' group has charm, but is somewhat romantic. I mean the charm is due to a romantic sort of exaggeration. It is not unlike the Georgian Anthology; though modernized. Or, it is tired Chinese—if that has any meaning to you—which the mood cannot condone. Williams is a sound satire, but seems to lack firmness.

Pound's emphasis was still, as it had been to Harriet Monroe, on the disparity between his side of the wet and the American side, but unlike Miss Monroe, Margaret Anderson eagerly endorsed this emphasis in managing her part of the magazine.

But if the poetry in the *Little Review* was disappointing, so was the verse published in *Poetry* in 1917 and 1918. The problem was general: all the poets were foundering, except for Yeats, Sandburg, and Marianne Moore. Even Pound's "Three Cantos" give evidence of the almost universal malaise. These poems are remote from the Cantos I, II, and III that appeared in 1925 in *A Draft of XVI Cantos*; the garrulity that had marked Pound's style in "To a Friend Writing on Cabaret Dancers," as he tried to feel his way into a longer form after years of emphasizing "the intaglio method," marks the first draft of the *Cantos*. Most of *Poetry*'s Cantos I and II is a long harangue addressed to the shade of Robert Browning, and a mulling over the material of Provence, which is the common subject matter of Browning and Pound; the uncanny resurrection of Andreas Divus, Canto I in its final form, is buried at the end of *Poetry*'s Canto III. The magnificent Canto II of the final version was not written until 1922, although the original poems play with images of intersections of light and perspective over water.

The final version of Canto II, which returns to Pound's aboriginal theme of metamorphosis and triumphantly relates it to intersecting levels of being and levels of language, brought together in the splendid and various imagery of the sea, would have earned a more vigorous response than the first draft of "Three Cantos" got. Alice Corbin Henderson's reaction to the 1917 versions in a letter of April 16, 1917, seems just: "I liked Ezra's poem—in spite of its being a tuning up of fiddles, it seems to have some body of its own. Of course if nothing crystallized further on, I can't say it would be a sufficient excuse for itself, except in method and quality. It is a preparation, and a linking up of times and classics, etc., preparatory, let us hope, to an individual vision."

If Pound was still feeling his way into a poem that he was to bring to triumphant achievement, the work of Lindsay and of Masters in 1917 and 1918 indicates that the brief glory of the middle-western renaissance was over. Vachel Lindsay had viewed 1917 in prospect with misgiving; he wrote December 9, 1916: "I think this next year I am in for a skinning, Harriet. I feel it coming. Many people who misapprehended me vaguely, but in a friendly way, will begin to realize I am but mortal, and jump me hard. See if they don't. And please counsel me to take my skinning like a man when it comes, and not get sore and hit back." His publications in *Poetry* in 1917 and 1918 required a good deal of editorial sifting and rejecting, and do not represent his best work.

Edgar Lee Masters was also depressed in 1917, with reason. The work he had been publishing after the *Spoon River Anthology* failed to come up to the same standard, and his closest allies were forced to admit this by 1917. He wrote in March that William Marion Reedy did not like his recent poems, and on September 8, in returning proof of "The Canticle of the Race," which *Poetry* published in October, 1917, he remarked: "I wish a big critic would come along, and if I can't write I wish he'd say so. I'd quit so quick everybody could hear the silence."

Unlike his fellows in the Chicago Renaissance, Carl Sandburg continued to write effective verse in this wartime era. Indeed, Sandburg hit a peak of lyric power about 1918, just when it became fashionable to talk down the Chicago school of 1914; commentators made a temporary exception of him, and went on talking down. His "Four Brothers" in *Poetry* for November, 1917, attracted admiration not only from Alice Corbin Henderson but also from Amy Lowell and John Quinn. William Carlos Williams praised him vividly in the same year: "Sandburg's 'In the cool tombs' [in the "Chicago number" of *Others*, June, 1917] is a splendid thing. I hope with all my power to hope I may meet Sandburg soon. He is, if I am not mistaken, really studying his form. Few men are making any progress in their art. They are adding new decoration or repeating the old stuff, but Sandburg is really thinking like an artist. He seems to me to know his America, and to be getting it in. Give him my best wishes."[2]

Among the foundering poets of 1917–18, one must list the would-be impresario of American letters, Amy Lowell. Miss Lowell gave herself away by using too many different voices: her talent began to seem more histrionic than poetic. She moved from short "intaglios" in the manner of Pound to long polyphonic prose narrative, to dramatic monologues like "Patterns," to brief impressions from the Japanese, to historical pageants like "Malmaison," to New England dialect monologues in imitation of Frost. One of the latter, "The Landlady of the Whinton Inn Tells a Story," appearing at the head of the January issue, got *Poetry* off to a disastrous start for 1918. It provoked an unprecedented intervention in editorial affairs from Henry Blake Fuller:

> If "Postponement" [his free-verse narrative in *Poetry* for February, 1916] "isn't poetry" as you said (and of course it isn't) still less so is the "Landlady's Story"—tho' interesting and arresting enough as a narrative. Yet, as poetry, it doesn't hold a candle to Carlos [Wallace Stevens' *Carlos among the Candles* in *Poetry* for December, 1917]. Heaven grant you more power to stand out against longwinded coadjutors, whether Amy, or Ezra, or me. Don't let *Poetry* become a Liberty Hall for mere clique. You and Mrs. J. just *must* discover a couple of new poetical geniuses within the next few months.[3]

William Carlos Williams does not belong in a list of failing poets in 1917–18. He continued to work along his own line, without much recognition but with increasing self-confidence. In 1917 he published *Al Que Quiere!* Wallace Stevens seems similarly detached from the confusion of the era, but his poetic direction seems less clear. Stevens had been lured away from short poems by the difficulty and interest of verse drama, but he was discouraged by failure of his play *Carlos among the Candles* as staged by Laura Sherry's Wisconsin Players: he almost had to be persuaded to publish it in *Poetry*. Like "Sunday Morning" and *Three Travelers Watch a Sunrise* earlier, *Carlos among the Candles*, in

2. Letter of July 17, 1917, in Thirlwall, *Letters*.
3. Undated letter.

Poetry for December, 1917, got very little reaction from *Poetry*'s readers. Most observers, like Pound, could not formulate an attitude toward Stevens' early work. Stevens, however, made little effort to promote himself. "Lettres d'un Soldat" in the May, 1918, issue of *Poetry* is not his strongest work, and the group at the head of the *Little Review*'s American number of June, 1918, is less than vintage Stevens—"Anecdote of Men by the Thousand," "Metaphors of a Magnifico," and "Depression before Spring." He gave his best poems in this period to *Others*, which appeared so irregularly, under such a variety of editors, that probably few interested readers noticed "Thirteen Ways of Looking at a Blackbird," "Valley Candle," "The Wind Shifts," "Meditation," and "Gray Room" in the December, 1917, issue edited in Chicago by William Saphier, the first number of *Others* to appear since June, 1917.

Considering the disasters that accumulated at the *Poetry* office about the time Alice Corbin Henderson left it, considering the occasional comment from Pound that he felt her more sympathetic than Harriet Monroe, considering that Pound sent Mrs. Henderson the manuscript of "Three Cantos," one is tempted to locate in her the editorial genius that accounted for *Poetry*'s showing in its great years. Pound's latest comments on *Poetry* attest to his idea of her efficacy: "NO CAUSE for me to have any pleasant recollection of any of Harriet's hams save Alice Corbin who was not a ham but did try to educate dear old Harriet, who was DUMB but honest, and honesty is a form of intelligence."[4] Possibly Pound felt greater faith in Mrs. Henderson because he respected her poetry: creative ability was often a touchstone to human worth for him. After Mrs. Henderson left Chicago for New Mexico, she tried to reassure Pound about Harriet Monroe. If like Joshua she needed hands to hold the trumpet if she were to breach the walls of Jericho,[5] she was doing the best she could, and Pound did not need intermediaries with her:

4. Letter of March 22, 1959, to Harry M. Meacham, in Meacham, *The Caged Panther*, p. 172 (copyright 1967 by Ezra Pound). Reprinted by permission of New Directions Publishing Corporation and Faber and Faber, Ltd., publishers and Agents for the Trustees of the Ezra Pound Literary Property Trust.

5. Alice Corbin Henderson to Pound, January 4, 1917, in Ezra Pound Archive,

But your influence with *Poetry* hasn't *waned*, you know, except as *you* have been willing to let it wane! I didn't know Harriet was grumped with you? What have you been doing or saying that she should be? I'm sure she's not really. She was much concerned a while back lest you should get a false interpretation of some sort of split between herself and Bodenheim (Bodenheim is really very much of what you call over there "a bounder.") I mean that she cares very much what you think. I don't think there's the least use or necessity of your addressing E.T. Carl is better than anyone in Chicago, and then there's Masters. And there's still ME. But Harriet herself is a good deal of a brick, all things considered. I don't know anyone of her generation who would prove so elastic—unless it might be Hen. Fuller, who has always been a joy to me personally. . . . But as I was saying, you have a perfectly good stand-in with Harriet direct. I'm sure of it.[6]

The tradition, fostered by Pound, that Harriet Monroe printed the new poetry reluctantly, early put observers to hunting for someone else who would account for *Poetry*'s openness to the movement. In his memoirs John Gould Fletcher articulated the view that Mrs. Henderson made the publication record possible. Out of a long acquaintance with *Poetry*, he chose to isolate a moment, sometime in 1914, when he traveled to Chicago to find Harriet Monroe, a humorless and forbidding presence, puzzled over "Prufrock" and wishing she could find a great middle-western poet. By contrast he found Alice Corbin Henderson sympathetic and sensitive, and felt it was her influence that accounted for the policy of the magazine.[7]

The question of Mrs. Henderson's contribution to *Poetry* cannot be settled so categorically. Her letters and her prose criticism make it indisputable that she had a lively literary intelligence, one that would be a great asset to any magazine. The verse she published still has life, and possibly she had a better abstract intelligence than either Ezra Pound or Harriet Monroe: she seems the only person who was able to make the necessary distinctions of idea in the vexed audience controversy. In her review of Sherwood Anderson's *Mid-American Chants* in *Poetry* for June,

Collection of American Literature, Beinecke Rare Book Room and Manuscript Library, Yale University.

6. Mrs. Henderson to Pound, February 17, 1917, in ibid.
7. *Life Is My Song*, pp. 191–94.

1918, she found art both international and local by necessity; she could relate nationalism in American art to nationalism in Irish art without losing sight of the fact that all art is also "cosmopolitan." If the debate between Ezra Pound and Harriet Monroe had been open to solution by intellectual analysis, Mrs. Henderson might have settled it for them.

But one cannot make a case that Alice Corbin Henderson was the one spokesman for an international standard in a nest of rabid middle-western chauvinists. She was as enthusiastic for an art that expressed America, or Mid-America, as Harriet Monroe. It was her editorial "Too Far from Paris," in *Poetry* for June, 1914, that opposed Yeats's advocacy of a learned tradition and of French criticism in his *Poetry* banquet speech, and insisted that the American poet must realize himself in direct relation to experience, holding up Lindsay as an ideal. In 1917, when Lindsay and Masters were floundering, Mrs. Henderson urged a more permissive editorial attitude toward the middle-western poets. In April, 1917, she strongly recommended the publication of Lindsay's "The Tiger Tree." She wrote on April 16 that *Poetry* had been too demanding in its treatment of Lindsay:

> There is one danger that we must guard against as publishers, and that is expecting a poet's work to be all up to his top-notch. Consider this poem in relation to a great deal that we have printed lately in *Poetry* (the fragmentariness of much of it) and you'll see what I mean. The danger of discarding what seems the second best of a poet like Lindsay (who always has something to say) for the *very best* of a poet whose *very best* is not equal to the third or fourth best of Lindsay! Imagine this to be the first thing you had ever had from Lindsay. I think we've been guilty perhaps of doing the same thing with some poems of Masters. And this attitude of the critics toward a poet who has made a mark (towards his subsequent work) is very noticeable. A familiarity a little too easily assumed. And it is a tendency to guard against.

But Harriet Monroe continued firm against "The Tiger Tree."

A little later Mrs. Henderson became freshly enthusiastic for middle-western regionalism, in the new verse of Sherwood Anderson, whom she introduced to *Poetry*. The group of poems that she sent June 9, 1917, commenting, "I tell you it is a great relief to read something real again!" was printed in *Poetry* for September, 1917, but Harriet Monroe again resisted Mrs. Henderson's enthusiasm for the regional cause, for her recommendation that Anderson get the Levinson Prize for the group was ignored, and two more groups of Anderson poems sent in by Mrs. Henderson in the year were not printed. *Poetry* never published Anderson's verse again, although the associate editor felt he was "the most important since Lindsay, Masters, and Sandburg." Harriet Monroe also discouraged Mrs. Henderson's enthusiasm for cowboy ballads, particularly the work of Charles Badger Clark, when she decided against publishing the article "Western Verse." Alice Corbin Henderson was irritated by the rejection, writing March 24, 1918: "I am sorry you didn't publish Western Verse. . . . I suppose you will wait until someone else 'discovers' Charles Badger Clark. Of course he is not the precieuse kind—but you have devoted far too much space to these lately—and the Others people are not really important—going to seed."

Balancing Mrs. Henderson's growing preoccupation with the West was her growing distrust of "the Others people." The verse of Alfred Kreymborg inspired in her something like contempt. She wrote July 3, 1916, of the poems published in *Mushrooms*: "Most of them are supposed to mean something—but they don't really. This kind of stuff, I think, does definite harm; for the moment, that is. . . . His versicles have an *implied* meaning, like much of the modern, very modern art. Do you get it? Yes, I get it! (No, you don't.) You can make as much or as little of it as you like." Here she seems fairly in accord with Harriet Monroe, who was never, as Kreymborg candidly recorded in his memoir, a believer in Kreymborg's verse, but about Wallace Stevens they were in mild disagreement. Mrs. Henderson was afraid that his verse would go soft: "I don't mean that Stevens' work is not worth while, but he does seem to me lately to have more tendency towards the precieuse or precieux than formerly, he always had it somewhat. I like him, you know, but I am sometimes afraid that he may wear a little thin."[8] Finally, she was flamingly, and very quotably, antagonistic to Amy Lowell, both as a poet and as a literary politician, and kept complaining that Har-

8. Letter of May 2, 1918.

riet Monroe should take a stronger line against her: "I note what you say on proof in regard to my criticism of Amy Lowell. *Honestly*, why should there be this 'Hands-Off' attitude towards Amy? She ain't the Kaiser—even if she is a relative of James Russell, sister of the President of Harvard, etc. etc."[9]

It seems quite reasonable to argue that Harriet Monroe was a better editor when she had Mrs. Henderson, with her sharp and immediate reactions, her keen sense for what worked in individual poems, at her side in the Chicago office. It was Mrs. Henderson who had discovered Sandburg when she fished "Chicago Poems" out of the incoming mail, and noticed *Spoon River* in an exchange copy of *Reedy's Mirror*. Harriet Monroe could not replace her when she left for New Mexico. There was not a comparably sensitive or stimulating literary intelligence among the circle of people who worked for *Poetry*. But Mrs. Henderson's predilections, if left to operate without resistance, would probably have made *Poetry* a regional bazaar where only middle-western wares were welcome. To publish Lindsay, Masters, and Sandburg, with Sherwood Anderson, at length, while deriding a "precieux" tendency in Kreymborg, Williams, and Stevens and declaring war on Amy Lowell, would have produced that effect, even if the magazine had remained open to everything Pound sent from London. At any rate, Mrs. Henderson was far from restraining middle-western chauvinism in Harriet Monroe: the restraints were applied in the other direction.

The news of the breakdown of the Poetry Renaissance, which the most informed observers began to trade among themselves in 1916, traveled out in widening circles; by 1918 it became general knowledge. With her usual good instinct for public relations, Amy Lowell published *Tendencies in Modern American Poetry* at the moment when the whole literary world discovered that some new definition of the renaissance was required. Her book brought her back into public notice just as the furor over *Some Imagist Poets* died down. In essays on Edwin Arlington Robinson, Robert Frost, Edgar Lee Masters, Carl Sandburg, John Gould Fletcher, and Hilda Doolittle, she described the new

9. Letter of May 29, 1918.

poetry as a peculiarly American phenomenon, a search for new national self-awareness and unity such as the *Seven Arts* promoted, which was also related to an international drive for a fresh, integrated view of reality in which man would see himself as part of a natural whole, "all falling into place in a vast plan, the key to which is natural science." Her treatment of the middle-western poets was rough. Masters in *Spoon River* she found a "Dostoievsky in *vers libre*," but she dismissed his later books and found him personally a pathological case, a man who "sees life through the medium of sex," representing a breakdown of values, an alteration of the racial type typical of America in transition, on its way to renewal. If she was blunt about Masters, she annihilated Lindsay: ". . . I think a closer attention will find him to be rather popularizing the second stage of the movement than heading a completely new tendency of his own." Only Carl Sandburg received relatively kind notice.

This brisk dismissal of the chief personalities of the Chicago Renaissance galvanized Harriet Monroe into exuberant praise of Lindsay, in a review in *Poetry* for December, 1917:

> Mr. Lindsay is no corollary of his Chicago confreres, and any discussion of American poetry which leaves him out is in danger of being discarded by the next age. If the thesis is not big enough to account for him, then the thesis has to be scrapped. Mr. Lindsay represents a tendency much richer and more indigenous than that personified by the Imagists, for example, however fine and high theirs may be. His roots run deep into the past of American literature; Mark Twain and Riley and Brer-Rabbit Harris were his collateral relatives, and all the wild lore which is in our western blood—our love of the wilderness, the folk-sense of magic in nature and life, the instinct of sympathy with all kinds and races of men—all this is in Vachel Lindsay's tendency, and he carries a good share of the new movement on his shoulders.

Although Harriet Monroe went on to describe other "tendencies" that Miss Lowell ignored or slighted, among them Pound's, Stevens', and Masters', the review as a whole put too much emphasis on Lindsay. T. S. Eliot was classified with Alfred Kreymborg, William Carlos Williams, and Helen Hoyt as an experimenter in moods and rhythms, in a tendency at the tail end of the movement. Masters was grateful for Miss Monroe's support, but felt that she had not dared to speak the whole truth. He wrote December 3, 1917:

> I feel impelled to write you this letter because of the very generous friendship which you maintain for me against the critics, including the tremendous Amazon who for the time being is rampaging through the flower gardens of America. In reading your criticism of A. Lowell's book I somehow got the impression that you did not feel free to go at the book as thoroughly and critically as you inwardly desired to do. . . . I cannot detach the book from the woman, or from what she has said to me respecting some of the subjects discussed. For example, I hardly know how to take her estimate of Frost, namely that he is an immortal equal to Burns and Synge, in view of her remark to me that he was "just a hay-seed"; nor do I know what to make of her eulogy of Sandburg as a lyricist when I remember that she said that Sandburg was "just a cobbler". . . . I wish that you had felt free to handle her book more drastically for this offense and for other offenses as well. I agree with you that Lindsay may be the founder of *the* movement; and every one who is a tendency, that is points somewhere in an original way deserves to be in a book of *tendencies*. In my own case I cannot help but extract a certain malice from her discussion of me. Her references to my mother's people were not only untrue but were in execrable taste. My mother was never a school-teacher.

Miss Lowell's dashing maneuver stirred up sharply conflicting critical currents. Harriet Monroe in 1918 simultaneously defended the primacy of aesthetic over social criticism in a controversy with Randolph Bourne, who had praised Amy Lowell's book, and denounced expatriate literature. Her reply to Bourne, in *Poetry* for October, 1918, is a fiery assertion of the artist's freedom to be himself:

> The artist, of course, can express only himself. If his vision is limited by the drawing-room, his utmost achievement will be a delicate miniature or a finely turned out *vers de societe*. If his vision embraces the medieval world and its religion, his achievement will be a *Divina Commedia*. The critic may rank the artist and define his work, but it is easier by thinking to find out God than by

criticizing to change a poet's scope and product. The critic may legitimately indulge in "discussion of a larger scope," examine the art "in relation to the larger movement of ideas and social movements and the peculiar intellectual and spiritual color of the time," but his discussion, if it is just, will have to estimate values at last by the strictly aesthetic standard. The poem or picture will stand by its aesthetic adequacy in the triumphant expression of the vision in the artist's soul, whether this vision be minute or cosmic. And if it is aesthetically inadequate the most illuminating social wisdom will not save it. . . .

Movements pass, but beauty endures. Our age will endure in the beauty it creates, and in that beauty its essential movement will be expressed. It may be—as indeed I believe—that certain of our living poets will be remembered in that ultimate record; but if they fail it will be through lack of power to feel or to express, or both, and not through lack of social criticism.

Poetry in the same year was caricatured as a hotbed of literary nationalism. In the *English Review* for May, 1918, Edgar Jepson, the English writer in whose refusal to publish his own poetry Pound had seen fine critical discrimination, published an attack on "Recent United States Poetry." Jepson called *Poetry* the seat of a western school in a pastiche of the recent prose of Mrs. Henderson and Miss Monroe. As he described it, the new school was securely rooted in native soil, genuinely national, creating a new diction that would be more fluid than English critics could fathom. The poets were autochthonous and unique: the subtle forces that shaped them included steel rails, moving pictures, world's fairs, and popular ballads. They would force United States art from its eastward gazing and its preoccupation with feudal Europe. American art would resume the habits of Mark Twain and Whitman, obeying the needs of the people.

Jepson's article made a peculiar selection of the poetry published in Harriet Monroe's magazine over the previous three years, to substantiate the charge that it was the house organ of a western school. He seems at first glance justified in taking poets awarded the Levinson Prize, particularly Vachel Lindsay for "The Chinese Nightingale" in 1915 and Edgar Lee Masters for "All Life in a Life" in 1916, as the magazine's favorites. But in his western school he included Robert Frost, who had not received a

Levinson Prize, but a second prize, for "Snow" in 1917, and who had published two poems altogether in *Poetry*. Other winners of second prizes and special prizes were ignored. The western school was defined rather captiously, especially since Carl Sandburg was excluded from it, although he had won the Levinson Prize in 1914 and published several times in *Poetry* over the span of three years that Jepson took under specific consideration. Sandburg's reputation in 1918 was apparently too good; reference to him would have botched the case against recent United States poetry.

The article was an intemperate and contemptuous attack that picked up evidence with no effort to be fair to American poetry, to *Poetry*'s publishing history, or to the publication record of individual poets. Masters was pompously condemned as if "All Life in a Life" were the pinnacle of his achievement. Frost was dismissed on the basis of "Snow," said to be a "maundering dribble" without music, suggesting no sense of music in its writer, who communicates only a nasal whine. Jepson speculated that American writers in general lacked all sense of beauty in words because of the ugliness of American speech. He took in a wider range of work in condemning Lindsay. "The Chinese Nightingale" and "The Fireman's Ball" were dismissed as slipshod, the work of a shirker. Jepson contrasted to these "ploppeyed bungaroos," gawky cowboys in the art, a true United States poet, expressing the true United States soul: T. S. Eliot. "Prufrock" was the perfect image of the thin, sophisticated, hyper-refined spirit that celebrates a beauty it dare not possess, the exquisite expression of the modern spirit shrinking from life. The paradox of finding T. S. Eliot the essentially American poet makes the conclusion of the article more interesting than its main argument.

Harriet Monroe reacted too sharply to this attack. She wrote a long reply for the *English Review* that made too many concessions to local newspaper comment. Burton Rascoe in the *Tribune* for May 25 had put down Jepson as an infuriated scribbler, but he and Bert Leston Taylor in the *Tribune* for May 28 both recognized the type of the ploppeyed bungaroo, and were entertained by Jepson's phrase making. But Miss Monroe indicated effectively that Jepson had misrepresented the individual poets, *Poet-*

ry's publication, and *Poetry*'s prizes. She questioned Eliot's value as a representative American, but not the quality of his work. She only wondered about "the discrimination of a critic who finds so much to say for him and nothing for two or three poets whose art is quite as delicately creative: Wallace Stevens, for example, a wizard with fine ironies and solitary grandeurs set in curious rhythms. . . ."[10] But Austin Harrison refused to print her article—he told Jepson that it was merely a personal attack[11]—and she wrote another reply in *Poetry* for July, 1918, that was largely an attack on Eliot. She found that Eliot's choice of exile had narrowed the range of his art, making a "wandering cosmopolite" of him and condemning him to repetitions of "Prufrock."

There was enough localism in Harriet Monroe's management of *Poetry* to give a color of truth to Jepson's extravagant attack. Read from London, *Poetry* must always have had a strong middle-western twang. One remembers how violently Pound suffered in 1913 and 1914 over its failure to make the impression he wanted. D. H. Lawrence remarked of *Poetry* in 1919: "I always like to see it. The American tone usually sets the English back up: and I suppose the English tone sets the American back up: in literature, I mean. But I do believe that America has a real will-to-live, and that attracts me most."[12] But read from Chicago or Saint Louis, *Poetry*'s tone was not local, but cosmopolitan; this seems one effective refutation of the charge that it functioned as cheerleader for the local team. Llewellyn Jones in the *Chicago Evening Post* for October 13, 1916, like Lucian Cary in the *Little Review* in 1915, praised *Poetry* primarily for bringing the world to Chicago, citing the printing of Tagore and Yeats, before the introduction of Lindsay and Sandburg, and valuing Pound's London correspondence above any other prose printed. In the *Mirror* for February 11, 1916, William Marion Reedy wrote an idiosyncratic account of Miss Monroe's achievement, which

10. A copy filed with the Jepson correspondence.
11. Jepson to Harriet Monroe, October 2, 1918.
12. Letter of February 1, 1919, excerpt printed by permission of Laurence Pollinger, Ltd., and the Estate of the late Mrs. Frieda Lawrence, of the Viking Press, Inc., and of William Heinemann, Ltd., publishers of *The Collected Letters of D. H. Lawrence*, ed. Harry T. Moore. All rights reserved.

came down to the judgment that she had had the courage to see poetry where no one else saw anything but madness, in the work of Ezra Pound as well as in the work of Vachel Lindsay:

> . . . some of the pieces accepted by her suggested at first to the curious observers of this literary phenomenon the necessity of a commission *de lunatico inquirendo* for this Chicago lady. The works of Ezra Pound had fallen dead-born in England, but when his bare, esurient, rhymeless and almost rhythmless writings appeared in *Poetry*, he found an audience that understood. His own countrymen, seeing with the eyes of Miss Monroe, discovered him, and their discovery reacted upon England with happy results for Mr. Pound. To her belongs also credit for the courageous acceptance of the peculiar poetry of Mr. Nicholas Vachel Lindsay. The more conservative editors had "passed up" this poet as being probably a little "cracked," but the editor of the Chicago "magazine of verse" saw Lindsay's writings for what they were, namely, an effort at interpretation of American life, reverting of set purpose to the origins of poetry in the chant or croon.

Read from New York or Boston, *Poetry* could set the back up almost as quickly as it set backs up in London, but in the American East reactions were for a long time ambiguous. Conrad Aiken was the aboriginal detractor of Harriet Monroe's achievement, and had published, the year before Jepson's attack on *Poetry*, a review of *The New Poetry* titled "The Monroe Doctrine in Poetry," which found that the policy of the magazine had been "unfortunately provincial in tone: toward all that she has felt no sympathy with Miss Monroe has manifested too frequently a cocksure intolerance."[13] Aiken's prime piece of evidence for intolerance was the publication of Pound's "Status Rerum" in 1913, with its lighthearted refusal to mention the existence of the Georgians; in 1917 the fact functioned against Harriet Monroe, but Aiken did not see fit to identify the author of the article. Aiken had a stronger case when he went on to mention the confusion Miss Monroe had displayed about "realism" in poetry:

> Miss Monroe, if she is really a radical at all, is chiefly so as regards form; as regards the material of poetry. . . . she suffers from many of the curious inhibitions, for the most part moral, which played havoc with the Victorians. The truth must not be told

13. *Dial*, May 3, 1917, pp. 389–90.

when it is disagreeable or subversive. One's outlook on life must accord with the proprieties. Above all, one must be a somewhat sentimental idealist—anthropocentric, deist, panpsychist, or what not, but never, by any chance, a detached and fearless observer.

But Alfred Kreymborg, whose *Others* in 1915 seemed the first sign of an eastern reaction against *Poetry*, wrote a review of *The New Poetry* for Harriet Monroe in July, 1918, that was an explicit refutation of Aiken's attack. He emphasized the fairness of *Poetry*'s editorial selections—"The portcullis of Carl Sandburg's 'hog-butcher of the world' has been lowered in democratic fashion to an hundred and one men and women"—and their effective value of promoting the new movement:

> And toward this renaissance, for the most part six or seven years old, the editors have contributed more than the combined efforts of the commercially endowed editors of *The Atlantic*, *Harper's*, *The Century*, et al. When I say this, I say something, for no one person has quibbled more valiantly with this or that phase of the "Harriet Monroe doctrine" than your humble servant. I say this or that, because I have never doubted the general policy of *Poetry*, even though my particular breed of poetasting was politely rejected for three consecutive years.

The Kreymborg review got a magnificently mixed response from William Carlos Williams. He wrote Harriet Monroe on July 17, 1918: "I hope you had a real rest on your vacation . . . and that all is going well with *Poetry*. I liked Alfred's article. He spoke fearlessly and succinctly, in places he revealed splendid flashes of style—what does it matter what he said. Ha, ha!"

Like the status of many of the poets involved in the renaissance, *Poetry*'s status in 1918 combined too many elements to be easily defined. Edgar Jepson's attack reduced this confusion to a confidently simple definition of the magazine. The attack did not attract much explicit comment; as Harriet Monroe wrote Jepson on September 12, 1918, no one paid any real attention. Alice Corbin Henderson wrote in June: "You really don't need to defend yourself, because he has made out no case. His stuff is quite ridiculous and sloppy. . . ."

The most amusing of the confused literary affairs of 1918 was the unmasking of a group of fake free versifiers called the Spectrists. "The Spectric School" was a prolonged masquerade by

Witter Bynner and Arthur Davison Ficke, two poets generally rated conservative on the free-verse issue, who had been writing free verse under the pseudonyms Emanuel Morgan and Anne Knish and sending it around to the magazines since 1916. Marjorie Allen Seiffert, writing as Elijah Hay, was a third and minor member of the school. The chief instrument of the deceit was the anthology *Spectra*, published by Mitchell Kennerley in 1916, and the only outright victim was *Others*, which gave a whole issue over to "The Spectric School" in January, 1917, during the era when it appeared irregularly. The *Little Review* had published a poem or two of Morgan's in July, 1917, with this editorial comment: "Banish / Anne Knish / Set the dog on / Emanuel Morgan." *Reedy's Mirror* had printed some Elijah Hay in March, 1917, and reprinted a solemn description of the purpose of the school by Anne Knish and Emanuel Morgan from Kennerley's magazine, the *Forum*, in June, 1916. *Poetry* had barely given the Spectrists editorial mention; they were judged to be more "elliptical" than the Imagists in a survey of the schools in the August, 1916, issue. The anthology *Spectra* went to Helen Hoyt for review, but she found a review very difficult to write, and if it was completed, it was not used.

Witter Bynner had written May 21, 1916, encouraging Miss Monroe to print some Emanuel Morgan: "Why don't you publish samples of the Spectric stuff. Even I can see the raison d'etre for some of the Morgan-Knish experiments." Again on September 15, 1916: "in their poems I find a certain quality not in any of the other newcomers—perhaps because they have been closer to the continental sources. At any rate they started me up." She accepted a number of Morgan poems for publication, the first as early as January 4, 1917,[14] but she heard about the hoax through gossip before publishing any of the poems or making any significant editorial comment on *Spectra*.

14. William Jay Smith, *The Spectra Hoax*. The more serious poets do not seem greatly influenced by the Spectric affair; there is little comment on it in the *Poetry* Papers. Masters in a letter of December 1, 1916, praised the anthology, and Williams in a letter of January 26, 1917, asked Harriet Monroe's opinion of the Spectrists—possibly feeling for reaction to the Spectrist number of *Others*, in which he had a hand. After the hoax was exploded, Ezra Pound in a letter of December 17, 1918, inquired after the identity of Marjorie Allen Seiffert; she had recently written to him but was unknown to him, although he had mentioned her work in a letter to the *Little Review* for April, 1916, p. 36.

When the masquerade had ended, Witter Bynner gave Harriet Monroe the graceful explanation that the alter ego he had acquired in Emanuel Morgan was a poet of genuine value. But the effect of the hoax was to make the Poetry Renaissance ridiculous. Thus the *Dial*, which broke the story on April 25, 1918, judged it: "The history of our so-called poetic renaissance will contain no sprightlier chapter than the tale of the Spectrist school." The 1916 *Spectra* anthology had appeared at the right time: "The Muse was on the make hereabouts: patronesses had been discovering her; prizes were multiplying; newspapers were giving critics their head; poetry magazines, mushrooms or hardier plants, were springing up overnight; it was raining anthologies—boom times!" A public that had accepted Cubists, Futurists, Imagists, Vorticists, and Others would not hesitate to swallow Emanuel Morgan and Anne Knish when they were served up by Mitchell Kennerley.

Alice Corbin Henderson in *Poetry* for June, 1918, congratulated *Poetry* on escaping the hoaxers, without revealing how narrow the margin of escape, and declared the joke rather pointless. It went without saying, she thought, that critics were unselective, especially in the presence of anything new; if the same hoax had been played with insincerely written lyrics in conventional form, no one would have seen a joke at all, "for this happens every day." Emanuel Morgan replied in the August, 1918, issue, explaining that his motive was the destruction of fussy pretense, and remarking that he awaited with impatience the publication of the poems accepted by *Poetry*. Harriet Monroe, who wrote in her autobiography that she discovered the imposture with only one Morgan poem in her accepted file, had apparently amused herself by hoaxing the hoaxer with further acceptances, and was able to slide away from his demands with "Thanks for your thanks, Emanuel! But has *Poetry* ever printed you? or so much as mentioned Spectra? It was a pleasure to 'accept' the poems of so clever a joker, but why all this hand clasping?"

In refusing to concentrate on an elite, Harriet Monroe gave someone else the chance to define the movement in a way that would subordinate her magazine. This opportunity Ezra Pound seized when he republished Edgar Jepson's attack on *Poetry*, "The Western School," at the head of the *Little Review* for September, 1918. The Jepson attack, which had provoked little reaction in its first publication in Austin Harrison's *English Review*, had a devastating effect when it reappeared under Pound's sponsorship. Since much of the material in *Poetry* that a reader might recall to ascertain the unfairness of the article had come from Pound, Pound's endorsement of the attack removed its effect of bias. The legend of "hammering stuff into *Poetry*" was rebroadcast, a legend that had first developed out of Pound's efforts to get Robert Frost's poems published in 1913. Now Pound made a gift to *Poetry* of the career of Frost, with the careers of Lindsay and Masters. By implication, everything else in *Poetry* that was not autochthonous had been imported by Pound over the agonized protests of the Chicago office.

Pound gave the reprint of the article an extra edge by adding a note that the survey of *Poetry*'s prize poems had been "ordered" by the editors, who "having asked for criticism, when they were ready for nothing but eulogy, refuse to publish the criticism." And the appearance after the article of Eliot's first poems in more than a year, "Sweeney among the Nightingales," "Whispers of Immortality," "Dans le Restaurant," and "Mr. Eliot's Sunday Morning Service," did something to strengthen Jepson's case: the peculiar, beautiful, and sardonic effects of the first two poems in particular added luster to the argument that Eliot was *the* significant United States poet.

The facts about Harriet Monroe's ordering the article are not entirely clear, although one can see the beginning of the whole episode in Pound's innocent question in a letter of July 2, 1917: "? do you want any more prose by Jepson?" Edgar Jepson approached *Poetry* under Pound's auspices, wondering out loud in a letter of September 28, 1917, which covered a poem, if *Poetry* would like an appreciation of the native poets based on several months' reading of its files. Harriet Monroe responded by offering some "characteristically American" back numbers, which Jepson gratefully accepted. He sent the article February 20, 1918, requesting immediate notice of date of publication. After Harriet Monroe rejected the article, Jepson wrote July 4, 1918, apologizing for his stupidity in assuming that the editors of *Poetry* were seriously interested in the art. Harriet Monroe explained in *Poetry* for November, 1918: "Our letter to Mr. Jepson saying that we might wish to use his proposed 'appreciation' of American poetry was not an 'order,' and our rejection of it was not due to its 'lack of flattery,' but to its cheap incompetence. By the reprint Mr. Pound freshens up, so to speak, the article's attack on *Poetry*, a magazine which, during the past six years, he has so amiably represented in London. Evidently this poet obeys the scriptural injunction not to let his right hand know what his left hand is doing." The leading article in the same issue, "A Century in Illinois," was a passionate restatement of Harriet Monroe's belief in the need for a confident Americanism in letters:

> Chicago, Illinois, the Middle-West—this vital and vitalizing section—needs only, in art, the spirit it has shown in other things—the spirit of active and immediate response to the need of the hour. It is in this spirit that Chicago invented the sky-scraper, in this spirit that she brought forth *The Spoon River Anthology* and *Chicago Poems*, in this spirit—let us hope—that *Poetry* was founded and that many greater things will be achieved in the future of our dreams. . . .
>
> Every artistic venture . . . meets the facile temptation to become itself colonial. When *Poetry* began, for example, two courses were open: it could have become, what the *Little Review* is now, the organ of a choice little London group of super-intellectualized ultimates and expatriates; or, as I hope it has become, the organ of a higher and more conscious, concentrated and independent imaginative life in this country. The first course would have been comparatively easy—I remember with what cordial kindness a poet in exile once offered to conduct from London our entire prose section!—and, since the editorials would no doubt have been very clever, and very scornful of most things American, we should unquestionably have been praised by some of the choicest spirits on both sides of the water, and should have acquired by this time a much longer list of subscribers. . . .
>
> The word coterie is perhaps over-despised. Coteries having proved necessary and effective in Athens, Rome, Florence, Paris and London, they are of course equally necessary, and may prove

equally effective, in Chicago. A coterie is but a group of people working together, and teamwork is required in the arts, as in everything else, if anything save benumbing isolation is to be accomplished. If *Poetry* can help to develop and make articulate the imaginative life of the nation . . . then its editors will be more proud than of having introduced the imagists, important as that episode was in our earliest history and the literary history of our period.

The editorial was a declaration of war from Chicago to London. It was unfair to *Poetry*'s past: Harriet Monroe's great achievement had not been the rejection of an expatriate point of view in favor of a local point of view; the excitement of *Poetry* in 1914 came from the welding of the two into a unity, so that Sandburg seemed to follow from Pound as Masters seemed to follow from Sandburg, and Yeats praised "strange beauty" in the work of Lindsay while reproaching Chicago for being "too far from Paris." It was untrue to Chicago's present, for it exaggerated both the unity and the sense of purpose of the middle-western poets who were regarded as belonging to *Poetry*. Masters' letter denying that *Poetry* had been important in inspiring his verse or in recognizing it had been printed in the magazine only two months before. Once again Harriet Monroe reacted emotionally to attack, and imprudently adopted the enemy's division of the poetic schools. But middle-western chauvinism was foisted upon her, not freely adopted. In her inmost editorial citadel she remained unchanged. She returned Lindsay's latest poems to him in October, 1918, with the comment that they needed revision; Lindsay wrote back October 16 to say that he disagreed and had sent them to *Others*. In the same month she asked T. S. Eliot for verse; he wrote November 7, 1918, "As for verse—I have so very little nowadays that I have been able to provide enough only for one issue of the 'Little Review' in the past year." The judicious side of Harriet Monroe's personality was as determined as usual to publish the best she could get of all the schools.

And if Miss Monroe was ready to do battle in her November, 1918, editorial, the home office of the *Little Review* did not wish to see war declared along the lines described by Jepson. In its

November issue the *Little Review* reprinted Harriet Monroe's paragraph of protest and explanation, and Jane Heap added a long comment:

> Judging from the reverberations a great many people got excited over Mr. Jepson's article and a great many more suffer loudly and continually over Mr. Pound.
>
> Miss Monroe is not the first to tell us that the *Little Review* is under the dictatorship of Pound. Our idea of having a foreign editor is not to sit in our New York office and mess up, censor, or throw out work sent to us by an editor in London. We have let Ezra Pound be our foreign editor in the only way we see it. We have let him be as foreign as he likes: foreign to taste, foreign to courtesy, foreign to our standards of Art. All because we believe in the fundamental ideal back of our connection with Mr. Pound: the interest and value of an intellectual communication between Europe and America. If anyone can tell us of a more untiring, efficient, better-equipped poet to take over the foreign office let us hear from him.[15]
>
> I cannot understand how anyone with enough intelligence to read the *Little Review* could have thought of Mr. Jepson's article as aesthetic criticism. . . . Of course I don't know what may have been Mr. Jepson's idea, but Pound calls his article criticism in a footnote. Cursing, endless repetitions of abuse of all outsiders, and a mutual advertising agency for themselves, seem to be a popular kind of in-door sport of the literary lizards in London. They call it criticism.
>
> Neither can I quite see literature reduced to a profession of the mind in just the way these men do it. . . .

Edgar Jepson was moved to reenter the fray several months later, in the *Little Review* for February–March, 1919, explaining that Miss Monroe had sent him twenty-eight numbers of her magazine in which the typical United States poems were marked. How could she call his comments "uninvited and undesired"? Taking three of the poems as typical, he had pointed out as politely as he could that they were punk. None of *Poetry*'s defenders had made a reasonable answer: Miss Monroe and her

---

15. "Pounding Ezra," in *The Little Review Anthology*, ed. Margaret Anderson (copyright 1953). Reprinted by permission of the publisher, Horizon Press, New York.

cohorts had simply burst into abuse. Jepson closed with the speculation that the touchiness of his Yankee victims came from their consciousness that United States art was negligible: in artistic achievement the United States ranked lowest of all civilized nations of all time. Its writers and painters developed only if they were Europeanized.

After Harriet Monroe's editorial reply in November, 1918, *Poetry* left the Jepson controversy alone. But not even the support of the intimidating Jane Heap could shield it from the effects of Pound's sponsorship of Jepson. At the *Poetry* office, the roof fell in. The evidence of this is not only the swiftness, the anger, and the directness of Harriet Monroe's reply, but the quantity of comment sent in correspondence.

Vachel Lindsay was greatly pleased by the editorial "A Century in Illinois," for the explicit championing of a Chicago coterie was welcome to him, and represented an editorial line he had encouraged without success in 1914. He wrote a long letter November 3, 1918, his first serious effort to influence the editorial policy of *Poetry*:

> I want to congratulate you on the editorial section of your last number. I laid it down with the feeling that you were on a new tack, more deliberately and clearly Middle-western, more deliberately and reasonably and definitely the advocate of your coterie, more deliberately against the expatriates, and more definitely the champion of the poet as an American public figure. . . .
>
> I think I see a new tone in the Poetry magazine, less of tart personalities and more of a platform, and you cannot go too far in this policy. It was plain to me in the past that some of the Eastern people got your goat too much, when you were really at your best in the bland and the judicial, and now you are in a position to be these and more. The place of the poet as a person who is or is not conscripted, who is or is not receiving an income, who is or is not expressing America are points on which you can keep your paper bristling for some time to come. It seems to me that hereafter technical considerations should come fourth in importance, remembering that the other critics are threshing them out endlessly, and doing about all the service needed along this line. But your paper is still the model for all others, the only one planted in a sure place, and envied of all the rest. I am quite sure of that.

Lindsay was as unclear as usual about the attitudes of his contemporaries. Several observers who had been viewing *Poetry* with distrust for some time were pushed by the Jepson attack to the conclusion that the general weakness in the poets was the fault of *Poetry*'s editor. John Gould Fletcher was one of these. He wrote November 21, 1918, that something fundamental had gone bad. Was the trouble with the poets or with *Poetry*? Was American poetry set on a steep downhill course? He and others had hoped that America would fulfill all the hopes *Poetry* had aroused in the years 1913–16. But now he found all his expectations draining away. A week later, on November 28, Fletcher thought he had arrived at the diagnosis of the trouble: Harriet Monroe had a peculiar editorial bias—she instinctively preferred a poet's second-best work. She had steadily rejected all his finest poems, with only two exceptions. This diagnosis must owe something to the quarrel Fletcher had picked in 1914 about the poetry in regular form that he sent in to *Poetry* after the acceptance of "Irradiations." His work in *Poetry* after "Blue Symphony" is undistinguished and unmemorable, but his correspondence gives no indication that Harriet Monroe was at fault in this.

Amy Lowell wrote in response to Harriet Monroe's editorial in November, 1918. She felt vindicated in her assertion that *Poetry* showed scandalous partiality. In 1916 she had cited Vachel Lindsay and Ezra Pound, but the reprint of the Jepson attack in the *Little Review* simplified *Poetry*'s identity in a way Miss Lowell found quite satisfactory. In a letter of November 2, 1918, she read Harriet Monroe a long lecture on her regional bias.

Not all the comment was negative, of course. Alfred Kreymborg wrote September 2, 1918, apropos of nothing explicit: "Pound has fallen behind. A recent re-reading of Whitman's prose proves this. Ezra's constant sneer in re America looks pale in the fierce glow of Walt's prophecy. Pound was once a leader—but now that he has gone to school in London—he has turned pedant. It is a seriously sorrowful spectacle." Richard Aldington wrote December 8 from London: "'Poetry' must not fall down if it can be helped. You have done a great deal in the past years. It would be absurd to expect you to print masterpieces each month and no one but a blind partizan would expect you to cling to one school of poetry; but you can claim, I think, to have published work by very nearly every living poet of talent. And that is more than most journals can say." William Butler Yeats made no comment, but his agent sent the manuscript of *The Only Jealousy of Emer* to Harriet Monroe on November 21, 1918. Yeats had been out of contact with Miss Monroe since he sent "Ego Dominus Tuus" more than a year before. It seems fair to infer that he did not quite like Pound's attack on *Poetry*.

The immediate reaction of William Carlos Williams is hard to classify. Of the serious poets writing in America, he felt most threatened by the *Little Review* attack. Lindsay and Masters were the quarry of every critic by 1918, and it made little difference to their poetic careers. The injustice of Jepson's treatment of Frost was so evident that the article had little power to harm him. But the division of poets into cowboys who wrote out of American backgrounds and superintellectuals who had lost all attachment to place left no room for Williams' notions of a poetry that was committed to the here and the now, in Rutherford, New Jersey, on grounds that had nothing to do with traditional appeals to a national or regional audience. "Preface to *Kora in Hell*," which Williams published the next year in the *Little Review*, was an effort to force some room for his own work in the highly polarized critical field created by Pound and Jepson. A letter that he wrote Harriet Monroe on February 10, 1919, discusses his poems published in *Poetry* for March, 1919, and indicates the strain of the *Little Review* quarrel on both of them. Williams lumped Miss Monroe with his wife, the attitude he usually adopted when he labored to forgive her:

> Neither in my house nor out of it must I ever speak my mind—it seems. If I said anything that seemed to injure you set it down for the true utterance of a damned fool.
>
> As far as the poems are concerned I think some of them are the best short things I have ever done—some I do not like so well— but to intimate that I have condemned them beforehand is to have been a crooked listener, to say the least. . . .
>
> As far as the Little Review is concerned: it has given me the kind of an entré I have lacked everywhere else [with the publication of *Kora in Hell*]. I like the attitude Jane Heap has taken toward

the American Issues and I feel that her work is to that extent important. I do not approve of Pound nor of the English hero-worship of
M.A.—

   Do you realize the narrowness of the opening through which I
must crawl?

Of all the commentators on the *Little Review* reprint, Alice
Corbin Henderson had the bleakest reaction. She had been contending for some time that *Poetry* had too much secondhand
Imagism in it, too much of the "precieux," which she distrusted
even in Stevens. Her first response to the *Little Review* attack,
dated November 7, 1918, showed a continuing tendency to
blame degenerate Imagism for a slump in *Poetry*:

> I find the Little Review very disappointing. But I also find *Poetry*
> disappointing, but not for the same reason, thank God. Don't
> think I'm fussing for the sake of fussing. Iris Tree was the best
> thing in the last number except for the Indian things [Lew Sarett's
> "The Blue Duck"]. Max Michelson and Helen Birch not there at
> all, the kind of thing that weakens the magazine. The dregs of
> imagism. Have you got anything in the file you're holding back
> the way you used to, for fear the good things might give out? For
> heaven's sake don't be afraid of printing the good things all at
> once! That's the only way to get more! . . . Certainly the
> present state of poetry is pretty rotten. What has become of the
> good stuff, is nobody writing it anymore? . . . I am afraid that
> they [the poets] think what you like is the imagism-primer stuff
> exclusively. . . .
>
>   P.S. Don't keep Ezra on your staff if he is not doing anything
> for you. He has his own *organ* now and *leave him have it*.

The affair wore on her self-confidence, and on November 18 she
wrote bitterly depressed:

> I am afraid, Harriet, that you are surrounded by people who are
> willing to say the pleasant thing and the easy thing about *Poetry*,
> instead of the honest thing and the hard and possibly bitter thing.
> . . . I found it an awfully hard job to find something in the last
> year's file good enough to give the prize to! And I doubt if I
> succeeded! . . .
>
>   *Poetry*—you, me and all of us—has a tendency to harp back to
> what we've published, mostly in the past tense, and too much on

the corn-fed poets of the middle states. It has got to be an obsession. But what we ought to do is look ahead. And if you don't, you'll find yourself a back-number as sure as you are born. Things are likely to start up now that the war is over, and there will surely be new magazines on the order of the Seven Arts, etc. Another thing, try to get rid of the parochial tone in the prose. I have begun to loathe the first person in reviews—Sounds like The Little Review and the naked "I" comes to be almost indecent. When it doesn't sound patronizing. It is a skillful person who can use the *I* without sounding undressed, these days.

A week later she was restored to a better mood. Harriet Monroe, who on November 1 had not heard from Pound since he returned a receipt for his review of Gosse's *Swinburne* without comment in March, 1918,[16] seems to have asked Mrs. Henderson if she knew anything of him. Mrs. Henderson replied:

> Your letter just arrived and I am truly surprised to find you so patient and forbearing. It is very good that you should remind me of the trials of an editor, now that I am in the petulant poet class! I never criticize the magazine that I don't feel sorry afterwards.
>
> Of course, I share your predilection for the middle western poets, and why shouldn't one? But we must try to find others.
>
> About Ezra. . . . I haven't written to him or heard from him since he went over to The Little Review. He said he trusted I could see why, etc. etc. hoped the Little Review justified etc. etc. Well, I couldn't see why or see any justification for the Little Review—I sent him a card once I think. No break. Just stopped. Of course he has his virtues, which many have appropriated to better use. But I can't follow him into his little cul-de-sac.[17]

However, irritation with what appeared in *Poetry* and a rather panic-stricken search for alternatives were the note of her correspondence for the rest of the winter.

Mrs. Henderson's complaint about the difficulty of voting the prize for the 1917–18 publishing year brings one's attention to the final misfortune of the Jepson attack on *Poetry*. Just at the time when it focused attention on *Poetry*'s prize awards as symptomat-

---

16. Pound wrote John Quinn that he broke off relations because Harriet Monroe deleted a story about protest against Christian rites at Swinburne's funeral. (Letter of June 4, 1918, in *Letters*, #153, p. 138.)

17. Letter of November 25, 1918.

ic of parochial editorial judgment, a dubious award of the Levinson Prize, to John Curtis Underwood for "Song of the Cheechas," was announced. Harriet Monroe described the awards in November, 1918, in no grandiloquent spirit. She justified her prizes on the ground that poets got some money by them: "'Poetry' would like to be rich enough to pay for poems at least a living wage. . . ." "'Poetry,' as we have often said, is a current exhibition; no more than in other current exhibitions can we hope to show numerous masterpieces, or to manifest impeccable justice in our awards." Still, the effect was dismal when in the issue for January, 1919, she had to print a letter from Paul Fortier Jones with an excerpt from his book, *With Serbia into Exile*, which contained most of the material and much of the language of John Curtis Underwood's "Song of the Cheechas." Jones felt that in not acknowledging his source, Underwood had wished to deceive the public. Miss Monroe attributed Underwood's failure to acknowledge a source to his being "the most distrait and least explicit of men."

The strong reaction to the reprint of the Jepson article indicates the importance of the affair for *Poetry*'s history. Ezra Pound's motive in it all is puzzling. He wrote Jepson, discussing a rewriting of the *English Review* article for the *Little Review*, as if they both felt an attack on Frost, Masters, and Lindsay was badly needed: "The thing was (obviously) aimed at *Poetry*'s readers. The L.R. lot don't need it at the same length. . . . For us, it does too much honour to Frost, Masters, and Lindsay to take 'em so seriously."[18] But the whole group of critics associated with the *Seven Arts*, Randolph Bourne, Van Wyck Brooks, Amy Lowell, and Louis Untermeyer, along with Conrad Aiken and T. S. Eliot, had disparaged Lindsay's achievement by mid-1918, and attacks on Masters had been mounting since 1916. Jepson's attack was new in associating Frost with the two middle-western poets, but his article was not constructed as if he saw any special need to explain that association. The essay was not needed, nor seriously planned, to correct rampant American nationalism in the arts; nor was it useful as a promotion of T. S. Eliot, although probably this was part of Pound's

18. Letter of "? May, 1918," in *Letters*, #151, p. 135.

motive in printing it. Pound perhaps felt in presenting Eliot's new poems in the *Little Review* some of the difficulty he had felt in 1912 about presenting H.D.'s five poems, the problem of properly dramatizing a very slender production. Thus he chose to associate them with an essay in appreciation of the poet. But Jepson's version of Eliot was almost as much a caricature as his version of Lindsay or Frost: the true United States poet comes on as a clinical curiosity, detached and sophisticated to the point of inanition. In any long view, the Jepson essay was an unworthy introduction to Eliot's poems, and Pound should have known it.

Some of the sensational impact of the reprint came from the taint of malice in it, as if Pound desired to inflict injury, to re-inflict injury, on Harriet Monroe. If it was necessary, as he wrote William Carlos Williams in a retrospective explanation, "to penetrate Harriet's crust. That silly old she-ass with her paeons for bilge," [19] her crust had been penetrated in May, 1918, when the original article appeared in the *English Review*, and a reply had been duly made in *Poetry* for July, 1918. If Harriet Monroe had been unwilling to take a strong editorial line since 1916, Pound in 1918 had the *Little Review* in which to create his own clarities. He did not need to operate in a roundabout way through Jepson. And his management of the *Little Review* had done nothing to clear up confusion about the new poetry, but had added to it. There was something gratuitous in the attack on Harriet Monroe.

The excessive force with which Pound attacked *Poetry* seems directed against old ghosts, the dead hopes of 1913 and 1914, the brief illusion in 1915 that Masters would contribute ideas based on life in arrangement. The inclusion of Frost in the attack, so inappropriate to the publishing history, suggests such an interpretation, that Pound was rolling up into one ball all the "Amur'k'n" poets for whom he had ever felt a stirring of rivalry, and sacrificing them to seal his new loyalty to T. S. Eliot. As he had written from London in 1912, Pound was following the track of the real, sorting out the rare truths from among the many falsehoods, and reality for him always meant the line along

19. Letter of September 11, 1920, in *Letters*, #170, p. 157.

which valid poetry could be written. In 1918 that line led through the work in rhymed quatrains after Gautier, and through the experiments in longer forms that he shared with Eliot (one can find echoes in "Gerontion" of discarded bits of the "Three Cantos" of 1917), and to define it he denied all the past associated with *Poetry*, including his own relatively unsuccessful experiments in satire, and the dead causes from Imagisme to *Spoon River*. There is an effect of exaggeration about this, because Pound was killing something of himself: the Pound of 1912–15 who had written his poetry without reference to the existence of the poetry of Eliot.

Among the letters that arrived at the *Poetry* office in November, 1918, with a variety of reactions to the Jepson reprint, the most improbable seems a small note from Ezra Pound's father, H.L. Pound, dated November 5: "I have Mss—of Ezra's on New Poetry—and he wishes me to ask you if you [*sic*] 'Does she want it?' Payment to be made to him—Why do I have it? Well I made a sort of muddle over this MSS—thinking I was doing him a favor. Before sending it to you I thought it best to hear from you. I have not seen anything of his in Poetry for some time, I suppose 'there's a reason.'" Not even Pound's nearest and dearest could believe that he could want to publish again in *Poetry*, or that Harriet Monroe would want to take him back. But he did, and she did. She wrote Pound on November 25 to acknowledge a letter enclosing his "Propertius" poems, her first word from him in over eight months, and asked to publish four of them.

Her response to "Propertius" was not overenthusiastic. It shows the marks of the Jepson quarrel, in her comments on libraries and withdrawal from present realities: "You are getting to be a regular eighteenth-century literary man—sinking into a quiet corner of an old library and poring over poets long dead. Propertius! Well, I can't pretend that I am glad or that it's the kind of thing *Poetry* is particularly interested in. I admit the delicate handling—a kind of 'spirit-translations' I suppose they are, as Max Michelson said—but I'd rather have Eliot's Hippopotamus—or Sarett's wild-Indian things. *Are* they translations, by the way?"[20] Pound wrote Marianne Moore that his interest in resuming relations with Miss Monroe was purely financial:

> As Richard said only six weeks ago (re *Poetry*): It's that on the cover that has beaten you. If you could have got that off (the silly question third-truth from Whitman) you could have made something of it.
>
> Now, one buys leisure to work by selling one's stuff for what one can. Harriet (Monroe) is too old to learn. Thank heaven I have conducted some of her funds to a few authors who needed emolument.
>
> I have repeatedly resigned. And it took a six month's struggle to get her to print Eliot's "Prufrock."
>
> I have nothing but my name on the cover. And the prospects of a very mutilated piece of my Propertius appearing in her paper, because it would be criminal of me to refuse £10 / 10; and because it don't matter. It don't matter in the least what appears or does not appear in that magazine. The elect will see, ultimately, the English publication of the series.
>
> (All of which is for your ear and no other. The woman is honest, and can not help her obfuscations.)[21]

That Harriet Monroe was willing to take Pound back is most surprising. It is almost as surprising that Pound thought she might be willing to take him, although he probably had no notion of the degree of uproar created at the *Poetry* office by the Jepson reprint. She seems self-abnegating to a heroic or foolish degree, and he seems callous to a corresponding degree. But both had personalities that operated on more than one level. Each of them could come back with positive and disinterested action from a strong inner self, after actions of surprising stupidity. Perhaps they knew that about each other: underneath all the stupidities, cruelties, and confusions, both Harriet Monroe and Ezra Pound were dedicated to poetry, the art, with an impersonal zeal that swallowed up every other consideration.

However, *Poetry* no longer had any real chance of capturing the best work of the new movement. The Jepson attack gen-

20. Harriet Monroe to Ezra Pound, November 25, 1918, in Ezra Pound Archive, Collection of American Literature, Beinecke Rare Book Room and Manuscript Library, Yale University.

21. Letter of February 1, 1919, in *Letters*, #159, pp. 147–48.

uinely paralyzed Harriet Monroe, and rendered her old balancing act between the schools unworkable. Only some good new work from Lindsay and Masters could have restored freedom of action to *Poetry*, and both of them were through as serious poets. They remained fastened to Harriet Monroe's neck; her notions of loyalty made repudiation impossible. Her sponsorship of the "Westerners," however much she tried to keep it in proportion, gave reality to Jepson's caricature. When she gave *Poetry*'s June, 1919, number over to Masters' "Domesday Book," and made a special defense of him in a survey of the schools in October—Masters, "who, of all our modern poets, has the most epic vision—shall he be denied free symphonic range within his large horizon, even though staccato poets and careful critics object to his smashing paces?"—she was animating the scarecrow created by Jepson. It is particularly irritating to see *Poetry* wrecked for Masters' sake, because he had done so little in his brief prime that had helped *Poetry*, and had been so quick to separate himself from the magazine when the Chicago Renaissance began to lose its glamour.

However, it was not the relationship with Masters, but the relationship with Ezra Pound, that was always crucial to the magazine's identity. The return of Pound, with his "Propertius" poems, was of very short duration. In April, 1919, the month after Sections I, II, III, and VI of "Homage to Sextus Propertius" were printed, Harriet Monroe published a letter from William Gardner Hale of the University of Chicago, a distinguished student of the Latin language, that was a violent attack on Pound's "translation." This attack on Pound reinforced the polarizations created by the Jepson article.

The issue in Hale's letter, "Pegasus Impounded," was not the simple one that had arisen early in the magazine's history when another University of Chicago classicist, Paul Shorey, objected that H.D. and Richard Aldington were inaccurate translators of Greek. Hale tended to the scholar's prejudice, that no one should attempt to translate a text before he is the easy master of its language. He rebuked Pound: "I beg him to lay aside the mask of erudition. And, if he must deal with Latin, I suggest that he paraphrase some accurate translation, and then employ some respectable student of the language to save him from blun-

ders. . . ."[22] Pound's defense against Hale, in a letter to A. R.
Orage that has been printed in Paige's edition of the *Letters*,
implies that the professor was insisting on an absolutely literal
translation, except that he was zealous to expunge every sexual
reference. But the argument was more complex and more intelligent than Pound would acknowledge.

Hale began by deploring the way in which Pound's poems
distorted Propertius' tone, substituting the flippant, the colloquial, and the obvious for what the original is "almost
academic," "consciously artistic." He was not so much concerned to bowdlerize Propertius as to defend a subtle, highly
mannered poetic tone. It is true that he called "devirginated
young ladies" a "decadent" meaning for the Latin "tacta puella,"
but he surely thought it an outrageous pun on "virgo intacta"—
"tacta puella," whose peculiar hilarity arises from the fact that
nothing special has happened to the lady or ladies; it is the adjec-
tive that has lost its chastity. Hale objected further that if he
granted Pound's right to make a translation in a colloquial tone,
the tone was not consistently maintained in the poem. He also
objected to comments and explanations dragged in to pad the
text. And he went on to cite a number of elementary blunders
that Pound had made in reading the Latin text.

Pound's defense against the attack was simply that his "Propertius" was not a translation. He wrote April 14, 1919, to

> Editor,
>
> Poetry.
>
> Cat-piss and porcupines!! The thing is no more a translation than
> my "Altaforte" is a translation, or than Fitzgerald's Omar is a
> translation.
>
> Poor brute naturally can't make much of the fragment of the
> poem you have used; but he misses a number of avoidances of
> literal meaning, including that unfortunate (from his presumable?
> point of view) misstatement about Thebes.
>
> In final commiseration,
>
> E. Pound

22. "Pegasus Impounded," *Poetry*, April, 1919 (copyright 1919 by Harriet Monroe,
renewed 1947 by the Modern Poetry Association). Reprinted by permission of the Editor
of *Poetry*.

Eliot put Pound's defense more quietly in 1928: "If the uninstructed reader is not a classical scholar, he will make nothing of it; if he be a classical scholar, he will wonder why this does not conform to his notions of what translation should be. It is not a translation, it is a paraphrase, or still more truly (for the instructed) a *persona*."[23] But these distinctions between translations, paraphrases, and *personae* avoid the point of Hale's attack: whether or not "Homage to Sextus Propertius" is a translation, Pound was caught out in a series of *mis*translations, many of which serve no very clear poetic purpose in English, most of which show Pound up as a person who was not easy with the Latin language. The first line of section II is the simplest illustration: "I had been seen in the shade, recumbent on cushioned Helicon." The Latin for "I had been seen" is "visus eram," and a Latinist would render it by some formula that would reflect the ingrained knowledge that the passive of the Latin "to see" is not rendered in English "to be seen" but "to seem." The instances Hale cited are only the most quotable or the most amusing; any uninstructed reader armed with the Loeb Library edition of the *Elegies* can hunt out fifteen or twenty more blunders for himself. And so many of them occur in lines that are lyrically and imaginatively neutral that one cannot imagine important poetic motives for the bad rendering, and concludes that Pound wrote his English line because he misread the Latin line.

The quarrel between Latinists and Poundians does not admit of solution, because both sides are right. Pound scholars can celebrate in "Propertius" Pound's first confident control of a larger rhythmic unit, the poem that marks a crucial stage in his poetic development,[24] the solution to the garrulity that marred the first drafts of the *Cantos*. But they do not meet the challenge that William Gardner Hale made. No one can properly dispute Pound's right to make a good poem that is a bad translation, but Hale was not unreasonable in treating "Propertius" as a translation. As a scholar at home in the Latin, he could not possibly read Pound's language without seeing the Latin in it: Latin torn to shreds, genders and cases wildly mismatched, English word

23. T. S. Eliot, Introduction to *Ezra Pound: Selected Poems*, reprinted by permission of Faber and Faber, Ltd.

24. Hugh Kenner, *The Poetry of Ezra Pound*, p. 156.

order brutally imposed on it. Hale's attack was overbearing; his
fury may have been a disillusioned disciple's. He quoted "Sor-
dello" in his letter to *Poetry*, and the Browning poem may have
been fresh in his mind because he had looked it up after a reading
of "Three Cantos." He refused to consider that Pound's linguistic carnage could create poetic value. One can imagine Pound
writing "Propertius," the mind sleeping over the Latin line, ob-
serving anything but the grammar, groping for something that
could strike fire, and creating language that was genuinely
Pound.[25] Pound came through with special vividness in section
VI, of the four sections Harriet Monroe selected:

> When, when and whenever death closes our eyelids
>
> Moving naked over Acheron
> Upon the one raft, victor and conquered together,
> Marius and Jugurtha together,
> > one tangle of shadows.[26]

But Ezra Pound could not afford to wave away the attacks of
scholars, "bald heads forgetful of their sins," with the serene
awareness that he had made a good poem. He could not expect to
be left alone by people like William Gardner Hale, for his long
campaign for accuracy, precision, and clarity in poetry did not fit
with the image of a mind sleeping over a line of text, waiting for
its own intuition to arise out of a cloud of hashed Latin. When he
published the poem without smoothing out the inaccuracies, he
was endangering the laboriously constructed *persona* of Ezra
Pound— the fiercely dedicated saint of the library who figured in
"Three Cantos," the "Mr. Pound, who has devoted some years
to an exhaustive study of metrical forms and variations in the
poetry of eleven languages." And William Gardner Hale's letter
seems to have smashed that mask, and brought Pound down to

25. Richard Aldington had said something like this about Pound's translations as early
as 1915: "In his many translations, among which is some of his best work, it is the
sudden, impulsive, emotional piece of translating which is successful; and the failure is in
the attempt to produce a piece of sustained hard work, like the translation of Guido
Cavalcanti and Arnaut Daniel." (*Egoist*, May 1, 1915, pp. 71–72.)

26. Excerpts from "Homage to Sextus Propertius" reprinted from *Personae* and *Collected Shorter Poems* (copyright 1926 by Ezra Pound) by permission of New Directions
Publishing Corporation and Faber and Faber, Ltd., publishers and Agents for the Trustees of the Ezra Pound Literary Property Trust.

the note of *Quia Pauper Amavi*, the title of the volume in which "Homage to Sextus Propertius" was published.

Harriet Monroe's motive in printing Hale's attack is open to question. She could have been retaliating for the drubbing that Pound, through Jepson, had given her six months before in the *Little Review*. But there is every evidence that she acted without malice in the affair. She felt that Hale's argument had reason in it, and that ordinary fair play required printing it. In 1930 she defended herself against a comment by Pound that she had mutilated "Propertius" by refusing to print the whole poem:

> . . . I did not "mutilate" his translation of Propertius; in fact, the four accepted sections of it were printed straight, exactly as they now stand in Mr. Pound's *Collected Poems*. These four sections covered nine *Poetry* pages, which would seem to be a fair showing of the anglicized Latin poet; to have used the entire series of twelve sections would have required a whole number, and perhaps agitated the censor. In fact, it was Mr. Pound who "mutilated" Propertius, for, according to the late William Gardner Hale, the distinguished University of Chicago Latinist, the translator made "excisions here and additions there." And in the next number of *Poetry* Mr. Hale listed certain school-boyish errors in an urbane and unanswerable letter which Mr. Pound has never forgiven.[27]

A fragment of the manuscript first draft of the above letter is preserved, which makes it clear that Hale had seen "Propertius" in manuscript or in proof before its *Poetry* publication, and that Harriet Monroe had printed Pound's poem over his strenuous protests: ". . . I printed the accepted portions of it straight, against the emphatic protest of my friend, the late Professor William Gardner Hale, [a few words here have been erased and are illegible] me in horror, begging me not to desecrate our pages with a translation guilty of numerous school-boyish errors. Nevertheless I printed it as it stood, over his protests, suggesting that Mr. Hale put his criticisms in a letter to the next issue of *Poetry*." There is a faint suggestion of the springing of a trap here. Ultimate loyalty would have required immediate notice to

27. Letter to W. Wilbur Hatfield, November 22, 1930, a copy in the Pound correspondence.

Pound. Harriet Monroe did send Pound a copy of the attack a few days in advance of its publication, and invited a rebuttal if he could keep it polite, though she did not think, she wrote, that he could have much to say in reply.[28]

But given the strained relation between them, it does not seem fair to expect ultimate loyalty. She felt that the printing of "Propertius" was an endorsement of Pound's point of view, and that the printing of Hale's letter was a necessary countergesture. The situation has vague analogies to the confusion over John Curtis Underwood's prize-winning poem in January, 1919, when *Poetry* printed Paul Fortier Jones's letter charging plagiarism, in a gesture that clearly hurt the editor and hurt the magazine's prestige. A sense of fair play forced Harriet Monroe to print Jones's letter, and one need look no further for her motive in printing Hale's letter. A scrap written by Carl Sandburg about the matter suggests that the discussions in the *Poetry* office were sometimes sympathetic to Pound: "Also there is Dr. Hale's handling of Pound. These two pieces ought to be printed to show what Americanese is and how a faithful literal translation wouldn't get by while a free slangy one makes a poem."[29] Finally, Harriet Monroe's reply to Pound's "resignation" was full of goodwill:

Nov. 1, 1919

My dear Mr. Pound:

Your last letter to me, received in May, was signed under the words, "In final commiseration."

I have taken this, as you doubtless intended, as a resignation from the staff of Poetry, a resignation emphasized by your subsequent silence. But as I am about to make an arrangement for a London correspondent, it may be as well for me to say this word in formal acceptance of the situation.

I feel unfailing gratitude for all that you did to help the magazine along during those difficult first years, and deep regret that we have had to come to a parting of the ways. I cordially hope that you will continue to contribute to *Poetry*, and that poems finer

28. Harriet Monroe to Ezra Pound, March 29, 1919, in Ezra Pound Archive, Collection of American Literature, Beinecke Rare Book Room and Manuscript Library, Yale University.
29. Note dated "June 1."

than you have ever written—which is saying a great deal—may be yours next year and the years after.

> With all good wishes, I am
>
> Yours sincerely,
>
> Harriet Monroe

The relatively few observers who could evaluate Hale's attack may have felt some brief satisfaction that Pound had been brought down from an exaggerated perch of erudition, but no one in the movement wanted Ezra Pound reduced or humiliated. It was Pound who kept things going, who emphasized development, who opened the door to new beginnings. One can sense love and fear for Ezra in William Carlos Williams' "Belly Music" in *Others* for July, 1919. It seems reasonable to take Williams' remarks in the last issue of *Others* as reaction to the "Propertius" attack, as a qualified rejection of Harriet Monroe and *Poetry* for Ezra's sake. Not that his stand in "Preface to *Kora in Hell*" had endorsed "Harriet, with the swirl of the prairie wind in her underwear,"[30] but he had belonged on *Poetry*'s side of the division between westerners and internationalists if he had to accept such a division. However, praise of Margaret Anderson in *Others* for July seems by implication a rebuke of Harriet Monroe's too inclusive editorial policies, of her deference to what everybody—including classical scholars—expected of a magazine of verse:

> Whatever can be said against her, and whatever can be said for Harriet Monroe who dug up good work when everyone else was sleeping, Margaret Anderson is the only one of them all who gets up a magazine that is not a ragbag. . . . I feel that M.A. has definitely made up her mind as to each thing she prints and that to the best of her ability she is striving to express in this way a definite SOMETHING, a something moreover that is the *best* that she knows how to do and not a conglomerate of what-is-expected of her. And being so the Little Review can never be a mere bundle of snippets, its aim to purvey the *best* tidbits, its great purpose to

30. Ezra Pound to William Carlos Williams, in *Letters*, #137, p. 124, quoted by Williams in "Preface to *Kora in Hell*."

have something of everything on its bill of fare. It is at worst the expression of M.A.'s personality, the personality of a woman of complete lack of judgment in literary matters. . . . I find matter for serious attention in Ezra Pound's discordant shrieking: to hell with singing the States and the plains and the Sierra Nevadas for their horses' vigor.

It is the NEW! not one more youthful singer, one more lovely poem. The *New*, the everlasting *New*, the everlasting defiance. Ezra has the smell of it. . . . If it must come to that I prefer Ezra Pound to anyone. Say the man is dead, say he began to die the first time he set foot on a gangplank. He at least went abroad rather than do something worse. He went because he had to. He went because it was too easy to remain in this country. I wish he were here today. He was not always dead and so *he cannot be dead now.*[31]

If Williams had to take sides, if the literary war were to become so bloody that no neutral ground was left, "If it must come to that I prefer Ezra Pound to anyone." Williams also rebuked Harriet Monroe's newest discovery, H. L. Davis, whose poems appeared in *Poetry* for April, 1919, disparaging the "loveliness" of his songs. In the same issue of *Others*, however, he passed on the torch to Emanuel Carnevali, Harriet Monroe's discovery of the year before and briefly associate editor of *Poetry* in 1919 and 1920, so that the net effect of his outbursts in *Others* is not a direct attack on Harriet Monroe.

William Carlos Williams is hard to interpret in this era because his own work was coming clear to him. In the midst of the general confusion he experienced some memorable euphorias, and his reactions were more mercurial than ever. He wrote Harriet Monroe on April 28, 1919, after a lecture he gave in Chicago:

I was insane while I was in Chicago. I flung myself about like a silly wave. . . . I cannot say that I shall ever recover from that rain sodden but vicariously sunshiney week! It was as if, or rather it was actually—I had never in my life before had an opportunity to be just a poet, the one thing I want to be. I was, to the vulgar

31. "Belly Music," *Others*, July, 1919, pp. 27–31 (copyright 1919 by Alfred Kreymborg). Reprinted by permission of New Directions Publishing Corporation, publishers and Agents for Mrs. William Carlos Williams. All rights reserved.

eye at least, a poet! I was at least as near to being a poet as I had ever been and it was as if new bones had been put into me, etc. etc. etc. We are only beginning. I feel that barring death I shall see some work done in the next five years that will be unrivalled anywhere at any time. We are at the opening of a golden age of poetry HERE.

Criticizing some war poems by Richard Aldington and D. H. Lawrence published in *Poetry* that summer, Williams came up with his clearest description yet of his relation to New Jersey: "Poetry is not a despairing cry of defiance. It is not a bottle to nurse. It is an assertion: I am here today in the midst of living hell! I equal to any hell. . . . The poet must use anything at hand to assert himself. If he cannot do so he is less than great. The proof that I am I is that I can use anything, not a special formula but anything. That is the first necessity."[32] Connecting the poet's relation to a locale with the assertion of his isolated uniqueness, Williams short-circuited to his own satisfaction Jepson's polarity between nationalists and internationalists.

In the *Little Review* for April, 1919, Margaret Anderson printed a response to the "Propertius" attack in *Poetry* that is a good example of the allusive and personal way in which she liked to manage literary controversy:

> Harriet Monroe came to town. . . . I had a little talk with her one morning which we could have made into a "solemn" discussion, until I promised to spare her the bordeom of my repetitious remarks about what is and what is not Art. She was saying "And you don't like Galli-Curci? To me she is really an artist in her slight, rococo way." And, when I objected: "I mean just as Louis Quinze furniture is art." I objected again. "Of course that is an unfortunate example: I didn't mean anything so artificial as Louis Quinze." I objected again. And then we laughed and let it go.
>
> But all this might serve as an explanation of why I wanted to start a *Little Review*: namely, that when you talk of Galli-Curci or Caruso or McCormack, etc., etc., you are not talking of anything that has to do with the old fiery fountains except to remind you

32. "Four Foreigners," *Little Review*, September, 1919, p. 38 (copyright 1919 by Margaret C. Anderson). Reprinted by permission of New Directions Publishing Corporation, publishers and Agents for Mrs. William Carlos Williams. All rights reserved.

again that they are far off; that when you think of Louis Quinze
furniture as Art you are destroying all separations between craft
and aesthetics; and when you call such furniture or such a period
artificial you are destroying all the finer possibilities of thought.
A group of Russians killing themselves over the problems of the
universe can be just as artificial as the spectacle of Louis' court
laughing its way to death. Manners are not the criterion of arti-
ficiality.[33]

The difference between craft and aesthetics: the "Propertius"
attack, which Miss Anderson would not dignify by acknowledgment, showed *Poetry* unable to distinguish the essential
spiritual activity of the artist from his accidental activity, just as
Poetry's emphasis on nationalism, in Jepson's account, distracted
attention from what is essential to what is accidental in poetry.
Thus the Hale attack on Pound reinforced the polarizations
created by the Jepson attack, although it seems paradoxical that
the home base of ploppeyed bungaroos had suddenly become the
locus of misplaced academic precision.

It is not possible, in the postwar atmosphere, to trace reactions
to Hale's attack accurately, just as it is not possible to be precise
about the effect of the Jepson attack. Harriet Monroe in any case
would have been displaced from the forefront of the movement.
Not only were her attitudes on the censorship question out of
date after the publication of *Ulysses*; her peculiar blend of democratic idealism and devotion to the artist did not belong to the
twenties. Perhaps the crucial difference between the twenties
and the "generation of 1914" was the elimination of the political
note. Earlier, Margaret Anderson could espouse both art and
anarchism in the *Little Review*, the *Masses* could promote socialism
and free verse as if they were somehow the same thing, *Poetry*
could expect that new vigor in the art would renew the nation.
The twenties seem expressed by Scofield Thayer's *Dial* and by
the post-1917 Margaret Anderson: the ultimate appeal is personal, not social or political. The twenties were in their turn
superseded, of course, and the detached aestheticism of Thayer
came to seem remote from the later social philosophies of Eliot
and Pound, and from the radical politics of the thirties. Harriet

33. "As One Would Not," *Little Review*, April, 1919, pp. 57–58.

Monroe's political idealism can be related to Pound's persistent philosophy, and even to Eliot's. But her particular version of democratic aspiration was out of date in 1919. There was nothing theoretical about her feeling for the western landscape; she had hiked and camped in Arizona, New Mexico, and the Sierras for years. But when she returned in *Poetry* for September, 1919, to some of her favorite old themes, the note of Emerson and Whitman seemed dowdy, and her rhetoric simplistic in the postwar atmosphere:

> Will not the spiritual renewal of the race, especially of this rainbow-hearted race of ours which is forming out of the union of many strains—will not the spiritual renewal of the race, out of which great art must spring, come rather from a more direct appeal to more original sources—through the immediate contact of our people with nature in her sacred and intimate reserves? And will not the new art take its hint from aboriginal art—perhaps from the art of the Aztecs and the Pueblos—rather than from derivations of pseudo-classic derivations long separated from their primitive Greek source?
>
> In the love of our people for Nature lies the highest hope of the race. Out of this will develop, we may hope, spiritual freedom and an indigenous and self-expressive art.

The files of *Poetry* for 1920 give the impression that all the poets ran away to the *Dial* the moment Scofield Thayer opened up his shop, but clearly the drift away from *Poetry* began in 1919. By January, 1920, Harriet Monroe's file of accepted verse was almost empty of interesting work, and many of the important lead-off and closing spots during the year went to poets who used to be lucky if they were included in the mob in the middle of the leaflet. Contrast 1920 in the *Dial*. Scofield Thayer headed his first issue in January with a group of poems by E. E. Cummings that announced a significant new poet in the loudest terms. In April, Marianne Moore appeared. Cummings had five more poems in the next month. Ezra Pound in June affirmed the value of the *Cantos* with number four—"Palace in smoky light," substantially as it was printed in *A Draft of XVI Cantos*. Six poems by William Carlos Williams in the next issue are among the very best of his early short poems; indeed, they threaten to overflow into "loveliness." Six sections of Pound's "Mauberley" were printed in September, and William Butler Yeats appeared in November with a group that raises the hair on the head, ending with "The Second Coming." These are only the most brilliant of the poets published over the year in the *Dial*. Scofield Thayer apparently achieved this record by luck; at least the arrangement for Pound's foreign editorship was not completed until March, 1920, and was instigated by Eliot, who was worried because Pound had lost most of his magazine connections in London.[34] The full story of the *Dial* has not been told yet; someone on the paper was a discriminating reader of the new poetry, but Thayer found the *Cantos* "silly" and *The Waste Land* "very disappointing."[35] Probably no editor makes a publication record as good as Thayer's without the assistance of a great deal of luck.

The generation of the twenties saw none of the old glamour of renaissance in *Poetry*; its place in the movement seemed to them altogether marginal. James Sibley Watson, publisher of the new *Dial*, did some archeological research into the history of American letters in 1921 and came up with this account of the beginnings of the new poetry:

> This book [*Des Imagistes*, published in 1914 by Kreymborg's *Glebe*, with liberal unacknowledged reprints from *Poetry*] is still a pleasure to read, and seems older than the Golden Treasury. . . . *Des Imagistes* was followed by *The Egoist* in England and *The Little Review* and *Others* in this country. Only a little farther west *Poetry* turned up Sandburg; Amy Lowell and Vachel Lindsay gave readings. Of other poets to whom the public has paid out from time to time a little rope Edgar Lee Masters has hanged himself thoroughly and often . . . and Robert Frost has continued meritoriously.[36]

Poetry in Watson's account was on the western margin, discovering a Chicago poet or two, vaguely associated with Amy Lowell, while the *Little Review* and the *Egoist*, the two chief outlets for Amygism, were with *Others* the main carriers of a movement that originated in *Des Imagistes*. This account, which especially exaggerates the importance of the poetry published before 1917 by the

34. Reid, *John Quinn*, pp. 434–35.
35. Nicholas Joost, *Scofield Thayer*, p. 111.
36. W. C. Blum [pseud.], "American Letter," *Dial*, May, 1921, p. 564.

Little Review and the *Egoist*, has remained ever since a commonly accepted one.

A rather pathetic note of isolation, of exhaustion from the mere clerical problems of getting out the magazine, is sounded in several of Harriet Monroe's letters at this time.[37] These strains reflect problems in staffing the *Poetry* office. Helen Hoyt, who became associate editor in the fall of 1918, left in a year. Her place was filled by Emanuel Carnevali, but his tenure was brief and tragic, since he was troubled by the first symptoms of a nervous disease that was to incapacitate him. Marion Strobel became associate editor in the spring of 1920, beginning a relation with *Poetry* that was to last for many years. Eunice Tietjens in this era returned to Chicago and became a member of *Poetry*'s advisory board, replacing Edith Wyatt in April, 1919; she contributed a fair amount of prose over the next few years.

But none of these de facto associate editors replaced Alice Corbin Henderson. None of them had her critical trenchancy, and none of them could challenge and debate Harriet Monroe as a peer. When the worsening of Mrs. Henderson's illness in 1920 cut the stream of comment that had been emanating from Santa Fe since 1916, the loss to Harriet Monroe seems more serious than the value of the comment, as criticism, can express. She was losing the mind that had shared *Poetry* with her since the beginning, and there was no other mind with which she could enter into an unconstrained dialogue. She was moving toward the Harriet Monroe whom Vachel Lindsay described in the twenties, in a letter to a young writer and would-be editor: "you need Harriet, and, if I may be plain, she needs you. She is a tired, hard-fighting valiant woman. Because she is so plain-spoken, all but the hardy leave her alone in that office. . . . If you could persuade her that your magazine was a real rival of hers you would do her more good than a barrel of hooch. She has seen them live and die in three months so long, it is not good for her."[38]

37. Letter of April 21, 1919, to Maxwell Bodenheim, a copy in the Bodenheim correspondence; letter of February 3, 1920, to Yvor Winters, a copy in the Winters correspondence.

38. Letter of February 16, 1925, to Harry A. Maguire, a copy in the Lindsay correspondence.

The gap left by another lost *Poetry* correspondent, Ezra Pound, was filled briefly by Richard Aldington, who acted as *Poetry*'s foreign correspondent from the fall of 1919 to the summer of 1921. He seems to have come back from the war full of malaise. His comment on Edward Storer in *Poetry* for May, 1921, that his book showed "that unavowed but deep despair which holds so many sensitive minds in a distracted Europe," reads like a comment on himself. The fading away of Aldington represented for Harriet Monroe the loss of yet another link with the old days; he had been the first of Pound's Imagistes published in *Poetry*. And while counting the old associates who fell away, one must notice the news in *Poetry* for October, 1920, of the resignation of H. C. Chatfield-Taylor from the advisory board. The dean of Harriet Monroe's guarantors and the first of her advisors broke the connection because he was retiring from Chicago and rearranging his affairs.

But although the movement had moved over to the *Dial*, although *Poetry*'s subscription list dwindled by a third during 1920, although most of her original associates broke off connection with the magazine, Harriet Monroe did not bow to fate and gracefully retire. Her commitment to editing *Poetry* predated the movement, was prior to all the euphoria about renaissance and all the bickering about concentration. In the darkness of 1911, when everyone knew there was no market for books of poetry, she had conceived the idea of a magazine that would give the poet a place of his own, where hopefully he could develop a sympathetic audience for his work and come to earn a modest living by it. Her efforts had been rewarded by a development of poetry beyond any possible anticipation.

It is not surprising that Harriet Monroe decided, on the whole, that she had some reason to be proud and little reason to feel defeat. It is not surprising that she came at times to exaggerate *Poetry*'s role in the movement so that she had everyone discovered and first published in the pages of her magazine. It was the vision that her experience with the magazine left with her, after the movement became established and the established poets moved away from her: she had nursed a feeble spark against the darkness, which had gradually grown in strength and power until the fire spread away in all directions. If in 1920 she found herself again in darkness, she nerved herself and asserted a continuing strength in herself. She quietly raised her subscription rate and weathered *Poetry*'s sharpest financial crisis without a public appeal for funds. Perhaps a new contact with Ezra Pound, who wrote in October, 1920, suggesting that *Poetry* publish a long poem by Ford Madox Hueffer that the *Dial* had rejected, put some of the old zest back into her. But the vigorous new development of Wallace Stevens' poetry was probably her strongest prop in the crisis.

Of all the poets of the new movement, Wallace Stevens felt the most unconstrained friendship for Harriet Monroe. He had sympathized in an understated way when Williams had attacked *Poetry* in *Others* for July, 1919, damning the "loveliness" of H. L. Davis' work. When he sent a big group of poems to Harriet Monroe on August 16, 1919, he commented, "As part of the campaign against the horrors of beauty, I write on this pumpkin-colored paper."[39] And when Alfred Kreymborg asked to reprint the poems from *Poetry* in an *Others* anthology, Stevens felt that *Others* owed some gesture to *Poetry*. He wrote October 8, 1919, that his poems published in *Poetry* that month "evoked a note from the long-lost explorer, A. Kreymborg, who wants to put the thing in this year's *Others* anthology. I said that he might do as he liked, but thought he should first procure your consent."[40]

Stevens expressed pleasure and pride in "Pecksniffiana," the poems Harriet Monroe published in October, 1919. Harassed by business trips to Washington, he called the poems a "leaf in a storm," but also wrote October 8: "now . . . I must confess, or boast, that that one leaf doesn't look so rotten, when examined with care. True it is under the curse of miscellany, but in parts I am satisfied." The group includes "Fabliau of Florida," "Homunculus et la Belle Etoile," "The Weeping Burgher," "Peter Parasol," "Exposition of the Contents of a Cab," "Ploughing on Sunday," "Banal Sojourn," "The Indigo Glass in the Grass,"

39. In *Letters*, #232.
40. Ibid., #233.

"Anecdote of the Jar," "On the Surface of Things," "The Curtains in the House of the Metaphysician," "The Place of the Solitaires," "The Paltry Nude Starts on a Spring Voyage," and "Colloquy with a Polish Aunt." The bulk, variety, and timing of this publication presented Stevens more effectively than earlier publications had done, and Harriet Monroe had reason to be pleased with it. A strong Stevens group should have been particularly effective in breaking the Jepson stereotype of *Poetry*—no poet writing had less of the cowboy in him.

Poetry did not claim any special relation to Stevens, whose reticent and subtle personality abhorred literary grouping and clubbing. His description of a visit with William Carlos Williams, a few years later, suggests the complexity of his attitudes toward his fellows in the movement: "Williams drove through town a few weeks ago on his way to Vermont with one of his children and a dog. It was a blessing to see him although we were both as nervous as two belles in new dresses."[41] Stevens belonged to *Poetry* only in the sense that he admired Harriet Monroe as an editor, felt a friendly confidence in her, and valued her praise.

At the beginning of this friendship, in 1915, Harriet Monroe had made the biggest single blunder in her editorship, the failure to recognize the unity of "Sunday Morning," the printing of it as a rearranged fragment. One could expatiate at length on the unworthiness of such treatment of Stevens, but Stevens did not resent it. The sum total of Harriet Monroe's editorial gestures at the beginning of his career pleased him, and it is difficult to work up more indignation on his behalf than he felt himself.

His embarrassment about the praise Harriet Monroe gave "Pecksniffiana" demonstrates the confusion of his attitude toward his own poetry. She not only managed the award of the much controverted Levinson Prize to the group, but took advantage of the necessity of reviewing the *Others* anthology, in *Poetry* for December, 1920, to give Stevens a recognition she felt he had been evading:

> At last a chance to say a word about this reticent poet, who refuses to print a book and thereby prove himself the peer of any poet

41. Letter of August 24 [1922], ibid., #252.

now living, and of many a famous one now dead and enshrined. I well remember the amazed delight with which we received his contribution to our "war number" of November, 1914—a new and significant note from a man then unknown—and crowded it in although the magazine was already made up. And since then his every appearance in our pages has been, for us, a distinguished honor, of which the recent award of the Levinson Prize to his *Pecksniffiana* is too slight an acknowledgment.

One risks banality in any comment on works of art of complete and perfect beauty, but the public should be reminded that no less than that is what Mr. Stevens often achieves. . . . Here is a poet as unapologetically modern, and as generous and self-content, as the Elizabethans were in their day; a poet rich and humorous and profound, provocative of joy, creative of beauty in those who can respond to him.

This review, with the Levinson Prize award announced the month before, was enough to prove that *Poetry*, although abandoned by the international elite, was not to be discounted. Stevens was rather overwhelmed, writing December 2, 1920:

I am much more modest than you think, or than the overblown bloom I am suggests. Really, the bouquet in this month's Poetry will drive me to back alleys and the suburbs. I wrote you such a rotten letter about the prize, but it was only because I always write letters of that sort when they happen to be letters that I feel obliged to write. You know as well as I do that I should much rather not have written anything. I rather thought you might reply, and when I failed to hear from you I feared that my letter had got on your nerves. But there is nothing in this month's Poetry to indicate it. I shall be sending you another batch of things bye and bye, but prefer to allow your panegyrics to fade a little out of mind before I reappear.[42]

In October, 1921, *Poetry* published another big Stevens group, including "Palace of the Babies," "From the Misery of Don Joost," "The Doctor of Geneva," "Gubbinal," "The Snow Man," "Tea at the Palaz of Hoon," "The Cuban Doctor," "Another Weeping Woman," "On the Manner of Addressing Clouds," "Of Heaven Considered as a Tomb," "The Load of Sugar-Cane," and "Hibiscus on the Sleeping Shores." The

42. Ibid., #240.

269

surest evidence that this publication had impact is the *Dial*'s notice of it in November, 1921, the first attention given *Poetry* since James Sibley Watson had pushed it off to the western fringes of the movement: "Twelve poems by Wallace Stevens in *Poetry* for October are the best single chance one has had of estimating this *farouche* author." The comment, which is not particularly accurate, probably should be interpreted as a signal to Stevens that the *Dial* would like some of his work, and the next year the *Dial* published a Stevens group that included "The Emperor of Ice Cream." But if Stevens followed almost all of *Poetry*'s old contributors into Scofield Thayer's fold,[43] the moral victory remained Harriet Monroe's.

Stevens' modesty about his work is extraordinary. When he finally got to work to make a volume, he felt more self-reproach than self-approval during his preparation of *Harmonium*. He wrote Harriet Monroe on October 28, 1922: "Gathering together the things for my book has been so depressing that I wonder at Poetry's friendliness. All my earlier things seem like horrid cocoons from which later abortive insects have sprung. The book will amount to nothing, except that it may teach me something."[44] And he wrote two months later, on December 21: "I have omitted many things, exercising the most fastidious choice, so far as that was possible among my witherlings. To pick a crisp salad from the garbage of the past is no snap."[45] In his talk of cocoons and garbage, he seems to cringe away from the dead selves entombed in the poems; his attitude toward his own work seems a variant of Williams' "what I have done clings to me horribly." But unlike Williams, Stevens did not feel that publication freed him of a poem, although the delicate, unforced response of readers was precious to him. For both reasons he found the mechanics of literary promotion unpleasant. His reticence kept his poetic status undefined for much longer than the quality of the work deserved.

43. Stevens apparently resisted Scofield Thayer's efforts to promote him. Thayer wrote him in December, 1923, asking for poems to print that winter along with a review of *Harmonium* by Marianne Moore, and did not get "Sea Surface Full of Clouds" in time to print before July, 1924. Thayer regarded this as a "rebuff," according to Joost, *Scofield Thayer*, p. 200.

44. In *Letters*, #254.

45. Ibid., #256.

Some other factors may have confused the reception of Stevens' early poetry. Bynner and Ficke pushed the Spectric hoax beyond the limits of a good joke when they associated Stevens with their fictitious school in the preface to *Spectra*. Perhaps Ezra Pound's long silence about Stevens' poetry, in his criticism as well as in his correspondence, contributed something to its poor reception. Many critics took their cues from Pound, even the ones, like Lowell and Untermeyer, who abused him. Williams in his final editorial blast in *Others* for July, 1919, "Gloria!" joyfully denounced the magazine's entire publication: somehow the sewer no longer ran free, and the *Others* poets were living in their own filth.[46] He did not make an exception for "Le Monocle de Mon Oncle," which appeared in *Others* for December, 1918. Stevens felt with some justice that Harriet Monroe had been his principal sponsor. He wrote August 24, 1922, about plans for *Harmonium*, "This, by the way, is confidential for the present; but I don't know of anyone more entitled to first news of it than yourself."[47]

Harriet Monroe's praise of Stevens as "provocative of joy, creative of beauty," reminds one of the strain she had admired in Pound's work, the "oblation to pure beauty." As criticism, her talk about beauty does not throw much light, but it seems an index to her most personal, least theoretical preferences in poetry. Her ideal of response to the needs of the moment seems attractive when she emphasizes precise and delicate choice, and her editorial response as a whole shows very keen perception of the poetry of her day. But elevated to an abstraction, the mystique of the moment left her helpless against her passionate hopes for America. While her judgment was often stampeded by hope for the poet in the Promethean role, when she talked about beauty she was responding directly to poetic language, and her choices were the right ones. This double response accounts for her contradictory enthusiasms, especially for her simultaneous promotion of Pound and of Lindsay.

In 1921 Harriet Monroe's persistence was rewarded. The outlines of *Poetry*'s new place in the literary world began to come

46. "Gloria!" *Others*, July, 1919, pp. 3–4.
47. In *Letters*, #252.

clear. If it was less glorious than the old, it was an improvement over the vacuum in which the magazine seemed suspended in 1920. The contrast with the *Dial* was still embarrassing for *Poetry*, but in 1921 the *Dial* was already haunted by its past; the effect of its poetry publication was not so stunning as the effect of 1920. A number of poets seem ordinary. And the surprise was gone: there was no new discovery to match E. E. Cummings, and the new strength in Pound, Yeats, and Williams was no longer news. The universe of *Dial* poetry was one in which *Poetry* could coexist, poor as its record continued.

Poetry's role in the twenties began to emerge in 1921. First, it was a place for the occasional good poem rejected by a more prestigious magazine. *Poetry*'s history made it an outlet that a poet of reputation could use without disgrace. Recognition of this fact was implicit in Ezra Pound's return to the editorial counsel of the magazine. After his furious resignation in April, 1919, Pound stayed out of contact for eighteen months, during which he took on the foreign editorship of the *Dial*. He wrote October 11, 1920, to suggest that *Poetry* publish Ford Madox Hueffer's "A House," the best poem he had written since "On Heaven." The *Dial*, Pound implied, could not print the poem in time to synchronize with English publication; to protect the copyright he reluctantly offered the poem to *Poetry*. Having printed "On Heaven," Harriet Monroe had a right to the next chance at "A House." She replied offering to print a shortened version of the poem, which appeared in *Poetry* for March, 1921. Hueffer on February 10, 1921, wrote a charming letter of acknowledgment, overburdened with politic qualifications:

> I am sure that there will be a special niche for you on Parnassus, or the Heaven of Good Poets, wherever it be. I don't know the United States well enough to lecture you about yourself— but . . . at least for its periodicals, that nation is infinitely ahead of all its Anglo-Saxon brethren. And, if that periodical literature has a little peak, a little crown, raising it to the best of European cosmopolitanism, or at any rate in that direction, it is because you and your small paper showed how it could be done. It is a fine achievement.

About the same time he sent the Hueffer poem, Pound in a letter of November 28, 1920, offered Harriet Monroe those sections of

Mauberley that the *Dial* had not used. Since the whole poem had been published by the Ovid Press, Harriet Monroe would in any case have refused to reprint, and one cannot make anything of her refusal of this offer. Three weeks later Pound sent the apologia on the occasion of his departure from England that appeared in *Poetry* for March, 1921, as "Thames Morasses." After December, 1920, he did not write again until the spring of 1922, but the channel was open, and he kept up some correspondence through the twenties.

Poetry's second function in its new phase may be inferred by a glance at the poets published in 1921 and 1922. It was what Pound called in 1930 "a very meritorious trade journal,"[48] a clearinghouse for the work of the young and the relatively unknown. One notices publications by Elinor Wylie, John Peale Bishop, Elizabeth Madox Roberts, Glenway Wescott, Ernest Walsh, Louise Bogan, and Yvor Winters. The two most pretentious "discoveries" of the era were Genevieve Taggard and Edwin Curran, who do not add up to much in the permanent record.

Under the head of "discoveries" Harriet Monroe probably deserves a credit for the editorial intuition that sent her looking early in the twenties for new poetry written out of southern regional traditions. The fruit of this was the southern number of April, 1922. Unfortunately, she had inquired into the wrong corner of the South; her issue features DuBose Heyward, Hervey Allen, Beatrice Ravenel, and other members of the Poetry Society of South Carolina. By a rather stunning coincidence, April, 1922, was the month of first publication of the *Fugitive*. Harriet Monroe's patronage was rather resented by the Fugitives. An unsigned editorial note by Donald Davidson in their magazine for June–July, 1923, bids her bon voyage on her trip to Europe: "one supposes that American Poetry will have to limp along as best it may in her absence." Noting Miss Monroe's directions to southern poets in a recent review of DuBose Heyward, Davidson protested that poets "will create from what is nearest and deepest in experience—whether it be new or old, North, South, East, or West—and what business is that of Aunt

48. "Small Magazines," p. 692.

Harriet's?" Allen Tate wrote a courteous explanation of the motives behind the comment June 22, 1923: "we fear very much to have the slightest stress laid upon Southern traditions in literature; we who are Southerners know the fatality of such an attitude—the old atavism and sentimentality, even at this late date, are always imminent." Much later, in 1932, Tate himself edited another southern number for Harriet Monroe, by way of healing the breach.

Certain writers in the twenties made an occasional contribution to *Poetry* for motives that fall under no general category. Robert Frost sent a poem in July, 1920, his first contribution since his acknowledgment of the prize award for "Snow" in 1917. Frost may have felt, in the year that was *Poetry*'s nadir, a chivalrous sympathy for an old acquaintance in distress, but there is no evidence of such a motive in his correspondence. Harriet Monroe asked him for more poems, to make up a group, and November 12, 1921, Frost sent "The Witch of Coös" as a substitute for the poem on hand. The image of the skeleton balancing its way up the stairs from the cellar was a possible symbol for *Poetry* at this time, as it was a symbol for Frost himself, who was supposed to lie quiet with the rest of the western school. Although probably neither she nor Frost read the poem that way, Harriet Monroe published it quickly at the head of the issue for January, 1922, and awarded it the Levinson Prize for that publishing year. Frost had one other *Poetry* publication during the twenties.

William Carlos Williams was surprisingly slow to break off connection with *Poetry* in the twenties, considering how loudly he had suffered and continued to suffer under Harriet Monroe's editorial policies. Apparently the side of him that forgave her transgressions in the name of his wife was as real as the side of him that liked to denounce her vicious methods, and he meant the affection that he occasionally expressed for her in his correspondence. Nothing else explains his continuing as a *Poetry* contributor in this era when he had the *Dial* available to him, although Williams, like Wallace Stevens about the same time, felt rather abandoned by the Lost Generation's rush for Europe. One Williams letter in particular, written November 21, 1921, gives an eerie sense that the American poetry renaissance was coming into its fullness in New Jersey just as everybody was distracted away to Paris: "New York is very delightful this fall with all the neurosis in Paris. One walks the streets in quiet enjoyment knowing there is no one of importance to be met at the next corner. . . . I believe, really, that I am learning how to write at last. Perhaps I am even learning out of what to make up my pellets. This is all very uncertain." And he wrote the next month, pleased by his poems in the forthcoming *Poetry*, "I hope to live to grow old for really life is barely beginning."

The correspondence between Williams and Harriet Monroe continued to have a slapstick quality, with alternations of attitude too rapid to follow. After Williams' attack on *Poetry* in *Others* for July, 1919, Harriet Monroe was vigorously angry, judging by her response to Alfred Kreymborg's requests for his *Others Anthology*,[49] but she did not express her anger to Williams. Instead, Williams angrily withdrew all his manuscripts from the *Poetry* files at the beginning of 1920, asking her not to inquire into his reasons. He wrote June 10, 1920, asking for a "final and direct answer" to his question whether she would agree to print his work as written. When she reluctantly agreed to print his lines without capital letters at the beginnings, he replied October 4, 1920, with a tirade against mere formalism: "You yield to me in this as if you were granting me a favor. Is it possible that a person who even lets such a matter enter his consciousness can matter at all as an editor." But he submitted "A Goodnight," which was printed in *Poetry* for January, 1921, "as in copy."

He reappeared as a *Poetry* contributor the next spring, May 14, 1921, with a farcical little note: "After May 1st all poems by William Carlos Williams will be $50.—a piece mmmm—so get a thrill by rejecting a five or six hundred dollars worth while you may." Harriet Monroe had a marginal note on this letter, "These ac'd—if at our *usual* rates." Williams replied June 25: "Of course I am glad to have you take the four poems which you have selected—and at your own terms. It isn't you at whom I am

49. Kreymborg's letter of October 31, 1919, makes it clear that her first impulse was to deny permission to reprint *Poetry* poems in an *Others* anthology, but Kreymborg's next, undated letter agrees to forget it: "And no apologies—let's call it a hasty misunderstanding—that's all."

aiming when I set a high price on the poems I write. It is simply that it is time I settled this matter for myself—etc. There is nothing I would not do for you if I could. Mrs. Williams, who is your staunch champion, is always made content by my appearance in Poetry. She thanks you." The group that appeared in *Poetry* for January, 1922, showed the power of which Williams was becoming more and more confident—"Wild Orchard," "The Lonely Street," "Spouts," and "The Widow's Lament in Springtime." This work by Williams is so much more realized than most of the poems in *Poetry* at the time, the magazine gained so much from Williams as a contributor, that it is surprising that Harriet Monroe returned his next contribution, a group he sent April 15, 1922, with the comment "perhaps it is too soon." Judicious in extremis, Miss Monroe apparently did not wish to show special favor to Williams, and he seems to have given her up. The correspondence grew occasional in the twenties, although *Poetry* printed some poetry by Williams.

The blandness of much of the work in the *Poetry* of the twenties brings attention to Harriet Monroe's greatest editorial vice: her consistent kindness to the polished, well-bred poet who seems to be operating between firmly fixed limits—"who hasn't the *germ* of development, who will never *get* anywhere," as Mrs. Henderson wrote in 1916. Grace Hazard Conkling, Grace Fallow Norton, Louise Ayres Garnett, Florence Wilkinson, Louise Driscoll, Marjorie Allen Seiffert, and Antoinette DeCoursey Patterson seem examples of this type, among the poets published in 1921–22. Highly literate, intelligent, even ambitious, as these ladies were, their poetry fades into background music; their poems are memorable only when they blunder into fatuousness. There seems too much of this sort of work in *Poetry* at every stage of Harriet Monroe's editorship, and it is the inclusion of this work, rather than the inclusion of a "western school," which seems the excess of her "open door" policy. Probably one motive behind her sympathy for the minor poet was her knowledge that she was this kind of poet herself. The effect on her own verse of Pound's reform of style had been a loss of pontification, but also a loss of aspiration: she no longer wrote the kind of poem that asserted itself ambitiously. To a great degree Harriet Monroe was the person whom Pound had wondered about in 1913, who would "stand for a level of criticism even when it throws out most of their own work," but she could not go the whole way and block the lesser poets out of the magazine. There are at least two poets, moreover, whose publishing history in *Poetry* justifies her inclusiveness.

Sara Teasdale is the luminous example of the poet who worked a small conventional vein to come up with poems of constantly increasing excellence. The *Dial* in March, 1921, judged that she wrote in "an unimportant genre; the same impulse produced it that drives most women to needlework." But she moved over the years a long way from mock pastorals of girlish emotion like "Strephon kissed me." When one reads through the files of *Poetry*, Sara Teasdale's later poems stand out from the horde of dramatizations of feminine experience, partly because of a greatly superior tact, partly because of an intensity that lifts them out of the category altogether.

The movement passed over Sara Teasdale because she shut herself away from it, preferring the friendships that she formed in the New York Poetry Society of America with people who did not excite her admiration as poets.[50] Her inner life was extraordinarily lonely and she shrank from sharing it. She was once tempted to enter the free-verse quarrel, but withdrew her little article March 27, 1919, commenting, "it was borne in upon me that I had no business engaging in controversies." Also, her fellow poets found her work annoyingly popular. Her *Love Poems* received the first Poetry Society of America–Columbia Prize in 1918, precursor of the Pulitzer Prize for poetry, and "every old magazine" would take her poems, as she wrote Harriet Monroe on May 3, 1919.

But Sara Teasdale was something more than the most admired of magazine poets. The space and the setting for a good-sized group of poems were not easily available to her outside the pages of *Poetry*, and she valued *Poetry* publication for that reason. And the increasing strength of her work, first noticeable in "Songs Out of Stress" in *Poetry* for June, 1917, was related to the move-

50. Her letter of October 24, 1918, describes the P.S.A. as "a hopeless place if one is expecting any spiritual awakening," but "entertaining from the human standpoint."

ment, because it reflected the influence of Yeats. "I've been reading Yeats furiously again. He is the greatest poet living without the shadow of a doubt and wonder of wonders, he has never written better poems than those in his new book," she wrote April 6, 1919, of *The Wild Swans at Coole*. Since the book got a patronizing review in *Poetry* for October, 1918, from Marianne Moore, Sara Teasdale wrote a note on the excellence of the later Yeats, printed in *Poetry* for February, 1920, as the anonymous comment of a distinguished poet, expressing surprise that the reviews of Yeats's last book were so lukewarm.

Sara Teasdale's response to Harriet Monroe's suggestions for revisions in her poems was entirely amiable, but showed her the conscious literary artist. She wrote May 13, 1919, about revisions to the group "Memories," published in *Poetry* for September, 1919: "You are entirely right about the song 'It is not a word,' and I am enclosing it in a much improved version, thanks to your ideas. It is good now and I think you will wish to put it into the group. The group should be called 'Memories' and read with that title it gains weight and effectiveness. . . . You are right, 'Let it be forgotten' is one of the best songs I've ever done, and comes nearer in music and a sort of silence at the end, to what I mean by a lyric, than anything else of mine that I can think of." She found the revision process, which many poets resented from Harriet Monroe, a valuable opportunity to rethink the poem, and she respected Miss Monroe's reactions to her lines. The depth of Sara Teasdale's respect for Harriet Monroe came through in a paragraph she wrote March 13, 1931, a few years before her death: "I have often wanted to tell you—but have been shy about it—that I consider you one of the three straightest people I have known in my life. I prefer that quality, straightness, to any other, but if I were to add one for you, it would be valor."

In *Poetry* in the twenties, the poet who might be automatically rejected by the avant-garde magazines, and who would be read without attention in the "big" magazines, had a chance of a respectful hearing. Harriet Monroe felt that the minor poet had a right to a decent hearing on his own terms. Not very many writers profited as Sara Teasdale did from the opening that

Poetry offered. John Hall Wheelock was perhaps one. He patiently and gratefully endured years of Harriet Monroe's blue-penciling and set a very high value on her literary judgment. At the very beginning of the magazine, he wrote requesting the review of his books. About 1920 Wheelock seems to have emerged into a new, if rather bleak, understanding of himself as a poet. He wrote Harriet Monroe on March 29, 1920:

> You indicated that you felt I had made some progress in my statement of what I had to say—and the review throughout was encouraging to me in many ways. Perhaps I need that now more than you think, if my work is of the sort that is worth encouraging at all. I see the flaws of my past performance almost too clearly for comfort, and can agree with my bitterest critics in heart at least—except for "The Human Fantasy." . . . However 1920 finds me a very humble and doubtful man indeed as far as my own work is concerned.

Like Sara Teasdale's, his respect for Harriet Monroe was deep. He wrote December 12, 1925, to quiet her worries over a small circulation: "However, you have the only satisfaction that really matters in the long run of a fine piece of work carried through with passion and restraint, and a service to poetry, as a living and growing art, which outranks any service rendered by any other organ or individual."

In October, 1922, *Poetry* passed another milestone: Harriet Monroe completed ten full years of publication. Plainly, in the pages of *Poetry* the new poetry that began in 1912 had come to a conclusion, although the end of the movement itself was not in sight: the publication of *The Waste Land* in the *Dial* for November, 1922, signified that much at the least. Harriet Monroe was unable to account for what had happened in her magazine. Her two retrospective articles in the fall of 1922 make that clear. In September, 1922, she published the confessional article "Mea Culpa," which expressed her regret that *Poetry* had fallen away from its old standard and her fear that she had wasted a "great opportunity." She regretted most keenly her failure to build up a circulation large enough to make the magazine self-supporting and to pay the poets a living wage.

Since the much more heavily subsidized *Dial* had a peak circulation of about fourteen thousand in 1922, which sank in later years to between two and four thousand,[51] Harriet Monroe's circulation does not seem discreditable. She seems also to have done rather well with her rate to contributors, compared to Scofield Thayer. In 1922 *Poetry* was averaging about six dollars a page, while the far more affluent *Dial* paid ten dollars a page for poetry.[52]

Harriet Monroe's grief over lost opportunities was real but did not define the history of the magazine for her, although when she tried to give that history a positive definition, she did not succeed very well. Her editorial of October, 1922, in formal celebration of the ten-year anniversary, describes the movement as a boisterous procession instigated by Ezra Pound: ". . . Ezra Pound, with much tumult and shouting, buried the dry bones of the past and sounded the tocsin for a new era. In singles and pairs and cohorts they came trooping: Vachel Lindsay, Robert Frost, Carl Sandburg and Edgar Lee Masters; Wallace Stevens, D. H. Lawrence, and T. S. Eliot; Conrad Aiken and Rupert Brooke; Sara Teasdale and Edna St. Vincent Millay; the imagists—H.D. and Amy Lowell, Richard Aldington, John Gould Fletcher; the ironists—Carlos Williams, Alfred Kreymborg, Maxwell Bodenheim, Marianne Moore." In the middle of the twenties, oppressed by the dominance of Eliot and Joyce, whose art she felt was a "note of dissonance," a belated literary reaction to Victorian thought, she looked longingly back to 1914, to a prewar era of clarification and positive achievement in a poetry that had since been muddled and confused: "During *Poetry*'s first years the simplification process was going on. The imagists and vers-librists were 'stripping the art bare' of rhetoric, eloquence, grandiloquence, poetic diction—of all the frills and furbelows which had over-draped, over-ornamented its beauty. They brought it closer to life, to modern subjects, people and interests; they rebelled against its traditional prosody; they made it sing in new rhythms, and in the English of modern speech."[53]

51. Joost, *Scofield Thayer*, pp. 41, 254.
52. Ibid., pp. 40, 161. The twenty-dollar page rate that Joost gives for *Dial* poetry on page 59 did not apparently apply until after 1922.
53. "Looking Backward," *Poetry*, October, 1928, p. 36.

In 1928 it seemed to her that the Pound of the *Cantos*, William Carlos Williams, Hart Crane, Allen Tate, Laura Riding, and Yvor Winters represented a return to the opposite pole from simplification, to "the doctrine of the folding-in, the closure, the esoteric—the aristocratic conception of The Poet, the ancient spirit of caste." Her democratic sympathies were particularly outraged. She cried out that the poets "seem as scornful of the *profanum vulgus* as any aristocrat of the Augustan Age, as profoundly convinced that great art must arise above all contact with the common people, all sympathy with—nay, all interest in— their manner of speech, and their petty preoccupations, emotions, dreams."

She was reacting in accordance with the division of the schools that Pound had made in the Jepson attack: aristocratic intellectuals on one hand, and democratic simplifiers on the other. The paralysis imposed on her by that attack remained with her to the end. In the next year René Taupin's book, *L'Influence du symbolisme français sur la poésie américaine*, gave a clear public expression to the definition of *Poetry*'s early history that this division implied. Taupin concluded that Ezra Pound had given the magazine its revolutionary tone, and that the magazine had fallen back to the level of its editress the day he abandoned it. One of the difficulties with this view is fixing the limit of Pound's influence, putting a date on the day he abandoned *Poetry*. Taupin solved it by naming 1920 the year of Pound's departure; he remarked that about 1920 *Poetry* ceased to be an important magazine. Harriet Monroe appears in his account as a person of limited intelligence but of great good faith, devoted entirely to an ideal of democratic art: she had illusions about the heart of American democracy, about the voice of the West, and about the soul of Chicago. Since Pound departed with his friends, she had given herself over entirely to these nugatory entities.[54] In fact, *Poetry* in the twenties had relatively little middle-western content; between 1920 and 1930 Lindsay was published once, Sandburg twice, and Masters five times. But Harriet Monroe could not or would not make an adequate answer to Taupin's remarks. As Yvor Winters complained of her review of the book,

54. (Paris: Librarie Ancienne Honoré Champion, 1929), pp. 247, 255, 257.

in a letter of October 1, 1930, she could have shown up Taupin's asininity; instead she had rambled on about Lindsay and Masters.

Most of the poets were not willing to let the emptiness of *Poetry* in the twenties testify against the value of Harriet Monroe's earlier work. In the thirties, after Taupin's book, every one of the major poets except T. S. Eliot—Yeats, Stevens, Williams, Pound, and Marianne Moore, conspicuously—renewed the connection with Harriet Monroe and published something in her magazine. The reasons for this revival of *Poetry* as an outlet for the movement before Harriet Monroe's death in 1936 are beyond the scope of this study, and undoubtedly involve some complexities in the literary politics of the thirties. But it seems plain that part of the motive of this return of the major poets was a desire to render justice to Miss Monroe. Marianne Moore's testimony about Harriet Monroe is particularly detached, because *Poetry* in its first ten years had not been hospitable to her. She wrote to Harriet Monroe on March 28, 1932, about her editorial review of *Poetry*'s twenty years of publication, "this comment is eloquent, and more than that, affects one—by example might I say—in one's sense of loyalty to unselfish accomplishment." A little later, April 27, 1932, she wrote again: "The thought of your terminating this great work of yours, begun twenty years ago, that has had throughout, your particular individuality, saddens me." A younger poet, Allen Tate, made a similar comment when he wrote of Harriet Monroe in the southern number that he edited for *Poetry* in May, 1932: "she alone has come from the beginning of the late renascence to the present, with all the vigor of a new start. No single comment could do justice to her services to the American poet."

Pound published Canto XXXVII in *Poetry* for March, 1934, and flirted with the idea of renewing his foreign correspondence, but he was always in substantial agreement with the account of the first ten years of *Poetry* that appeared in Taupin's book. He, Ezra Pound, originated everything in the files worth printing, while Harriet Monroe was a good-hearted donkey who provided the means for printing his movement, but also presented annoying obstacles to its effective promotion. The memory Pound retained was that he "hammered stuff" into *Poetry* over Harriet Monroe's obstinate and repeated resistance. Her dislike of "Prufrock" and her crucial rejections and cuttings in 1916 seem the valid substance of this impression of Pound's, but from the beginning he overdramatized himself as the magazine's sole source of vitality.

In the end, his principal complaint against Harriet Monroe was that she could not and would not publish a journal of criticism, would not help to clarify or even describe the complexity of the twentieth-century world:

> Miss Monroe never pretended to adopt either a contemporary, European, or international criterion. Certain principles that Europe had accepted for eighty years have never penetrated her sanctum. It is possible that the recognition of these ideas would have prematurely extinguished her magazine. On the other hand she may never have grasped these ideas. She has repeatedly protected her readers; i.e., she has assumed that the intelligence of her readers is so far below that of the authors whom she has printed that the readers are at certain points not permitted to read and to judge for themselves what the writers believe.[55]

But here he seems to have described Harriet Monroe's strength as an editor of a poetry magazine: she had no desire to push the poets out of her space so that she might develop a lot of extraneous premises that would explain or present the poetry. She was not gifted with a keenly analytical mind, but she knew it, and resisted several suggestions that *Poetry* go in more heavily for prose. *Poetry* cannot be condemned for not being what it never wanted to be. Partly, of course, Pound's remarks glance at the censorship issue. On that question Harriet Monroe seems at fault for evading a problem that was crucial to the development of poetry.

Pound's summary in 1930 was about the best tribute he felt he could make to Harriet Monroe: "Miss Monroe has occasionally mutilated a work by excisions and has occasionally failed to see the unity of a longer work and given it in fragments. Nevertheless, she has done valuable work by reason of the purity of her intentions. She meant to provide a place where unknown poets could be printed; she has done so. Where new ideas and forms

55. "Small Magazines," p. 691

could be tried, she has done so. She has provided a meal ticket when the meal ticket was badly needed."[56] But this cheerful Dame Durden who kept a house furnished clean for poems to lodge in and provided poets with a frugal sustenance, this well-meaning housewife who took in all but dirty or annoyingly complicated poems, seems to have no relation to the dragon that Pound described in the same article, an editress who invited contributions from no one but Vachel Lindsay:

> She has printed on her own motion Mr. Lindsay's "General Booth Enters Heaven." She has printed, after six months' argument with me, Mr. Frost. She printed (after Marion Reedy had with great difficulty persuaded him to write Spoon River) some poems by E. L. Masters. She printed after six months' argument with me, Mr. T. S. Eliot's *Prufrock*. She printed me a year or so after Mr. Mencken had done so [in *Poetry*'s first issue]. She printed without protest the early work of "H.D." and of Aldington; work by Yeats, F. M. Hueffer. She also mutilated my "Homage to Sextus Propertius" at a time when I had to take what I could get, and long after I had ceased to regard *Poetry* or its opinion as having any weight or bearing or as being the possible implement or organ for expressing any definite thought.[57]

There was too much stress, too much "hammering" in the early years of *Poetry*. "Those were strenuous days, when we had to 'buck' the poets on the one hand and the public on the other," reminisced Alice Corbin Henderson about her four years as active associate editor, 1912–16.[58] Harriet Monroe could not possibly have sustained herself through those years if she were not something more steely than the good-hearted fool that Pound suggested. A dragon theory of Harriet Monroe makes more sense than a housewife theory. Pound wrote a late undated letter in which he guessed that she had "an inferiority complex that has upheld your hatred of having good stuff in the magazine, even when you have tolerated and permitted it." There is some appeal in a theory that she understood just enough about good poetry to envy the work of poets she could not emulate, and that she secretly wished them harm and did the little she could to harass

56. Ibid., pp. 691–92.
57. Ibid., p. 692.
58. *Poetry*, October, 1922, p. 56.

them, while printing them to sustain her magazine's reputation. But in the whole long course of her editorship, there is no evidence of malice, not even in the crippling attack on Pound's "Propertius" that *Poetry* printed. And Harriet Monroe began to print the new poetry before most of the poets had a reputation: no pressures of public or literary opinion could have controlled her editorial choices. If the history of her editorship of *Poetry* suggests that she had a good deal of inner strength, it was not fueled by malice or envy.

If Harriet Monroe was something more than an editorial housewife, Ezra Pound was something less than the sole source of energy and vitality in the pages of *Poetry*. Here one becomes involved in a distinction that seems niggling, except that Pound's account of Harriet Monroe seems to force it. His foreign correspondence was immensely stimulating for *Poetry*. Harriet Monroe has been the principal witness to that fact, with her consistent reminiscence of the "cordiality" of his cooperation from abroad. His letters radiate energy and emotion, but "cordial" is not the word most readers would use to characterize their tone. Harriet Monroe must have decided early to take Pound, and everything he wrote, impersonally, in the light of his devotion to the cause of poetry, and to register her gratitude for the service he rendered her:

> He looked on *Poetry* almost as his organ during its first year or two; indeed, it *was* partly his organ because, through his contacts in London, he sent to Chicago not only his own poems and articles, but poems by people otherwise mostly inaccessible—Yeats, Tagore, the Aldingtons and the other imagists, Ford Madox Ford, and others. He didn't mind being "didactic" in his letters even to the point of violence; and, since he was born to be a great teacher, the editor felt herself being rapidly educated. . . . At the beginning he was our most powerful aid and our keenest stimulus. He gave of his best freely in letters and influence, and sent to *Poetry* many of his most beautiful poems—poems now mostly in *Lustra*.[59]

One could describe Pound's early contribution less enthusiastically by saying that he sent in to *Poetry* the fifty or so poems

59. "*Poetry*'s Old Letters," October, 1935, pp. 38–39.

that constituted his movement—the same fifty poems that functioned in 1914 as the movement in the *Egoist* and again in *Des Imagistes*—that all the excitement of the reform of style to which Miss Monroe and Mrs. Henderson responded was an overstrained piece of literary politicking. Nor was Pound particularly a good judge of the new poetry as it developed. He dismissed William Carlos Williams as "a suburban physician" in a survey of the poets in 1915.[60] Eliot rather than Pound gave the first clear statement of the importance of Marianne Moore in 1918.[61] Pound ignored the work of Wallace Stevens in his every appearance in *Poetry*, from 1914 to 1921. He dismissed Yeats in 1920,[62] as he came into the period of his greatest strength, possibly because Yeats returned to Ireland as a subject in some of the poems he published that year, the *Dial* group climaxing in "The Second Coming." But this criticism is fishwifery, plainly unfair to the whole of Pound's contribution to poetry. One indulges in it to demonstrate the unfairness of Pound's treatment of Harriet Monroe, for that seems motivated by the same niggling zeal to spotlight every weakness, error, and hesitation in ten years of editorial decisions.

The truth about the first ten years of *Poetry* is that there really was a renaissance in poetry, beginning about 1912—a renewal of the art so vigorous and so profound that the fullness of it cannot yet be appreciated. So many poets of such durable reputation and tenacious skill appearing within two years, where no meaningful poet except Robinson had appeared for more than a generation: the phenomenon in America defies ordinary explanations, and Yeats's career is almost as mysterious. The cyclical forces to which Yeats liked to appeal must be behind the development of Robert Frost, Wallace Stevens, Ezra Pound, William Carlos Williams, T. S. Eliot, and Marianne Moore. Viewed from a decent

60. Letter of December 15, 1915.

61. Eliot, reviewing the second *Others Anthology* in the *Egoist* for May, 1918, pp. 69–70, classified Miss Moore as a "living writer" with Pound, Joyce, Lewis, and de Bosschère. Pound, reviewing the same book in the *Little Review* for March, 1918, p. 57, praised Miss Moore for logopoeia, but was more interested in defining his concept than her work, and did not clearly distinguish her from Mina Loy.

62. Letter of December 16, 1920, to Harriet Monroe: "Yeats . . . one hardly studies in reference to new developments." On September 11, 1920, Pound wrote Williams, "now that Remy and Henry are gone and Yeats faded. . . ." (*Letters*, #170, p. 158.)

historical perspective, the first ten years of the new poetry, after 1912, take on a symphonic grandeur as each poet introduces himself, explores, hesitates, then announces clearly his own theme and meaning, and is answered by the recognition of his fellows. At closer perspective, an appalling amount of daily irritation and personal suffering underlay each of these developing careers, but such disparity between the idea and the act is something every life endures. The confusion of 1916–19, which is so distressing in the chronicle of *Poetry*'s affairs, seems almost necessary to the development of those poets who found their own meaning in the midst of a bickering chaos. The poetic voice had to recognize its own reality in the isolation that followed the first excitements of the renaissance. One feels this in particular in the growing strength of Williams and of Stevens around 1919. Something similar happened to Pound and to Eliot.

The symphonic effect in the development of the movement is so compelling that one wants a conductor, a mind responsible for guiding the poets through struggle and disharmony to triumph. But no one was impresario for the new movement in poetry. The poets made themselves, they were not created by the sympathetic understanding of any editor or any audience, and they were not controlled by the brilliant literary journalism of Ezra Pound. The timing of their development was personal, unpredictable, and uncontrollable. This seems the chief reason that the effort to get the movement into a literary periodical was so exhausting and ultimately so unsuccessful. After 1920–22 in the *Dial*, the phenomenon was recognizably too complex to fit into one magazine; the poets were too various and their careers too diverse. But the chief reason that the first ten years of *Poetry* are exciting is that more of the new poetry got into Harriet Monroe's magazine than into any other except the *Dial*, and the development of it—the flux, the change of manner—is more clearly visible from the perspective of *Poetry* than from any other vantage point.

Ezra Pound deserves much of the credit for *Poetry*'s record. He provided the focus that got everything started, with his Imagisme and his reform of style. Imagisme in *Poetry* sent Amy Lowell to London with a letter of introduction to Ezra Pound from Harriet Monroe. Pound's reform of style influenced the change in Yeats, and in *Poetry* it helped to form the work of Sandburg and the *Spoon River Anthology*. Just before the Poetry Renaissance became a rather annoying institution, Eliot sought Pound out in London with "Prufrock" already written, and the two of them began the mutual development that was to dominate poetry for years. Ezra Pound was like a field of force in which everyone else danced in the early years of *Poetry*. But his movement was a personal invention: he was most sensitive to those poems and those poets that seemed to contribute something to his own work, or to answer to his own work. Thus he was intermittently sensitive to Yeats, insensitive to Williams, and deaf to Stevens, while brilliantly alert to Eliot. He followed the track of the real through the early work of Aldington, H.D., John Gould Fletcher, Skipwith Cannell, through the new work of Yeats, not really articulate about what he recognized in them. *Spoon River* and "Prufrock" burst on him as fulfillments of things he had dimly intuited. His excitement in 1916 over his "Cabaret Dancers," with the line that leads from Masters to it to his own later work and Eliot's in rhymed quatrains, indicates the pattern of Pound's movement: it was usually related to the development of his own work. The poets felt they were discovering a new form, recognizing it only as they created it, perfecting it in terms of their responses to each other's work—a state of affairs that is clearest in the interrelationships between Pound and Yeats and Pound and Eliot.

But the movement was larger than Ezra Pound's part in it, and his tendency to incorporate it into himself and the needs of his own work, while brilliant and unmalicious, did no good to those poets who were distinct from Pound. Notably it posed hardships for Frost, Williams, and Stevens. This seems the most important contribution of Harriet Monroe as editor of *Poetry*: she made Pound available, spread his influence abroad, but was not swallowed up by him. While she managed to sustain it, her balancing act between the poetic schools allowed a space in which a number of different poetic tendencies could grow, Stevens' as well as Lindsay's. One must not underestimate the stamina required to sustain openness to Pound in the early days. Amy

Lowell's campaign against him was shrewd and relentless; she was eager to take advantage of difficulties created by his high-handed management of the foreign correspondence. Nothing but a profound and impersonal commitment to the art explains the success with which Harriet Monroe resisted the blandishments of Amy Lowell and the tactlessness of Pound, while remaining open to new work coming in from unknown writers—Sandburg, Masters, Wallace Stevens.

The record of *Poetry* in 1914–15 depended on a great deal of good luck, but Harriet Monroe earned that luck, just as she earned the bad luck that began to accumulate about the magazine after 1916 by her insensitivity to the censorship question. Contemplating her decisions of 1916, one longs to push her out of her editorial chair. But even after she lost Pound and Eliot, her management of *Poetry* took in a large part of the movement, as the comparison between Pound's editorship of the *Little Review* and the corresponding issues of *Poetry* suggests. On the whole, Harriet Monroe cannot be given credit for sponsorship of William Carlos Williams, but the outlines of Williams' early development are in *Poetry*, and not many of the poems came through Pound. For an editor who liked to say that she never asked anyone for verse, Harriet Monroe after 1916 positively courted Williams, within the limits imposed by her feelings on the censorship issue. The early history of Wallace Stevens is beautifully represented in *Poetry*, but marred by the cutting up of "Sunday Morning."

That editorial gesture, like the reception Harriet Monroe gave T. S. Eliot, makes it clear that she was not an editor of legendary brilliance, that she lacked intuitive quickness with difficult work. And her zeal in defending Lindsay shows that emotion could interfere with her judgment. Her achievement as editor of *Poetry* was a triumph of will as much as a triumph of mind. But Pound's formulas about courage and goodwill yoked to a dim intelligence are hardly adequate to describe her. They make her a comic dragon. Pound must have felt that himself when in 1959 he added a new note to his stock portrait: "honesty is a form of intelligence." A more old-fashioned term than intelligence fits Harriet Monroe's mind when she set aside irritation or disappointment to attach herself to beauty, to the good of poetry itself: again and again she showed wisdom.

Much of Pound's retrospective complaint about *Poetry*'s failure to adopt an international standard came from his conviction that there was only one acceptable way to relate a poet's spiritual activity to his community, his place, his time. Whether the question is put in terms of the audience, as Harriet Monroe liked to put it, or in terms of a chosen locale, as Alice Corbin Henderson put it,[63] or in terms of the "now," "a vision into the desolate PRESENT," as William Carlos Williams liked to put it,[64] the relation between the artist and the other seems crucial to the development of the new poetry. The implications of it were worked out by the poets in lifetimes of discovery. Against the careers of Eliot, Yeats, Stevens, Pound, Williams, and Marianne Moore, the demands for definition of 1918 seem ludicrously impatient. The poets neither needed nor wanted to solve the problem, to come up with an answer that would end it. Their use for it as poets was to live out solutions to it in their poems. Ezra Pound's solution in the *Cantos*, the construction of an ideal metropolis populated by the great poets of the ages who were both his audience and his milieu, was no more universal or final than Harriet Monroe's appeal for a great audience. And when it worked, it worked only for himself and Eliot.

The solutions that seem most durable are the ones that allow the poet to straddle the alternatives of bondage to a community, a time, a place, on the one hand, and isolated spiritual activity, on the other. Eliot, who began in "Prufrock" with a brilliant and frightening picture of the spirit paralyzed by the difficulty and the futility of relation to the other, found eventually that he had "to construct something upon which to rejoice."[65] He left the school of pure intelligence to adopt an Anglican set of values, and a qualified, incarnational reverence for ties of time and circumstance and blood. Pound made the stiffer stand for the ideal metropolis, in which the artist recognizes no necessities beyond

63. Review of Sherwood Anderson's *Mid-American Chants*, in *Poetry*, June, 1918, pp. 157–58.
64. "Belly Music," *Others*, July, 1919, p. 30.
65. Excerpt from "Ash Wednesday" reprinted from *Collected Poems, 1909–1962* by T. S. Eliot by permission of Harcourt Brace Jovanovich, Inc., and Faber and Faber, Ltd.

those of his art and no community beyond the brotherhood of the elite who triumph over time. Although the early *Cantos* show many developments from an ideal of life in arrangement, the history in the poem seems patterned by Pound's ideology; it is a world closed in on itself. But in the *Pisan Cantos* he genuinely mastered circumstance, by writing the sort of poem that William Carlos Williams would have written, if William Carlos Williams were Ezra Pound: "The poet must use anything at hand to assert himself. If he cannot do so he is less than great. The proof that I am I is that I can use anything, not a special formula, but anything."

The failures of Lindsay and Masters testify to the importance of the relation of the artist to the other in the genesis of the new poetry. Lindsay met disaster because he tried to accept the America of 1900 on its own terms, and the massiveness of his failure, the unquenchable callowness of his poetry, demonstrates the futility of an uncritical relation between the artist and community in the twentieth-century world. One says twentieth-century world, because Frost evaded the problems that overwhelmed Lindsay, perhaps because he found his chosen locale in a backwoods New England, which had been left behind after the Civil War as truly as the South, and was unimproved and unreduced by the norms of a modern industrial society. Harriet Monroe's ideal of organic, harmonious relations between bard and audience required a community that had strong traditions and was unselfconscious about them. A number of critics about 1918 pointed out the need of the traditions, but nothing could supply the unselfconsciousness. This organic ideal, however, may explain Masters' isolated achievement in *Spoon River*. Perhaps his boyhood memories of Lewiston, Illinois, had a coherence that no other material available to him possessed.

But the poet who was writing in the twentieth century, and not depending upon a lucky accident of background, could not afford to be simple or trusting about his relation to community or locale. The development of Yeat's work was a shifting series of lights thrown on the relation of the passionate individual to country, time, or circumstance. Yeats was like Frost, and unlike

Pound and the early Eliot, in requiring relation to a countryside and a popular tradition in his verse, but he showed a splendid skill in evading the traps of Irish nationalism and Gaelic glamour. And the developed work of Stevens, Williams, and Marianne Moore explores the relation of the passionate mind to the other, the effort to satisfy the mind without the literary and learned tradition that is important in Yeats, Pound, and Eliot.

The variety of poetic developments outruns the formula, which can, however, serve as a definition for the movement in its largest sense, as it applies to all the poets. The poets cooperated to find a voice for the human spirit in a world that had despaired of spiritual significance, and had lost the support of unselfconscious tradition. The voice of the spirit was uttered in those poems that did not cheat or oversimplify the problem, that were written neither out of despair nor out of a pretense that dead tradition was alive; and the meaning of any utterance did not extend beyond the creation of a poem. Harriet Monroe's audience ideal, which prescribed more durable meanings, extending ultimately into the reformation of society, put her at cross-purposes with the new poetry at times, but her emphasis of it was not inappropriate to the poets' situation in the twentieth century. Under one aspect, her ideal poet was Stevens' glass man, "responsive as a mirror with a voice,"[66] who sums up men in a million diamonds: she pointed to a problem that was at the heart of the development of the movement. Possibly the sad element in her democratic idealism, her precommitment to the community, to the common understanding, to the certainty of the defeat of dreams, has something to do with the breakdown of the poetic impulse in her generation. A further erosion of the traditional American community, stripping away the defensive loyalty that was prominent in Harriet Monroe, perhaps created a release for poets of a younger generation.

Harriet Monroe's characteristic mood was not the contemplation of "the last trench and the last despair," but the glorious energy of reaction with which she fought the intuition of defeat, and this energy she put at the service of poetry. If the movement

66. Excerpt from "Asides on the Oboe" reprinted from *The Collected Poems of Wallace Stevens* by permission of Alfred A. Knopf, Inc., and Faber and Faber, Ltd.

inevitably traveled beyond her, it seems most regrettable that the separation of the avant-garde from *Poetry* was full of distress, because while she lasted Harriet Monroe put up a splendid fight for her cause. For anyone who shares the fascination for life in arrangement that Ezra Pound once expressed, there is a salty interest to Harriet Monroe's editorship. She bridged a great gap in American literary and intellectual life; she was stretched to the utmost to make the connection between the America of William Jennings Bryan and the America of William Carlos Williams that her editorial career represents. It does not seem surprising that she could not herself pass over the bridge, and adopt all the values of the America of the twenties. There is even something humanly appealing in her failures, because the irrevocable consistency with which she was Harriet Monroe accounts for her essential success as much as it occasioned her mistakes. Ezra Pound made it clear that he would have preferred a different sort of editor, but it seems absurd to deny her a substantial share of the credit for the publishing history of *Poetry*.

The history of the first ten years of *Poetry* is the history of a beginning. Its meaning can be assessed only in retrospect, when the full meaning of the modern movement in poetry is assessed. Most recent evaluations of the modern revolution are plainly inadequate: they separate out individual poets and relate them to perennial English and American poetic traditions, or start from the poets' situation in the postsymbolist world as if it had a street address. It was the contemporary conviction that this poetry was new. Possibly the tension between the poet and the other, which is clear in the new poetry and in the immediate reactions to it, is part of most interesting poetry: poetry lives on the frontier where the mind finds itself in what is not itself. But the poets who wrote about 1912 were uniquely without support in exploring that frontier. Their courage withers to an attitude in the tradition established by their success; perhaps this explains a weakening of the modern movement since the passing of the great generation. For those who lived through it, the Poetry Renaissance was full of exhilaration, but also of contradiction and confusion. It required extraordinary intensity of purpose to survive without bitterness or compromise. As much as the poets of the movement,

Harriet Monroe was a successful survivor of that time. Her testimony to the early years emphasized always the excitement and joy of a new age, a renaissance. It was her hope and her faith that *Poetry* had ushered in a great era of poetry, and that faith was justified.

Appendix: Figures on *Poetry*'s Income, Expenditures, and Circulation 𝄞

TABLE 1. INCOME

Year Ending	Income from Guarantors	Income from Sales, Subscriptions, and Advertisements	Total
Aug. 1, 1913	$5,746.50	$1,598.26	$7,344.76
Aug. 2, 1914	5,595.00	2,202.74	7,797.74
Aug. 1, 1915	5,280.00	2,324.81	7,604.81
Sept. 1, 1916	5,330.00	2,907.32	8,237.32
Oct. 1, 1917	5,990.00	3,015.33	9,005.33
Oct. 1, 1918	4,605.00	3,644.38	8,249.38
Oct. 1, 1919	4,300.00	4,196.84	8,496.84
Oct. 1, 1920	3,627.00	5,413.91	9,040.91
Oct. 1, 1921	3,825.00	5,181.28	9,006.28
Oct. 1, 1922	4,045.00	5,674.56	9,719.56

TABLE 2. EXPENDITURES

Year Ending	Payments to Contributors	Printing Including Paper	Rent, Office Supplies, Postage	Salaries	Miscellaneous	Total
Aug. 1, 1913	$2,466.31	$2,774.76	$ 771.75	$ 616.75	$ 70.80	$ 6,700.37
Aug. 1, 1914	2,961.34	3,156.74	835.75	990.90	124.19	8,443.92
Aug. 1, 1915[a]						
Sept. 1, 1916	3,149.75	2,837.31	902.74	1,422.00	123.14	8,884.94
Oct. 1, 1917[a]						
Oct. 1, 1918[a]						
Oct. 1, 1919	2,486.35	3,003.24	913.05	1,603.00	176.42	8,532.06
Oct. 1, 1920	2,532.07	3,113.98	1,043.87	2,094.35	462.05	9,646.32
Oct. 1, 1921	2,495,25	3,734.80	1,216.27	2,035.00	138.86	10,020.18
Oct. 1, 1922[a]						

[a] Figures not filed in the Business Papers of the magazine.

TABLE 3. CIRCULATION

Year	Figure Reported to Guarantors[a]	Calculated Figure[b]	Figure Reported to N. W. Ayer & Son Newspaper Annual	Subscription Price
1912–13	1,030	1,065	. . . .	$1.50
1913–14	1,101	1,468	. . . .	1.50
1914–15	1,169	1,549	2,000	1.50
1915–16	1,401	1,938	2,250	1.50
1916–17	. . . .	2,010	. . . .	1.50
1917–18	. . . .	1,822	3,000	2.00
1918–19	1,564	2,098	3,000	2.00
1919–20	. . . .	2,706	3,000	2.00
1920–21	1,708	1,727	3,000	3.00
1921–22	1,638	1,891	3,000	3.00

[a] In one year, 1913–14, this reported figure is said to represent a total of paid subscriptions, "besides copies sent to guarantors, etc." In a special "Statement of Circulation" dated January 22, 1915, a total "mailing list" of 1,233 is broken down into 790 paid subscriptions, 254 guarantor copies, 149 copies for exchange and press, and 40 for advertisers, contributors, and miscellaneous. The meaning of the figures in the Annual Reports to Guarantors is thus ambiguous.

[b] A maximum possible circulation arrived at by dividing the total of "income from sales, subscriptions, and advertisements" by the subscription price. Newsstand sales ran about 400 or 500 a month, according to a 1915 report. Advertising revenue was never much of a factor.

Bibliography ⟨≈

Aldington, Richard. *Life for Life's Sake*. New York: Viking Press, 1941.
Anderson, Margaret. *My Thirty Years' War*. New York: Covici, Friede, 1930.
Art (Chicago). Scattered issues, October, 1912–April, 1915.
Blast. No. 1, June 20, 1914; no. 2, July, 1915.
Braithwaite, William Stanley, ed. *Anthology of Magazine Verse for 1913*. Cambridge, Mass.: Issued by William Stanley Braithwaite, 1913.
———. *Anthology of Magazine Verse for 1915*. New York: Gomme and Marshall, 1915.
———. *Anthology of Magazine Verse for 1916*. New York: Lawrence J. Gomme, 1916.
Brooks, Van Wyck. *Days of the Phoenix: The Nineteen-Twenties I Remember*. New York: E. P. Dutton and Co., 1957.
Broom. November, 1921–November, 1922.
Buttel, Robert. *Wallace Stevens: The Making of Harmonium*. Princeton, N.J.: Princeton University Press, 1967.
Carpenter, Margaret Haley. *Sara Teasdale: A Biography*. New York: Schulte Publishing Co., 1960.
Coffman, Stanley K., Jr. *Imagism: A Chapter for the History of Modern Poetry*. Norman: University of Oklahoma Press, 1951.
Contact. No. 1 (December, 1920)–no. 4 (September, 1921).
Contemporary Verse. January, 1916–November, 1922.
Damon, S. Foster. *Amy Lowell: A Chronicle*. Boston and New York: Houghton Mifflin Co., 1935.
de Nagy, N. Christoph. *The Poetry of Ezra Pound: The Pre-Imagist Stage*. Bern: Francke Verlag, 1968.
The Dial. October, 1912–November, 1922.
Dolmetsch, Carl R. "A History of the *Smart Set* Magazine." Ph.D. dissertation, University of Chicago, 1957.
———. *The Smart Set: A History and an Anthology*. New York: Dial Press, 1966.
The Double-Dealer. January, 1921–November, 1922.
Duffey, Bernard. *The Chicago Renaissance in American Letters*. East Lansing: Michigan State College Press, 1954.
Earle, Ferdinand, ed. *The Lyric Year*. New York: Mitchell Kennerley, 1912.
The Egoist. January, 1914–December, 1918.

Ellmann, Richard. *James Joyce*. New York: Oxford University Press, 1959.
Fletcher, John Gould. *Life Is My Song*. New York and Toronto: Farrar and Rinehart, 1937.
Ford, Ford Madox. *Return to Yesterday*. New York: Horace Liveright, 1932.
Gallup, Donald. *A Bibliography of Ezra Pound*. London: Rupert Hart-Davis, 1963.
Gregory, Horace. *Amy Lowell*. New York: Thomas Nelson and Sons, 1958.
————. and Zaturenska, Marya. *A History of American Poetry, 1900–1940*. New York: Harcourt, Brace and Co., 1942.
Hansen, Harry. *Midwest Portraits*. New York: Harcourt, Brace and Co., 1923.
Hoffman, Frederick J.; Allen, Charles; and Ulrich, Carolyn. *The Little Magazine: A History and Bibliography*. Princeton, N.J.: Princeton University Press, 1947.
Hughes, Glenn. *Imagism and the Imagists*. Stanford, Calif.: Stanford University Press, 1931.
Jepson, Edgar. "Recent United States Poetry." *English Review*, May, 1918.
Joost, Nicholas. *The Dial: Years of Transition, 1912–1920*. Barre, Mass.: Barre Publishers, 1967.
————. *Scofield Thayer and the Dial*. Carbondale: Southern Illinois University Press, 1964.
Kenner, Hugh. *The Poetry of Ezra Pound*. London: Faber and Faber, 1951.
————. *The Pound Era*. Berkeley and Los Angeles: University of California Press, 1971.
Kreymborg, Alfred, ed. *Others: An Anthology of the New Verse*. New York: Alfred A. Knopf, 1916.
————. *Others: An Anthology of the New Verse (1917)*. New York: Alfred A. Knopf, 1917.
————. *Others for 1919: An Anthology of the New Verse*. New York: Nicholas L. Brown, 1920.
————. *Troubadour*. New York: Boni and Liveright, 1925.
Lidderdale, Jane, and Nicholson, Mary. *Dear Miss Weaver: Harriet Shaw Weaver, 1876–1961*. London: Faber and Faber, 1970.
The Little Review. March, 1914–Autumn, 1922.
Lowell, Amy. *Some Imagist Poets, 1915*. Boston and New York: Houghton Mifflin Co., 1915.
————. *Some Imagist Poets, 1916*. Boston and New York: Houghton Mifflin Co., 1916.
————. *Tendencies in Modern American Poetry*. New York: Macmillan Co., 1917.
McAlmon, Robert. *Being Geniuses Together*. London: Secker and Warburg, 1938.
Macdougall, Allan Ross, ed. *Letters of Edna St. Vincent Millay*. New York: Harper and Bros., 1952.
Marsh, Edward, ed. *Georgian Poetry, 1911–1912*. London: Poetry Book Shop, 1912.
Martin, Wallace. *The New Age under Orage*. Manchester: Manchester University Press, 1967.
Masters, Edgar Lee. *Across Spoon River*. New York: Farrar and Rinehart, 1936.
Meacham, Harry M. *The Caged Panther: Ezra Pound at St. Elizabeth's*. New York: Twayne Publishers, 1967.

The Measure. March, 1921–September, 1922.

Middleton, Christopher. "Documents on Imagism from the Papers of F. S. Flint." *Review*, April, 1965, pp. 35–51.

Monroe, Harriet. Introduction to *The Congo and Other Poems*, by Nicholas Vachel Lindsay. New York: Macmillan Co., 1914.

———. *John Wellborn Root: A Study of His Life and Work*. Boston: Houghton Mifflin Co., 1896.

———. "Looking Backward." *Poetry*, October, 1928, pp. 34–36.

———. "An Open Letter." *Chicago Daily News*, June 20, 1915.

———. The Personal Papers of Harriet Monroe, in the Harriet Monroe Modern Poetry Library of the Joseph Regenstein Library, the University of Chicago.

———. "*Poetry's* Old Letters." *Poetry*, October, 1935, pp. 38–39.

———. *A Poet's Life*. New York: Macmillan Co., 1938.

———. "A Retrospect." *Poetry*, October, 1927, p. 34.

———. "Volume Forty." *Poetry*, April, 1932, pp. 30–34.

———, with Henderson, Alice Corbin, eds. *The New Poetry*. New York: Macmillan Co., 1917.

Mott, Frank Luther. *A History of American Magazines, 1885–1905*. Cambridge, Mass.: Harvard University Press, 1957.

Norman, Charles. *Ezra Pound*. New York: Macmillan Co., 1960.

Others. July, 1915–July, 1919.

The Pagan. Scattered issues, 1916–20.

Paige, D. D., ed. *Selected Letters of Ezra Pound, 1907–1941*. New York: Harcourt, Brace and Co., 1950.

Paul, Sherman. *Louis Sullivan: An Architect in American Thought*. Englewood Cliffs, N.J.: Prentice-Hall, 1962.

Poetry: A Magazine of Verse. October, 1912–November, 1922.

———. The Papers of *Poetry: A Magazine of Verse*, in the Harriet Monroe Modern Poetry Library of the Joseph Regenstein Library, the University of Chicago.

The Poetry Journal. December, 1912–March, 1918.

The Poetry Review (Cambridge, Mass.). August, 1916–February, 1917.

Pound, Ezra. "Harold Monro." *Criterion*, July, 1932, p. 590.

———. *Literary Essays*. London: Faber and Faber, 1945.

———. *Lustra*. New York: Alfred A. Knopf, 1917.

———. *Patria Mia*. Chicago: Ralph Fletcher Seymour, 1950.

———. *Pavannes and Divisions*. New York: Alfred A. Knopf, 1918.

———. *Ripostes*. London: Stephen Swift, 1912.

———. "Small Magazines." *English Journal* 19 (November, 1930), 689–704.

———, ed. *Catholic Anthology, 1914–1915*. London: Elkin Mathews, 1915.

———. *Des Imagistes*. *Glebe*, February, 1914. New York: Albert and Charles Boni, 1914.

Putzel, Max. *The Man in the Mirror: William Marion Reedy and His Magazine*. Cambridge, Mass.: Harvard University Press, 1963.

Reed, Forrest, ed. *Pound/Joyce*. London: Faber and Faber, 1968.

Reedy's Mirror. February, 1912–June, 1915. Scattered issues, 1916–20.

Reid, B. L. *The Man from New York: John Quinn and His Friends*. New York: Oxford University Press, 1968.

Ross, Robert H. *The Georgian Revolt, 1910–1922: Rise and Fall of a Poetic Ideal*. Carbondale: Southern Illinois University Press, 1965.

Ruggles, Eleanor. *The West-Going Heart: A Life of Vachel Lindsay*. New York: W. W. Norton, 1959.

Russell, Peter, ed. *Ezra Pound*. London and New York: Peter Nevill, 1950.

Selver, Paul. *Orage and the New Age Circle*. London: Allen and Unwin, 1959.

Sergeant, Elizabeth Shepley. *Robert Frost: The Trial by Existence*. New York: Holt, Rinehart and Winston, 1960.

The Seven Arts. November, 1916–October, 1917.

Seymour, Ralph Fletcher. *Some Went This Way*. Chicago: R. F. Seymour, 1945.

Slatin, Myles. "A History of Pound's Cantos I–XVI, 1915–1925." *American Literature* 35 (May, 1963), 183–95.

Smith, William Jay. *The Spectra Hoax*. Middletown, Conn.: Wesleyan University Press, 1961.

Stevens, Holly, ed. *The Letters of Wallace Stevens*. New York: Alfred A. Knopf, 1966.

Stevens, Wallace. *The Necessary Angel*. New York: Alfred A. Knopf, 1951.

Stock, Noel. *The Life of Ezra Pound*. London: Routledge and Kegan Paul, 1970.

Sullivan, J. P. *Ezra Pound and Sextus Propertius*. Austin: University of Texas Press, 1964.

Tate, Allen. "Editorial Note." *Poetry*, May, 1932, p. 94.

Taupin, René. *L'Influence du symbolisme français sur la poésie américaine de 1910 à 1920*. Paris: Librairie Ancienne Honoré Champion, 1929.

Thirlwall, John C., ed. *The Selected Letters of William Carlos Williams*. New York: McDowell, Obolensky, 1957.

Thompson, Lawrance. *Robert Frost: The Early Years*. New York: Holt, Rinehart and Winston, 1966.

———. *Robert Frost: The Years of Triumph*. New York: Holt, Rinehart and Winston, 1970.

———, ed. *Selected Letters of Robert Frost*. New York: Holt, Rinehart and Winston, 1964.

Tietjens, Eunice. *The World at My Shoulder*. New York: Macmillan Co., 1938.

Untermeyer, Louis. *From Another World*. New York: Harcourt, Brace and Co., 1939.

———. *The New Era in American Poetry*. New York: Henry Holt and Co., 1919.

Wasserstrom, William. *The Time of the Dial*. Syracuse, N.Y.: Syracuse University Press, 1963.

Williams, William Carlos. *I Wanted to Write a Poem*. Reported and edited by Edith Heal. Boston: Beacon Press, 1958.

Yeats, William Butler. "'American Literature Still in Victorian Era?'—Yeats." *New York Times*, February 22, 1914, p. 10.

———. *The Trembling of the Veil*. London: T. Werner Laurie, 1922.

Index

Abercrombie, Lascelles, 19, 24, 35
"Abu Salammamm" (Pound), 121
"Acon" (H.D.), 69
"The Adventurer" (Shepard), 169
Advisory board of *Poetry*, 23–24, 81, 159, 212, 265, 266
"Agathas Intacta" (Pound), 121
Aiken, Conrad, 20, 34–35, 36, 71, 72, 140, 170–71, 178–79, 197, 198, 236–37, 249, 280; quoted, 35, 140, 171, 178–79, 198, 236–37
"Aladdin and the Jinn" (Lindsay), 106
Alden, Raymond M.: quoted, 152
Aldington, Richard, 32, 34, 38–41 *passim*, 64, 69, 82, 86, 92–96 *passim*, 99, 120, 130–39 *passim*, 146, 147, 155, 156, 164, 167, 168, 245–46, 252, 253, 256n, 261, 266, 280, 284, 285, 288; quoted, 69, 82, 94, 131, 132, 139, 147, 155, 245–46, 266
Aldis, Mary, 179
Aldrich, Thomas Bailey, 5, 10
Allen, Hervey, 273
"The Allies" (Lowell), 144
"All Life in a Life" (Masters), 180, 233, 234
Al Que Quiere! (Williams), 86, 217, 225
"Amitiés" (Pound), 121
"Ancora" (Pound), 48, 74
Anderson, Margaret, 42, 52–53, 103, 145–49, 205, 206, 207, 222, 223, 247, 259–60, 261–62; quoted, 145–46, 147, 207, 261–62
Anderson, Sherwood, 52–53, 227–30 *passim*

"Anecdote of Men by the Thousand" (Stevens), 226
"Anecdote of the Jar" (Stevens), 268
"Another Weeping Woman" (Stevens), 269
Anthology of Magazine Verse (Braithwaite), 7–8, 87, 169, 170, 171, 201–2
"Anticipation" (Lowell), 144
"Apology" (Lowell), 60
"Apology" (Williams), 181
"Appellate Jurisdiction" (Moore), 155
"April" (Pound), 48
"Arabel" (Masters), 152–53, 157, 166, 180
Arensberg, Walter Conrad, 149, 188
"Arides" (Pound), 45
Atlantic, 4, 9, 12, 66, 68, 212, 237
At the Goal (Monroe), 12
"The Audience" (Pound-Monroe), 95, 160–62, 214, 215, 228

"Banal Sojourn" (Stevens), 267
Barnsdall, Aline, 180
Barry, Iris, 181, 222
"The Bath" (Lowell), 169
"The Bathtub" (Pound), 44
"The Bellaires" (Pound), 121
Bellman, 5, 87
"Belly Music" (Williams), 259
Benet, William Rose, 19, 22, 49–50, 54, 71, 72, 87
"Beyond the Stars" (Towne), 49
Beyond the Stars (Towne), 141
Bezruč, Petr, 40, 71
Birch, Helen, 247
Bishop, John Peale, 273

"The Black Cottage" (Frost), 69
"The Blackhawk War of the Artists"
    (Lindsay), 106
"The Blacksmith's Son" (Lindsay), 104
Blast, 130, 131–32, 133
"A Blockhead" (Lowell), 60
"The Blue Duck" (Sarett), 247
"Blue Symphony" (Fletcher), 71, 91, 94,
    144, 245
Bodenheim, Maxwell, 92, 134, 144–48
    passim, 167, 193, 195–97, 204, 222, 227,
    280; quoted, 146, 193, 195–96, 197
Bogan, Louise, 273
"The Bombardment" (Lowell), 144
Bourne, Randolph, 232–33, 249
A Boy's Will (Frost), 6, 54, 66, 68
Braithwaite, William Stanley, 7–8, 26,
    85, 87, 169–70, 171, 178, 179, 194,
    198, 201–2, 211; quoted, 85, 201–2
Bridges, Robert, 87
"Broken Dreams" (Yeats), 209
Brooke, Rupert, 25, 35, 92, 154, 168, 280
Brooks, Van Wyck, 249
Brown, Edmund R., 171
Brown, Robert Carlton, 151
Brown (Bodenheim), 195, 198
Browne, Francis Fisher, 5, 10, 50
Browne, Maurice, 34
Bryan, William Jennings, 11, 293
"The Bungler" (Lowell), 144
Burr, Amelia Josephine, 85, 87
Burton, Richard, 5, 19
Bynner, Witter, 19, 22, 33, 54, 148,
    238–39, 271; quoted, 148, 238

"The Cabaret Dancer" (Hagedorn), 164,
    167, 183
"Cabaret Dancers" (Pound). See "To a
    Friend Writing on Cabaret Dancers"
Cabell, James Branch, 118, 215; quoted,
    200
"Cafe Sketches" (Ficke), 148
Campbell, Joseph, 20, 22, 33, 54
Cannell, Skipwith, 32, 33, 41, 55, 75, 80,
    91, 92, 94, 124, 149, 177, 192, 288
"The Canticle of the Race" (Masters), 224
Cantos (Pound), 166–67, 183, 255, 264,
    281, 282, 290–91; "Three Cantos," 183,
    203–4, 205n, 208, 223–24, 226, 251,
    256

Carlos among the Candles (Stevens), 225
Carman, Bliss, 5, 20, 22, 26, 71, 72, 93
Carnevali, Emanuel, 260, 265
Carpenter, Rhys, 87
Cary, Lucian, 117, 235; quoted, 10, 117
Cathay (Pound), 43
Cather, Willa, 20
Catholic Anthology (Pound), 108, 110,
    134–35, 188
Cawein, Madison, 5, 10, 26
Censorship: in Poetry, 117–23, 163,
    189–91, 199, 283, 289; of Pound's
    "Cabaret Dancers," 186, 189–90; of
    Pound's "Phyllidula" and Eliot's "Mr.
    Apollinax," 190–91; of Williams'
    "History," 215–18
Century, 5, 7, 8, 49, 87. 114, 212, 237
"A Century in Illinois" (Monroe), 241–42
Chapbook, 10
Chatfield-Taylor, Hobart C., 12, 15, 16,
    23–24, 81, 266
Chicago Evening Post, 9, 10, 48, 235
"Chicago Poems" (Sandburg), 91, 99–101,
    104, 230
Chicago Poems (Sandburg), 194, 242
Chicago Renaissance, 4, 51–53, 102, 104,
    146, 147, 213, 224, 231, 242, 244, 253;
    and Alice Corbin Henderson, 228;
    Jepson attack on, 233–34; Harriet
    Monroe on (1918), 241–42
Chicago Tribune, 9, 48, 124, 234
"The Chinese Nightingale" (Lindsay), 92,
    104, 106, 109, 151, 158, 233, 234
The Chinese Nightingale (Lindsay), 105
"The Choice" (Pound), 48
"Choricos" (Aldington), 69
Clark, Charles Badger, 229
"A Coat" (Yeats), 91
Coates, Florence Earle, 87
"The Cocked Hat" (Masters), 166
"The Code" (Frost), 67, 91, 180
"The Collar Bone of a Hare" (Yeats), 209
"Colloquy with a Polish Aunt" (Stevens),
    268
"Colonialism Again" (Monroe), 143
Colum, Padraic, 92, 94, 99, 167
"Columbian Ode" (Monroe), 8, 98
"The Coming of War: Actaeon" (Pound),
    192
"Commission" (Pound), 43, 44

"The Condolence" (Pound), 43
"The Congo" (Lindsay), 103, 104, 108, 110
The Congo (Lindsay), 13, 104, 106
Conkling, Grace Hazard, 27, 33, 54, 276
"Conquest" (Williams), 122–23, 154
"Conseil to a Bachelor" (Moore), 155
"Contemporaria" (Pound), 31, 43–51 *passim*, 54, 80, 84, 100, 121
Contemporary Verse, 178, 198
"The Conversation" (Masters), 157
"Conversation Galante" (Eliot), 182
"The Cool Fingers of Science" (Pound), 48
"Cool Tombs" (Sandburg), 224
Corbin, Alice. *See* Henderson, Alice Corbin
Cournos, John, 38
"Cousin Nancy" (Eliot), 156
Crane, Hart, 222, 281
"The Cuban Doctor" (Stevens), 269
Cummings, E. E., 263, 272
Curran, Edwin, 273
Currey, Margery, 52
"The Curtains in the House of the Metaphysician" (Stevens), 268
"The Cyclists" (Lowell), 144

Damon, S. Foster, 222
"Dance Figure" (Pound), 43, 45
"The Dance of the Seasons" (Monroe), 12
"Dans le Restaurant" (Eliot), 240
"Dans un Omnibus de Londres" (Pound), 182
Dargan, Olive Tilford, 5, 19
Davidson, Donald: quoted, 273–74
Davies, W. H., 35, 71, 72
Davis, Fannie Stearns, 19, 60, 87
Davis, H. L., 260, 267
Dawson, Mitchell, 147; quoted, 148
The Death of Agrippina (Neihardt), 54–55, 123
"Death of St. Narcissus" (Eliot), 182
"The Death of the Hired Man" (Frost), 83
de Bosschère, Jean, 182, 203
"A Deep Sworn Vow" (Yeats), 209
de Gourmont, Remy, 83, 117
de la Mare, Walter, 25, 35, 121
Dell, Floyd, 10, 19, 48, 52; quoted, 48
"Depression before Spring" (Stevens), 226

Des Imagistes (Pound-Kreymborg), 39–43 *passim*, 86, 97–99 *passim*, 130, 131, 134, 147, 150, 264, 285
Dial, 5, 7, 10, 25, 54, 84, 87, 103, 152, 168, 198, 202, 215, 221, 239, 262–67 *passim*, 270–74 *passim*, 277, 285, 286; attacks Pound (1913), 48–50; attacks Sandburg (1914), 100–102; attacks Eliot (1915), 156
Dickinson, Emily, 165
"Le Directeur" (Eliot), 221
"The Discarded Imagist" (Upward), 138
Dismorr, Jessie, 222
The Divine Fire (Sinclair), 105
"The Doctor of Geneva" (Stevens), 269
"Dogmatic Statement Concerning the Game of Chess" (Pound), 153
"Domesday Book" (Masters), 253
"Don'ts by an Imagiste" (Pound). *See* "A Few Don'ts by an Imagiste"
Doolittle, Hilda. *See* H.D.
Dorr, Julia C. R., 5, 19
Drama, 133
Drinkwater, John, 19, 24, 35, 71, 72
Driscoll, Louise, 144, 276
Dudley, Dorothy, 34
Dudley, Helen, 27, 34
"Dum Capitolium Scandet" (Pound), 58

Earle, Ferdinand Phinny, 25
Eastman, Max, 87
"Ego Dominus Tuus" (Yeats), 222, 246
Egoist, 59, 93–99 *passim*, 117, 125, 129–33 *passim*, 136, 138, 139, 147, 150–55 *passim*, 192, 198, 215, 264, 265, 285
Eliot, T. S., 3, 91, 92, 114, 123, 129, 134, 135, 145, 149, 151, 153, 156, 158, 159, 164, 167, 182, 199, 203, 209, 211, 212, 214, 221, 222, 231, 234, 235, 240, 242, 249–51, 255, 262, 264, 280, 282, 285–92 *passim*; publication of "Prufrock," 125–28; Pound's influence on, 183–85; "Mr. Apollinax" censored, 190–92; quoted, 99, 242, 255
"The Emperor of Ice Cream" (Stevens), 270
English Review, 56, 67, 233, 234, 240, 249, 250
"Epigram" (H.D.), 69
"Epilogue" (Pound), 45

"Epilogue: To My Five Books" (Pound), 44, 80

"Erinna" (Pound). *See* "The Patterns"

"Eros Turannos" (Robinson), 91, 99

"Exile's Letter" (Pound), 91, 137, 145, 153, 166, 186

"Exposition of the Contents of a Cab" (Stevens), 267

"Fabliau of Florida" (Stevens), 267

"Fallen Majesty" (Yeats), 62

"The Father" (Pound), 120, 121

Fawcett, Edgar, 9

Fenollosa, Ernest, 43, 91, 94, 133, 144, 166

"A Few Don'ts by an Imagiste" (Pound), 40, 41, 62, 139, 166

Ficke, Arthur Davison, 19, 20, 22, 27, 33, 34, 54, 148, 188, 193, 238, 271

Field, Eugene, 5, 11, 61

"The Fight for the Crowd" (Monroe), 116, 162

"La Figlia Che Piange" (Eliot), 182

"The Fireman's Ball" (Lindsay), 106, 109, 234

"The Fish and the Shadow" (Pound), 182, 186

Fisher, Mahlon Leonard, 87

Fiske, Isabelle Howe, 87

Fletcher, John Gould, 32, 60, 70–71, 75, 80, 86, 91, 92, 94, 96, 124, 125, 131, 135, 137, 139, 141, 143, 144, 146, 148, 163, 178, 188, 194, 198–202 *passim*, 227, 230, 245, 280, 288

Flint, F. S., 32, 39, 41n, 54, 64, 72, 76, 86, 92, 96, 131, 135, 137, 146

"Flood" (Joyce), 182

"A Flower Given to My Daughter" (Joyce), 182

"Fodder" (Pound), 121

Ford, Ford Madox. *See* Hueffer, Ford Madox

Ford, Webster. *See* Masters, Edgar Lee

"The Foreigners" (Lowell), 144

"The Forsaken" (Lowell), 118–19, 144

Fortnightly Review, 12, 133

Forum, 5, 87, 238

"Four Brothers" (Sandburg), 224

Freer, Agnes Lee, 140

Free verse, 18, 24, 38, 39, 45, 54, 57, 59, 66, 70, 87, 117, 134, 164, 169, 183, 188, 207, 277; "Contemporaria" criticized as example of, 48–51; Sandburg attacked for, 100–101; in *Spectra* hoax, 237–38

"From Chebar" (Pound), 73, 74

"From the Misery of Don Joost" (Stevens), 269

Frost, Robert, 3, 6, 20, 54, 64, 80, 86, 91, 96, 99, 124, 141, 143, 152, 159, 164–70 *passim*, 180, 188, 199, 201, 202, 203, 225, 230, 232, 233–34, 240, 246, 249, 250, 264, 274, 280, 284, 286, 288, 291; first publication in *Poetry*, 66–69; quoted, 64, 66–67, 68, 203

Fugitive, 273–74

Fuller, Henry Blake, 9, 11, 12, 23–24, 52, 179, 225, 227; quoted, 11, 225

"Further Instructions" (Pound), 47, 48

"The Garden" (Pound), 43, 45

Garland, Hamlin, 10, 33, 50, 52, 80–81

Garnett, Louise Ayres, 276

"The Garret" (Pound), 43, 45, 46

Garrison, Theodosia, 6, 19

Garvin, Margaret Root, 87

Gaudier-Brzeska, Henri, 133

"General William Booth Enters into Heaven" (Lindsay), 33, 38, 49, 50, 54, 102, 104, 110, 284

General William Booth Enters into Heaven (Lindsay), 86, 87, 105, 141

"Gentildonna" (Pound), 48

Georgian Poetry, 25, 40, 223

Georgian revival, 19, 25, 34, 71, 86, 170, 236

"Gerontion" (Eliot), 184–85, 251

Gibson, Wilfred Wilson, 19, 22, 24, 35

"A Gift" (Lowell), 144

Gilder, Jeannette, 7

Gilder, Richard Watson, 8, 9

Gilmore, Louis, 222

"The Gipsy" (Pound), 153

Glebe, 97–98, 264

"Gloria!" (Williams), 271

Goldring, Douglas, 92, 134

"The Goodly Fere" (Pound), 230

"A Goodnight" (Williams), 275

Graves, Alfred Perceval, 26
"Gray Room" (Stevens), 226
Gregg, Frances, 38
Gregory, Augusta, 266
"The Grey Rock" (Yeats), 31, 49, 54
Grotesques (Head), 179
Guarantors of Poetry, 16–17, 102, 118, 186, 199, 200, 201, 205, 211, 213, 214
Guarantors' Prize, 69, 77–78, 82, 124
"Gubbinal" (Stevens), 269

Hackett, Francis, 10
Hagedorn, Hermann, 19, 87, 164, 167, 182–83
Hale, William Gardner, 253–57, 259, 262; quoted, 253–54
Hark to These Three (Moore), 153
Harland, Henry, 8
Harmonium (Stevens), 270, 271
Harper's, 5, 66, 68, 87, 212, 237
Harrison, Austin, 235, 240
Harte, Bret, 5, 61
H.D. (Hilda Doolittle), 32, 34, 38, 39, 40, 41n, 60, 64, 69, 75, 80, 86, 92, 96, 99, 131, 135, 137, 139, 143, 147, 158, 159, 167, 191, 230, 250, 253, 280, 284, 285, 288
Head, Cloyd, 179
Heap, Jane, 206, 207, 222, 243, 244, 246–47; quoted, 207, 243
Hecht, Ben, 147, 222
Heinemann, Alfred, 86
Henderson, Alice Corbin, 22–23, 24, 38, 61, 62, 66, 69, 74, 100, 111, 112, 114, 133, 134, 138, 152, 167, 180, 192–94, 197–98, 202–8 passim, 223–24, 233, 237, 239, 247–48, 276, 284, 285, 290; leaves Chicago, 186–88; importance of to Poetry, 226–30, 265; quoted, 114, 138, 187–88, 194, 197–98, 202, 203, 204, 207–8, 223–24, 227–30 passim, 237, 247, 248, 284
"Hermes of the Ways" (H.D.), 32, 69, 147
"Hermonax" (H.D.), 69
Hervey, John L., 156, 168
Heyward, DuBose, 273
"Hibiscus on the Sleeping Shores" (Stevens), 269

"The Hippopotamus" (Eliot), 221, 251
"History" (Williams), 216–17
"History of Imagism" (Flint), 39, 41n, 43
Hodgson, Ralph, 121
Holley, Horace, 151, 177
"Homage to Quintus Septimius Florentis Christianus" (Pound), 182
"Homage to Sextus Propertius" (Pound), 251–62 passim, 284, 285
"Homère Mere Habite Sa Maison des Planches" (de Bosschère), 182
"Homunculus et la Belle Etojle" (Stevens), 267
"The Hotel" (Monroe), 12
"A House" (Hueffer), 272
Hovey, Richard, 5, 7
Hoyt, Helen, 147, 149, 194, 207, 231, 238, 265
Hueffer, Ford Madox, 32, 34, 38, 39, 54, 55, 75, 76, 79, 81–82, 83, 91–94 passim, 97, 117, 123–24, 127, 130, 131, 135, 144, 158, 159, 164, 167, 176, 188, 267, 272, 284, 285; quoted, 81–82, 272
Hulme, T. E., 39, 40, 64, 134, 135
The Human Fantasy (Wheelock), 279
Hunt, Violet, 92

"I Am the Woman" (Moody), 27, 49
"I Live among Men" (Flint), 72
"Image from D'Orleans" (Pound), 153
Imagism(e), 34, 53, 92, 108, 133, 134, 136, 138–40, 142, 146–47, 152, 165–66, 169, 170, 188, 238, 247, 251, 266, 287; in Poetry (1912–13), 38–43; Amy Lowell's schism, 129–31; Some Imagist Poets (1915), 135–40
"Imagisme" (Flint), 39, 41
"Impressionism" (Hueffer), 32, 55
"Impressions of François-Marie Arouet" (Pound), 182
"In a Station of the Metro" (Pound), 43, 45
"Incense and Splendor" (Lindsay), 104
Independent, 6, 87
"The Indigo Glass in the Grass" (Stevens), 267
"In Memory of Byron Lathrop" (Masters), 180

"In Memory of William Pollexfen"
(Yeats), 209
"In Shadow" (Crane), 222
International, 117
"In the Garden" (Flint), 72
Iris, Scharmel, 146, 147
"Irish Spinning Songs" (Colum), 99
"Irradiations" (Fletcher), 32, 70, 75, 96,
245
"Isaac and Rebekah" (Moore), 153, 188
"Ite" (Pound), 48
"It Is Not a Word" (Teasdale), 278

Jepson, Edgar, 202–3, 237, 249, 251,
252–53, 257, 262; attacks *Poetry* (1918),
233–35; reprinted in the *Little Review*,
240–51
Johns, Orrick, 20, 55, 75, 93, 94, 99, 124,
134, 149
Johnson, Robert Underwood, 87
John Wellborn Root (Monroe), 11, 13
Jones, Llewellyn, 235
Jones, Paul Fortier, 249, 258
Joyce, James, 39, 129, 133, 167, 181–82,
214, 221, 280
Judgment (Burr), 85
Jurgen (Cabell), 118

Kaufman, Reginald Wright, 96
Kaun, Alexander S., 42
Kemp, Harry, 87
Kennerley, Mitchell, 12, 238–39
Kilmer, Joyce, 20, 33, 87
Kora in Hell (Williams), 222, 246
Kreymborg, Alfred, 42, 71, 72, 86, 97, 98,
129, 134, 135, 154, 168, 177, 187,
192–96 *passim*, 199, 202, 222, 229, 230,
231, 237, 245, 264, 267, 275, 280;
begins *Others*, 149–51; quoted, 42, 150,
193–94, 237, 245

"A Lady" (Lowell), 144
"The Lake Isle" (Pound), 182
"The Landlady of the Whinton Inn Tells
a Story" (Lowell), 225
"Langue d'Oc" (Pound), 222
"Lapis Lazuli" (Yeats), 115–16
Lawrence, D. H., 55–56, 60, 75, 76, 86,
91, 92, 96, 99, 131, 135, 141, 166, 167,

198, 235, 261, 280; quoted, 235
"Lead Soldiers" (Lowell), 138, 148
Ledoux, Louis V., 22, 169
Lee, Agnes, 4, 33, 34, 54, 140
LeGallienne, Richard, 26, 71
Leonard, William Ellery, 87
"Lesbia" (Aldington), 94, 120
"Lesbia Illa" (Pound), 120, 121
"Les Millwin" (Pound), 48
"Let It Be Forgotten" (Teasdale), 278
"Lettres d'un Soldat" (Stevens), 226
Levinson, Salmon O., 124n
Levinson Prize, 78n, 106, 124n, 151, 153,
166, 229; to Sandburg (1914), 123–24;
to Lindsay (1915), 158; attacks on, 171,
233–34; to Head (1917), 179; to Masters
(1916), 180; to Underwood (1918), 249;
to Stevens (1920), 268; to Frost (1922),
274
Lewis, Wyndham, 38–39, 131, 132, 133,
163, 214, 222; quoted, 38–39
"L'Homme Moyen Sensuel" (Pound),
151n, 212
Lindsay, Vachel, 3, 7, 13–14, 19, 22, 26,
33, 34, 38, 42, 49, 52, 54, 55, 60–61,
69, 77, 81, 86, 87, 91, 93, 94, 99, 101,
110–11, 117, 124, 128, 135, 141–48
passim, 151, 158, 159, 171, 180, 187,
188, 193, 199, 224, 228–36 *passim*,
240–46 *passim*, 249, 250, 253, 264, 265,
271, 280, 281, 284, 288, 289, 291; and
Harriet Monroe, 104–10; quoted, 42,
61, 105, 106, 107, 109, 128, 148, 187,
224, 244, 265
Lippincott's, 5, 87
Little Review, 42, 83, 103, 117, 118, 151,
155, 159, 166, 185, 198, 199, 216, 226,
235, 238, 249, 250, 257–65 *passim*, 289;
publishes poetry (1914–16), 145–49;
and Pound, 205–14, 221–23; attack by
Jepson (1918), 240, 242–43, 244–48
Little Room, 9–10, 16, 23, 49, 52
"The Load of Sugar-Cane" (Stevens), 269
Lodge, George Cabot, 5
"London Night" (Rodker), 94, 120–21,
128
"The Lonely Street" (Williams), 276
"The Loop" (Masters), 152
Lorimer, Emilia Stuart, 27

Love Poems (Lawrence), 56, 60
Love Poems (Teasdale), 277
"Love Song" (Williams), 181
"The Love Song of J. Alfred Prufrock" (Eliot), 91, 145, 148, 151, 155, 158, 159, 181, 192, 227, 234, 235, 252, 283, 288, 290; published in *Poetry*, 123, 125–28
Lovett, Robert Morss, 10
Lowell, Amy, 19, 22, 33, 39, 41, 59–60, 82, 86, 87, 92, 93, 96, 108, 118–19, 125, 130–35 *passim*, 146–49 *passim*, 163, 169, 170, 179, 188, 194, 199, 202, 207, 208, 222, 224, 225, 229–32, 245, 249, 264, 271, 280, 287, 289; and Harriet Monroe, 135–45; quoted, 83, 119, 130–31, 136–44 *passim*, 147, 149, 169, 170, 179, 231
Loy, Mina, 149, 286n
"Lune de Miel" (Eliot), 221
"Lustra" (Pound), 46, 47
Lustra (Pound), 86, 120, 122, 133, 285
The Lyric Year, 25–26, 85

McCarthy, John Russell, 118
McClure, Jack, 96
MacKaye, Percy, 5, 22, 71, 87
Macmillan Company, 104, 136, 188
"Madonna Mia" (Williams), 57n
"The Magi" (Yeats), 91
"The Malay to His Master" (Rice), 70
"Malmaison" (Lowell), 225
Manning, Frederic, 20, 38, 54, 188
Markham, Edwin, 5, 20, 22, 26, 71, 87, 169
"Marriage" (Williams), 181
Marsh, Edward, 25
Marshall, John, 192
Masefield, John, 19, 24, 35, 38, 71, 86, 92, 141
Masses, 52, 262
Masters, Edgar Lee, 3, 7, 9, 20, 52, 92, 100, 102, 111–17 *passim*, 128, 134, 143, 147, 151–53, 157, 159, 164–70 *passim*, 180, 183, 184, 188, 193, 195, 199, 200, 202, 207, 213, 224, 227–34 *passim*, 238n, 240, 242, 246, 249, 250, 253, 264, 280, 281, 284, 288, 289, 291; quoted, 9, 52, 111–15 *passim*, 224, 232
Mathews, Elkin, 19, 22, 120, 133

Mauberley (Pound), 167, 183, 264, 273
"Mea Culpa" (Monroe), 279
"Meditatio" (Pound), 45
"Meditation" (Stevens), 226
"Mélange Adultère de Tout" (Eliot), 182, 221
Men, Women, and Ghosts (Lowell), 207
Mencken, Henry Louis, 87, 118, 284; quoted, 87
"Men Improve with the Years" (Yeats), 209
"Metaphors of a Magnifico" (Stevens), 226
Metropolitan, 104, 118
Mew, Charlotte, 71, 96
Meynell, Alice, 20, 22
Meynell, Francis, 71
Michelson, Max, 194, 222, 247, 251
Mid-American Chants (Anderson), 227
"Middle-Aged" (Pound), 34
Middleton, Scudder, 119
Millay, Edna St. Vincent, 26, 280
Miller, Joaquim, 5
"Mr. Apollinax" (Eliot), 182, 190–92, 195
"Mr. Eliot's Sunday Morning Service" (Eliot), 240
"Moeurs Contemporaines" (Pound), 222
"Le Monocle de Mon Oncle" (Stevens), 271
Monro, Harold, 20, 22, 25, 94, 127, 134, 135, 155, 167, 168
Monroe, Harriet, *passim*; motive for launching *Poetry*, 3–7, 12–15, 18, 20–21; background, 8–13; and ideal of modern art, 11–12; and Lindsay, 13–14, 102–10, 231; finances *Poetry*, 15–18; early relation to Pound, 34–37, 44–46, 51, 53, 61–62, 72–74, 78–81, 82; and Williams, 56–59, 177, 181, 196, 215–18, 259–60, 274–76; prunes MSS, 62–65; and Frost, 66–69, 203, 274; money worries, 83–84, 124, 170, 176, 189, 208, 214, 218, 266–67, 279–80; censors MSS, 94, 118, 122–23, 190–91, 216–17; replies to *Dial* (1914), 101–2; and Masters, 111, 114–15, 152–53, 231–32, 253; and Stevens, 113, 157–58, 180, 267–71; on poet's mission (1915), 116; objections to "Prufrock," 123, 125–27; and Amy Lowell, 135–45; and

Imagism (1915), 139–40; and
"Audience" controversy, 160–64;
distracted (1916), 186–89; and
Bodenheim, 195–97; relation to Pound
after 1917, 205–6, 208–11, 233–35,
240–42, 251–52, 257–59, 276–77,
282–84, 285; editorial ideal and
accomplishment, 215, 266–67, 271,
288–94; and Alice Corbin Henderson,
227–30, 265; quoted, 9, 13–14, 14–15,
20–24 passim, 33–34, 37, 38, 44, 46–51
passim, 55–60 passim, 63–66 passim, 69,
72, 78–79, 82, 98–99, 101–5 passim,
111, 113, 115, 118–21 passim, 126–27,
128, 135, 138–39, 140, 143, 150,
161–62, 180, 182, 189, 197, 200–201,
202, 208–11 passim, 214, 215, 216,
231–35 passim, 239, 241, 249, 251–52,
253, 257, 258–59, 263, 268–69, 280,
281, 285
"The Monroe Doctrine in Poetry"
(Aiken), 236–37
Moody, Harriet, 27, 214
Moody, William Vaughn, 4, 27, 33, 49
"Moon Poems" (Lindsay), 60–61, 104
"The Moon Rises" (Masters), 152
Moore, Marianne, 92, 151, 154–55, 158,
159, 195, 223, 252, 263, 278, 280, 282,
285, 286, 290, 292; quoted, 155, 282
Moore, T. Sturge, 92, 153, 162–63, 167,
176, 185, 189
"Morning at the Window" (Eliot), 182
Mosher, Thomas Bird, 66
"Mother Earth" (Monroe), 49
"The Mountain Tomb" (Yeats), 62
Mushrooms (Kreymborg), 229
"Music" (Lowell), 144

"Naked" (Williams), 181
"Near Perigord" (Pound), 91, 153, 166
"Needle Travel" (Patton), 169
Neihardt, John G., 19, 22, 33, 50–51,
54–55, 122; quoted, 51
New Freewoman, 80, 150
The New Poetry (Monroe), 188–89, 201,
204, 216, 236–37
New York Times, 86, 156, 169
"Night Piece" (Joyce), 182
Nishikigi (Pound), 91, 94, 95

"Nogi" (Monroe), 49
North American Review, 5, 84, 87
North of Boston (Frost), 69, 141, 169
"The North Star" (Lindsay), 104
Norton, Grace Fallow, 276
Noyes, Alfred, 19, 22, 24, 33, 86

"Of Heaven Considered as a Tomb"
(Stevens), 269
"The Old South" (Fletcher), 148
"The Old Worshipper" (Williams), 181
"On Heaven" (Hueffer), 91, 94, 117, 124,
144, 176, 272
The Only Jealousy of Emer (Yeats), 246
"On the Manner of Addressing Clouds"
(Stevens), 269
"On the Surface of Things" (Stevens), 268
"The Open Door" (Monroe), 37
Oppenheim, James, 169, 202
Orage, A. R., 152, 254
"Ortus" (Pound), 43, 45
O'Sullivan, Seamus, 92, 94
Others, 129, 149–51, 154, 155, 157, 159,
169, 170, 177, 178, 192–95 passim, 198,
202, 215, 218, 224, 226, 229, 238, 242,
259–60, 264, 267, 271, 275
Others Anthology, 150, 192–94, 267, 268,
275, 286n
"Our Respectful Homage to M. Laurent
Tailhade" (Pound), 44
Outlook, 87

"A Pact" (Pound), 43
"Pagani's" (Pound), 182
"Palace of the Babies" (Stevens), 269
"The Paltry Nude Starts on a Spring
Voyage" (Stevens), 268
"Paris" (Pound), 76
"Passing" (Pound), 121
Patria Mea (Pound), 13
"Patterns" (Lowell), 147, 148, 169, 225
"The Patterns" ("Erinna") (Pound), 45,
120, 121
Patterson, Antoinette DeCoursey, 276
Patton, Margaret French, 169
"Pax Saturni" (Pound), 43, 44, 45
Peabody, Josephine Preston, 5, 87
"Peace on Earth" (Williams), 56
"Pecksniffiana" (Stevens), 267–68

Perry, Bliss, 4
"Peter Parasol" (Stevens), 267
"Peter Quince at the Clavier" (Stevens),
    149, 155, 170, 199
"Phases" (Stevens), 113, 157
"Phyllidula" (Pound), 120, 121
"Phyllidula and the Spoils of Gouvernet"
    (Pound), 190–91
"The Place of the Solitaires" (Stevens),
    268
Players' Producing Company, 180
"Ploughing on Sunday" (Stevens), 267
Poems (Eliot), 183, 191
"Poems to Be Chanted" (Lindsay), 106
"Poetry" (Ficke), 27
Poetry and Drama, 67, 94, 127, 131
Poetry Journal, 25, 26–27, 85, 87, 119,
    140, 159, 170, 178, 179
Poetry Renaissance, 3–4, 7–8, 12, 18, 22,
    24–25, 56, 73, 91, 108, 143, 150, 175,
    187–88, 213, 230, 237, 239, 260–61,
    264, 280, 286–87, 293–94; and Lyric
    Year, 25–26; in 1912–13, 84–87; in
    1915, 168–70; in 1916, 192, 198–99;
    Braithwaite on (1916), 201–2
Poetry Review, 170, 178, 194, 198
Poetry Society of America, 168, 169, 198,
    277
Poetry Society of America–Columbia
    Prize, 191n, 277
"Portent" (Williams), 57
"Portrait of a Lady" (Eliot), 128–29, 149,
    151, 155, 199
Portrait of the Artist as a Young Man
    (Joyce), 129, 167
"Postlude" (Williams), 32, 56, 64
"Post Mortem Conspectu" (Pound), 44
"Postponement" (Fuller), 179, 225
Pound, Ezra, passim; first correspondence
    with Harriet Monroe (1912), 33–37;
    early Imagiste campaign, 38–43, 53;
    "Contemporaria," 43–46, 48–50; and
    Smart Set, 47–48, 75–76; correspondence
    with Harriet Monroe revives (1913),
    54–56; and Williams, 56, 59, 259–60,
    285; as the "Divine Ezra," 61; and Yeats,
    62n, 82, 104, 285; prunes MSS, 62–64;
    and Frost, 65–69; "hammers stuff into
    Poetry," 68–69, 70–71, 94, 240; early

relation to Harriet Monroe, 72–74;
    quarrel with Harriet Monroe (1913),
    74–79, 80–81, 82; and Amy Lowell,
    82–83, 93, 130, 131, 135–36, 140–41; on
    censorship, 94, 189–91 passim; and
    Masters, 110, 112, 114, 117, 128, 152,
    153, 166, 180, 195; and Eliot, 123, 125,
    183–85, 249–51; and Imagist schism,
    129–31; and money, 133, 175, 189,
    212–13, 214, 252, 284; situation in
    London (1914–16), 133–34; on "life in
    arrangement" (1915), 159, 164–65; and
    "Audience" controversy, 160–64;
    Cantos, 166–67, 223–24, 290–91; and
    rejection of "Cabaret Dancers" (1916),
    182–86; and the Little Review, 208–9,
    211–12, 214, 221–23; and Jepson attack
    on Poetry (1918), 240, 249–51; and
    "Propertius" quarrel, 251–57 passim;
    contribution to Poetry, 285–88 passim;
    quoted, 7, 17–18, 22, 35–40 passim,
    43–47 passim, 50, 54, 55–56, 61–83
    passim, 93–99 passim, 108, 110, 112, 114,
    116, 120–29 passim, 132–35 passim, 145,
    146, 153, 154, 159, 160–66 passim, 175,
    176, 179, 182–86 passim, 189–90, 191,
    195, 202–6 passim, 221, 222, 226, 240,
    249, 250, 252, 254, 283–84, 286n
Pound, Homer Loomis: quoted, 251
"Preface to Kora in Hell" (Williams), 246,
    259
"Presences" (Yeats), 209
"Priapus" (H.D.), 69
"Printemps" (Pound), 121
"Proof of Immortality" (Williams), 57
"Propertius" (Pound). See "Homage to
    Sextus Propertius"
"Provincia Deserta" (Pound), 153

Quia Pauper Amavi (Pound), 257
Quinn, John, 83, 130n, 133, 185, 210,
    212, 213, 224

Rascoe, Burton, 234
Ravenel, Beatrice, 339
"Recent United States Poetry" (Jepson),
    233–34, 244–51
Reed, John, 33, 45, 49, 67
Reedy, William Marion, 7, 85, 111, 112,

152, 168, 224, 235–36, 284; quoted, 84–85, 152, 168, 236
Reedy's Mirror, 6, 84–85, 111, 114, 117, 152, 166, 168, 198, 230, 235, 238
Reese, Lizette Woodworth, 5, 19
"The Renaissance" (Pound), 162, 168
"Renascence" (Millay), 26
"The Rest" (Pound), 48
Rhys, Ernest, 20, 33
"Rhythms of English Verse" (Monroe), 32, 60
Rice, Cale Young, 4, 22, 65, 70; quoted, 65
Rice, Wallace, 48, 49–50, 100
Riding, Laura, 281
Riley, James Whitcomb, 4
Ripostes (Pound), 39, 40
"The Road Not Taken" (Frost), 170
The Roadside Fire (Burr), 85
Roberts, Elizabeth Madox, 273
Robinson, Edwin Arlington, 5, 6–7, 20, 87, 91, 99, 152, 169, 230, 286
Rodker, John, 92, 94, 96, 110, 120, 121, 128, 135, 167, 222
"Room 634" (Masters), 152
Root, John Wellborn, 9
Ryerson, Edward L., 214

"Salutation" (Pound), 43
"Salutation the Second" (Pound), 43
"Salutation the Third" (Pound), 44, 54
"Salvationists" (Pound), 121
Sanborn, Robert Alden, 151, 222
Sandburg, Carl, 3, 20, 91, 92, 102, 103, 104, 108, 111–17 passim, 123–24, 134, 143, 149, 167, 171, 180, 188, 194, 195, 199, 200, 201, 202, 222–25 passim, 229–37 passim, 242, 258, 264, 280, 281, 288, 289; first Poetry publication, 99–100; attacked by Dial, 100–102; quoted, 258
"Sangar" (Reed), 45, 49
"The Santa Fe Trail" (Lindsay), 106–7, 108
Saphier, William, 195, 226
Sarett, Lew, 24, 247, 251
"Scented Leaves from a Chinese Jar" (Upward), 43, 96
Scollard, Clinton, 5, 19

Scribner's, 5, 68, 87, 212
"The Second Coming" (Yeats), 264, 285
"The Seeing Eye" (Pound), 121
Seiffert, Marjorie Allen, 238, 276
Selver, Paul, 39, 40, 71
Seven Arts, 198, 202, 231, 248, 249
Seymour, Ralph Fletcher, 24
Shaw, Frances, 99
Shepard, Odell, 169
Shorey, Paul, 38n, 253
"Sicilian Emigrant's Song" (Williams), 56
"Silence" (Masters), 92, 112, 152
"Simples" (Joyce), 182
Sinclair, May, 105
Six French Poets (Lowell), 140, 142
Skinner, Constance Lindsay, 158, 159
Smart Set, 47–48, 67, 75–76, 80, 87, 88, 129, 145, 213
"Smell" (Williams), 216
Smith, Clark Ashton, 87
"Snow" (Frost), 180, 203, 234, 274
"The Snow Man" (Stevens), 269
"Sobriety and Earnestness" (Monroe), 95, 160
Some Imagist Poets, 131, 134–40 passim, 169, 188, 230; Harriet Monroe's response to, 135–40
"Song from the Player Queen" (Yeats), 91
"A Song of Degrees" (Pound), 48
"Song of the Cheechas" (Underwood), 249
"Songs of Deliverance" (Johns), 55, 94
"So We Grew Together" (Masters), 166
Spectra hoax, 237–39, 271
Spoon River Anthology (Masters), 100, 111–17 passim, 151–52, 167, 168, 169, 213, 224, 230, 231, 241, 251, 284, 288, 291
"Spouts" (Williams), 276
"The Spring" (Pound), 153
"Status Rerum" (Pound), 34–36, 40, 170, 236
Stedman, Edmund Clarence, 5, 9
Stephens, James, 20, 35, 92
Stevens, Wallace, 92, 135, 144, 149, 151, 166, 180, 188, 195, 200, 222, 225–26, 229, 230, 231, 235, 268, 274, 280, 282, 285–92 passim; first Poetry publication, 112–14; publishes "Sunday Morning,"

157–58; and Harriet Monroe, 267–71;
quoted, 14, 157, 158, 267–71 passim
Stickney, Trumbull, 5
Storer, Edward, 39, 266
Stork, George Wharton, 87
"The Street in Soho" (Pound), 48
Strobel, Marion, 265
"The Study in Aesthetics" (Pound), 121
Sullivan, Louis, 9; quoted, 11–12
"Summer Song" (Williams), 181
"Sunday Morning" (Stevens), 91, 113,
157–58, 166, 225, 268, 289
"Surgit Fama" (Pound), 48
"Sweeney among the Nightingales"
(Eliot), 184, 240
Sword Blades and Poppy Seed (Lowell), 136
"Symphony in a Mexican Garden"
(Conkling), 27

Taggard, Genevieve, 273
Tagore, Rabindranath, 31, 34, 38, 49, 51,
53, 54, 63–64, 67, 86, 87, 101, 117,
135, 209, 235, 285
Tarbell, Ida M., 5
Tate, Allen, 274, 281, 282; quoted, 274,
282
Taupin, René, 40, 281, 282
Taylor, Bert Leston, 48, 234
"Tea at the Palaz of Hoon" (Stevens), 269
Teasdale, Sara, 20, 26, 34, 81, 92, 99,
105, 187, 277–78, 280; quoted, 277, 278
"The Teashop" (Pound), 44, 80
"The Temperaments" (Pound), 120, 121,
122
Tendencies in Modern American Poetry
(Lowell), 230–32
"Tenzone" (Pound), 43
"That Harp You Play So Well" (Moore),
154
Thayer, Scofield, 221, 262, 263–64, 270
"Thirteen Ways of Looking at a
Blackbird" (Stevens), 226
Thomas, Edith, 5, 19
Thomas, Edward, 203
Thompson, Francis, 87
"Three Cantos" (Pound). See Cantos
"The Three Poets" (Pound), 182
Three Travelers Watch a Sunrise (Stevens),
158, 180, 225

The Thunderstorm (Monroe), 13
Tietjens, Eunice, 52, 147, 186, 187, 207,
208, 227, 265
"The Tiger Tree" (Lindsay), 228
"To a Child Dancing upon the Shore"
(Yeats), 62, 63
"To a Friend Whose Work Has Come to
Nothing" (Yeats), 91
"To a Friend Writing on Cabaret
Dancers" (Pound), 167, 182–86, 189,
195, 223, 288
"To an Intramural Rat" (Moore), 154–55
"To KALON" (Pound), 121
"Too Far from Paris" (Henderson), 228
Torrence, Ridgely, 5, 26
"To Whistler, American" (Pound), 27, 53
Towne, Charles Hanson, 49, 141
"The Tradition" (Pound), 76, 114
"The Traveler Heart" (Lindsay), 104
Tree, Iris, 247
"Trees" (Kilmer), 87
Trench, Herbert, 20
Trend, 113
"The Turbine" (Monroe), 12
Turbyfill, Mark, 222
"Tutto è Sciolto" (Joyce), 182
"The Two Kings" (Yeats), 31, 75

Ulysses (Joyce), 118, 221, 262
Underwood, John Curtis, 249, 258
Untermeyer, Louis, 19, 128, 169, 187,
249, 271
"Upon a Dying Lady" (Yeats), 209, 211,
222
Upward, Allen, 33, 42–43, 75, 96, 130,
134, 138

"Valediction" (Pound), 121
Valeria (Monroe), 8, 10
"Valley Candle" (Stevens), 226
van Dyke, Henry, 19, 87, 114
"Various Voices" (Monroe), 143
Vers libre. See Free verse
"Vers Libre and Metrical Prose" (Lowell),
60
Viereck, George Sylvester, 117
Vorticism, 131–33

Waley, Arthur, 214, 222

Walsh, Ernest, 273
"The Wanderer" (Williams), 59, 80, 96
Ward, Susan Hayes, 6
The Waste Land (Eliot), 264, 279
Watson, James Sibley, 264, 270
Weaver, Harriet Shaw, 130n
"The Weeping Burgher" (Stevens), 267
Wescott, Glenway, 273
"The Western School" (Jepson). *See*
 "Recent United States Poetry"
"Western Verse" (Henderson), 229
Wheeler, Edward J., 33, 112
Wheelock, John Hall, 19, 22, 33, 71, 72,
 81, 87, 279; quoted, 279
"Whispers of Immortality" (Eliot), 240
White, J. R., 222
Whitman, Walt, 7, 11, 13, 21, 51, 55, 73,
 77, 156, 161, 169, 233, 245, 252, 263
Widdemer, Margaret, 33, 54
"The Widow's Lament in Springtime"
 (Williams), 276
Wilcox, Ella Wheeler, 5, 19–20
"Wild Orchard" (Williams), 276
"The Wild Swans at Coole" (Yeats), 209
The Wild Swans at Coole (Yeats), 278
Wilkinson, Florence, 4, 56
Wilkinson, Marguerite, 19, 87
Williams, Florence, 178, 217, 246, 274,
 276
Williams, William Carlos, 3, 20, 31, 32,
 37–38, 39, 59, 61–62, 64, 80, 86, 92,
 96, 122–23, 128, 132, 134–35, 149, 151,
 154, 155, 158, 160, 167, 177, 178,
 180–81, 187, 188, 190, 194, 196–97,
 201, 207, 222–25 *passim*, 230, 231, 237,
 238n, 250, 259–61 *passim*, 264, 267,
 270, 271, 272, 280, 281, 282, 285–94
 passim; first *Poetry* publication, 56–58;

on *Others* and Kreymborg, 192–93; on
 censorship and money, 215–18; and
 Jepson attack on *Poetry*, 246–47, 259;
 and Harriet Monroe, 274–76; quoted,
 57, 58, 59, 62, 122, 154, 177, 178, 181,
 192, 193, 196, 197, 216, 217, 218,
 224–25, 237, 246–47, 259–61 *passim*,
 272–76, 290
"The Wind Shifts" (Stevens), 226
Winters, Yvor, 273, 281
"The Witch of Coös" (Frost), 274
With Serbia into Exile (Jones), 249
"The Wizard in Words" (Moore), 155
Woodberry, George Edward, 5, 26, 87
"Words and the Poet" (Jepson), 203
Wright, Willard Huntington, 47, 87
Wyatt, Edith, 4, 23–24, 27, 34, 179, 180,
 265
Wylie, Elinor, 273

"Xenia" (Pound), 46, 47

Yale Review, 87
Yeats, William Butler, 6, 20, 22, 31, 33,
 34, 38, 47, 49, 53, 54, 65, 69, 75, 76,
 80, 85–86, 87, 91–97 *passim*, 108, 115,
 116–17, 122, 124, 128, 129, 134, 144,
 153, 156, 159, 162, 164, 165, 167, 171,
 176, 181, 188, 199, 209–14 *passim*,
 221–22, 223, 228, 235, 242, 246, 264,
 272, 278, 282–92 *passim*; emended by
 Pond (1912), 62–63; and Guarantors'
 Prize, 77–78, 82; and *Poetry's* banquet,
 102–4; quoted, 82, 86, 102–3, 181, 222
You and I (Monroe), 11, 86, 114
"Young Lady" (Pound), 121

Zorach, William, 151